The International Companion to Scottish Poetry

INTERNATIONAL COMPANIONS TO SCOTTISH LITERATURE

Series Editors: Ian Brown and Thomas Owen Clancy

Titles in the series include:

International Companion to Lewis Grassic Gibbon
Edited by Scott Lyall
ISBN 978-1-908980-13-7

International Companion to Edwin Morgan
Edited by Alan Riach
ISBN 978-1-908980-14-4

International Companion to Scottish Poetry
Edited by Carla Sassi
ISBN 978-1-908980-15-1

The International Companion to Scottish Poetry

Edited by Carla Sassi

Thomas Owen Clancy, Gaelic adviser

Scottish Literature International

Published by
Scottish Literature International
Scottish Literature
7 University Gardens
University of Glasgow
Glasgow G12 8QH

Scottish Literature International is an imprint of
the Association for Scottish Literary Studies

www.asls.org.uk

ASLS is a registered charity no. SC006535

First published 2015

Text © ASLS and the individual contributors

All rights reserved. No part of this book may be
reproduced, stored in a retrieval system, or
transmitted in any form or means, electronic,
mechanical, photocopying, recording or otherwise,
without the prior permission of the
Association for Scottish Literary Studies.

A CIP catalogue for this title
is available from the British Library

ISBN 978-1-908980-15-1

**Kingston
University**
London

ASLS acknowledges the support of Kingston University
towards the publication of this book.

Contents

Series Editors' Preface vii
Acknowledgements ix
A Note on the Text xi

Introduction 1
Carla Sassi

PART 1: LANGUAGES AND CHRONOLOGIES

1. Early Celtic Poetry (to 1500) 6
   Thomas Owen Clancy
2. Scots Poetry in the Fourteenth and Fifteenth Centuries 15
   R. D. S. Jack
3. Poetry in Latin 23
   Roger Green
4. Poetry in the Languages and Dialects of Northern Scotland . . . 31
   Roberta Frank, Brian Smith
5. The Sixteenth and Seventeenth Centuries 44
   Sim Innes and Alessandra Petrina
6. The Eighteenth Century 54
   Ronald Black and Gerard Carruthers
7. The Nineteenth Century 64
   Ian Duncan and Sheila Kidd
8. The Poetry of Modernity (1870–1950) 74
   Emma Dymock and Scott Lyall
9. Contemporary Poetry (1950–) 83
   Attila Dósa and Michelle Macleod

PART 2: POETIC FORMS

10. The Form of Scottish Gaelic Poetry 94
    William Gillies
11. Scots Poetic Forms 109
    Derrick McClure
12. The Ballad in Scots and English 121
    Suzanne Gilbert

Contents (continued)

PART 3: TOPICS AND THEMES

13. Nature, Landscape and Rural Life 132
    Louisa Gairn
14. Nation and Home 144
    Carla Sassi and Silke Stroh
15. Protest and Politics 156
    Wilson McLeod and Alan Riach
16. Love and Erotic Poetry 169
    Peter Mackay
17. Faith and Religion 179
    Meg Bateman and James McGonigal
18. Scottish Poetry as World Poetry 190
    Paul Barnaby
19. The Literary Environment 202
    Robyn Marsack

Endnotes 213
Further Reading 261
Notes on Contributors 269
Index 275

Series Editors' Preface

When in 2009 the first of the series of *Companions to Scottish Literature* under our editorship appeared under the aegis of the Edinburgh University Press, we had a vision of the scope and range of the series which extended to nineteen potential volumes, some based on literary periods, some on overarching themes and some on specific authors. As the years passed, other topics were recognised and added. By 2013, fifteen volumes in the series had appeared, but Edinburgh University Press had also decided that it no longer wanted to continue publishing new titles in the series. We remain grateful to them for their support for those first volumes and the community of Scottish literature scholars and lovers worldwide must be grateful to the Association for Scottish Literary Studies, which after reviewing the position, decided to take on completing the original vision for the series under the aegis of its academic imprint, Scottish Literature International. After the gap of a year to manage transitional matters, the 2015 tranche, therefore, represents under the series title, *International Companions to Scottish Literature*, the continuing fulfilment of the series editors' original vision, with the welcome addition of further topics. These will take the number of volumes produced well beyond twenty.

The 2015 tranche includes two volumes originally envisaged: the thematic volume on Scottish Poetry edited by Carla Sassi, which complements the 2011 volume edited by Ian Brown on Scottish Drama, and the volume on Edwin Morgan, edited by Alan Riach. The third volume, on Lewis Grassic Gibbon, edited by Scott Lyall, is an addition to the original vision, and one highly appropriate. Gibbon studies have developed strongly in recent years and this Companion is much needed.

As readers will see, these volumes continue to attract contributors of international standing and the highest quality. From the start, we have argued the complexity and profundity of the issues that Scottish literature embodies and addresses. The editors and authors of the 2015 volumes play a full part in helping fulfil the vision with which the series in its initial form began, to problematise in the most positive and creative way any easy notion of what Scottish literature is. The generic and linguistic complexity of the poets, poet-playwright and novelist these volumes address illustrates that vision.

Ian Brown
Thomas Owen Clancy

Acknowledgements

The project behind this volume is the outcome of over two decades of research and teaching, in the course of which many friends, poets and/or colleagues, have contributed in different ways to my appreciation and understanding of Scottish poetry, providing me with invaluable inspiration and support. While I could not attempt to list them all here (many of them are indeed contributors to the present volume), I do wish to thank them collectively.

Scotland is a country that nurtures and supports literary culture to an extent that is rare elsewhere. Its extraordinary literary institutions and events – especially the Scottish Poetry Library and StAnza, Scotland's annual poetry festival – have provided a unique source of inspiring ideas and concepts for the *Companion*.

Acknowledgements are due to the School of Critical Studies of the University of Glasgow, and in particular the colleagues of the department of Scottish Literature, for generously hosting me as an Honorary Research Fellow in 2010–11. It was there, in one of the friendliest and most stimulating professional environments in my life so far, that the project of the present volume took shape. I am especially grateful to the series editors, Ian Brown and Thomas Owen Clancy, for their support throughout the stages of preparing the book, and to the ASLS Director, Duncan Jones, for overseeing its production.

Finally, a special thanks goes to my mother, who taught me love of words and beauty. To her memory, this volume is dedicated.

A Note on the Text

Quotations from poems and the titles of poems written in languages other than English and Scots are provided in the original language in regular type, followed by translation in italics.

Gaelic poets are indicated by their Gaelic name, followed by its English version in parenthesis. An exception has been made for those poets who are internationally known by their English name: in these cases, it is the Gaelic name that follows parenthetically.

The collections of poems or anthologies whose full bibliographical details can be traced freely on the Internet are indicated in the text only by title and publication date. Fuller details are provided in endnotes for old and rare primary sources. Secondary sources are regularly referenced in endnotes.

Introduction

Carla Sassi

When Liz Lochhead was appointed Scots Makar – National Poet for Scotland – in 2011, she formally accepted her new role 'on behalf of poetry itself, which', she explained, 'is, and always has been, the core of our culture, and in grateful recognition of the truth that poetry – the reading of it, the writing of it, the saying it out loud, the learning of it off by heart – all of this matters deeply to ordinary Scottish people everywhere'.[1] Lochhead's words are not mere rhetoric, as indeed in Scotland the status of poetry is high and the love for it strong and widespread. Her statement, however, while it indeed expresses a sense of national pride, does not imply any national closure. Very much like her predecessor, Edwin Morgan (the first to hold the post of Scots Makar between 2004 and 2010), in her work she constructs nationhood as a democratic and inclusive polity, envisaging poetry as a medium to express local as well as planetary consciousness. In Anne Varty's words, 'she has taken Scotland beyond its borders and brought home new worlds, transforming both her native landscape and its global position'.[2]

Like all scholarly endeavours, and especially those that engage at some level with the 'national', even the present volume, encompassing approximately fifteen centuries of poetic production and thus engaging with writers and texts from ages when 'Scotland' did not exist, or its geopolitical configuration was very different from that of today, is inevitably retrospective in nature and informed by contemporary concerns. Scotland has changed dramatically in the past twenty years, socially, culturally and politically, and today seems to be on the verge of further radical change. In this period of dramatic transformation poets and poetry have often played an active role, not simply by voicing or representing contemporary hopes and demands, but by questioning conventional political language and taking a 'poethical' perspective on the possible future of their country – most visibly so during the 2014 referendum campaign. *The International Companion to Scottish Poetry*, conceived and written in the course of the past five years, could not and does not refrain from partaking in such a changed ideological and political landscape – that of a country that has gone a long way, in comparison with many European nations, to rethink its identity as that of a cosmopolitan 'post-nation', ready to revision its past as much as to imagine a new future. Very much like Lochhead's 'glocal' project, then, the present volume aims at accounting for a genre that indeed matters deeply to contemporary Scottish readers and scholars and is perceived by many of them as a centrally meaningful expression of their national identity, and at the same time to take it beyond its borders, to estrange it from its cultural moorings and to have it fruitfully engage in a dialogue with the world.

It may be worthwhile to point out that the present volume is the first of its kind to engage with Scottish poetry as a whole. Innumerable scholarly works on specific poets, regions and periods are available. An impressive range of anthologies illustrate its many chronological, linguistic or thematic facets or indeed provide an overview of the history of Scottish poetry. Histories of Scottish literature, of course, devote ample sections to this genre. But no companion to, or history of, Scottish poetry has been produced before. The variety of reasons for this may be wide, and to assess them fully is beyond the scope of this introduction. They may have to do with the fact that 'history' and 'poetry' stage two antithetically different 'grammars' and aims – denotative versus connotative, a quest for 'objective' data and information versus a 'subjective' focus on form and language. They may also have to do with the complex history of 'Scottish literature' as a field of studies and with the markedly controversial process that has characterised the formation of its literary canon in the twentieth century – both aspects that somehow concur in making the weaving of a consistent critical narrative more challenging. They are surely to do with response to Scotland's multilingualism: the ways in which at different periods poetry in Gaelic, Brittonic, Norse, Latin, French, Scots and English have been seen as separate, Gaelic literature distinct from Scottish literature, literature in English as not really 'Scottish' or Scottish literature as a subdivision of 'English literature'. These are indeed issues that have been faced and carefully considered by the present editor, and that inevitably underlie this project. A companion, however, is not a history – it is, more humbly or more ambitiously, a tool that aims to support any would-be 'traveller', professional or occasional, into a field of studies. It may thus be compared to a map in the hands of someone who ventures into a new or partly new territory. It will yield precious, even though, by necessity, incomplete, information, as well as options of orientation and indications of possible routes and paths. A map, very much like a companion, will provide an abstraction – an overview that leaves numberless local details uncharted, and yet offers a picture someone travelling on ground level would otherwise miss.

Readers already aware of the richness and complexity of the history of Scotland's poetry will know in advance that the present volume cannot aim, given its very size, at exhaustiveness. It does, however, aim at inclusiveness: spanning across fifteen centuries, it accounts for texts written in Celtic, Romance and Germanic languages and dialects, it engages, albeit succinctly, with the work of some of the best-known world poets – the makars, Robert Burns, James Macpherson, Walter Scott, Edwin Morgan, among others – as well as with authors (quite often women) whose work has been less visible at both a national and an international level. It also attempts to highlight, when possible, international affiliations, as indeed poetry (or any literary and artistic expression) can never be confined in the exclusive space of a single nation – it will trespass borders, and come back enriched and changed. And the history of Scotland's poetry is extraordinarily rich in such journeys: contaminations, hybridisations, borrowing and reappropriations, across three families of European languages and through contact with different cultures, within and outwith its national borders, are possibly one of its most notable and valuable features. The instability and complexity of Scotland's political history over the centuries may have had a negative impact in some aspects of its national life, but they have arguably represented an extraordinarily fertile field for poetic creativity – a wealth that has been fully evaluated only in the past twenty years or so, when the literatures of Scotland, in three main languages (Gaelic, Scots and English), have been recognised on the same standing, as all contributing in equal measure to the definition of the Scottish canon. Roderick Watson's critical anthology *The Poetry of Scotland: Gaelic, Scots & English 1380–1980*, published in 1995,[3] represents an important milestone in this respect.

The *Companion*, then, responds to and furthers the ongoing quest for a pluralist representation of Scottish literary history, both by foregrounding an inclusive approach (rather than a strictly canon-oriented one, that would have focused on a select number of established writers), and by accounting for the different languages in which poetry was written in the course of centuries: from the early Celtic languages, Old and Middle Scots, Latin and Norse, to Scotland's modern languages and dialects. In particular, it aims, innovatively, at providing an integrated and comparative approach to the three linguistic strands – Gaelic, Scots and English – that have been mostly treated by academic practice as separate, even incommunicable, fields of investigation. To this end, most of the chapters of the *Companion* have been co-authored by a Scots/English studies scholar and a Celtic studies specialist, or by a single contributor who has competence in both literary areas. This very structural choice – one that it is hoped will be opted for more frequently in the future – bestows a fresh perspective on the conventional chronological and thematic categories in which the *Companion* is articulated. It also aims to encourage the reader to see Scotland's poetry as a continuum of voices and to pursue further comparative exploration.

Because the purpose of the present volume is not to provide a history, but rather a flexible tool in the hands of students and scholars, it has been structured in three parts, representing three different standpoints from which Scotland's poetry can be investigated. While each part (and indeed each chapter) can be read individually, the three sections are also meant to work on a larger scale, and create a sense of the many ways in which poetry can be read and categorised, as well as yield a picture which is broader and more articulated than a single approach would have provided. The first part, 'Languages and Chronologies', is divided into nine chapters and provides a timeline based on conventional literary periodisation, while at the same time accounting, as explained above, for Scotland's heterogeneous linguistic voices. In this section, individual chapters are devoted respectively to early Celtic, early Scots and Latin poetry, as well as to the poetry in the languages and dialects of northern Scotland, seen as a linguistically and culturally specific region. The remaining chapters chart the parallel/intersecting poetic voices in Gaelic, Scots and English from the Middle Ages to the present day. The second part, 'Poetic Forms', divided into three chapters, focuses on the formal aspects of Gaelic and Scots poetry – metre, rhyme, sound patterns, stanza – and on the shape of a quintessentially 'Scottish' genre, the ballad in English and Scots. The third part, 'Topics and Themes', consisting of seven chapters, identifies five 'universal' subjects ('Nature, Landscape and Rural Life', 'Nation and Home', 'Protest and Politics', 'Love and Erotic Poetry', 'Faith and Religion') and concisely charts the specific meanings these take in specific historical and cultural contexts, from the medieval to the contemporary age. The two concluding chapters focus on two professional practices that are crucially related to poetic production and that also present interesting national specificities – respectively charting the translation of a select number of Scottish poets into world languages ('Scottish Poetry as World Poetry'), and providing a survey of the support to poets and poetry offered by contemporary institutions ('The Literary Environment').

A final, methodological note is in order with respect to the 'national' perspective foregrounded by the *Companion*. Each reader will of course bring his/her own distinct cultural baggage, interests and expectations to the appreciation of the present volume, and will predictably leave it with a slightly different set of impressions. And yet, for all its structural open-endedness, the *Companion* does pinpoint at least two national 'truths'. The first is the objectively extraordinary richness and diversity of Scotland's poetic heritage and contemporary scene. The second is the existence of a relevant number of specific features – cultural, formal, thematic – that create important lines of continuity across regions, languages and centuries, and that allow us (specialists in Scottish studies as well as occasional visitors) to deem the macro-category 'Scottish poetry' as a highly meaningful and productive one. T. S. Eliot and F. R. Leavis's notions of a monolithically or organically defined 'Great Tradition', with capitals, are by now superseded and anachronistic. And so is the idea of a 'pure' and transcendent form of art, untouched by local processes, or the possibility of a purely 'cosmopolitan' literary utterance. The *Companion* eschews such views and attempts instead a balanced approach between a notion of nation that is purely 'territorial' or, to borrow and adapt a term used by Christopher Whyte, a stance that is 'agnostic' in relation to 'nationalist ideology',[4] and the observation and recognition of recurring specific features, ideas and emotions that indeed have concurred in shaping the present idea of 'Scotland'.

PART 1: LANGUAGES AND CHRONOLOGIES

CHAPTER ONE

Early Celtic Poetry (to 1500)

Thomas Owen Clancy

The contribution of the Celtic languages to the poetry of Scotland is arguably the earliest and, certainly in the case of Gaelic, the most sustained of all Scotland's languages. Despite this, the situation of any one piece of poetry can often be hard to determine, in terms of the extent to which we would be happy to describe it as 'Scottish'. Up to and beyond the twelfth century, the remains of poetry in Celtic languages that we have are often preserved in manuscripts of other countries, in particular those of Wales and Ireland, and in many instances it is difficult, if not impossible, to judge whether poetry which relates to Scotland was composed in Wales or Ireland, rather than in Scotland. Before going on to consider the nature of this poetry, it is necessary to get a proper sense of the problems in determining a genuine corpus of texts.

A brief case in point will illustrate the complexity of the problems surrounding attribution, preservation and 'Scottishness': two of the finest poets practising the strict-metre praise poetry of Classical Gaelic, both working around the year 1200, acquired the Gaelic epithet 'Albanach' ('*Scottish, the Scotsman*'). One, Muireadhach Albanach Ó Dálaigh, was certainly Irish. His family was intimately involved in the linguistic and literary revolution which gave rise to Classical Gaelic poetry and language.[1] The traditions relating to him recount that he was exiled from Ireland as a result of murdering the steward of his local lord; poetry he writes fifteen years later suggests a very extended period of exile. During, or perhaps even before, this time, he worked as a poet for patrons in Scotland, particularly in the area of the Lennox (Loch Lomondside), and seems to have settled here during his exile, and he is the ancestor of the most distinguished line of medieval Scottish Gaelic poets, the MacMhuirichs. However, he also spent time on the Fifth Crusade (1213–21), alongside the other contemporary poet to bear this epithet, Gille-Brighde Albanach. For this poet, aside from verses relating to his Mediterranean sojourn, we have preserved only poems for Irish patrons, though in one of these he makes clear that his native land was Scotland. Almost all the poetry of these two poets is to be found in Irish manuscripts, where it is treated, rightly, as part of the corpus of Classical Irish Bardic poetry. In such instances – and they are many – we must sit reasonably lightly on the ascription of 'Scottishness'. This situation, however, mirrors also many of the Scottish poets of the modern and contemporary period, who may be seen as Scottish by birth, residence or affiliation, but often not all three, and who are sometimes not themselves willing to accede to the 'Scottish' label.[2]

The problem is particularly acute for the early poetry of the Northern British tradition, composed in a language closely akin to Welsh, and preserved entirely in later medieval Welsh manuscripts. It should be emphasised that the material here relates to a language which, certainly by 1200, and quite probably by 1100, was no longer spoken in Scotland, and so it stands to reason preservation of any texts in that language would lie elsewhere. The long poem or series of poems called *Y Gododdin*, preserved in one late-thirteenth-century Welsh manuscript now known as Llyfr Aneirin (the Book of Aneirin), is a good example of the issues involved. Once capable of being described (albeit controversially) as 'the Oldest Scottish Poem', its antiquity has come under sustained scrutiny in recent years, and some scholars would now see it as largely a product of Wales, at a much later period than once thought. On the basis of this revision, one scholar has even gone so far as to claim exaggeratedly (and not taking into account literature in languages other than Welsh): 'I have left the Scots with nothing – bereft at a stroke of both their literature and their history of the sixth century.'[3]

The matter is far from decided, however, with other scholars maintaining *Y Gododdin*'s origins in the early north, where its events are certainly set.[4] The work, which we have preserved in two interrelated versions in the same manuscript, consists of elegies for fallen warriors, who are said to have died in a battle at a place called Catraeth, now usually identified with Catterick in North Yorkshire. The text's name, however, relates to the kingdom of Gododdin, which in the poem and elsewhere looks to have centred on what is now Edinburgh. The dead warriors in the poem are said to have feasted on mead in Din Eidyn (where Edinburgh Castle now sits), before going forth to their doom. Some of the verses, intruded into what must have been the original poem at some early date, certainly relate to Scotland, as, for instance, verses on the Battle of Strathcarron, which took place in 642, when Domnall Brecc, the king of the Gaelic region of Dál Riata (modern Argyll), was slain in an encounter with the king of Dumbarton, Owain: 'Gueleys y wyr tylluavr gan wavr a doyn, / a phenn Dyuynwal Vrych, brein ae knoyn' ('*I saw stalwart men, they came at dawn, / And crows picked at the head of Dyfnwal Frych*').[5]

This poetry has been termed 'heroic', in that it celebrates, by way of praise or mourning, masculine warrior exploits. This is true even where praising kings in a more courtly mode – Urien of Rheged, in a series of poems uncertainly attributed to Taliesin, and perhaps more related to northern England than Scotland, is profiled as a war-leader even amongst praise for his generosity to his retainers and poets. This same stance pervades a good deal of the fragmentary material from the early Gaelic corpus. Praise poetry predominates, whether this be praise of kings, warriors or saints, a fact highlighted in Robert Crawford's recent treatment of this period.[6] Here we must confront the fact that the poetry of this period is rarely the unfettered product of poets free to compose their own original thoughts. Poets were constrained by the economy of praise. This was true whether we look to the court poets of kings and lords, whose poetry is composed directly for patrons, in anticipation of reward and remuneration; or whether we consider religious poetry, which often overtly refers to its quest for heavenly patronage from its saintly subjects. Poetry from Scottish contexts provides good examples of both these aspects. However far we wish to accommodate the poetry in praise of King Urien of Rheged into either a Scottish or an early medieval literary history, it undoubtedly provides some of the classic tropes of the court poet–patron relationship. 'Lleuuyd echassaf / mi nyw dirmygaf: // Uryen a gyrchaf, / idaw yt ganaf. // Pan del vy gwaessaf / kynnwys a gaffaf // Ar parth goreuhaf / ydan eilasaf.' ('*A ruler most valiant / I'll not abandon: // It is Urien I seek, / To him will I sing, // When my warrant comes / I will find a welcome // In the best of regions / Beneath the best of rulers*').[7]

Likewise, verses from *Y Gododdin* show that even in the midst of praising the heroism of warriors and their gallant and tragic defeat in battle, poets would opt to nod in the direction of such patronage. 'Trwm en trin a llain yt ladei. / gwaro rybud o gat dydgei / gant; can yg calan darmerthei' ('*In hard fighting he'd slash with his blade: / A hundred bore a bitter warning from battle. / He would furnish song for New Year's*').[8] Two Classical Gaelic poems are the most explicit about this relationship. Muireadhach Albanach composed a stinging poem for Amhlaoibh of the Lennox, complaining that he was still owed the price of a poem (now lost) for his father, and about his current treatment:

> Mairg thrégeas inn, a Amhlaoibh,
> An ghuirt uaine ubhallmhaoil,
> > Giodh mór do ghnaoi 'gus do ghráin
> > Ní lór mur taoi 'gum thógbháil.

Woe to him who neglects me, Amhlaoibh, / of the green orchard of apple-trees, / although great your charm and your malice, / not sufficient are your retaining-fees.[9]

Similarly, a poem of c. 1250 by an Irish poet for Aonghus, the Lord of the Isles (d. 1296), explains in a witty and artful way that that noble patron owed him his father's arrears for his poetry: 'Ceannaigh duain t'athar, a Aonghas, [...] adéara cách dlighi a dhíol' (*'Pay for your father's poem, Aonghas, [...] Everyone will say you ought to pay'*).[10] The implication of all this is that faulty patrons could be shamed by satire. Muireadhach implies as much when he judiciously mentions the reputations of Amhlaoibh's ancestors as very much being in Amhlaoibh's hands. We have some evidence of such satire from the late medieval period; and one brief glimpse of a more politically driven polemic thrust to Gaelic poetry of the earlier period in a fragment written c. 1113 commenting acerbically on the actions of the future King David I:

> Olc a ndearna mac Mael Colaim,
> > ar n-aimhleas re hAlaxandair;
> do-ní le gach mac rígh romhainn
> > foghail ar farastAlbain.

It's bad, what Mael Coluim's son has done, / dividing us from Alexander; / he causes, like each king's son before, / the plunder of stable Alba.[11]

As noted, religious poetry also deals in the same economy of praise. It envisages saintly patrons as capable of giving poets protection in this life and beyond. Beccán mac Luigdech, perhaps to be identified with the Beccán of Rum who died in 677, author of two poems in praise of St Columba of Iona, gives us some excellent examples of this. In these finely crafted poems, he invokes the power of Columba to grant him protection (*snádud*), a legal term which transposes onto the heavenly otherworld the conventions of earthly status in Gaelic law.[12] More striking, perhaps, is the nature of the portraiture in one of these poems, called in the manuscript in which it is contained 'Tiughraind Bhecáin' (*'Beccán's Final Verses'*).

It builds up a picture of the saint and his virtue by recourse to short (usually four-syllable), linked images, roving from image to image and idea to idea.

> Búachail manach, medam cléirech, caissiu rétaib,
> Rígdaib sondaib,   sonaib tedmann, tríchtaib cétaib. [...]
>
> Techtaiss liubru, léicciss la slán, selba aithri,
> ar seirc léigind, léicciss coicthiu, léicciss caithri.

Shepherd of monks, judge of clerics, finer than things, / Than kingly gates, than sounds of plagues, than battalions. [...] / He possessed books, renounced fully claims of kinship: / For love of learning he gave up wars, gave up strongholds.

The stance of praise also predominates in poetry that is not ostensibly court or panegyric poetry. The twelfth-century poem in praise of the island of Arran is a good example.[13] This is fundamentally an idealised vision of place. It attacks its subject, however, via the same sort of 'collage' or perhaps 'montage' aesthetic which pervades the court poems of Muireadhach or Gille-Brighde, or indeed Beccán's poems on St Columba.[14] The aesthetic here can be difficult to comprehend at first. There is little attempt to structure an argument: rather we are given brief flashes of images, often quite disparate or even contrasting, and from these poetic pixels we are expected to construct the portrait of king, or saint, or island. A related phenomenon, in court poetry, or indeed some devotional poetry, is the extraordinary use of synecdoche, with rulers or saints being referred to simply as their hair, or their hand. Muireadhach Albanach's poem in praise of the Virgin Mary has some striking examples of this – there she is addressed as 'a gheal déadghlan' (*'white tooth'*).[15]

Holding these poems together is the linguistic resonance of them, and, often, their metrical virtuosity. Here we must allow for the fact that formal aspects sometimes take precedence in the Gaelic poems, especially of the later medieval period, over the content. In a few cases, indeed, we owe our knowledge of the fragments of Gaelic verse from Scotland to the preservation of poems in treatises on poetic metres. One example is a poem treasured by the compilers of the text it is found in surely only for its tight metricality and perfect four-syllable full rhymes; it praises one or another of the early medieval kings of Scotland called in Gaelic Óengus (probably Unust son of Uurgust, king of Picts, 729–761).

> Fó sén dia ngab Óengus Albain,
>   Albu thulchach trethantríathach
> tuc do chaithrib costud clárach
>   cossach lámach lethanscíathach.

Good the day when Óengus took Alba, / hilly Alba, with its strong chiefs; / He brought battle to towns, with boards, / with feet and hands, and with broad shields.[16]

The poetry from the early medieval period is extremely fragmented.[17] We have, as noted earlier, little on the British side that is not, essentially, Welsh poetry by virtue of its preservation and current linguistic state. On the Gaelic side, much of what we have from before 1150 is a somewhat random selection of poems that need to be argued into their 'Scottishness', and the quality here, outside the early Iona poems, is quite patchy as well. The situation changes markedly in the later Middle Ages, owing mainly to the preservation in one manuscript – the Book of the Dean of Lismore – of a great amount of Gaelic poetry primarily of the fifteenth and very early sixteenth centuries.[18] This can make it quite hard, from a critical standpoint, to get a firm hold on the period and its products.

Bearing this in mind, we are fortunate to have a few poets with a substantial corpus attributed to them and, if these attributions can be trusted, we are then in a position to get a better viewpoint on the workings of individual poets. One such is Mugrón, abbot of Iona from 964 until his death in 980, as well as ruler of the Columban family of monasteries in Ireland. The corpus here is small and very diverse, but still more than we have for any other poet before 1200. We have four poems attributed to him. Perhaps the two most likely to be genuinely his are a 'breastplate' poem in which he girds on the cross of Christ across every limb and organ of his body, to preserve himself safe from harm and sin; and a long litany invoking the Trinity. More skilful as poetry, though perhaps less certainly his, is a poem in praise of Columba, invoking him as 'matchless barque of bards' rewards, / eager author, high heaven's noble seal'. (The 'seal' in this verse is *rón*, the animal, an extraordinary way to describe the saint). An as yet unedited elegy on the death in battle of the king of Tara, Congalach mac Maíle Mithig (d. 956), is also attributed to him.[19] Taking these together, we can see the potential output of a clerical poet, situated on Iona (though probably part of the time in Ireland), as encompassing devotional verse, spiritual hymns and prayers, but also secular panegyric and elegy.

The combination of panegyric and devotional verse is also present in the work of Muireadhach Albanach Ó Dálaigh, although the balance is in the other direction, and in his case he was clearly not a cleric – indeed, he is amongst the first of the major Gaelic poets to belong to a new phenomenon, linguistically and poetically, that of Classical Irish verse, the training for the writing of which seems to have taken place largely outwith the Church. Nonetheless, as we have briefly seen, Muireadhach has devotional poetry, not only on the Virgin Mary, but also late poems (if genuine) of renunciation and a deathbed poem. As noted, with a companion he set off on the Fifth Crusade, and his and Gille-Brighde Albanach's poems on their 'tonsuring' before leaving, and some verse which, *inter alia*, invokes the aid of saints, has survived from this journey.[20] The bulk of Muireadhach's poetry is witty and impressive praise poetry – his 'bill of sale' poem to Amhlaoibh of the Lennox has already been mentioned; he has a marvellous calling-card poem to a Munster patron on his return from the Mediterranean, and a poetic plea to be allowed to return to Ireland at the end of fifteen years' exile. Perhaps no poem best exemplifies his reach and depth than his finely wrought poem on the death of his wife.[21] Throughout, the poetic demands are controlled perfectly, and somehow through the metrical skein the deep emotion is channelled to resonant effect. It is a rare example of personal poetry from the period.

The period 1200–1500 in a Gaelic context is dominated by the professional poetry within the Classical, strict-metre mode, in which Scottish practitioners and Irish ones were clearly being trained in the same schools and participating in the same regulations and aesthetic. By the end of this period, however, it is possible to see more local arrangements and developments. This is largely thanks to one manuscript, the Book of the Dean of Lismore, written in the early sixteenth century, and containing the bulk of what we know of late medieval Gaelic poetry from Scotland, as well as a great deal of Irish material. There is not space to do this manuscript and its contents justice here, but it has been well treated recently, especially by scholars such as William Gillies and Martin MacGregor.[22] As well as panegyric, some very much the product of local schools of activity in Perthshire and Argyll, there are heroic ballads, bawdy satire, love poems, and other poems which escape from the net of regulation, either metrically or linguistically. Study of the manuscript is made more challenging by its rendering of Gaelic verse in Middle Scots orthography; but the bicultural environment lying behind the scribal system also underpins what is a highly international, European, whilst still distinctively local anthology of poetry. There are some important phenomena it bears witness to, for instance, poetry by women – love poetry, as well as an important poem on the death of her husband by an aristocrat named Aithbhreac inghean Coirceadail.[23] We see in this collection for the first time the presence of female voices in the Gaelic tradition strongly represented, and this will continue to be a feature of Gaelic poetry until the late nineteenth century.

Without the Book of the Dean we would be ignorant of much of Scotland's Gaelic verse of the Middle Ages, and also of various aspects of its relationship with Ireland. But there are poems from the later Middle Ages beyond it. Two poems may be noted in closing, to illustrate that for all the sparsity of the Scottish material, there is power in what is there. Sometime before 1500, a man we know only as Ó Maoil Chiaráin composed a lament for his young son, his only child. Internal evidence reveals the poet to be Scottish. His son had died on a poetic tour in Ireland, and there can be few poems so starkly grief-stricken – it deserves to be known as one of the great poems of Scottish literature, though it has not yet attained that status. In its closing stanzas, as elsewhere in the poem, the poet comes close to blasphemy in his imprecations against God:

> An filise 's an fear thríd,
> > mo chridhise an béal gan bhréig,
> an tshaorshlat gan mhuirn gan mhóid,
> > caolbhrat fóid ghuirm ar an ngéig.
>
> Guilim ar a los gach laoi
> > ní fhuilim anos do ní;
> as í a mharbhnaidh do mheasg mé
> > a Dhé, is leasg lem anmuin í.
>
> Níor ghabh dhíom an Coimdhe cead
> > fan ngníomh – mur do-roighne rug;
> diomdhach mé don Rígh do-rad,
> > mur do ghad din an té tug.

This poet, grass growing through him, / my heart, the deceitless mouth, / fine branch, without wish or joy, / green earth's thin cloak on the bough. // I weep for him every day; / nothing occupies me now. / His elegy maddened me, / God, it's a chore for my soul. // God got no permission from me / for the deed: He took, as He made. / I don't thank the King who gave him: / He stole from me the one He gave.[24]

We are fortunate to have an example of his son's poetry. Fearchar Ó Maoil Chiaráin is author of a metrically tight but thematically light poem, 'The Blackthorn Brooch', which praises a woman by lamenting that the blackthorn brooch in her cloak is not worthy of her stature.[25] It is a sign of the range of poetry by Gaelic poets during the period before 1500, of their full participation in Irish and international poetic conventions, and also of how much we may have lost amongst the fragments that remain.

CHAPTER TWO

Scots Poetry in the Fourteenth and Fifteenth Centuries

R. D. S. Jack

The richness and diversity of late fourteenth- and fifteenth-century Scottish poetry is best understood within appropriately attuned critical contexts. These should be attentive to its European influences, the nature of its linguistic and dialectal range, which frustrates any assumption that this poetic culture represents a victory of Scots over English, and the ways in which it reflects the intellectual and philosophical currents of the period which are related to the powerful movement of Christian humanism, from the twelfth until the late fifteenth centuries.

The rise, in fullness and subtlety, of Middle Scots from John Barbour to William Dunbar and Gavin Douglas is one of the most striking features of this period, but it is important to remember that vernacular Scots began as a branch of Northumbrian English. The *Kingis Quair* of James I of Scotland (c. 1424) illustrates the inaccuracy of treating English and Scots as quite separate languages at this time as Northern English and Scots forms still combined, while expansive techniques (e.g. 'faire, bright and schire') sought to develop Scots vocabulary. James I's lengthy English imprisonment means that English forms are especially prevalent in the *Quair*. James also varies between Scots and English forms in a self-consciously artificial, rhetorical style:

> For as the foulere quhistlith in his throte
> Diversely to counterfete the brid,
> And feynis mony a swete and strange note
> That in the busk for his desate is hid,
> Till sche be fast lokin his net amyd;
> Ryght so the fatoure, the false thief I say,
> With swete tresoune oft wynnith thus his pray.
>
> (*Quair*, stanza 135)

The courtly 'maker' aimed to highlight his skills, not to conceal them. Kurt Wittig's search for radical, down-to-earth views[1] is, therefore, doomed to anachronistic failure in an age which welcomed hierarchy and artifice. Diachronic evidence not only discredits the simple Scottis versus Inglis assumption, it reminds us that other 'rivals' existed. In Holland's *Buke of the Howlat* (c. 1450) it is Gaelic, whose power is obliquely acknowledged when the rough language of 'A bard out of Ireland' is mocked (794–806). Latin is the other language Holland discusses: like his contemporaries, however, he views it as a long-term ideal rather than present competition (248–49).

A Scottish chivalric romance, *Golagros and Gawane* (c. 1470), offers two further diachronic insights into the development of fifteenth-century Scots. Its author has chosen to translate and adapt two separate episodes in the Old French *Perceval* – the embassy of Kay and Gawain to Chastel Orgueilleux (16,323–634) and Arthur's attempt to make Golagros vow fealty (18,209–19,456).[2] The thematic links he introduces will be studied in the next section; meanwhile, the European context to the romance mode and the popularity of translation in the fifteenth century warrant attention. If in the *Bruce* the Scottish hero is compared to foreign romance worthies drawn from the Matters of Rome, France and England, *The Taill of Rauf Coilyear* (c. 1475) celebrates Charlemagne, while *Golagros* derives from a French romance. The motivations for translation in the Renaissance are also important. The most common analogy employed at the time placed 'colonising' of foreign words on a patriotic par with Drake colonising new lands.[3] This helps to explain why the first use of 'Scottis', meaning the language of the Scottish nation, comes in Gavin Douglas's translation of the *Aeneid* – *Eneados* (c. 1513) – along with a condemnation of Caxton's rival English version. Latin generally, and Virgil's genius in particular, Douglas argues, makes his task particularly ambitious. He therefore confesses that he has been 'constreynt' to use coinages from many languages, including English, French and Latin (*Eneados* I, Prologue, 117). The same rhetorical tradition means that when Douglas calls his language 'plain' (*Eneados* I, Prologue, 110) this is again a modesty *topos*, indirectly drawing attention to his rhetorical skills.

Dunbar's welcoming of 'Inglis' as his language and Chaucer as his major source in stanza 29 of *The Goldyn Targe* (c. 1508) also has positive competitive undertones as it reflects an optimistic view of decorum. Scottish writers saw vernacular Scots as an additional linguistic resource. From highest, Latinate English as the appropriate register for the high style, and noble topics via English and Anglo-Scots for the middle high and middle levels respectively, down to the thick Scots employed for flytings and other 'low' topics, they appeared to feel particularly well endowed to meet any of the stylistic levels prescribed by Horace. In short, the comprehensive approach of Christian–Humanist analysis makes it easy for Dunbar to get the best of both worlds. Decorously, Scots matches English on all stylistic levels but itself adds another, unique 'word-hoard'. Viewed nationalistically, this implies a double heritage of the kind still being urged in the eighteenth century by Allan Ramsay when demanding an English (Isaac Bickerstaff) and a Scottish pen-name (Gavin Douglas) for entry into the Easy Club.[4]

As the Scottish nation gradually emerged, patriotic and chivalric romances celebrated it. Following the *Bruce* (c. 1375) came *Golagros and Gawane*, already mentioned, and the *Wallace* (c. 1477) while even the light-hearted *Rauf Coilyear* has serious comments to make on hierarchy and fealty. While these tales can be enjoyed for the adventurous deeds, their full meaning is only revealed diachronically and allegorically.

This is first of all because the effective persuading of your audience to moral action was the accepted *causa finalis* ('moral persuasion') in classical times. This is part of what is known as the Aristotelian causal line. Aristotle's view that rhetoric's role was confined to 'observing the available means of persuasion' (*Rhetoric*, I. 1) meant that the final test of any work was whether it effectively moved a given audience to moral action or not. This belief remained constant, repeated in the medieval commentary tradition, and remained a strong line in Dante's thinking.[5] As that view remained, with minor adaptations, into the later medieval and Renaissance periods, its practical implications remain important. It follows, for example, that, when historical 'truth' obscures the moral message, it is history which has to change its grounds. Barbour, for example, knew that his perfect patriotic icon had fought on the English side. This he excludes from his poem, instead substituting patriotic deeds from the lives of Robert's father and grandfather, thus creating (literally) a Christian hero 'three-in-one'. The same persuasive motives produce exaggerated ethical character contrasts. The poem opens and closes with contrasted pilgrimages. Bruce's final posthumous crusade did occur and effectively ends the poem, but the account of Edward I returning from an earlier crusade for worldly reasons in Book I is entirely fictional, the exaggerated villainy of England's ruler being invented to strengthen the 'moral' cause for war.

In claiming for Bruce the status of romance worthy, Barbour regularly compares him to his rivals in the Matters of Rome, France and England.

The author of the *Wallace* follows his example while the European background to essentially Scottish arguments is also illustrated in the major chivalric romances of the period. *Rauf Coilyear* celebrates Charlemagne but raises questions which were of major concern in fifteenth-century Scotland.

Golagros and Gawane centres on Arthur but, as noted earlier, has a French source. As Larry Benson notes, it is also a late Arthurian romance and so emphasises 'religious virtues at the expense of chivalric ones'.[6] In that context, however, it is the Scottish writer who highlights the Christian elements within that code more explicitly. For example, the Middle Scots Arthur is first encountered on a pilgrimage, while his French equivalent is not. The Scottish poet loosely translates two separate episodes from the French romance *Perceval* in order to evaluate the later Arthur and his knights. The judgement begins when Kay and Gawain visit the Lord of Chastel Orgueilleux (*Perceval*, 16,323–634), as does the more explicit Christian bias of the Scottish poem. In his redaction, Kay's rudeness, pride and anger make him the exact countertype to Gawain's virtuous gentility and chivalric behaviour. The second section concentrates on Arthur's determination to make Golagros vow fealty to him (18,209–19,456). Verbal and thematic links between the two sections encourage us to link and compare them. The effect of this is to draw him away from Gawain's virtues onto the side of worldly power and pride earlier exhibited by Kay. The final outcome, however, is unambiguously Christian and redemptive. Aided by his wise counsellor, Spynagros, Arthur repents:

> [The king] prayt to the grete God to grant him his grace,
> Him to save and salf that is our Soverane. (792–93)

His return to God is signed in the poem's circular form as recommended for anagogical themes. Further, as in *Gawain and the Green Knight*, King Arthur's fall from great heights and final triumph are linked at each stage. For example, the comfort and good fortune of the first castle and its respectful lord are recalled in the later movement when bad fortune, a different castle and a much less accommodating lord pose a much more difficult test. That the second movement also highlights fealty has another, this time nationalistic, implication. As English attempts to claim suzerainty continued until 1364, a Scottish audience's sympathy with Golagros was practically guaranteed.

As earlier suggested, the Aristotelian causal line guided critical questioning and poetic practice in fifteenth-century Scotland. The

Aristotelian concepts of *causa formalis* and *causa materialis* can help us to understand the intricate relationships between form and meaning which can be perceived in this poetry. For the Christian writers of the late medieval period, poetic form and structure were imbued with theological significance. Interrelationships and analogies are therefore the only means of representing a God who contains all being within him.[7] Like the medieval commentators they not only valued the greater artistic challenge represented but saw that the particular ordering of material might 'sign' the theme.[8]

The *Quair* is another example of significant linking of form to meaning. Indeed, arguably, it does so more overtly and thoroughly than any other Scottish poem of the period. It begins anagogically ('Heigh in the hevynnis figure circuler', stanza 1), and ends on a variation of that phrase ('Hich in the hevynnis figure circulere', stanza 196). In the early, youthful period of his life the circle image is also employed. As he wanders heavy with care he describes his neurotic thoughts as 'rolling to and fro'. And after he has been taught by the pagan gods, it is the wheel of Fortune which is introduced to sign the eternal movement of human fate. Even those like James who have been placed high on it, will have to strive against the counter-motion downwards. The same analytic approach underlines the poet's final victory and reveals a second formal sign of divine unity. As in the martial context of the *Bruce*, we learn of the outcome of the war before the first battle begins. James's is not a physical but a mental conflict, yet the same principle pertains. He reads Boethius and is motivated by the Roman senator's victory over self to achieve the same end. The victories like the battles differ – Boethius can face death philosophically; James can find the will to love and marry – but the test is the same.

Personal, mortal and divine wheels – Boethius as classical guide and pagan gods teaching Christian truths – there is no doubt that this poem has to be read allegorically. Allegory, of course, is the fundamental means of imaginative, philosophical and theological signification in the Middle Ages. Hugh of St Victor imagines a writer raising different allegorical 'courses' from the literal narrative. The medieval 'maker' or 'word-builder' also has the potential to build upwards from politics to morality, spirituality and ultimately metaphysics,[9] thereby imaginatively encompassing all levels of allegoric concern. Dante is one of the very few to attempt all levels concurrently in *La Divina Commedia*, making his analyses of allegory particularly valuable.[10] Yet James offers the clearest of signs in the extended ship metaphor of stanzas 15–18. Indeed the *Quair* is so obviously 'planned' that the early critical attacks on its shapelessness now seem bizarre.

The *Buke of the Howlat* as a dream poem also has a circular form – from waking state via vision to waking state again. Indeed the relationship between form and meaning in this poem is of particular interest, as is the number of other poetic kinds it evokes. The May setting which opens and closes the poem evokes the Reverdie form, while the Bird Parliament and the case of the Owl being judged by spiritual and temporal powers points back to Chaucer and on to David Lyndsay respectively. As the Douglases were Holland's patrons, that family's formal position at the centre of the poem is understandable. By surrounding them with accounts of the Pope and the Church as well as the major crowned heads of Europe, Holland implicitly raises the family to that level. He also offers an early example of another form. Veiled allegories dealing with current European politics would prove especially popular in the following century as the many translations of Barclay's *Argenis* illustrate.[11]

The other major romance, the *Wallace*, also uses parallels and artificial orderings. Books I–VI celebrate Wallace's childhood, youth and early manhood while Books VII–XII trace his rise, fall and holy death. Formally, both adopt an artificial form which is at once retrospective and circular. Hary offers to retell an old, known story to inspire today's audience to moral action (I. 1–16). That God is on Wallace's side is also initially established ('Bot God abuff has maid thar [English] mycht to par', I. 14). His libertarian heroism and his holy death are also confirmed prophetically (I. 351–52; II. 349).

Hary also follows Barbour in setting his martial story within Scotland's mythic history, in relating Wallace's heroism to the regenerative powers of Nature, in changing the dates of battles to coincide with religious festivals (e.g. the Battle of Stirling Bridge moves to Assumption Day), deleting troublesome evidence such as Wallace's defeat at Falkirk and even crediting him with victories won by others (e.g. Bruce's triumph at Loudon Hill). *Wallace*, like *Bruce*, seeks to persuade Scots to continue their just war against England. Robert Burns recognised this when noting that the former poured a tide of Scottish prejudice into his veins.[12] Of course, Burns read William Hamilton of Gilbertfield's eighteenth-century 'translation' of the poem. This omits most of the specifically Catholic evidence. In particular, it excludes the account of Robert I's 'holy death'. By deleting it, Gilbertfield sidesteps a major problem which Hary faced head on. What kind of Christian moral advice advocates killing the English? Yet that is the persuasive end proposed. Hary answers the question by moving into heaven where God's *fiat* ends the argument before it can begin. A holy monk on his passage through purgatory finds his forward progression halted, so that a famous 'slaar [slayer] of men' may move in front of him. The privileged one proves to be Wallace, who, we learn, will stand on God's side at the Day of Judgement. And if God excuses Wallace's penance and welcomes him into heaven, then attacks on England are justified by the highest authority of all.

It is, however, the Prologue to Henryson's *Morall Fabillis* (c. 1475–90) which most clearly defines the basic tenets of Christian humanism. In linking that simple theoretical 'foundation' to the wide range of allegorical challenges encompassed within it, Henryson confirms the theoretical principles studied in this article. His study of range within one form – the beast fable – also illustrates microcosmically the variety of allegorical challenges implied by the method. The Prologue begins by noting the wide allegorical framework within which imaginative 'truth' is set. Literally and sensually, his work is justified by giving aural pleasure to its audience. Anagogically and philosophically, he hopes it will turn sinful men to good living and so save them from damnation. A common image for allegory, the nut and the kernel, follows. But Henryson's 'students' are warned that the casing of these nuts will be hard and the task of 'cracking' them will involve different techniques. The Prologue's rhetorical origins are then acknowledged via a modesty *topos*. As with James I, his protestation that his work is 'rude' follows an accepted convention. In accusing himself of rudeness and a lack of skill, he in fact conveys the opposite. Stanza 7 initiates a more particular account of the beast fable and its value as a vehicle for conveying lessons which are both appetitive and rational. After all, man and animals share an appetitive soul, while man adds reason into the equation. The opening 'Tale of the Cok and the Jasp' exemplifies this. In the tale, man and bird are both starving and sensibly reject the jewel in search of necessities. The *Moralitas*, however, moves the hermeneutic goalposts. Now life is normal and it is only man as rational animal whose rejection of the jewel is condemned. Against the harmonious ideal of reason ruling passion the jewel becomes knowledge and its rejection signs ignorance.

Different kinds of *versi strani*, set at different allegorical levels, characterise the collection. 'The Two Mice', 'The Sheep and the Dog' and 'The Lion and the Mouse' are all essentially political allegories: they test the reader's ability to uncover the kernel in different ways and each demands a different way of 'cracking' the allegorical kernel. Others raise religious and spiritual questions, while 'The Paddock and the Mouse' offers different 'morals' on every level of allegorical enquiry. The mouse's literal attempt to ride on the paddock's back teaches a practical moral lesson – avoid hypocrites – but also provides a negative philosophical mirror for the proper relationship between reason and passion. It also offers advice on the spiritual outcome of the Fall and an anagogical reminder of how far we are from salvation.

Taken together, the linguistic riches of Middle Scots and the high quality of the work being composed at the turn of the century is at once a legitimate source of pride and a difficult qualitative act to follow. In the mid-sixteenth century David Lyndsay and Alexander Scott would guarantee that their legacy was not forgotten. But increased anglicisation in that period already meant that Middle Scots would never again be so full and subtle a medium for poetry as in the 'Golden Age' of Henryson, Dunbar and Douglas.

CHAPTER THREE

Poetry in Latin

Roger Green[1]

Early in the second century AD, the Roman satirist Juvenal joked that 'Thule' (often taken to mean the northern tip of Scotland) was talking of hiring a rhetorician.[2] If poets had then followed rhetoricians, as was not unknown in ancient Rome, and if Roman control of northern Britannia had been prolonged, the story of Scottish Latin poetry might have begun with the Romans. In fact, it begins with a strong impulse from Ireland. The present short account begins on the island of Iona, long after the Romans had left Scotland, with the arrival of the Irish monk Columba, whose name will long remain a very present help, invoked for protection against plague, bad weather, and invading English armies.[3] From the manifold verse attributed to him pride of place must be given to the amazing poem 'Altus Prosator' (*'Creator on High'*), which has often been considered to be his, though there are reasons for doubt, particularly regarding its date.[4]

Each of the twenty-three stanzas of this long but consistently powerful poem begins with a new letter of the alphabet (in case the reader is wondering, the last three stanzas begin with the words 'Xristo', 'Ymnorum', 'Zelus').[5] There is rhyme between the endings of each pair of eight-syllable lines (aa, bb, and so on), or, if sixteen-syllable lines are printed – both configurations are found in the manuscripts – internal rhyme in each line;[6] and the poet also revels in the assonance produced by Latin's substantival morphemes. Remarkable words abound, sometimes locked, like boulders in some great wall, by weighty pairings such as 'protoplastum praesagmine' and 'parasito praecipites'; they include loan words from the Greek such as 'cenodoxiae' (*'vainglory'*), and at least one from the Hebrew ('iduma', apparently *'hand'*), and long Latin words chosen, or devised, for effect, such as the word 'fatimine' developed from the short word 'fari' (*'to speak'*), or 'flammaticus' (this would be comparable in tone with *'flammatical'*).[7] Indeed, there is in general a fondness for long words, to an extent unusual in iambic or trochaic metre, with which the metrics of this poem, rightly or wrongly, are sometimes equated.

The poem resounds with knowledge of the Bible – the prophecy and narrative of the Old Testament, the Psalms (which, as will appear, are a long-continuing feature of Scottish Latin poetry), and especially the Book of Revelation – and with doctrine forthrightly presented: on the Trinity, on angels, and on an indubitably unpleasant hell. As the poem moves from Creation to Judgement, with its terrifying *dies irae*, it unfolds a series of remarkable images, none more brilliant in visual and acoustic terms than that of Moses ascending to meet the Lord on Sinai (stanza 16). Even in the untypically calm and lyrical praising of God's measured gift of fructifying water (stanza 11), the danger of furious cloudbursts is felt, reminding one that, as Clancy and Márkus point out, delight in nature is not an especially prominent or dominant feature of Celtic verse.[8] A fragment of another, earlier, poem that begins *Noli Pater* ... prays that God will not wish 'to indulge the thunder and lightning'. There are other dangers; human sin is bewailed in *Parce, Domine* ('Spare us, O Lord'), a work of the sixth century though ascribed to the shadowy Mugint (probably of Whithorn), assembled from multifarious biblical and liturgical matter.[9] Prayers for protection from threats physical and spiritual, and praise of protectors human and divine, form a constant thread in Scottish Latin poetry.

Another poem attributed to Columba, *Adiutor laborantium*, has recently been tentatively assigned to Adomnán, biographer of Columba and abbot of Iona in the late seventh century.[10] In this poem, closely united by its abecederian format and by the final rhyme in every line, the first fifteen lines are titles of God; the rest issue a humble prayer for the safety of the Christian rowing through life's storm.[11] Early in the next century there is a poem by a monk of Iona, Cú Chuimne (no Latin name is attested), *Cantemus in omni die*, that displays evidence of the gradual cross-fertilising of poetic traditions: various features, such as 'binding rhyme', recall Irish poetry,[12] while from another angle the hymn anticipates the wealth of Marian verse that will flower in the liturgical Sequence of twelfth- and thirteenth-century Europe. Later in the eighth century there is a hymn for St Nynia (Ninian), who was at Whithorn before Columba came to Iona, but left no poetry. This hymn is written in what are sometimes called echoic, or serpentine, elegiac couplets (in this format, found also in some classical poets and in a work cited by Bede, the second half of the second line repeats exactly the first half of the first line). In the manuscript it follows a longer poem, *Miracula Nynie episcopi*, which was sent by scholars of York to Alcuin, now at the court of Charlemagne.[13] Written in undistinguished Latin hexameters, this is heavily dependent on the poetry of the Anglo-Saxon Aldhelm and others; broadly speaking, it belongs to a genre developed by Christian poets such as Juvencus (a copy of his epicising version of the gospel narratives was in the Iona library),[14] and by Late Antique writers of saints' lives. No doubt more books, and perhaps writers and owners (but at this time the word 'Scoti' denotes Irishmen), made such a journey abroad. Mention should be made, as we proceed into the Middle Ages, of some noteworthy presences of St Kentigern. It is not impossible that the context of a poetic tribute to Kentigern from Columba (*Scotichronicon*, III. 30) was an actual meeting, but notwithstanding the inlay of Greek and Hebrew vocabulary the metre points to a later date and another author. Rather later, William, a clerk of Glasgow, tells how Kentigern answered his people's fearful prayers, and removed the threat of Somerled, the dangerous rebel who attacked Renfrew in 1164.[15] From the following century there exists a rhymed office for St Kentigern, of which the music and Latin text have been recently edited.[16]

Poems on 'kings and battles', and the deaths of kings, and their saintliness or wickedness, abound in the sixteen-book prose history entitled *Scotichronicon* authored by Walter Bower, who developed and amplified earlier work (notably that of Fordun).[17] As well as occasional lines of classical poets, there are extensive passages taken from medieval poems; these sources include the *Chronicon Elegiacum* of the mid-thirteenth century, which commemorates kings from Kenneth I to Alexander III, and the longer and later composite work *Chronicon Rhythmicum*. The Latin hexameter is adapted (without sacrificing leonine rhyme) to give precise dates (for example, 'M semel et c ter simul x I iungito quater' is 1314),[18] but dates are also given in words, as are details such as the inflated figures cited from Bernard of Arbroath for the size of the English army, 300,000 cavalry and 40,000 foot soldiers. The climactic narratives of the battle of Bannockburn are vivid and vigorous. One of them (*Scotichronicon*, XII. 23) was actually written by an Englishman, no doubt glad, at least temporarily, to be counted as a writer of Scottish Latin poetry: this is Robert Baston, a Carmelite monk who had come north to praise an English triumph, but was compelled to sing of their defeat 'without any ambiguity'. With a clever variation of rhyme-schemes the poem counters the sing-song tendency of leonine rhyme, and ingeniously represents the pace and chaos and clatter of warfare. Like the various other poets, he is an accomplished 'metrista'; the word is in no way derogatory but parallel to uses such as 'legista' and the later 'umanista' ('*one who studies the law/ humane letters*'). To appreciate these experts in metre, one should ignore any frisson of fear at the sometimes complex nature of classical and medieval Latin versification and their terminology; the skills of the metrist were carefully taught and greatly admired. A much less happy poem lamented the Black Death of 1349 (XIV. 7), but there is another feast of metrical and rhythmical versatility from the Glasgow canon Thomas de Barry to celebrate the victory at Otterburn in 1388 (XIV. 54).

Another plague features in the varied set of poems by John Foulis (Follisius), printed and sold in Paris, and now reliably dated to 1512.[19] Its first and longest poem, almost five hundred lines of elegiac couplets, was occasioned by the plague that had just caused Foulis to flee from Paris to Orléans with his tutor, the Italian humanist Jerome Aleander; but Foulis chose to describe a plague that had devastated Edinburgh, perhaps in the 1490s. This slim collection also includes a praise of St Margaret, in sapphic stanzas, and a poem in the Asclepiad metre, 'De mercatorum facilitate' ('*On the obligingness of merchants*': they are easily cuckolded). Some neat networking poems give some indication of his friends or contacts, including humanists like the Scot Patrick Panter and Remaclus Arduenna from Liège. In another poem from Orléans, in the elegiac metre – this technical term seldom has a connotation of mourning or melancholy – he warmly praises Scotland. Returning there soon afterwards, perhaps in the year of Flodden, perhaps a few years later, Foulis was to become secretary to James V in 1529; ten years after that he is still celebrated as a poet.[20] In such an apparently double career there is no conflict; it is typical in the world of Renaissance humanism. Skills concerned with the elegant manipulation of the prose or verse structures of classical Latin, and the knowing exploitation of its prestigious intertexts, its generic richness and its grammatical solidity, excellently equipped a person for the arts of diplomacy and publicity. Another such person was the busy diplomat Adam Otterburn, praised as a poet by Buchanan; the short-lived William Hay might have become another.[21]

Increasing numbers of Scots make their presence felt abroad. Erasmus, himself once tutored by Boece, the first principal of Aberdeen University, in a letter of 1517 mentioned with pleasure the growing numbers of Scots studying in France.[22] It was not long after this that there came to Paris a young scholar from Stirlingshire, George Buchanan. Eager to hear the philosopher John Major, perhaps, rather than any elegant humanist, he admits in his short autobiography his surprise at the stress laid on verse composition,[23] though in the event it was this more than anything that would make him famous. Many years later, but before the title was common, Buchanan would be called 'easily the prince of poets' by a Parisian publisher, and, not unreasonably, the tribute has stuck.[24] The young Buchanan soon flung himself into the intellectual life of Paris, winning esteem and laying the foundations of his bewilderingly varied political oeuvre. In France he also met like-minded Scots, such as Florens Wilson,[25] and in Scotland, where he spent most of the years 1535–39, he met others who had been abroad, including probably the aforementioned Foulis and possibly Roderick MacLean, future Bishop of the Isles, who would in 1549 publish a polymetric sequence of poems based on episodes from Adomnán's *Life of Columba*.[26] During this Scottish phase Buchanan wrote his *Somnium*, adapted from Dunbar, followed by a tongue-in-cheek recantation, and made a first version of his famous satirical poem *Franciscanus* – evidently not biting enough for James V, who, he claims, had commissioned it.

The patronage of James V proving less than robust, Buchanan came back to France, and ended up happily teaching in Bordeaux in the years 1539–43, a period notable for his dramas, two translated from Euripides, with help from Erasmus's translations, and two original plays on biblical topics but not unlike those of Seneca. His next home, Coimbra, where he taught in the Colégio das Artes from 1547, is linked with his poetical Psalm paraphrases, which he was able to bring on considerably during his confinement by the Portuguese Inquisition. After a doubtlessly distressing trial, things turned out well: not only was he released after eight months in a monastery, but these months had given him a time of relative tranquillity to continue with his learned and thoughtful psalm-poems, using no fewer than thirty classical metres in a poetic masterpiece that was to be so important later to the spiritual and cultural life of Scotland. The poems need not be read as the anguished outpourings of a prisoner, though they are often so read today; it is naive (or at least unmethodical) to ignore the fact that the anguish is that of the psalmist, whose thoughts are closely followed, and not necessarily Buchanan's.

On his release and throughout the 1550s he seems to be once more, but with more caution, a typical French neo-Latin poet. He wrote a sophisticated celebration of the regaining of Calais from the English and an epithalamium on the marriage of the Dauphin and Mary, Queen of Scots – to whom he was soon to become, when both were back in Scotland after 1561, first her Latin tutor and then, at the end of a tumultuous decade, her accuser. It is in this decade that the bulk of his religious and secular poetry was published, in Paris, Antwerp, Geneva and other centres. The 'secular' poems are fronted by the expanded *Franciscanus* and neatly, but somewhat uninformatively, arranged under titles such as *Silvae* (a label harking back to Statius, much used in the Renaissance), *Elegies* or *Epigrams*. There are a few omissions, some squibs being perhaps considered unsuitable for one who became Moderator of the Church of Scotland in 1567. Some poems would follow posthumously, mainly under the rubric of *Miscellanea*.[27]

The fact that his works were printed furth of Scotland will not have reduced their impact on readers in Scotland, who had ready access to continental publishers. Admirers included Thomas Maitland, a promising and skilful poet, as well as the interlocutor in Buchanan's *De Iure Regni*, Andrew Melville, who enthusiastically taught Buchanan's Psalms in Paris and Geneva,[28] and paid him the tribute of imitation in his own, less memorable, verse; Adam King, who became a professor of philosophy and mathematics in Paris, who sought to complete Buchanan's unfinished didactic poem *De Sphaera*, and later Arthur Johnston, who staunchly defended the integrity of Buchanan's Psalms, which he genuinely admired, but chose not to imitate stylistically.[29] Many other poets claimed or have been claimed to be pupils or followers of Buchanan in some way. Leaving aside his regal pupil King James,[30] they include James Crichton, who was to die young after a brawl in Mantua, and only later was made 'admirable'; Hercules Rollock, author of a poem on yet another plague in Edinburgh, and of various religious verse;[31] David Hume, poet and political philosopher; and Alexander Yule, commentator on Buchanan's Psalm paraphrases.[32] But Buchanan was by now a man with many official duties, and one should think in terms of 'services to education' rather than face-to-face teaching. Wisely, scholars have not sought to construct or describe a 'school' of Buchanan, though he led the way in many fruitful areas, not least occasional poetry, and is generally mentioned with awe and admiration.

To summarise or categorise the wealth of poetry written by Scots in the fifty or so years after Buchanan's death in 1582 cannot be attempted here. In an early survey Adams tried to construct a framework in terms of religious allegiance, but in some cases allegiances are not known to us, and their strength indeterminate, and where they are known there is a danger of giving them undue significance.[33] Other critics have sought to use genre for this purpose, though the regular, conventional titles such as *Silvae*, *Elegies* and *Epigrams* may be misleading; some works are hard to place or liable to be misrepresented in the attempt to do so.[34] The label of 'Ovidians', a grouping largely based on the use of the elegiac metre, was not very helpful, for although Ovid's letters of heroic lovers and other amatory works were models for some poets, others had nothing in common with him other than metre. For all his merits, Arthur Johnston is hardly 'Ovidian' in any other sense. An attractive, and picturesque, solution to the problem of classification, though not an analytical one, was made by John Leech, who, in a pastoral context, introduces some thirty poets, almost all alive at the time. Mildly disguised by pastoral names such as Corydon, or by Latinate approximations (for example, 'Cyllocus' is David Kinloch, the medical writer), or by places associated with them, the poets are led into this pastoral Hall of Fame by Buchanan, the bard of the Blane, followed by his royal pupil James under the name Daphnis (the name once associated with Julius Caesar) and then the rest. These include certain vernacular writers, with no sense that there was any contest, or incompatibility, between users of English and Latin.

Indicative at least of the rude health of verse composition, and of its utility, is a substantial volume printed in 1618, *The Muses' Welcome* (the main title is in fact in Greek). The goddesses are welcoming James VI and I back to Scotland in 1617, on what would be a short visit, though it took in many towns in his Scottish kingdom. In each place the king was received with recitations of specially composed Latin poetry, and, in all, no less than sixty-two poets joyfully pour out praise; there is even a poem signed *Pons Perthanus* (Perth Bridge), elegantly requesting funds for its repair. There is no recycling, either of poems or poets, and apparently no ghosting. Perhaps tactfully, a much smaller volume marked the king's regretted departure.

A much more important sign of the strength and scope of Latin poetic writing is the *Delitiae Poetarum Scotorum huius aevi illustrium* (*Delights of Famous Scottish Poets of This Age*), printed in two volumes at Amsterdam in 1637. Planned and funded by Sir John Scot of Scotstarvit, and with Arthur Johnston playing a large role in the collecting and editing, this work is parallel to recently produced volumes of French, German, Italian and other national delights, whose compilers sought to showcase the work of their countrymen. Scot's two volumes include thirty-seven poets, some already in print, some newly presented, from almost two generations; the earliest poet, by some way, is Florens Wilson, who died around 1550 but was remembered and esteemed for his prose work *De Tranquillitate Vitae*. The principles of choice are not always obvious: one can understand the omission of a work such as Patrick Adamson's *De Papistarum superstitiosis ineptiis* (1564), but certain poets, such as the above-mentioned John Leech, are puzzlingly absent. The poetry of Buchanan, glowingly praised in the preface by Johnston, was probably reckoned too voluminous to include; it was easily available elsewhere, having been recently, for the first time, published in its entirety in 1615.[35] Given various evidence that he admired Buchanan, it is not credible that Johnston was moved, or persuaded, to leave him out for some other reason.[36] Only careful study of this massive collection – though those of the nations mentioned above are even more massive – will show what the currents and undercurrents are, and from such belated scrutiny a new picture of Jacobean literary culture may emerge.[37]

There is a pronounced lull after 1637, and a gulf begins to open between Scottish poetry and the more prolonged English poetic achievement. An eighteenth-century Scottish professor is said (albeit by a raconteur with a reputation for wit)[38] to have blamed the Solemn League and Covenant for Scotland's inferiority in 'longs' and 'shorts', and although this is a narrowly pedagogical viewpoint, the atmosphere of religious discord and civil conflict must have contributed. Somewhat later, there are poems on warfare, a *Bellum Bothuelianum* of 1679 and a *Grameid* on the rising of John Graham of Claverhouse in 1689; significantly, the former is extant only in a single manuscript, and although the latter has more, its first printing was in 1888.[39] Gentler Muses inspired, and caused to be read widely, the eight books of epigrams, both Christian and secular, of the minister Ninian Paterson, and Andrew Symson's *Octupla* of 1696 with its eight versions of Psalm 104, half of them recent. Of particular interest are the short poems of the learned Jacobite Archibald Pitcairne, a vigorous and entertaining collection now carefully edited with exemplary erudition.[40] The book of *Selecta Poemata* printed in 1727, which includes these poems and those of a few others, was read well into the next century. Its preface issues a short but sharp protest by the printer, Richard Freebairn, at patronising comments recently made about British, and by implication Scottish, Latin by a Dutch scholar. He states the obvious: that the majority of Dutch scholars had felt very differently, and the Scottish achievement, in quality and quantity, spoke for itself.

CHAPTER FOUR

Poetry in the Languages and Dialects of Northern Scotland

Roberta Frank and Brian Smith

At first sight there is not much similarity between the island societies of the Northern Isles of Britain in the twelfth and twentieth centuries, and the verse produced in them. Orkney in the earlier period was an aristocratic community, dominated by some of the most powerful earls in Scandinavia; eight hundred years later, at least until the arrival of the oil industry in the 1970s, Orkney and Shetland were economic and cultural backwaters of Scotland. (The islands became Scottish counties in 1468–69.)

There is, however, much to study from both eras, and there are now useful synoptic works about the literatures of both groups of islands.[1] Here Frank discusses the skalds of Scandinavian Orkney and their metrical experiments; Smith the dialect verse and the poets of Shetland and Orkney from Victorian times until the present.

The Norse Verse of the Orkney Earldom

The poetry composed in Old Norse between c. 1030 and c. 1230 in Scandinavian Scotland offers precious glimpses into a literary culture unknown to Barbour, Henryson, Dunbar and Douglas. This verse is subtle and sophisticated, metrically and generically inventive, learned, politic, colourful, witty and cosmopolitan. The Norse Earldom of Orkney, which at its height controlled most of northern and western Scotland, was a busy crossroads. Icelandic court poets, sails trimmed to power, made their way there in the eleventh century, treating its rulers to skaldic tributes. In the Orkney Earldom of the twelfth century, traditional Norse-Icelandic skaldic forms met and embraced Francophone literary culture and theory, a process usually expressed in terms of fission and fusion, cross-fertilisation, minglings, convergences, interpenetrations and feedback-loops.

Two sites on the Mainland of Orkney, one from the late Viking Age, the other from the twelfth century, recall the two golden ages of verse production in the Northern Isles. The first, a complex of windswept ruins visible today on and near the Brough of Birsay, marks what remains of the hall and church of Earl Þorfinnr Sigurðarson the Mighty (c. 1009–1065), powerful patron of the skald Arnórr jarlaskáld ('earls' poet) Þórðarson. The second, a red sandstone Romanesque cathedral, still towers over central Kirkwall. Begun in 1137 by the earl and poet Rögnvaldr Kali Kolsson (ruled c. 1135–58), the cathedral was conceived as a memorial to St Magnus (d. 1117), earl, family martyr, and soon symbol of Orcadian independence. Major additions and alterations to the Kirkwall minster were overseen by the skald and bishop Bjarni Kolbeinsson (1150–1222), who lived next door in the Bishop's Palace, still standing. Like skilled masons carving local stone into new, imported forms, the poets of the Orkney Earldom used their craft to expand the range and competitiveness of Old Norse skaldic verse.

This Norse poetry deserves to be considered part of Scottish literary history, even though neither poets nor patrons thought of themselves as Scottish, and their 'Scotland' was not the nation we call by that name today. For an eleventh-century earl of Orkney, the land of the Scots was the 'other' place, the enemy territory where you burned and harried, hurled weapons, coloured rivers red, and fattened wolf, raven and eagle with corpses. Arnórr's memorial stanzas for Earl Þorfinnr Sigurðarson mention Scots, Scotland and the Scottish realm as opponents at least four times, along with naming (a first) the Pentland Firth, and locating battles at Roberry in Hoy, Tarbat Ness, Deer Ness, Loch Vatten in Skye and Dornoch Firth. As place-names indicate, the Scandinavian imprint on maritime Scotland north of the Great Glen was strong and long-lasting.

Earl Þorfinnr had close personal relations with Scotland and the Western Isles. His mother was a daughter of Malcolm II of Scotland; his maternal grandfather fostered him and gave him the earldoms of Sutherland and Caithness (where he lived for a time), a realm which he expanded southward and westward. His skald Arnórr, son of a famed Icelandic court poet who composed for several princes of Britain, married into the earl's family, and spent a long period of time in Orkney, perhaps even settling down. Þorfinnr's Norwegian widow Ingibjörg briefly presided over a Gaelic-speaking court as the first wife of King Malcolm III of Scotland, himself an English- as well as a Gaelic-speaker, a hint that at least some Scottish kings found the Norse earls valuable allies. Malcolm's second wife, Margaret (c. 1045–1093), Scotland's only female saint canonised by Rome, was of royal Anglo-Saxon descent and not only spoke English, French, German and Hungarian, but was famed at the Scottish court for her Latin literacy. The earls and poets of twelfth-century Orkney were multinational in origin and outlook: their exploits are recounted in *Orkneyinga saga* (*Saga of the Orkney Islanders*), compiled by an Icelandic author around 1200. Rögnvaldr Kali Kolsson was born in Norway of a Norwegian father and a mother descended from an earl of Orkney; he partnered with Icelandic skalds, and sojourned in southern France on his voyage to Constantinople and the Holy Land. Bishop Bjarni Kolbeinsson, who initiated Earl Rögnvaldr's canonisation, was the son of a Norwegian chief in Orkney and related on his mother's side to the earls of Orkney; he travelled frequently to Norway and had close relations with Oddi in southern Iceland, where Snorri Sturluson was reared.

Viking-age skaldic court poems in 'dróttkvætt' (the meter fit for the 'drótt', the ruler's band of retainers) involve commemoration and celebration. Such panegyrics (called 'drápur') include an initial call for silence, a summary of the ruler's outstanding battles and achievements, and an affirmation that his fame has spread far and wide. The 'erfidrápa', or *'memorial ode'*, to which most of the Norse kings between 900 and 1100 were treated, often conclude with a statement to the effect that the departed was the best prince under the heavens: it will be long before one equally great is born. So Arnórr praises Earl Þorfinnr around 1065:[2]

> Bj<u>ǫ</u>rt verðr sól at sv<u>ar</u>tri;
> s<u>ø</u>kkr fold í mar d<u>økk</u>van;
> br<u>es</u>tr erfiði <u>Aus</u>tra;
> *all*r glymr sær á fj<u>ǫ</u>llum,
> <u>áð</u>r at Eyjum fr<u>íð</u>ri
> (*inn*dróttar) Þórf*inn*i
> (þ<u>eim</u> hjalpi g<u>o</u>ð g<u>eymi</u>)
> gœðingr myni fœðask. [stanza 24]

Bjǫrt sól verðr at svartri; fold søkkr í døkkvan mar; {erfiði Austra} brestr; allr sær glymr á fjǫllum, áðr gœðingr fríðri Þórfinni myni fœðask at Eyjum; goð hjalpi {þeim geymi inndróttar}.

The bright sun will begin to blacken; the earth will sink into the dark sea; {the toil of Austri} [SKY / HEAVEN] will split; all the ocean will roar over the mountains, before a chieftain more splendid than Þorfinnr will be born in the Isles; may God help {that guardian of his household retainers} [RULER].

This is the classical eight-line 'dróttkvætt' stanza; a syntactic break after the fourth line divides the whole into two symmetrical halves. The basic unit is the three-stress, six-syllable line, with a trochaic or 'falling' ending. Two alliterating syllables in each odd line chime with the syllable (all three printed here in bold) at the head of the following even line (all initial vowels alliterate with each other). In every line the next-to-last syllable rhymes with a stem in the same line: full rhyme (same vowel and following consonant) occurs in even lines and is here indicated by italics; half or slant rhyme (different vowel, same consonant) occurs in odd lines and is here underlined. (Of the forty-eight syllables in a stanza, normally twenty-four were stressed, twelve bore alliteration, eight had to form full rhyme and eight, half rhyme; there was no choice in the placement of eight rhyming and four alliterating syllables.) Syntax is skewed (hence the prose order provided above); skalds used a special language, which included kennings (or metaphoric circumlocutions), 'solved' above in square brackets. In line 3, the 'toil of Austri (easterly)' refers to the myth that the sky is held up by four dwarfs.

Arnórr was the first skald to use the Norse meter 'hrynhent' (*'flowing rhyme'*): its alliteration and internal rhyme remain the same as in 'dróttkvætt', but its rhythm, which came to dominate later Icelandic poetry, seems to show the influence of the Latin trochaic tetrameter. In his poems in praise of King Magnús the Good of Norway, Arnórr is lavish with Christian motifs and colouring; and in a couplet for Earl Rögnvaldr Brúsason of Orkney (d. c. 1045), the poet's concluding prayer is unambiguously Christian: 'true ruler of the sun-tents' [SKY > God], help wise Rögnvaldr' (3). But in his ode for Earl Þorfinnr, Arnórr seems more chameleon-like. The imagery of stanza 24 – sun turning black, sky breaking, earth sinking into the sea – belongs to both Christian apocalypse and pagan Ragnarök, a stirring blend of Christian and ancestral tradition. The skald's concluding prayer ('may God help ...') shows similar cultural hybridism. Christians in the hall-troops to whom the memorial ode was addressed would have heard the word 'goð' as a monotheistic singular; nativists, in their turn, might have heard it as the pagan plural: 'may the gods help ...'[3] Although Adam of Bremen credited Þorfinnr with bringing Orkney into 'European Christendom', many paganisms and Christianities would have been lurking in Þorfinnr's bodyguard. To a skald at the coalface of things, the directions of the winds above was not always clear.

Arnórr's stanzas for Þorfinnr occasionally startle: horns never before heard in 'dróttkvætt' sound; men carry standards ashore; dawn signals the start of battle; and the earl's retinue, bent on carnage, reddens the 'eagle's tongue' (17/4). Skaldic verse traditionally revels in the bloodied claws, beaks and 'whiskers' of carrion birds, but to celebrate, as the skald does, a bird's reddened *tongue* seems a bit over the top. Women are completely absent from Arnórr's commemoration of Þorfinnr, as they are from all tenth- and eleventh-century court 'drápur'; his poem is distinctly male-centred, celebrating a masculine pride of life.

The stanzas of Rögnvaldr Kali Kolsson, twelfth-century earl of Orkney, mark a sea-change. The formal praise poem is gone and in its place a loose collection of stanzas registering moments that today might be immortalised in a photograph or tweet: a woman's bizarre headdress, the colour of a corpse, seemingly cross-dressed Orkney monks, the chattering teeth of a female servant in Shetland, in Constantinople a drunk companion falling off a bridge into the muck below. Content has changed too. Love between a man and woman, *fin' amor*, now boldly raises its head. In the summer of 1151, on his crusade to the Holy Land, Rögnvaldr halted in Narbonne, at the court of Viscountess Ermingerðr (Ermengarde/Ermengarda), patroness of a half-dozen troubadours. In the stanza below, he addresses her directly, presumably to obtain not her body, but a *laissez-passer* into the rich world of her court:

> Vísts, at frá berr flestu
> Fróða meldrs at góðu
> vel skúfaðra vífa
> vǫxtr þinn, konan svinna.
> Skorð lætr hár á herðar
> haukvallar sér falla
> – átgjǫrnum rauðk erni
> ilka – gult sem silki. [stanza 15]

Konan svinna, vísts, at vǫxtr þinn berr at góðu frá vel flestu vífa skúfaðra {meldrs Fróða}. {Skorð {haukvallar}} lætr hár, gult sem silki, falla á herðar sér; rauðk ilka átgjǫrnum erni.

Wise woman, it is certain that your [hair-]growth surpasses in goodness [that of] pretty much most women with locks of {the meal of Fróði} [GOLD]. {The prop {of the hawk-field}} [ARM > WOMAN] lets her hair, yellow as silk, fall onto her shoulders; I reddened the feet of the food-greedy eagle.[4]

The gold-kenning 'meldr Fróða' ('*meal (or flour) of Fróði*') in Rögnvaldr's first half-stanza has a local Orkney sound: not only does it allude to the story of slave-giantesses grinding out gold for that Danish king beneath the sea (or, in one version, the Pentland Firth), but 'meldr' ('*meal*') is good Northern Isles usage, as in Iceland the word referred only to 'the act of grinding' (*SkP* 2: 593). The skald opens with a general eulogy of Ermingerðr, something quite foreign to traditional Norse court poetry, before turning attention back to himself and his battlefield prowess. His boastful aside – 'I reddened the foot-soles of the food-greedy eagle' (= I fed carrion birds with corpses) – is not typical of Occitan love-lyric. It is as if, halfway through the stanza, a traditional skaldic rule reasserted itself, that the female addressed watches while the addressing male acts: 'Notice me, admire me, advertise me – look, lady, how good I am at being a man'. Rögnvaldr is here replicating and innovating within a traditional poetic form.

In collaboration with the Icelandic skald Hallr Þórarinsson, Rögnvaldr composed a long verse *clavis metrica* called 'Háttalykill inn forni' ('*the old key to verse-forms*') that systematically illustrated different metrical forms, many unattested in earlier Norse poetry. 'Háttalykill', in addition to serving as a model for Snorri Sturluson's better-known 'Háttatal' ('*list of verse-forms*'), may have been the first Norse poem intended for readers. Earlier praise poetry had been composed for named contemporary princes or recently dead ones. Rögnvaldr and Hallr begin their poem in the distant past with ancient, legendary heroes, including characters from stories about Ragnarr loðbrók, a figure also commemorated in runic inscriptions in Maeshowe, Orkney. The latter part of 'Háttalykill' (now incomplete) treats the military adventures of the kings of Denmark and Norway. These poets' innovative backward-look led the way for subsequent developments in Norse royal chronology and history.

A similar focus on old lore and legendary heroes characterises the *Jómsvíkingadrápa* by Bjarni Kolbeinsson, bishop of Orkney. Two centuries after the event, he narrates a story of Viking war and love: a Danish attack on Norway c. 986, culminating in a famed sea-battle in Hjörungavágr (Sunnmøre); Vagn Akason, youngest member of the Viking band, is defeated on the battlefield but fulfils his vow to wed Ingibjörg, daughter of the Norwegian chief. A first-person speaker, identified as the poet, is prominent throughout and comments incessantly on both his authorial role ('I call upon no warrior to listen to my poem') and his own unrequited love: 'a woman with beautiful hands has bound sorrow to me'; 'the beautiful woman robs me of happiness'). In each refrain-stanza, the narrator confides that a married woman causes him sorrow; parenthetical comments trace the progress of the Vikings' war-expedition:

> Ein drepr fyr mér allri
> – ylgr gekk á ná bólginn –
> – þar stóð úlfr í átu –
> ítrmanns kona teiti.
> Góð ætt of kemr grimmu
> – gein vargr of sal mergjar –
> – gráðr þvarr gylðis jóða –
> gœðings at mér stríði. [stanza 31]

Ein kona ítrmanns drepr allri teiti fyr mér; ylgr gekk á bólginn ná; úlfr stóð þar í átu. Góð ætt gœðings of kemr grimmu stríði at mér; vargr gein of {sal mergjar}; gráðr {jóða gylðis} þvarr.

A certain nobleman's wife slays all happiness for me; the she-wolf stepped on the swollen corpse; the wolf stood there on the food. The good descendant of a chieftain brings cruel torment upon me; a wolf gaped over {the hall of marrow} [BONE]; the greed of the wolf's babies diminished.

The skald's 'I' gives the illusion of simultaneity, of a performance of oral poetry, as the speaker grotesquely interweaves his unhappy love and the carnage of battle. A light parodic wit mocks conventional skaldic clichés: rather than having a solitary wolf enjoying fresh carrion he calls up the entire family – a she-wolf, two males and a pack of hungry cubs. *Jómsvíkingadrápa* marks the first appearance in Norse literature of a love lament as both frame and refrain in a narrative poem. This 'device' becomes a habit in the later Icelandic 'rímur', whose conventional erotic introductions were called 'mansöngr', a word that in skaldic verse occurs only in *Jómsvíkingadrápa* and in *Málsháttakvæði*, the poem that immediately follows in the single manuscript preserving both. Both compositions juxtapose the grand passion of a hero from the Viking age with the skald/speaker's own disappointment in love.

As in *Jómsvíkingadrápa*, the speaker of the *Málsháttakvæði* or 'Proverb poem' (the title is modern) opens by lamenting his inadequacy as both poet and lover. The skald structures his catalogue of old lore as an erotic complaint, the frenetic, incoherent piling up of sayings mirroring his inner turmoil. The momentous – Norse gods and goddesses, golden pagan heroes – appears alongside the everyday: wave-washed skerries, frangible spring ice, foxes, cows, pigs, frogs and bad haircuts. The poem presents a kind of soap-opera version of the myth of Baldr, in which that god's tragic death is portrayed as an ordinary domestic tragedy rather than the beginning of the last days of the world:

> Friggjar þótti svipr at syni;
> sá var taldr ór miklu kyni;
> Hermóðr vildi auka aldr;
> Éljúðnir vann sólginn Baldr.
> Oll grétu þau eptir hann;
> aukit var þeim hlátrar bann;
> heyrinkunn er frá hánum saga;
> hvat þarf ek of slíkt at jaga. [stanza 9]

Þótti svipr at {syni Friggjar}; sá var taldr ór miklu kyni; Hermóðr vildi auka aldr; Éljúðnir vann Baldr sólginn. Þau ǫll grétu eptir hann; {bann hlátrar} var þeim aukit; saga frá hánum er heyrinkunn; hvat þarf ek at jaga of slíkt.

It seemed a sudden loss concerning {the son of Frigg} [= Baldr]; he was reckoned from a great family; Hermóðr wanted to extend his life; Éljúðnir [hall of Hel] had swallowed up Baldr. They all wept for him; {their ban of laughter} [SORROW] grew; the tale about him is very well known; no need for me to harp on it.

The narrator talks constantly about himself, trespassing on our field of vision like a family member whose toothy face obstructs every photographed wonder of the world. His self-referential asides evoke the impression that the poem is coming into existence before our eyes. Lovesick, he flirts shamelessly with the discourse of disease, mentioning minor miseries such as boils, cataracts, toothache and diarrhoea, along with the more exalted pestilence and mania. The refrain, forming the second half of four stanzas, alludes to the bewitchment of Norway's king, Haraldr hárfagri 'fair hair', famed Viking-age hero, by the Saami enchantress Snjófríðr:

> Stefjum verðr at stæla brag,
> – stuttligt hefk á kvæði lag –
> ella mun þat þykkja þula
> þannig nær, sem ek henda mula.

Ekki var þat forðum farald;
Finnan gat þó œrðan Harald;
hánum þótti sólbjǫrt sú;
slíks dœmi verðr mǫrgum nú. [stanza 11]

Verðr at stæla brag stefjum – hefk stuttligt lag á kvæði –, ella mun þat þykkja þula, þannig nær, sem ek henda mula. Ekki var þat farald forðum; Finnan gat þó Harald œrðan; hánum þótti sú sólbjǫrt; mǫrgum verðr nú dœmi slíks.

Poetry has to be fitted with refrains – I have an abrupt form in this poem – else it shall seem a rigmarole, almost as if I were grabbing at crumbs. It wasn't a malady in the old days; still, the Saami girl drove Haraldr out of his mind; to him she seemed bright as the sun; many a man has experience of such now.

The poem is composed throughout in an alliterating 'end rhymed' variety of 'hrynhent' metre first seen in Earl Rögnvaldr's 'Háttalykill'. (The linkage of 'farald', *'pestilence'*, with *Harald* in the refrain might not have struck the living king as comic.) In addition to a manuscript association, *Málsháttakvæði* shares some content, archaisms, dialect words and rare lexical items with *Jómsvíkingadrápa*; it may also share an author.

The anonymous twelfth-century poem *Krákumál* (*Kraka's Poem*) is on various grounds often taken to be an Orcadian composition as well: who else but an Orkneyman would report a naval skirmish in the Sound of Yell? Its speaker is the Viking leader Ragnarr loðbrók 'hairy breeches', who dies heroically, a smile on his lips. In 1636, Ole Worm published Ragnarr's 'Deathsong' with a Latin translation, launching it into the learned world; the phrase *ridens moriar* ('laughing I shall die') influenced views of northern heroism for centuries. In his *Orcades* (1697), the Icelander Thormod Torfæus quoted another anonymous poem, *Darraðarljóð*, battle-verses supposedly chanted by valkyries at their loom and overheard by a man in Caithness; Torfæus's textual source was Thomas Bartholin's *Antiquitatum Danicarum* (1689); both he and Bartholin lie behind Thomas Gray's version, *The Fatal Sisters* (1761), perhaps the most famous eighteenth-century English literary rendering of the Norse sanguinary sublime. The original milieu for *Darraðarljóð* was almost certainly the British Isles; a more precise localisation is impossible.

Although there is no evidence for a vibrant Norse literary culture in Orkney after the middle of the thirteenth century, oral traditions lingered on. In his novel *The Pirate*, Walter Scott tells, at third hand from a Mr Baikie of Kirkwall, the story of an eighteenth-century Orkney clergyman who

> remembered well when some remnants of the Norse were still spoken in the island called North Ronaldshaw. When Gray's Ode, entitled the 'Fatal Sisters', was first published, or at least first reached that remote island, the reverend gentleman had the well-judged curiosity to read it to some of the old persons of the isle, as a poem which regarded the history of their own country. They listened with great attention to the preliminary stanzas [...]. But when they had heard a verse or two more, they interrupted the reader, telling him they knew the song well in the Norse language, and had often sung it to him when he asked them for an old song. They called it the 'Magicians', or the 'Enchantresses'. It would have been singular news to the elegant translator, when executing his version from the text of Bartholin, to have learned that the Norse original was still preserved by tradition in a remote corner of the British dominions.[5]

It is a pretty story but, alas, not very reliable. Not folk memory but an early transfer to Iceland ensured the preservation of the extraordinary verse of the Orkney Earldom.

Roberta Frank

Modern and Contemporary Poetry in Northern Scottish Dialects

Dialect verse in Orkney and Shetland came into existence in the late nineteenth century. In Shetland the indispensable medium for its appearance, as for dialect writing elsewhere in Scotland, was the arrival of a local newspaper press in 1872.[6] The *Shetland Times* published dialect poetry and prose from the outset, and its rival, the *Shetland News* (1885–1963), vied with it in doing the same.

The Shetland pioneers George Stewart (1825–1911) and James Stout Angus (1830–1923) produced their first work in the 1870s. Whereas Stewart's work was sentimental and pawky, Angus's poem 'Eels' (published in the *Shetland Times* in 1877, but not reprinted until 1920) is a 'strange masterpiece':[7] lyrical and humorous at the same time. 'Eels' inaugurated a school and tradition of Shetland poetry.

The appearance of dialect verse in Orkney was less promising. There was and is no Orkney school: the pioneer Walter Traill Dennison (1826–1894), author of agreeable and genial verses, worked entirely on his own. By contrast, in the same period a group of Shetland poets, many of them exiles in Edinburgh, was publishing relatively unusual work. Jessie M. E. Saxby (1842–1940), L. J. Nicolson, the self-styled 'Bard of Thule' (1844–1901), and Basil R. Anderson (1861–1888) are key figures from that era.

It was not until J. J. Haldane Burgess (1862–1927) published his masterpiece, *Rasmie's Büddie*, in 1891, that the Shetland movement came of age. Burgess, a talented linguist and teacher, and a passionate socialist, had heard some superior men, as he put it, discuss how Shetland dialect was worthless for expressing abstract ideas.[8] He set to work to prove them wrong. His masterpiece is 'Scranna', a long poem about a duel between a Shetland crofter, Rasmie, and Satan: an amusing predecessor of Max Beerbohm's short story 'Enoch Soames' (1916), except that Rasmie is victorious in the contest.

On a more sombre level, Burgess's poem 'Da oobin [moaning] wind', Hardyesque in tone and written at the end of a 'doitin' (senile) year, confronts the dire problems and possibilities of the century's end.

The First World War created havoc in Orkney and Shetland, as elsewhere in the world, and the depression of the inter-war period was not conducive to serious literary work. It was not until 1947 that Peter Jamieson (1898–1976), a Lerwick Communist, founded the *New Shetlander* magazine, to publish prose and verse that anatomised the islands' post-war situation. Himself a poet, he had already sounded out and got on board others: William J. Tait (1918–1992), T. A. Robertson (1909–1973), writing under the pen-name 'Vagaland', and Stella Sutherland (1924–2015).

Tait, Robertson and Sutherland produced major work. Each of them was anthologised in Scottish collections, and each produced widely different material. Tait was cerebral, influenced by MacDiarmid and the modern English poets: his collected poems *A Day between Weathers* (1980) is a masterpiece. Robertson was intro-spective and sometimes (as in his poem 'Da Sneug wal') mystical. Sutherland is emotional – see her 'Celandine' – but her emotions are under strict control. Each of them also produced fine work in old age. They are arguably the best Shetland poets of any period.

The *New Shetlander* continued to attract good dialect verse after Jamieson demitted the editorship in 1956. He was succeeded by John J. Graham (1921–2008) and his brother Laurence Graham (1924–2009), themselves dialect poets; they attracted work by Jack Peterson (1898–1972), Rhoda Bulter (1929–1994) and many others. The tradition continued.

In Orkney, meanwhile, Robert Rendall (1898–1967) had emerged as a writer of fine dialect verse, first published in volume form in 1946. But in those islands, by contrast with Shetland at that point, there was deep pessimism about the viability of the local language for literary work. Writing in 1949, Ernest W. Marwick uttered the extreme opinion that '[t]he time for attempting to make the [Orkney] vernacular a vehicle of serious verse passed long ago'.[9]

Orcadians were envious of the *New Shetlander* and the renaissance in verse that it had fostered, and yearned to produce something similar. 'I do not insult or belittle my own Orkney people', wrote a youthful George Mackay Brown (1921–1996), 'when I say that the Shetland imagination and sense of purpose, which functioned triumphantly when in Orkney the spirit lay dark and cold, is even stronger than ours; and is even now due to speak out nobly and magically once more.'[10]

But Brown himself never essayed dialect verse, and no Orcadian equivalent of the *New Shetlander* appeared. It was not until 2008, when Morag Macinnes (b. 1950) published *Alias Isobel*, that Robert Rendall had a serious fellow practitioner in Orkney. That work, the curious tale of a woman who posed as a man while working at the Hudson's Bay Company, is the most adventurous and accomplished Orkney dialect poetry to date, comparable with the Shetland output. Macinnes has now produced *Street Shapes* (2013), a collection of dialect poems about her native Stromness.

She is alone in her achievement in her native islands. Shetland poetry, on the other hand, thrives in the present day. Christine De Luca (b. 1947), Laureen Johnson (b. 1949), Jim Mainland (b. 1952), John M. Tait (b. 1955), Robert Alan Jamieson (b. 1958), James Sinclair (b. 1961), Paul Ritch (b. 1967), Lise Sinclair (1971–2013), Mark Ryan Smith (b. 1976), and Jen Hadfield (b. 1978), who relocated to Shetland and makes occasional use of Shetland dialect, are representative dialect poets from Shetland's most recent literary renaissance. All of them are associated with the *New Shetlander*; most feature in Kevin MacNeil's anthology *These Islands, We Sing* (2011). Each writes verse that would have been intelligible and pleasing to Burgess in the 1890s: they are part of a tradition that he and his colleagues began to fashion, and which is still vibrant.

There is a final contrast between Orkney and Shetland that we must discuss. Amidst so much good writing, for a long time Shetlanders have been anxious about the long-term prospects for their dialect. In 1953 a local anthologist complained that it had been 'overwhelmed under the onslaught of east coast Scotch and board school English, until any effort at rescuing and restoring the old speech as a living tongue would be futile to the point of silliness'.[11] In 2004 Shetland Arts Trust went so far as to convene a conference to discuss the matter.[12] The poets were producing fine dialect verse, but they worried. There is no such breast-beating in Orkney. The question arises, in this case: does anxiety lead to creativity?

Brian Smith

CHAPTER FIVE

The Sixteenth and Seventeenth Centuries

Sìm Innes and Alessandra Petrina

Gavin Douglas's *Eneados* was concluded in 1513; in the same year James IV's reign reached its apogee, only to conclude disastrously with his attempted invasion of England and his defeat at Flodden. Just as Douglas represents a poet *in limine* between the medieval, courtly mode and the new humanist interests, so the Battle of Flodden Field marks the end of a period of great hopes of social and intellectual renewal for Scotland (in 1507 the king had supported Chepman and Myllar's project to set up a printing press in Edinburgh); but the apparent check gave way to a new phase of Scottish literature. The ninety years between Flodden and the Union of the Crowns (1603) have been hailed as 'an impossible, or improbable, first Scottish Renaissance';[1] they are a time of literary creativity and experimentation, in which lyric poetry undergoes great changes. Such changes, as far as literature in Scots or English is concerned, are inextricably linked with political power: both Mary Stuart and her son James VI were poets, and the latter's interest in literature fostered new poetic modes at the Scottish court. If Crown policy, particularly during and after the reign of James VI and I, rejected Gaelic literary production as alien to the royal court, the Gaelic nobility supported, and themselves produced, a wealth of Gaelic poetry, often transitional and innovative, against a background of Crown-promoted forfeiture, plantation, feud and strictures in the Gaelic world.

Manuscript Anthologies

James IV lost battle and life at Flodden, leaving on the throne the infant James V. The following years saw dissension and competition for power among the Scottish nobility; the court was no longer the unifying centre of intellectual life. Individual noblemen, in both the Highlands and the Lowlands, would patronise poetic efforts meant to support their cause or aggrandise their status, and writers would express their concern for the instability of the country. The literary production is thus dispersed and diversified.

In this confused situation, isolated poetic voices emerge, such as that of the court poet David Lyndsay of the Mount, discussed below, or of the scholar George Buchanan, one of the first poets to offer, in his (Latin) paraphrases of the Psalms, an instance of a genre that would be extremely popular throughout the Reformation. Even more interesting is the rise and establishment of literary manuscript anthologies, possibly the most precious testimony of late medieval and early modern poetry, not only showing the wealth of poetic production in early modern Scotland, but also offering a fascinating glimpse of the tastes of early modern readers.[2] Among the anthologies in Scots and English, the most notable are the early sixteenth-century Asloan Manuscript, the late sixteenth-century Bannatyne Manuscript and the Maitland Folio and Quarto, all presenting a richly diversified range of genres, and preserving for us much of the poetry of the makars (so much so that they have in fact been subsequently 'worked as a quarry')[3] as well as late medieval English poetry, particularly Chaucer's; but other collections, such as William Fowler's papers (Edinburgh, NLS, MSS Hawthornden 2063–67), are equally important as they reflect not only the literary production of the time but also the often collaborative nature of such production. In exceptional cases such as the Bannatyne Manuscript, an articulate, organised collection of uniquely wide range, they can also be read as the attempt to create a canon of national literature by exercising a surprising degree of editorial control on the collected material, showing the compiler's view of Scottish poetry, or, in some cases, the Scotticisation of English models.[4] Anthologies would play an important role in the canonisation of Scottish literature even in later years – one has only to think of the *Delitiae Poetarum Scotorum*, printed in Amsterdam in 1637.[5]

Manuscript anthologies of bardic and semi-bardic Gaelic poetry do not survive in large numbers for the period; those that do, however, are hugely significant. They include the Book of the Dean of Lismore (1512–42), NLS MS 72.1.48 (seventeenth century) and the Fernaig Manuscript (1688–93). Indeed, the Book of the Dean of Lismore, largely compiled during the reign of James V, may to some extent reflect the same collaborative desire to anthologise, as noted above, in the years following Flodden. Surviving Gaelic manuscripts compiled in sixteenth- and seventeenth-century Scotland preserve poetry belonging to the bardic and semi-bardic traditions but not the vernacular clan poetry tradition nor the folksong tradition. The clan poetry and folksong corpora datedto the sixteenth and seventeenth centuries come to us from a combination of Gaelic oral tradition and the papers and publications of collectors from the eighteenth century onwards. Therefore, the surviving evidence allows us to see that these four distinct, and yet interrelated, Gaelic poetic traditions all flourished concurrently during our period. As one instance of this, poetry from at least three Gaelic traditions, and maybe even from all four, survives eulogising or elegising the same chieftan: Dòmhnall Gorm Òg (d. 1643), chief of the MacDonalds of Sleat, who was created baronet of Nova Scotia in 1625 by Charles I. Cathal MacMhuirich, active during the first half of the seventeenth century, composed a sophisticated bardic eulogy for MacDonald: 'Mo-chean do chonnarc a-réir' (*'Welcome to him I saw last night'*) which survives in the poet's own manuscript hand in Dublin, RIA MS E i 3 (778).[6] On MacDonald's death Murchadh Mòr mac mhic Mhurchaidh MacCoinnich (Murdo MacKenzie), chief of the MacKenzies of Achilty, composed the semi-bardic elegy 'Sgeula leat, a ghaoth a deas' (*'You bring news, wind from the south'*).[7] A number of MacKenzie's poems survive in the Fernaig Manuscript.[8] A vernacular eulogy, again for the same Dòmhnall Gorm, 'A Dhòmhnaill an Dùin' (*'O Donald of the Dùn'*) (c. 1640), from early in the career of the 'clan' poet Iain Lom, comes to us from *Comh-Chruinneachidh Orannaigh Gaidhealach* (1776), the first printed anthology of Gaelic verse.[9] This collection is known as the 'Eigg Collection' and was edited by a son of the renowned Jacobite poet Alasdair mac Mhaighstir Alasdair. Further, a folksong, 'Tàladh Dhòmhnaill Ghuirm' (*'Lullaby for Donald Gorm'*), could also be for our Dòmhnall Gorm, as a young child.[10] Various versions of 'Tàladh Dhòmhnaill Ghuirm' were collected from tradition bearers in the nineteenth and twentieth centuries and subsequently published.[11] Thus, a wealth of Scottish poetry in a variety of registers of Scots, Gaelic, English and Latin from the sixteenth and seventeenth centuries survived in manuscript, in print and in the oral tradition. A select overview of poetic production during the reigns of James V and Mary will be followed by an examination of the reign of James VI and into the latter half of the seventeenth century.

After Flodden: James V and the Marian Period

David Lyndsay of the Mount (c. 1486–1555), whose poems (*The Dreme*, 1526–28, *The Complaynt*, 1529–30, and *The Testament and Complaynt of Our Soverane Lordis Papyngo*, 1530) testify to his concern with a potentially explosive political situation, is the single most memorable name in an age of political and social confusion. A poet, satirist and reformer, he is now best remembered as a dramatist.[12] Yet he had a very individual voice, often using popular speech and metre (though he is also familiar with the Chaucerian stanza), proverbs and colloquialisms in drama and poetry – remarkable traits that will find echoes in later poets. In his early *Dreme* he uses the convention of the dream-vision, beloved of late medieval poets, but rather than inserting in this frame an equally conventional love complaint, he inserts a striking vision of Scotland's plight; the central figure is not a Petrarchan lady, but 'Jhone of the Comoun Weill'. Later poems will be openly satiric, espousing the cause of the Reformation. The Bannatyne collection also preserves the works of Alexander Scott (*fl.* 1545–68), whose love poems, rather than mere expressions of individual emotions, should be seen as having a '*collective* function within a court community'.[13] Religious poetry also finds its Protestant voice in these years (though the Bannatyne manuscripts contain verse expressive of Catholic devotion), mixing translations (or 'paraphrases') from the Psalms and adaptations of musical and metrical setting from pre-existing non-religious verse: the most notable example doubtlessly is *The Gude and Godlie Ballatis* (published in 1546 and often reprinted), a collection of spiritual songs and ballads (often translations of Lutheran texts), including also a metrical translation of the Psalms. Here popular rhythms and images, through adaptation and appropriation, are set at the service of religious propaganda, making this the most popular volume of the Scottish Reformation.[14]

Women poets, in both the sixteenth and seventeenth centuries,[15] are a small but striking group, including the Calvinist poet Elizabeth Melville, Lady Culross (*fl.* 1599–1631) and the translator Anna Hume (*fl.* 1644). But the most individual voice undoubtedly belongs to Mary, Queen of Scots (1542–87). She is remembered (though her authorship is controversial) for a collection of secular love sonnets in French, the so-called Casket Sonnets, and for meditational or elegiac love poems. Her output also includes a collection of religious poems.[16]

A collective court function is also key to an understanding of Gaelic poetry in this era. A cluster of bardic poems by Fionnlagh an Bard Ruadh, a professional poet, addressed to Eoin Dubh, chief of the MacGregors (d. 1519), survive from the Book of the Dean of Lismore. The poet beseeches the chief for patronage, apparently following some misstep.[17] Patronage may indeed have become increasingly difficult to acquire since Gaelic poetic survivals from the sixteenth century are not plentiful. There is in fact a noticeable dearth of syllabic poetry by MacMhuirich poets for the sixteenth century.[18] However, much has been lost; on occasion we know of poets but have nothing of their corpus.[19] 'Linn nan Creach' ('*The Age of Forays*') witnessed much upheaval and saw the Crown extracting much higher levels of rental from the Western Highlands, as well as the Dòmhnall Dubh 1545 rebellion.[20] The Campbells of Glenorchy, whose participation as patrons and poets of Gaelic literary circles is evident in the Book of the Dean of Lismore, went into decline as a powerful kindred following Flodden and then appear not to have prioritised Gaelic literature on their return to strength from the 1550s.[21] A similar slump and then new wave of professional bardic poetry by the end of the sixteenth century is detectable in Ireland also.[22]

Indeed, consideration of the pan-Gaelic context can help to flesh out our understanding of the involvement of Scottish Gaels in poetic production and consumption during periods when Scottish evidence becomes scarce. The latter half of the sixteenth century saw a number of important marriage alliances between the noble houses of Ulster and the Western Highlands. These marriages give us a glimpse of the educational achievements of some Highland noblewomen. Catrìona (d. 1588), the daughter of Eachann Mòr MacLean of Duart (*fl.* 1527–70), was married twice in Ireland and twice in Gaelic Scotland.[23] She was reportedly 'not unlernyd in the Latyn tong, speckyth good French, and as is sayd, som lyttel Italyone'.[24] Anna/Agnes Campbell (d. 1590), daughter of Colin Campbell (Cailean Meallach), the third Earl of Argyll (d. 1529), married James MacDonnell (Seumas nan Ruaig, d. 1565) of Dùn Naomhaig and the Glens of Antrim, chief of Clann Eòin Mhòir. Both Anna and Fionnghuala (An Inghean Dubh, d. c. 1611), her daughter with MacDonnell, were important political players in Gaelic Scotland and Ireland, with further high-profile marriage alliances in Ulster. A report from 1569 tells us that both women were 'trained up in the scotts courte & spake both frenche and inglyshe'.[25] We might assume, although without any evidence either way, that this learning came at the expense of training in Classical Gaelic. Yet, although little bardic poetry from Scotland survives from the period, both Anna[26] and Fionnghuala are mentioned by name in bardic poems composed for their husbands by Irish poets and presumably acted as patrons. An Irish Ó hEóghusa poet, referring to Colla Uais, the purported fourth-century ancestor of the MacDonalds, describes Fionnghuala as 'Crú daghCholla nár dhiúlt cléir an Inghean Dubh dreach shoiléir' ('*Stock of good Colla who never refused a poet-troop is the Inghean Dubh of the shining countenance*').[27]

The reigns of James V and Mary provide us with works of note from the other Gaelic traditions. Indeed some of the earliest songs surviving in the Scottish Gaelic vernacular, rather than the pan-Gaelic high literary register, are from this period and in some respects also reflect the uncertain times. 'Caismeachd Ailein nan Sop' ('*War-Song for Ailean nan Sop*'), by the chief of the MacLeans of Coll, dated to around 1537, celebrates the deeds of a raider and pirate.[28] In 'Òran na Comhachaig' ('*The Song of the Owl*'), a long dialogue piece perhaps a little later, the owl is asked to record the troubled past of the Central Highlands:

> Bu lìonmhor cogadh is creachan
> Bha 'n Loch Abar anns an uair sin;
> C' àite am biodh tusa 'gad fhalach
> Eòin bhig na mala gruamaich.

Numerous were the conflicts and raids / In Lochaber at that time; / Where used you to hide yourself, / Little bird of the gloomy brow?[29]

To this period also belong a number of poems seen to be transitional between bardic poetry and the poetry of the vernacular clan poets, to be discussed below, such as 'An Duanag Ullamh' ('*The Finished Ditty*') and 'MhicPhàrlain an Arair' ('*MacFarlane of Arrochar*').[30] From the middle of the sixteenth century the collective court function of poetry remains vital in Scotland. As we shall see, James VI's own keen interest in poetry, and also Crown policy in Gaelic Scotland and Ireland, may also have further galvanised new and transitional literary modes in a number of Scotland's literary and vernacular languages.

The Reign of James VI

Though not the only early modern European poet-king, James VI (1566–1625) was unique in promoting poetry as part of a political agenda. Whatever the truth about the denomination 'Castalian band',[31] doubtlessly his determination to have a coterie of poets and translators resulted in a new attention to lyric poetry and non-Scottish literary modes: the poets surrounding him – Alexander Montgomerie, John Stewart of Baldynneis, William Fowler, Alexander Hume and the Hudson brothers – are the most significant voices of the late sixteenth century.[32] The fact that two of them, Thomas and Robert Hudson, were

Englishmen employed in Scotland as court musicians shows the closeness of music and poetry in Scottish early modern poetry,[33] but also the attention James paid to foreign literary models. However one may judge his own efforts as a poet,[34] he undoubtedly possessed technical competence and curiosity,[35] enough to complete 'Ane Schort Treatise conteining some Reulis and Cautelis to be observit and eschwit in Scottis poesie', published in 1584, a manual that (though indebted to Joachim Du Bellay's *Deffence et Illustration de la Langue Françoise*) is both didactic and political.

Among his closest followers was John Stewart of Baldynneis (c. 1550–c. 1605), who shared with William Fowler a preference for Italian literary models, leaving a manuscript of verse including an abridgement of Ariosto's *Orlando Furioso*, thirty-three sonnets and a long poem, *Ane Schersing Out of Trew Felicitie*. This interesting corpus shows two of the main characteristics of James's coterie: its use of lyric forms and its interest in translation. One cannot overestimate the importance of translation in the development of Scottish poetry, and its basis on literary imitation.[36] Though the most notable translations were of epic poetry (Thomas Hudson and James himself translating Du Bartas's *Judith* and *Uranie*, Baldynneis translating Ariosto), lyric poetry also played a role, in the translation of Petrarch's *Trionfi* undertaken by William Fowler (1560–1612) and conceived as an answer to the earlier English translation by Henry Parker, Lord Morley (an effort echoed half a century later by Anna Hume with her own version of the *Trionfi*). Such a translation, though not memorable, highlights an interesting facet of Petrarchism in Scotland. As happened in the British Isles, the Petrarchan work that most engaged translators was the *Trionfi* rather than the *Canzoniere*; the latter, though never translated in its entirety, became a powerful model, and inspired a vogue for the sonnet in Scotland that matched the English one.[37] All the poets at James's court engaged with this form, mainly using the so-called Spenserian sonnet. Fowler was more determined than any other 'Castalian' in his search for Italian models, looking at Petrarch but also at Giordano Bruno's *Eroici Furori* for his sonnet sequence, *The Tarantula of Love*.[38]

The most striking lyrical voice at James's court is that of Alexander Montgomerie (c. 1555–1597), whose fame, for a time depending only on single poems such as *The Cherrie and the Slae* (printed in 1597), has recently flourished again[39] thanks to the rediscovery of masterpieces such as his flyting with Polwart (echoing earlier examples of the genre), or *The Solsequium*, in which the lover is compared to a sunflower, evoking 'an allegory of longing for Christ's presence'.[40] Other, possibly minor, voices, such as that of Robert Ayton (1570–1638), author of epigrams and courtly, occasional verse, also add to the richness of the literary culture of the period.

The royal court of King James VI and I was apparently not a creative hub for Gaelic poetry. His rantings against his Gaelic-speaking subjects are well known. He also oversaw attempts at plantation of parts of the Hebrides with Lowland Scots. Yet this apparent 'lunatic racial prejudice'[41] against Gaels did not stop him turning to Scotland's Gaelic past when it served his own purposes. For instance, in 1614 he stated that he would not neglect the Irish situation since 'as King of England, by reason of the long possession the Crown of England has had of that land; and also as King of Scotland; for the ancient Kings of Scotland are descended from the Kings of Ireland', he had a duty to intervene.[42] The Lowland royal court was not closed to the Gaelic nobility during this period either. A number of prominent Gaels had houses in Edinburgh from the beginning of the sixteenth century and indeed some held positions of national importance, particularly the Campbell earls of Argyll.[43] Iseabail Mhòr, the daughter of MacDonald of Glengarry and wife of Ruairidh Mòr MacLeòid of Harris, is reported to have acted as a maid of honour for James's queen, Anne of Denmark (d. 1619).[44]

Outwith the royal court a burst of creativity and masterful Gaelic bardic poetry survives from the first half of the seventeenth century by the MacMhuirich and Ó Muirgheasáin poetic lineages. The prized product of the Gaelic bardic poet in Ireland and Scotland was the eulogy that set out the attributes and right to rule of the chief. As a conservative poetry of convention, bardic poetry, for and often by the nobility, can be portrayed as lacking political awareness and as 'anachronistic, particularist and elitist'.[45] Yet conversely we might celebrate the cultural vitality that allowed Cathal MacMhuirich to pepper his poetry with allusions to both medieval Irish and Classical literatures. He compares one patron to Guaire Aidne mac Colmáin, a seventh-century Irish king legendary for generosity;[46] another is compared to Cormac mac Airt, a third-century Irish king legendary for wisdom;[47] the soldiers of a third patron are likened to 'táin na Traoí' ('*the host of Troy*').[48] Also, bardic poetry can provide some evidence that the professional poet could act as praiser but also 'ambassador, spy, "native-bishop", chief counsellor, genealogist'.[49] For instance, MacMhuirich has one poem in which he calls on Coll Ciotach MacDonald (d. 1647) to bring his violent campaign to an end. He uses praise, and in that poem Gaelic proverbs, to this aim.[50]

Bardic poetry was 'a stylistic instrument of great delicacy and potentiality'[51] and perhaps this is nowhere clearer than in Scotland's bardic tradition of Gaelic *amour courtois*. Niall Mòr MacMhuirich's beautifully tense 'Soraidh slán don oidhche a-réir' (*'Hail and farewell to last night'*) exemplifies this:

> Nocha leigid lucht na mbréag
> smid as mo bhéal, a rosg mall
> tuig an ní adeir mo shúil
> agus tú san chúil úd thall.

The folk of lies do not allow / one peep from my lip, o languid eye: / understand the thing my eye says, / though you are in the corner over by.[52]

In the examples quoted above we see instances of poetry adapting a European poetic convention in uniquely Gaelic fashion. In addition, the sonnet found an original voice in Scotland, employed both for occasional verse in Scots (rather than Latin), as in the congratulatory sonnets appended to or prefacing longer works, and in the more complex form of the sonnet sequence, beloved of later poets such as William Alexander (*Aurora*, 1604), David Murray (*Celia*, 1611), and Alexander Craig of Rosecraig (*Amorous Songes*, 1606). But the greatest sonneteer is certainly William Drummond of Hawthornden (1585–1649). A poet of both religious and amorous poetry and a remarkable translator, he also wrote a striking meditation ('A Cypresse Grove', included in his 1623 collection *Flowres of Sion*). He occupies an isolated place in the Scottish canon: often accused of being derivative, and of writing an 'imitative poetry [that] hardly contains anything Scottish',[53] he strikes a singular note in that much of his work is detached from contemporary social or political concerns, and devoted to the enquiry upon beauty, whether the beloved's or God's.[54] Though his poetry appeared when in the rest of Europe Petrarchism was already declining, and though critics have considerable difficulties in locating it within a specific cultural setting,[55] Drummond in fact proposes an innovative elaboration of Petrarchan philosophy of love, freeing it from the 'ideological burden' superimposed by the love poetry of Mary Stuart.[56]

Mairghread nighean Lachlainn, active from the end of the seventeenth century, asks, 'Ach cò an neach a tha gun mhùtha, mar na nialaibh air an aonach' (*'But who can remain without change, as the clouds on the moorland must change?'*).[57] Indeed our period witnesses an 'inexorable revolution in Gaelic poetry' since from the middle of the seventeenth century we find more and more vernacular clan poetry and less and less bardic poetry.[58] The work of professional vernacular poets such as Eachann Bacach (d. post 1651), Iain Lom (d. post 1707), Màiri nighean Alasdair Ruaidh (d. c. 1707) and An Clàrsair Dall (d. 1713/14) can be supplemented by the work of noble non-professionals such as An Ciaran Mabach.[59] It has been noted of clan poetry that 'more-or-less formulaic praise of the chief continues to be a dominant theme'.[60] Thus, one poetry of convention, that of the bardic poets, is replaced by another poetry of convention, that of the clan poets – the search for innovations or the voice of the individual poet must be undertaken with an understanding of the panegyric code.[61] Yet, partly as a result of the use of the vernacular and the rise of polemic on political issues of local and national importance, clan poetry has also been described as 'radical' and of a 'popular orientation'.[62] Towards the close of the seventeenth century, in at least some parts of the Highlands, the opportunities for noble patronage which might allow a professional poet to perform his or her collective court function were dwindling. While some courts continued to thrive, An Clàrsair Dall famously longs for the 'dùn' which was once filled with song and beloved of poet bands. We learn that the new young chief of the MacLeods of Dunvegan prefers Edinburgh to the Gaelic literary and musical entertainments of home.[63]

Scotland can boast of a treasure trove of poetry in the sixteenth and seventeenth centuries. The corpus discussed here reflects the culturally and linguistically diverse nature of the country and the politically and socially tumultuous eras. We would not expect to see exact parallel trends in Scots and Gaelic poetry during the period, and yet a number of new literary forms come to light and flourish, along with more traditional forms, in both. This engenders a sense of the country as a crossroads of cultures and tongues, eager to import texts and genres from outwith its own borders, but at the same time reworking them and making them part of emergent national canons. In the same decades in which the Scottish nation finds its identity and negotiates its complex relationship with England and Gaelic Ireland, Scottish lyric poetry evolves in innovative, polyphonic ways which build on native traditions whilst also engaging with wider European modes.

CHAPTER SIX

The Eighteenth Century

Ronald Black and Gerard Carruthers

Eighteenth-century poetry in Scotland involves us in a rich set of varieties and critical approaches. When in Scots or English, it has been read rather narrowly against the supposed watershed date of 1707 (the Union of the Parliaments), and in Gaelic verse, where there is an obvious correlation between the clan system and the panegyric code, it is only too easy to see the key dates of 1715 and 1746 (the battles of Sheriffmuir and Culloden) as points of transition from codification to realism.

Much criticism, especially in the last hundred years, has tended to read Scottish eighteenth-century poetry as deeply unsatisfactory overall English, Gaelic, Latin and Scots are alleged to represent different ideological positions. Three of the most influential critics, Kurt Wittig, David Craig and David Daiches, speak of a broken culture, and see the Enlightenment, 'Augustanism' and 'Sentiment' as forms of cultural pollution that preclude the formation of a true and unified national poetry, notably through the synthetic depredations of the English language. In their view, Gaelic and Scots are the 'correct' literary channels of eighteenth-century Scotland, albeit impoverished by the general circumstances of a 'divided' national culture, while Scottish poetry in English is seen as artificial and almost completely unsuccessful. In some aspects Craig diagnoses an 'alienation from things native', and for Daiches the 'paradox' of Scottish literature in the period generally is its production of famous works on the basis of unpropitious national and cultural circumstances.[1] We prefer to argue, along the lines of a recent critical revaluation of this literary period, that Scotland's cultural diversity was, and is, its strength; that adverse circumstances bring vibrancy to literature; that there is a surprisingly high degree of political and social homogeneity across the four languages; and that the achievements of poets such as Allan Ramsay, James Thomson, Alastair mac Mhaighstir Alastair, Rob Donn MacKay, Duncan Ban Macintyre and Robert Burns are all worthy of celebration.

The eighteenth-century Latin poetic heritage of Scotland has (until recently) been largely neglected, but offers a crucial starting point in understanding a transnational or international dimension. Following the 'Glorious Revolution' of 1688–89, the work of Archibald Pitcairne (1652–1713) empowered the Tory, Jacobite opposition to Whiggism in Britain as a whole. As a claim to the intellectual high ground in the face of what he and those of his ideological stamp took to be the culturally barren puritanism of the Whig ascendancy, he wrote numerous Latin verses.

On the Gaelic side, as one type of international dimension was lost, another kicked in. The early eighteenth century witnessed the last compositions (by members of the MacMhuirich and Ó Muirgheasáin bardic families) in the learned written language shared with Ireland since c. 1200 and known to scholars as Classical Common Gaelic. One such poem, 'An Tánaiste Tais' ('*The Gentle Tanist*', 1719), celebrates a French-educated member of the Clanranald family who was, says the poet, no mere student prince, for '*he has been called a magister*' ('maighaisdir ar a ragh ris').[2] What we begin to find instead is the appearance of Augustan elements in songs composed in the largely unwritten vernacular language of Gaelic Scotland. In a brave attempt to persuade the chief of the MacLeods to give up expensive foreign ways, for example, An Clàrsair Dall, 'the Blind Harper' (Roderick Morison, c. 1656–c. 1714), personifies the spirit of the past as 'Mac-Alla' ('*Echo*'), while, in a similar strain, Lachlann mac Theàrlaich Òig (Lachlan MacKinnon, 1665–1734) finds three young orphans called 'Iochd, is Gràdh, is Fiùghantas' ('*Mercy, Generosity, and Love*') wandering in the hills.[3]

What the new century brings to Gaelic verse is above all the deepening and broadening of the pre-existing tradition of highly codified vernacular verse. This tradition was deprecated by the late Derick Thomson, a poet and critic of David Craig's generation, before being brilliantly expounded as the 'panegyric code' by Dr John MacInnes.[4] Its other main practitioners in this era were am Pìobaire Dall, 'the Blind Piper' (John MacKay, 1656–1754), Sìleas na Ceapaich (Cicely MacDonald, c. 1660–c. 1729), Iain mac Ailein (John MacLean, c. 1660–c. 1741), Mairghread nighean Lachlainn (Margaret MacLean, c. 1660–c. 1750) and Iain Dubh mac Iain mhic Ailein (John MacDonald, c. 1665–c. 1725).[5] None were 'published' (other than orally) in their day, but all were influential: their poetry was a social medium, and the test of a song was its practical effect. Of these five poets only Mairghread appears to have concentrated almost exclusively on eulogy and elegy, but she did so with magnificence. Sìleas, Iain mac Ailein and Iain Dubh mixed panegyric with incisive social and political commentary, while in 'Cumha Choire an Easain' ('*Corrienessan's Lament*') the Blind Piper produced one of those strange 'nature plus' songs that Gaelic does so well – a crucial link between 'Òran na Comhachaig' ('*The Owl's Song*', c. 1600) and 'Moladh Beinn Dòbhrain' ('*The Praise of Ben Dorain*', 1751–66).[6] He is the only one of all these poets of whose politics we know nothing – the rest were Jacobites.

Returning to Pitcairne, his particular scorn for the powers that be in contemporary Scotland is registered in his drama *The Assembly* (written 1690, three published editions in the eighteenth century) and *Babell* (written 1692, not published until the nineteenth century).[7] Both of these satirise Presbyterianism. Although neither was printed until after Pitcairne's death, as was the case also with much of his Latin work, they were part of a vibrant manuscript literary culture enjoyed by Tory Jacobites, including poets like James Watson (d. 1722), the editor and publisher Thomas Ruddiman (1674–1757), and Allan Ramsay (1684–1758).[8]

Watson, a Roman Catholic, produced a series of volumes, more often now cited than read, called *A Choice Collection of Comic and Serious Scots Poems* (1706, 1709, 1711). These featured medieval works such as 'Christis Kirk on the Green' (attributed to James V, who lived from 1512 to 1542), Alexander Montgomerie's 'The Cherrie and the Slae' from the same century, and, from the seventeenth, 'The Life and Death of the Piper of Kilbarchan, or the epitaph of Habbie Simson', credited to Robert Sempill of Beltrees. The 'Christ's Kirk' and 'Habbie' stanzas especially became signatures in the Scots poetry 'revival' over the course of the eighteenth century, and are sometimes read as elements in a new cultural nationalism.[9] If there is some truth in that view, nonetheless the crucial collective *mentalité* of Watson's volumes was pro-Stuart, anti-Whig. James V (Stuart monarch), Montgomerie (Catholic) and Sempill (anti-Catholic) do not make for a cogent grouping, but in their relishing of both high literary art and coarser 'folk' humour, all three are made to stand for a part of the Scottish literary voice that is, in the early eighteenth century, being opposed by the more puritanical Whigs in general, and by some Calvinists in particular. Often cited in criticism as a response to the debates surrounding the Union, these volumes are essentially part of a cross-border Jacobite outlook, and contain as many works in English and Latin as in Scots.[10]

Scottish humanism (betokening an allegiance to the classical culture of Latin and Greek) is the strongest part of Ruddiman's compass as publisher and editor in early eighteenth-century Edinburgh. When in 1710 he publishes Gavin Douglas's Virgilian *Eneados* (completed 1512), his revivalism is as much to do with Latinity as with medieval Scots. His Scottish humanism (and, indeed, internationalism) is also reflected by his publication of the works of George Buchanan, one of the great Latin dramatists of the sixteenth century. The Scots glossary of Ruddiman's *Eneados* is mined by Ramsay for his original Scots poems in the first decades of the eighteenth century, but its original purpose is not so much to set Scots up as a literary language in its own right as to speak to a Latin-Vernacular exercise demonstrating Douglas's literary prowess against the classical standard.

More important than the politics of 1707 as a context for the work of Ramsay and James Thomson is 'Augustan' literary sensibility. It helps explain their revivalism (for example the use of 'Habbie' and 'Spenserian' stanzas respectively), their use of landscape depiction (especially pastoralism) and their cultural experimentalism.[11] Cross-cultural fertilisation and individual genius were equally important in Gaelic literature – giving us the works of Alastair mac Mhaighstir Alastair and Rob Donn, speeding transition, and leading to Macintyre, Buchanan and Uilleam Ros.

Ramsay's career begins with the English poem 'Elegy for Archibald Pitcairn' (1713), which tucks pro-Stuart imagery and Scottish martial iconography into hexameters. It partakes, most generally, of a neoclassical, indeed Augustan idiom. Augustanism, harking back to a supposedly golden age of Roman cultural and civil prosperity, may be identified as a literary period in England, but speaks to a wider neoclassical milieu, part of a new age of European rationalism that arose in the late seventeenth century as the continent recoiled from an era of violent religious conflict. We see this neoclassical palette in Ramsay as he produces a set of poetic fables which owe more to the influence of John Dryden (a man of similar, pro-Stuart ideological stamp) and Antoine de la Motte (a Frenchman) than to the medieval Scots versions of Robert Henryson. In his Scots works from the second decade of the century, Ramsay also employs a number of standard neoclassical devices such as the pastoral idiom, a strong zeugmatic wit, urbanity of perspective, and the verse epistle. These characteristics have too often been relegated within his work by literary scholars intent on prioritising 'native' Scottish qualities.[12]

Similarly, Ramsay's pastoral drama *The Gentle Shepherd* (1725), often read for its 'folk' matter, is a celebration of the Stuart dynasty: set at the Restoration, it depicts a society in which aristocrats and peasants live in harmony. It fits well into the British literary context of the late seventeenth and early eighteenth centuries, when writers such as Dryden and Alexander Pope depicted a lost golden age of Stuart rule as well as the fashion for 'primitive' mores celebrated in pastoral by John Gay and others. In one of Ramsay's many ventures as cultural entrepreneur, he displayed over his bookshop in Edinburgh a sign showing the heads of William Drummond and Ben Jonson enjoying their 'Table-Talk', a famous moment in British literary history. Ramsay's British-wide ideological allegiances are clear: they are those of a party which was at once cultural and political, the Jacobites, most of whose leading members were in exile in France and Italy, and who included Pitcairne, who had studied at Paris and Reims, and was professor of medicine at Leiden.

Transnationalism is again evident with the publication in 1720 of the *Edinburgh Miscellany*, which includes work by many individuals including former University of Glasgow student James Arbuckle (1700–c. 1742). Born in Ulster, he eventually became part of the Dublin literary scene. To this volume he contributes Horatian satires, a form which in Scotland (as in many European countries throughout the century) was a strong part of the classical poetic palette, and was also practised by Ramsay. Arbuckle's Augustan verse, including *Snuff* (1717) and *Glotta, or the Clyde* (1721), constitute a highly interesting economic and landscape poetry centred on Scotland as seen through the eyes of an 'outsider' (although the east–west linkage of Ulster-Scots culture is a marked phenomenon in nineteenth-century verse).[13]

Another contributor to the *Miscellany* was James Thomson (1700–1748), in time author of the poetic suite *The Seasons* (1726–1730), one of the most internationally influential Scottish literary texts of all time, feeding as it did the aesthetic and construction of numerous works of art beyond literature – in music, painting and sculpture – across Europe in the centuries following its publication. Often spoken about for his authorship in 1740 of the words of 'Rule Britannia' in the play *Alfred, a Masque*, Thomson is not generally jingoistic, but rather a didactic poet who belonged to the Real Whig party, which was somewhat suspicious of the power of the state.[14] It is worth pointing out that the promotion of the name 'Britain' over 'England' for our island was, by the eighteenth century, a Scottish-led Stuart project, and that *Alfred* was co-written by another émigré Scottish writer, David Mallet (1700–1765), whose name had undergone a curious trajectory from the Gaelic epithet Mailgheach ('Beetle-Browed') via its Scots spelling 'Malloch'.[15] He was, no doubt, anxious to give his English friends something they could pronounce.

Having been a student at Glasgow University in the years following the Union, the Gaelic poet Alastair mac Mhaighstir Alastair (Alexander MacDonald, c. 1698–c. 1770) imbibed all of the contemporary influences mentioned above, in all four languages. His list of literary allegiances – sometimes explicit, sometimes implicit – includes Watson, Ramsay and Thomson, not to mention Homer.[16] His list of religious allegiances is just as long and every bit as representative. He was an Episcopalian, a Presbyterian and a Roman Catholic, in that order, and, as he fell out very publicly with his local priest towards the end of his life, it is probably fair to view him as a sceptic in the mould of David Hume.[17] These are splendid Enlightenment credentials, but there is another important biographical fact which would have sounded more appropriate in the era of Romanticism: having almost certainly fought beside his father at Sheriffmuir in 1715, he buckled on his sword again in 1745 and served Prince Charles as a captain in the Clanranald Regiment.[18]

For all the Jacobitism of our poets, very few put their lives at stake for the cause. One thinks mainly of Alexander Robertson of Struan (Tighearna an t-Sruthain, 1670–1749), who wrote in English and Latin, William Hamilton of Bangour (1704–1754), who wrote in English and Scots, and John Roy Stewart (1700–1749), who wrote in Gaelic and English.[19] On the other side we find two Gaelic poets, Fear Mhuthadail (John MacKay of Mudale, c. 1690–c. 1750), who distinguished himself by capturing the Earl of Cromartie, and Duncan Ban Macintyre (Donnchadh Bàn Mac an t-Saoir, 1724–1812), a Jacobite in spirit, who deserted the Argyll Militia at the battle of Falkirk.[20]

Mac Mhaighstir Alastair's work falls into two phases, separated by the '45, both full of innovation. From the beginning he set himself against the demands of the panegyric code. He was willing to praise anything *but* famous men – women, bagpipes, the Gaelic language, a pet dove, the seasons, whisky, the Muses, the 'Sugar Burn', a good penis. His 'Moladh Mòraig' (*'The Praise of Morag'*) is an erotic tour de force. Yet while he gives so much he holds something back: we cannot be sure that Morag is not an allegory for Jacobitism. And there are satires full of soaring imagery, including one of Morag herself in which her body becomes a rotting tree.[21]

After the '45 the mood changes. The fun is gone (mostly), but his blood is up. The Redcoats must be drubbed in urine, he says, as women do to cloth at waulkings.[22] Like Hamilton of Bangour, he has become a propagandist for the Cause, and song after song hammers out the same message – Prince Charles we love you, come back, bring French troops to help us in our anguish. In English he writes accounts of the campaign and of the Prince's wanderings.[23] In Gaelic he praises the Highland dress (now proscribed by law), viciously puts down a Campbell poetess who disagrees with him, and tries to drum up universal support for the next rising. Yes, from Campbells too.[24] In Gaelic script he writes out a Fenian tale, probably from Iain mac Fhearchair's (John MacCodrum, 1693-1779) recitation.[25] Financed by the Loch Arkaig Gold, he has his verse printed in a book with his name on it: in so doing, he is the first Gaelic poet ever to publish his own work.[26] Then, with a flourish, he writes his best poem of all, the Homeric 'Birlinn Chlann Raghnaill' ('*Clanranald's Galley*'), which is at once a tribute to the dignity of human labour, an allegory of the '45, and a hand outstretched to Gaelic Ireland for help in the next rising.[27] It is, arguably, Scotland's first socialist poem.

Mac Mhaighstir Alastair has been both loved and loathed, but no one has ever doubted the power of his work. On Rob Donn MacKay (1714-1778) the critics differ more profoundly. He has been seen both as second-rate and as the greatest Gaelic poet of the century.[28] He, too, turned his back on tradition. In his case the outside influences were Alexander Pope (mediated to him orally by his parish minister) and the value system of Presbyterianism, resulting in a focus so intensely local that the late Ian Grimble was able to base a parish history on his work.[29] Yet when push came to shove in 1745, his powerful sense of morality made him a Jacobite.[30]

After 1746 there is a parting of the ways. Writers in Scots and English such as Alexander Ross (1699-1784), Michael Bruce (1746-1767), Robert Fergusson (1750-1774) and James Beattie (1735-1803), whose 'The Minstrel' (1771 and 1774) was so admired by William Wordsworth, maintain and extend the new literary pathways in a manner that is both cosmopolitan and native, contributing to didacticism, nature-writing and sentiment.[31] In Gaelic perhaps only Uilleam Ros (William Ross, 1762-?1791), who was influenced by the Blind Piper and Burns, and Eoghann MacLachlainn (Ewen MacLachlan, 1773-1822), who also wrote in Latin, can be said to have done so.[32] In the specific situation of the Highlands, however, cross-culturalism was the benign face of a coin: with it came negative forces such as clearance, emigration, deracination, cultural tension, looming oblivion. By the end of the century most Gaelic poets are providing some sort of commentary on these forces, grafted onto the panegyric code, which they continue to practise to help them eke out a living. The greatest and best loved of them is Duncan Ban Macintyre, whose teemingly descriptive 'Moladh Beinn Dòbhrain' should be read as codified criticism of the political and social judgements made by many in the Highland leadership, particularly, in this case, the third Earl of Breadalbane.[33] Macintyre was a mighty satirist, but restricted himself (in print at least) to 'safe' targets like young men at home in Glenorchy, bad innkeepers and John Wilkes.[34] Iain mac Fhearchair, who did not use print, sympathised with the plight of emigrants, while Ailean Dall MacDhùghaill (Allan MacDougall, c. 1750–1828), who did use print, turned his fire on the Lowland shepherds who were colonising the Highlands.[35] The catechist Dùghall Bochanan (Dugald Buchanan, 1716–1768) exemplifies a completely different approach: as a poet, he turns his hearers' attention from the earthly to the heavenly paradise by blending traditional heroic imagery with scenes from the everyday life of Rannoch and the work of English hymn-writers like Isaac Watts. Other non-biblical influences that may be detected in his work are *Hamlet* and the 'Graveyard School' of Edward Young and Robert Blair. His *Spiritual Songs* (1767) was a best-seller, being reprinted about forty times.[36] His work has not stood up well, however, to modern critical examination.[37]

Along with *The Seasons*, the other most powerfully international English text from eighteenth-century Scotland is the 'Ossian' of James Macpherson (Seumas Bàn MacMhuirich, 1736–1796). Whether it should be called 'poetry' is a moot point, as it is laid out as prose. Macpherson's *Fragments of Ancient Poetry* (1760) and two other 'epics' of similar material were claimed by the author to be ancient work collected in the Highlands and translated from Gaelic, including ballads by Ossian about the pre-Christian times of the Fenian tales. The reality of these texts is a small core of original Gaelic verse reworked and supplemented by Macpherson.[38] Discussion sometimes concerns the traduction of their alleged originals (which are full of detail, colour, irony and boisterous humour),[39] their supposedly opportunistic appropriation of the culture of Ireland (though the Fenian tales and ballads are set in a cross-channel landscape that includes the west of Scotland), the detraction of attention away from the brilliance of contemporary Gaelic poetry, and the cross-border feuding between the cultural interests of Scots and English (David Hume was an early enthusiast; Samuel Johnson an angry debunker). But it is important also to note that Macpherson was a fluent Gaelic-speaking Highlander whose childhood was scarred and broken by the appalling events of 1746 in his native Badenoch. 'Ossian' was the work of a man who had personal experience of rape, murder, house-burning and starvation carried out by a government which routinely referred to his people as 'vermin'; here was a man to whom violence was no joke.[40] Seen like this, 'Ossian' was catharsis and revenge.

Sometimes adduced as part of synthetic, ersatz, Enlightenment cultural engineering (for instance, the Ossian texts revelled in a version of the 'noble savage'), Macpherson's work was, and is, highly influential across the artistic imagination of Europe. Goethe's protagonist in *The Sorrows of Young Werther* (1774) is consumed for a period by the poetry of Ossian, Napoleon was a great enthusiast for the martial qualities of the texts, and their influence can be traced down to the poetry of Tennyson and perhaps on to the fantasy of J. R. R. Tolkien. Macpherson's construction of a melancholic Celticism is a significant part of the proto-Romantic milieu, and can easily be traced in the work of Blake, Burns, Wordsworth, Scott, Byron and many others.

Less celebrated in their own time are several poets in Scots who are contemporaries of Macpherson. Alexander Ross's *Helenore, or the Fortunate Shepherdess* (1768) is the longest work in Scots during the century. It exemplifies the classical (pastoral) ambition of that language rather than the kind of 'folk' sensibility, with its back against the wall in the face of the literary predilections of Enlightenment Scotland, that criticism has sometimes seen in it. Alexander Geddes (1737–1802) writes a long narrative poem, 'Epistle to the President, Vice-Presidents and Members of the Scottish Society of Antiquaries' (1792), a sweeping history of Scotland in the context of European culture. No less sweeping in ambition is his *Three Scottish Poems with a Previous Dissertation on the Scoto-Saxon Dialect* (1792), which argues for the fuller potential of Scots over English and attempts to demonstrate its point via translations from classical pastoral poetry. Robert Fergusson's English work is much better than is sometimes claimed, and is equal in volume to his efforts in Scots. His view is pan-British at least, as he comments, from his pro-Jacobite perspective, on the cultural and political corruption of Hanoverian Britain. His use of the Spenserian stanza form in 'The Farmer's Ingle' (1773) also exemplifies a pastoral revivalism and experimentalism common to Scotland and England. In many ways his numerous Scots satires lampooning the mores of city-living and luxury are part of a pan-European critique that looks towards the protesting stance in Romanticism.[41]

By the late eighteenth century the question of influences upon Gaelic verse has become fraught. Almost all the Gaelic poets of the day appear to be directly influenced by mac Mhaighstir Alastair. This is obvious in the work of, for example, Coinneach MacCoinnich (Kenneth Mackenzie, 1758–1819) and Donnchadh Caimbeul (Duncan Campbell, *fl.* 1798).[42] If literate in English, they could also read James Thomson for themselves, and no doubt some did. The poems of Aonghas Caimbeul (Angus Campbell, c. 1740–1814), published in 1785, have much in common with those of Rob Donn and Robert Burns (1759–1796): the same sardonic humour, the same demotic localism, the same stress on personal morality, the same tension between lust and virtue.[43] But neither Rob Donn nor Burns were published as yet, and it seems a little unlikely that the ceilidh-house grapevine had reached all the way from Sutherland to Perthshire, so we must simply conclude that Campbell was reflecting the general mood of his time.

Burns, who becomes Scotland's most famous poet internationally, is a new bardic figure for the Romantic age, a poet who supposedly strongly expresses his indigenous culture.[44] He may be said to have learned something from all the figures previously mentioned in this chapter other than those whose work was in Gaelic. It is he, along with a little help from 'Ossian' and Walter Scott, who has given today's cosmopolitan world 'Scotland the Brand'. His sentimental Jacobitism, his defence of (and simultaneous satirising of) his cradle Presbyterianism, his Lowland fellow feeling for the Highlands and his sympathy with a wide range of people (including women, vagabonds, gypsies and Catholics) exemplify his ecumenical, transnational, Enlightenment-based perspective. Poems and songs which favour the American and French revolutions, and which sometimes display apprehension in the face of an 'improved' world that makes life more difficult for the little person, make him a new world poet suitable to a newly emerging age of mass politics. His universalism, whether in terms of 'Auld Lang Syne' (1788), a song about parting in a hugely increased age of human mobility, the psychology of human fear in 'Tam o' Shanter' (1790) or in 'Is there for honest poverty' (1795), which becomes one of the great world songs of the political left, help make him one of the very few who can aspire to the title of global writer. He is the only poet whose verse has been translated into Gaelic in its entirety.[45]

If Scots poetry after Burns, it is often argued, is a tale of diminishing returns, numerous diasporic writers in the Antipodes, North America, South Africa and Ulster attest to his enduring influence. Yet curiously, unknown to the world at large (or even to most Scottish literary historians), in Alastair mac Mhaighstir Alastair the eighteenth century has given the twenty-first a still more representative figure, a battling intellectual who loved life, lived it to the full, fought for his people's cause, campaigned tirelessly when it was lost, and gave us, in 'Birlinn Chlann Raghnaill', an epic celebration of the dignity of labour. Mac Mhaighstir Alastair is not a greater poet than Burns, but he is his equal.

CHAPTER SEVEN

The Nineteenth Century

Ian Duncan and Sheila Kidd

Although they share certain preoccupations – colonial emigration, the impact of urban and industrial experience, the status of a minority language (in the case of Scots and Gaelic), the transmission and reinvention of traditional forms – poets writing in Scots and English, on one hand, and poets writing in Gaelic, on the other, represent largely divergent traditions throughout the nineteenth century.

Scottish Gaelic poetry of the nineteenth century mirrors the breadth and diversity of Gaelic speakers' experiences, in the Highlands, Lowlands, and the more distant parts of the British Empire in which they settled. Gaelic poets had traditionally held a public role as commentators on behalf of their clan chief and clan or their local community and, while they would retain a public role through the century and beyond, this was to evolve, as too would their poetic output, to reflect and respond to changing relationships in Gaelic-speaking society. The range of modes and panegyric motifs which formed a core part of the traditional poetic repertoire was extended in response to new social circumstances, most notably in poetry and song of social protest, where sheep, factors, Lowlanders and the English language begin to carry metonymic weight, as they spoke to a Highland-wide experience of social and cultural dislocation.

In Ailean Dall MacDhùghaill (Allan MacDougall, c. 1750–1828) and Iain MacIlleathain/Bàrd Thighearna Cholla (John MacLean/the Laird of Coll's Poet, 1787–1848), whose lives spanned the eighteenth and nineteenth centuries, we have the final examples of official poets to clan chiefs, as they fulfilled their respective duties to Alasdair Ronaldson MacDonell of Glengarry and Alexander MacLean of Coll. While Ailean Dall composed no less than six poems and an elegy in praise of his chief, the tensions and contradictions inherent in what was, even in the poets' time, an anachronistic role, surface in 'Oran do na Cìobairibh Gallda'

('*Song to the Lowland Shepherds*'). In this biting satire the shepherds are unforgivingly depicted: 'Bidh sgread Ghallda 'm beul a chlèibh, / 'G èigheachd an dèidh a chuid chon; / Ceòl nach b' èibhinn linn a sgairt; / Bracsaidh 'na shac air a chorp; / E suainte 'na bhreacan glas; / Uaimh-mheulan 'na fhalt 's 'na dhos' ('*A Lowland screech will come from his chest, / calling for his pack of dogs; / his yell would be no sweet music to us; / There is a load of braxy on his body, / wrapped in his grey plaid; / lice are in his hair and forelock*').[1] Yet, with no apparent sense of irony, the poet ends with a toast to MacDonell, whose rental income is buoyed by those whom the poet has attacked in the preceding fourteen verses. MacIlleathain on the other hand chose to emigrate to Canada in 1819 at the age of thirty-two. When his poetry is viewed as a whole, we witness the process of adjustment, beginning with dislocation and isolation in 'Am Mealladh' ('*The Deception*') and 'Oran do dh'America' ('*Song to America*'), but moving through this to acceptance and assimilation into the Nova Scotian Highland community to the point where we find him composing 'Bronsachadh Roghnachaidh' ('*An Election Incitement*'), in which he urges his Gaelic-speaking audience to vote for his preferred candidate, in the vein of traditional battle incitements: 'Nuair rùisgeadh iad am brataichean, / 'S a sheinnt' a phìob gu tartarach, / Bhiodh cliù air luchd nam breacan, / Anns gach baiteal mara chualas'[2] ('*When they would unfurl their banners, / And the pipes would be played loudly, / The reputation of the tartan-clad men / In every battle would be heard*').

MacIlleathain was one of many emigrants for whom poetry served as a natural means of expressing their homesickness for their native land, both personally and communally.[3] The voices of Gaelic poets in the East and West Indies, North America, Canada, Australia and New Zealand open up new worlds of experience to Gaelic-speaking audiences. In a poetic tradition laden with conventional motifs, this emigrant voice brings flashes of the exotic, as in Raibeart MacDhùghaill's (Robert MacDougall, 1813–1887) lines sent from Australia to a Gaelic periodical published in Glasgow, which capture a different natural world from that in which he had grown up in northern Perthshire: 'Far am bi 'n Kangaroo criomadh fhlùr feadh nan tòm / A's an t-àl òg r'a chùl, ruith gu sùrdail neo-thròm; / Far am bi'n Cockatoo ga mo dhùsgadh à crann; / A's na h-eoin bheaga bhrù-dhearg, le'n ciucharan fann'[4] ('*Where the Kangaroo nibbles flowers among the bushes / And its young behind it, running eagerly, playfully; / Where the Cockatoo from a tree awakens me / And the scarlet robins with their faint lament*'). Compositions such as this by Gaels abroad sit comfortably within the Gaelic tradition and reflect the ways in which poem and song were often deployed to reinforce both links between an increasingly disparate Gaelic-speaking population and a sense of Highland identity.

The question of what makes a poem or poet Scottish became especially vexed, for poets writing in Scots and in English, in the vortex of Scotland's imperial and industrial integration into 'Greater Britain'. 'I am half a Scot by birth, and bred / A whole one, and my heart flies to my head', declared George Gordon, Lord Byron (1788–1824) in Canto X of *Don Juan* (1823) – the era's most glitteringly cosmopolitan of modern epics, with its Spanish hero who travels via Ottoman captivity and the court of Catherine the Great to the intrigues of an English country house. The occasion for Byron's confession is the phrase 'Auld Lang Syne', which brings back his 'boy feelings' and 'gentler dreams' of 'Scotch plaids, Scotch snoods, the blue hills, and clear streams'. Not even his quarrel with the Edinburgh literary establishment in 'English Bards and Scotch Reviewers' (1809) could 'quench young feelings fresh and early: / I "scotch'd not kill'd" the Scotchman in my blood, / And love the land of "mountain and of flood."'[5] That last phrase comes from Walter Scott's *The Lay of the Last Minstrel*: Byron's citations from Burns and Scott (and *Macbeth*) give Scotland a literary-historical location, in British Romanticism, as well as a somatic one, in the poet's 'heart', 'blood', and 'young feelings'. Even as Byron recognises a modern tradition of Scottish poetry, he sets Scottishness in the past, in childhood, in the body: a resource for nostalgic reverie rather than intellectual engagement.

Byron, Scott and Thomas Campbell, the most famous British poets (with the Irishman Thomas Moore) of the early nineteenth century, represented the last generation of a long Romanticism (c. 1760–c. 1830) in which Scotland stood in the vanguard of European literature. James Macpherson's 'Ossian' epics, Burns's lyrics and Scott's metrical romances made up the prototype of a modern national poetry (in Johann Gottfried Herder's influential account) founded on indigenous popular traditions of ballad and song. The Napoleonic wars infused these national genres with a British patriotism that entailed, as often as not, their abstraction from 'the people' – and potentially radical causes – and their enshrinement in antiquarian projects, or else their conscription for military and domestic sentiment. Byron's career can be understood, in part, as a cosmopolitan riposte to these nationalist projects. Childe Harold's farewell, 'My Native Land, Good-Night!' (*Childe Harold's Pilgrimage*, Canto I), wafted its author into self-imposed exile.

Of the three headline achievements, Campbell's (1777–1844) has worn least well. His condensed ballad imitations ('Lord Ullin's Daughter'), noisy martial eulogies ('Ye Mariners of England', 'Battle of the Baltic', 'Hohenlinden'), exotic elegiac idylls (*Gertrude of Wyoming*, 1809), and swaggering anapaestic tetrameters ('And coming events cast their shadows before' – 'Lochiel's Warning') modelled a nineteenth-century style of popular public poetry aimed at an imperial diaspora of soldiers and emigrants ('Lines on the Departure of Emigrants for New South Wales', 'Song of the Colonists Departing for New Zealand') as well as domestic readers. Campbell's light was outshone by Scott (1771–1832), who kindled his literary career with *Minstrelsy of the Scottish Border* (1802–03), the major traditional ballad collection of British Romanticism. It was followed by a 'modern-antique' original, *The Lay of the Last Minstrel* (1805), a work of bracing experimental vigour in the irregular tetrameter measure of Coleridge's 'Christabel', which makes the transmission and mediation of poetic energy – through magic spell, oral recital and printed book – its theme, within a nest of narrative frames. Scott's subsequent romances put aside that mediating apparatus and tell their story straight, achieving maximum romantic incident and scenic colour in the Highland tale *The Lady of the Lake* (1810). While Scott went on to greater heights writing historical novels (notable for their lyrical interpolations), his long narrative poems remained hugely popular, founding one of the signature genres of nineteenth-century poetry in English – Matthew Arnold dubbed it (disparagingly) the 'ballad-epic'.

Besides these high-profile careers, the Romantic-era flowering of Scottish poetry included other distinctive, in some cases subversive, reinventions of national forms. James Hogg (1770–1835) entered the field with original ballads and songs (*The Mountain Bard*, 1807), authenticated by his early career as a Border shepherd, and contended for the role of Burns's successor with his friend the Nithsdale poet Allan Cunningham (1784–1842). A third claimant, the Paisley weaver Robert Tannahill (1774–1810), made his debut in 1807 with *The Soldier's Return*, a dramatic interlude with songs and poems 'Chiefly in the Scottish Dialect'. Tannahill's songs enjoyed enormous nineteenth-century popularity, too late, however, to lift him out of poverty and obscurity: he committed suicide three years later. Hogg was more fortunate. After winning fame with his romantic ballad miscellany *The Queen's Wake* (1813), he tried his hand at an ambitious range of genres, from cosmological dream-poem (*The Pilgrims of the Sun*, 1814) to Caledonian epic (*Queen Hynde*, 1825). The cool critical response to these experiments kept pushing Hogg back into the ideologically more tractable role of the 'Ettrick Shepherd', a genial fount of Scottish song for *Blackwood's Edinburgh Magazine*.

Also writing against the grain was Anne Bannerman (1765–1829), whose *Poems* (1807) are notable for their 'dark' manner and technical polish. 'The Spirit of the Air' animates a fantasy of the poet as sublime demiurge of global social justice. 'Sonnets from Werter' ventriloquises a series of impassioned monologues by the protagonist of Goethe's novel, following the example of Charlotte Smith's *Elegiac Sonnets*. Bannerman's ballads – 'The Dark Ladie', 'Basil', 'The Prophetess of the Isle of Seam' – disconcert the reader with their central narrative opacity around themes of wronged womanhood and figures of a veiled female avenger.

Margaret Chalmers (1758–1827) was acutely conscious of writing from Shetland – the extremity of Scotland, the north of the north (as Penny Fielding puts it).[6] Chalmers's *Poems* (1813) make much of their 'Thulian' provenance. All are written in standard English poetic diction, apart from the 'Verses, In Humble Imitation of Burns', a witty essay in the female-apologetic tradition of Janet Little, modelled on Burns's own epistles to John Lapraik. Here, the shade of Burns addresses Chalmers, marvelling that poetry should issue from such a remote, obscure source:

> Amang thae awfu' eerie rocks,
> Whar selchies, otters, gang in flocks,
>   There dwalls a hizzie,
> Wha has the pertness 'mang the Nine
>   To be right bizzie.

The poet upbraids her presumption: "Twad set you better to clean fish, / Or knit your sock', than pretend to be 'a Poetess'. With ironical zest, Chalmers makes Burns (posthumously at ease on Parnassus) ladle out sexist discouragement, much as he had foreseen metropolitan critics dampening his own ambitions.

Romantic-era Scottish poetry flourished upon a robust infrastructure of native institutions, from colleges to reviews and presses, in Lowland Scotland, especially Edinburgh. As well as preserving Scotland's distinctive religious, legal and financial systems, the Union opened space for the 'separate public sphere' that Murray Pittock has diagnosed as essential to national cultural formation, by the sheer physical distance it interposed between Scottish civil society and the British political centre.[7] After 1830 that separate space contracted, for political, economic and technological reasons, and ambitious authors, editors and publishers went south. It is no longer so easy to speak of a 'Scottish literature' distinct from English or British literature in the Victorian age. One symptom is language. In

1870 Janet Hamilton (1795–1873) bears witness to the brain drain – 'I'm wae for Auld-Reekie; her big men o' print / To Lunnon hae gane, to be nearer the mint' – in a poem titled 'A Plea for the Doric'. Hamilton protests against the commonplace that Scots is an endangered literary language, while admitting, 'aft [the] dear Doric aside I hae flung, / To busk oot my sang wi' the prood Southron tongue'. By 1887 Robert Louis Stevenson (1850–1894) remarks, in a note to *Underwoods*, 'the day draws near when this illustrious and malleable tongue shall be quite forgotten'.

Stevenson, late in the century, makes for an interesting test case. There is a flavour of academic exercise in his Scots poems; they stick doggedly to one register, eschewing the stylistic and linguistic modulations within an individual poem of which Burns was the virtuoso. His English poems, typically of the age, tend to encase themselves in a standard Victorian poetic diction. *Underwoods* yields some good lines – 'Suburban ashes shivered into song' ('To Mrs Will. H. Low'), the onomatopoeia enriched by the pun on 'ashes' – but also bad ones: 'Of cobweb dew-bediamonded' ('The House Beautiful'). The best poems tend to be the simplest: those in *A Child's Garden of Verses* (1885) that have not cloyed to contemporary taste, or some of the *Songs of Travel* (1896), such as 'In Dreams, Unhappy' and 'Bright is the Ring of Words', which match the lyric concentration of A. E. Housman's *A Shropshire Lad*. One poem, 'The Woodman', sustains an intensely imagined, philosophically alert experiment in post-Darwinian georgic – its compass ranging between T. H. Huxley's 'Evolution and Ethics' and Aldous Huxley's 'Wordsworth in the Tropics'.

The case of the Doric points to the general problem of a Victorian calcification of Romantic styles and genres. The archive is cluttered with volumes of songs, lays and ballads, imitations of Burns and Scott, which reiterate their model without imaginative or technical renewal. Prolonged exposure to them can develop an appreciation of the 'bad' aesthetic of William McGonagall (1825–1902); a few still show signs of life, however. Carolina Oliphant, Baroness Nairne (1766–1845), the most accomplished songwriter after Burns and Hogg, gives the tradition a decisively sentimental-Jacobite tilt. Her comic lyrics ('The Laird o' Cockpen', 'Cauld Kale in Aberdeen') come up better than the religiosity of 'The Land of the Leal', while 'Caller Herrin' develops a motif from Scott's novel *The Antiquary* ('it's no fish ye're buyin', it's men's lives'). The best-selling Victorian 'collection of songs for the social circle', *Whistle-Binkie, or the Piper of the Party*, compiled by John Donald Carrick and Alexander Rodger in 1842 and much reprinted, recycles sub-Burns and *Blackwood's Magazine* styles of comic, sentimental and patriotic lyric in Scots and English.

The equivalent of *Whistle-Binkie* in the literary ballad tradition is W. E. Aytoun's (1813–1865) *Lays of the Scottish Cavaliers* (1849), a slick revision of Scottish history as Jacobite myth. Thomas Babington Macaulay's (1800–1859) once famous *Lays of Ancient Rome* (1842) undertakes, more adventurously, to appropriate the Roman republic as a national ancestor by casting it in ballad form. There are other experiments, not all of them successful. Stevenson adapts South Pacific oral tradition to the Victorian epic measure of dactylic hexameter in his 'Song of Rahero: A Legend of Tahiti'. John Davidson (1857–1909), the most interesting of *fin-de-siècle* Scottish poets, invigorates the genre in his *Ballads and Songs* (1894) by lightening the tone – acknowledging that it may all be tosh – and capsizing received moral and religious maxims: a woman commits suicide for love but stages a walk-out from hell when she realises she has been cheated ('A Ballad of Hell'); a composer starves his family for his art but is admitted to heaven when his symphony is adopted as the music of the spheres ('A Ballad of Heaven').

Just as the expansion in publishing through the nineteenth century created new opportunities and new readerships for poets composing in Scots and English, so too the voice of the Gaelic poet was extended far beyond his local community and, as the earlier examples have shown, between emigrant communities and Gaels in Scotland.[8] Linguistic and cultural change impacted significantly on many poets, and Calum Caimbeul MacPhàil (Calum Campbell MacPhail, 1847–1913) may not be unrepresentative when, in the middle of the century, he lamented the lack of interest in Gaelic songs at penny readings in Argyll's main town, Inveraray, in 'Oran do Luchd-fuatha na Gailig' ('*Song to the Haters of Gaelic*'): 'A measg naoidh òrain Bheurla / Chan éisdeadh iad ri aon 's a' Ghàilig; / Ach sionnaich Ghallda le'm miolaran Beurla / Am baile greadhnach Earra-Ghàidheil'[9] ('*Among nine songs in English / They wouldn't listen to one in Gaelic; / Only Lowland foxes with their English howling / In the magnificent town of Argyll*').

Poets frequently framed the fundamental economic and social changes in Gaelic-speaking society in terms of landscape, juxtaposing pre- and post-Clearances scenes. One of the most effective proponents of this strategy was Iain MacLachlainn (John MacLachlan, 1804–1874), a Morvern poet composing in the middle decades of the century. In 'A Ghlinn ud shios' ('*Oh yon Glen below*') he shares with his audience the visual impact of population loss upon the glen: 'Ach chì mi d'fhàrdaich air dol sìos, / 'N an làraich, fhalamh, fhuar; / Cha-n fhaic fear-siubhail far an stùichd / Na smùidean 'g éiridh suas'[10] ('*But I see your dwellings have declined / Into cold and empty ruins; / A traveller will not see from the hill / Smoke rising up*'). For the Glasgow-based Islay poet Uilleam MacDhunlèibhe (William Livingston, 1808-1870), the landscape of Argyll formed a backdrop for a number of historical epic poems drawing on Scottish and Highland history; the most memorable of all his poems, however, is arguably the measured control in 'Fios chun a' Bhàird' ('*A Message for the Poet*'), with the evil of the clearances embodied by the serpent, the sole occupant of the houses: 'Tha an nathair bhreac 'na lùban / Air na h-ùrlair far an d' fhàs / Na fir mhòr' a chunnaic mise; / Thoir am fios seo chun a' Bhàird' ('*The speckled adder is lying in coils / on the floors where once there grew / the big men that I saw there; / take this message to the Poet*').[11]

From the 1870s and the politicisation of the cause of the Highland crofters new vigour was breathed into the traditional poetic forms of 'moladh' ('*praise*'), 'diomoladh'/'aoir' ('*dispraise*'/'*satire*'), 'brosnachadh' ('*incitement*') and 'marbhrann' ('*elegy*') as they provided poets with a framework for praising crofting heroes, whether involved in confrontations with the authorities or campaigning on their behalf, and for criticising those who stood in the way of land reform. In the poetic vanguard was the Skye poetess Màiri Nic a' Phearsain (Mary MacPherson, known as Màiri Mhòr nan Òran/Big Mary of the Songs, c. 1821-1898), whose own (apparently false) imprisonment in Inverness for theft had both prompted her to begin composing songs and sharpened her sense of injustice, infusing her verse with a particular empathy for the crofters: ''S e na dh'fhuiling mi de thàmailt / a thug mo bhàrdachd beò'[12] ('*It is the shame I suffered / Which brought my poetry to life*'). In 'Òran Beinn Lì' ('*Song of Ben Lee*') she celebrates the crofters' victory in the Battle of the Braes in 1882 and the return of grazing land to them in 1887 in traditional terms, underlining the change in the focus of heroic praise away from the clan chief to crofters who 'Bha air tùs anns a' bhatail, / 'S nach do mheataich san strì'[13] ('*Who were in the forefront in the battle / And who weren't daunted in the conflict*').

Nic a' Phearsain was not unusual in being an urban Lowland Gaelic poet. The work of some of these poets veers towards the nostalgic and sentimental, lacking a specificity of location or occasion, but nonetheless appealing to contemporary urban audiences. Common among their compositions were songs in praise of Highland societies and associations in Glasgow and Edinburgh, celebrating and reinforcing their cultural identity. One poet who does not entirely fit this mould was Iain MacAonghais (John MacInnes, *fl.* 1875), from Lismore, whose work in the second half of the century also captures the less pleasant side of Glasgow life from his stance as social commentator. In 'Oran mu Dhaoine Posda a bhios a sgròbadh a chèile' ('*A Song about a Married Couple who attack one another*'), the poet blames alcohol for this domestic violence: 'Cha chluinn mi 'n diugh ach glaodhaich, / Mu fhear a's bean aig caornag, / 'S e bualadh bhreab uirr' agus dhòrn, / 'S i 'cur air thòrr nam maor dha'[14] ('*Today I only hear shouting, / About a man and his wife quarrelling, / With him showering kicks and fists upon her, / And she sending the police after him*').

MacInnes's gritty picture of nineteenth-century urban life is thoroughly in keeping with poetry written in Scots and English that flourished in the mid-Victorian popular press in Glasgow and its ports and suburbs – the ascendant industrial hub of the British Empire, displacing Edinburgh to claim the title of literary metropolis in the next century. The Glasgow newspapers provided a broader democratic forum, closer to their readers and to unfolding events, than upmarket periodicals like *Blackwood's*. They supported a public poetry engaged with social issues such as urban pollution, temperance, domestic abuse, workers' education, industrial action and women's rights. While the poetic traditions in Scotland may have been linguistically divided, in short, the poets' experiences and literary responses often converged. Working-class autodidact Janet Hamilton was taken up by John Cassells, the editor of *The Working Man's Friend*, in 1850, and published four book collections between 1863 and 1870, achieving national fame. Hamilton's poems address domestic problems (obsessively, temperance) as well as world events (the Crimean War and American Civil War, independence struggles in Italy and Poland) in pithy Scots: 'The South they'll keep the negro slave – they like the chain and collar, / The North tae trade, an' rug, an' reive, an' pouch the michty dollar' ('Advice tae Brither Jonathan: At the Beginning of the Ceevil War in America'). Her case may be compared with that of English-born Glasgow resident Marion Bernstein (1846–1906), who published her work in the *Glasgow Weekly Mail* and *Glasgow Weekly Herald* from 1874. In contrast to Hamilton's conservatism on gender issues, Bernstein was a staunch advocate for feminist causes (a marker, perhaps, of generational as well as class difference). 'A Woman's Plea' issues a call 'To vote for all that's right and just / To vote down all that's wrong; / These are our rights. For these we must / Cry out in speech and song.' In 'A Dream' Bernstein imagines that 'the nineteenth century / [Has] entirely passed away' and a female majority exerts benevolent sway in a reformed Parliament. 'On the Franchise Demonstration of the 6th Inst.' (1884) rebukes the women of Glasgow for their absence from the suffrage rally.

Tom Leonard includes Bernstein (but not Hamilton) in the 'Radical Renfrew' tradition of activist, mainly working-class poetry from the west of Scotland he brought back to light in 1990.[15] With French Revolution-era roots in Burns and Tannahill, the tradition, addressing contemporary industrial and urban experience, makes for a striking contrast with the *Scottish Cavaliers* and *Whistle-Binkie* vein of sentimental Scotchness. While the core work, published in the popular press, is frankly occasional, local and topical, its aesthetic refractions are visible in 'art' poetry – testing its own conditions as poetry – in the second half of the century. Alexander Smith's (1829–1867) 'Glasgow' (1857) attempts the idiom of 'Another beauty, sad and stern' for the industrial city:

> Draw thy fierce streams of blinding ore,
> Smite on a thousand anvils, roar
> Down the harbour-bars;
> Smoulder in smoky sunsets, flare
> On rainy nights; with street and square
> Lie empty to the stars.

James Thomson's (1834–1882) 'The City of Dreadful Night' (1874) guides the reader through the visionary metropolis of modern life, a hell, or rather limbo, stripped of theological meaning and thus of traditional sources of hope and faith, its inhabitants condemned to an interminable, monotonous melancholy – whose titanic effigy (based on Dürer's etching) is the 'City's Patroness and Queen'. To read Thomson's long poem is indeed to feel, for the duration, like a denizen of this Victorian prototype of Unthank, the purgatorially transfigured Glasgow of Alasdair Gray's novel *Lanark* (1981).

The poet who reckons most resourcefully with the challenge posed to poetic form by contemporary urban experience among those we have discussed, however, is John Davidson, who experiments with a mixed, flexible set of styles that range from high aestheticism (inlaid with jewelled diction) to street vernacular. 'Thirty Bob a Week', the dramatic monologue of a beleaguered clerk, invests the demotic voice with stoic, even tragic pathos. The remarkable *Fleet Street Eclogues* (1896) alternate lyric interjections of a pastoral world elsewhere with the pressmen's ironic banter, in what may be British poetry's most sustained attempt before high modernism to subdue its supposed antithesis – the news – to its own formal discipline.

CHAPTER EIGHT

The Poetry of Modernity (1870–1950)

Emma Dymock and Scott Lyall

The city is important to the beginnings of modern Scottish poetry. T. S. Eliot, whose *Waste Land* portrays the classic modernist city, was influenced by James Thomson (1834–1882) and John Davidson (1857–1909), who, like Eliot, were national outsiders in the English capital. The poetry of both Scots is characterised by pyschogeographical exile, then emerging as a condition of atomised modernity. Thomson's *The City of Dreadful Night* (1874), for Robert Crawford the 'greatest English-language urban poem of the nineteenth century',[1] maps 'places of the mind',[2] not of comfortable secularity, but despairing nihilism: 'I find no hint throughout the Universe / Of good or ill, of blessing or of curse'.[3] Davidson, like Thomson from an evangelical Christian background, also inhabits a Godless universe, one informed by evolutionary biology and social Darwinism. Regenia Gagnier calls Davidson's work a 'poetry of bipolarity [...] lurching between abjection and the sublime'.[4] His 'Thirty Bob a Week' questions Victorian progress, yet displays a zealous individualism borrowing from the self-help of Samuel Smiles and Nietzsche's will to power:

> No fathers, mothers, countries, climates – none;
> Not Adam was responsible for me,
> Nor society, nor systems, nary one:
> A little sleeping seed, I woke – I did, indeed –
> A million years before the blooming sun.[5]

The English-language poets Thomson and Davidson give the lie to George Bruce's claim 'that no Scottish poetry of great consequence was produced between the death of Burns in 1796 and 1922,'[6] the year C. M. Grieve (1892–1978) created his poetic persona as Hugh MacDiarmid and began publishing poems in Scots. Bruce (1909–2002) is here equating

Scottish poetry with Scots, although much of his own best poetry was written in lean English. MacDiarmid, who wrote in English and Scots, valorises Davidson in 'Of John Davidson'. Yet the influence of the nation-centric Scottish Renaissance movement spearheaded by MacDiarmid arguably exiled 'Anglo' poets such as Thomson and Davidson from the Scottish canon.

In contrast to modern Scottish poetry, it could be argued that any meaningful engagement with nihilism and modern images of destruction in Gaelic poetry came some time later, perhaps mainly due to early twentieth-century Gaelic poetry being influenced by the incantations of Alexander Carmichael's *Carmina Gadelica* (1900) and Marjory Kennedy-Fraser's *Songs of the Hebrides* (1909, 1917, 1921), embodied in the folkloric work of Katherine Whyte (Catrìona NicGhille-Bhàin, 1845–1928) and the poetry of Coinneach MacLeòid (Kenneth MacLeod, 1871–1955) and Donnchadh MacIain (Duncan Johnston, 1881–1947).[7] However, Donald Meek has recently presented significant scholarship on the 'industrial Gael', highlighting nineteenth-century urban Gaels and their interactions with industrial developments in the Scottish Lowlands, e.g. with poems about the 'iron horse' or 'an t-each iarainn', which showed that Gaelic experience leading up to the twentieth century was multi-faceted and not easily stereotyped.[8] Nevertheless, it was the experiences of the First World War which brought Gaelic poetry properly into the twentieth century and which led Gaelic poets to a more realist style in their work. Tradition and innovation meet in the poetry of both Donnchadh MacDhunlèibhe (Duncan Livingstone, 1877–1964), who composed poems about the Boer War, the Second World War and his emigrant life in South Africa,[9] and Dòmhnall Ruadh Chorùna (Donald MacDonald, 1887–1967), the North Uist-born 'Voice of the Trenches' who was wounded on the Somme in 1916. While many Gaelic poets from previous centuries had described battles, the sheer scale of the suffering during the First World War and the new weapons of war meant that poets such as Dòmhnall Ruadh had to adapt traditional styles and motifs to encompass these new experiences. 'Air an Somme' (*'On the Somme'*) and 'Dh'fhalbh na gillean grinn' (*'Off went the handsome lads'*)[10] recount specific memories of battles in traditional metres, and the refrain, well used in traditional Gaelic poetry, is given new life in 'Òran Arras' (*'The Song of Arras'*), in which Gaelic and English are employed almost simultaneously to remind listeners/readers that Gaelic soldiers were existing in a bilingual environment: "Illean, march at ease!' (*'Lads, march at ease!'*). In stanza five of this poem, the old panegyric vegetal motif of the warrior as part of a genealogical tree ('tìr nan geug') perhaps slightly masks the stark truth that so many Gaelic-speaking men failed to return to their communities from the trenches, with families 'Feitheamh ris an sgeul / Bhios aig a' chlèir ri aithris' ('*Waiting for news / That the clerk has to tell*').[11] As a woman's response to the more male-orientated experience of the First World War, Ciorstai NicLeòid's (Christina MacLeod, 1880–1954) 'Cuimhneachan 1914–1918' ('*In Memory of 1914–1918*') provides a fitting tribute to the debilitating grief of war.[12]

One of Dòmhnall Ruadh's most affecting war poems is 'Òran a' Phuinnsein' ('*Song of the Poison*'), in which the poet describes the horror of first-hand experience of chemical warfare: 'Ar leamsa gur e meal a bh'ann / Nuair theann e nall air còmhnard' ('*I had taken it for a shower / As it drifted across the ground to us*').[13] While this poem undoubtedly employs descriptive techniques for the benefit of an audience back home and can thus be viewed in relation to the Gaelic oral tradition, 'Òran a' Phuinnsein' is also notable for its underlying sense of threat and foreboding and its indication of a more intangible evil, symbolised by the invisible chemicals, which aligns it with a growing modernist sensibility.

MacDiarmid, who would later promote Gaelic, returned from the First World War with plans to rescue Scottish culture from parochialism. His early Scots poetry was in some measure a reaction to the Lallans (Lowlands) poetry of the late nineteenth and early twentieth century written by, for instance, Robert Louis Stevenson (1850–1894).[14] Stevenson published four volumes of verse and wrote in both English and Scots. *Underwoods* (1887) is divided between English and Scots poems and provides a glossary of Scottish vowel sounds. Stevenson, who admits 'that Burns has always sounded in my ear like something partly foreign', believes Scots to be a 'dying language'.[15] While his use of Scots can be satirical in a Burnsian vein, for example 'The Scotsman's Return from Abroad', Stevenson often betrays the nostalgia of the exile and Kailyard sentimentality, as in 'To S. R. Crockett', dedicated to the Kailyard novelist and written from Vailima: 'Be it granted me to behold you again in dying, / Hills of home!'[16] As Edwin Morgan points out, the poem uses just three Scots words; Stevenson is 'doing what he can with a thinned-out literary medium'.[17] Stevenson may have believed that Scots was moribund, but his own fame played a part in its revival. He expressed indifference to regional variations; however, as Colin Milton argues, Stevenson's Scots was drawn from his Lothian upbringing and 'belongs more to the regional tradition' preceding MacDiarmid than to the synthetic efforts at national linguistic integration pursued by MacDiarmid in the 1920s.[18] Milton claims persuasively that if C. M. Grieve was hostile to the regional revival, MacDiarmid's Scots owed it a debt.

The regional revival centred on the north-east. Its most successful protagonist was Charles Murray (1864–1941), who emigrated from Aberdeenshire to South Africa in 1888. Like John Buchan (1875–1940), who published *Poems, Scots and English* in 1917 and the anthology *The Northern Muse* (1924), Murray prospered as an imperialist. His *Hamewith* ('homewards'), first published in 1900 but running to several editions, shows Murray's ear for the spoken rhythms and words of Aberdeenshire. Other north-east poets in Scots include Mary Symon (1863–1938), who was taught by the Scots poet James Logie Robertson ('Hugh Haliburton'), and whose work was collected in *Deveron Days* (1933), and the sculptor-poet Pittendrigh MacGillivray (1856–1938), whose *Bog Myrtle and Peat Reek* (1922) impressed MacDiarmid. The places and people of Angus were important to Helen Cruickshank (1886–1975), Marion Angus (1865–1946), born to Scottish parents in Sunderland before moving to Arbroath, and the Montrose aristocrat Violet Jacob (1863–1946), author of *Songs of Angus* (1915). The Broughty Ferry-born Lewis Spence (1874–1955), a Scottish Nationalist and one of the earliest modern experimenters in Scots, writes in 'Great Tay of the Waves': 'The native airt resolves the man!'[19] This crucial connection of place to being was an essential ethos of the Scottish Renaissance, a modernist movement that, in contradistinction to the transnationalism of canonical modernism, was inter-national.

MacDiarmid wanted poetry in Scots to have a future that moved beyond the regional and the folkish to become a European literary language. The Doric should reach the same psychological and spiritual depths as Dostoevsky and Lawrence and strive for Joycean experimentation. MacDiarmid thought it 'necessary to go back behind Burns to Dunbar and the Old Makars', yet he wanted a Scots modernism.[20] This is no contradiction. For MacDiarmid, the modern Scottish Renaissance should be a unifying national movement, 'at once radical and conservative, revolutionary and reactionary'.[21] MacDiarmid promoted 'Scotland as a diversity-in-unity', seeking, too, a Gaelic revival.[22] The Scottish Renaissance was characteristically modernist in its desire for cultural rebirth, and in looking to the past to inspire the future. Roger Griffin defines modernism as a 'revolt against decadence'.[23] In *A Drunk Man Looks at the Thistle* (1926) MacDiarmid laments the perceived decadence of modern Scotland, where the Kailyard has sidetracked a Scottish poetic tradition 'And owre the kailyard-wa' Dunbar they've flung'.[24]

MacDiarmid wrote cosmological Scots lyrics in the 1920s, turned to Scots-inflected English for the harder-edged Leninist poems of the 1930s, and used a 'global English' full of uncited quotations and scientific terms for longer prose poems, such as *In Memoriam James Joyce*, that remained unpublished until the 1950s. This switching between Scots and English makes somewhat tendentious his falling-out with Edwin Muir (1887–1959) over Muir's *Scott and Scotland* (1936), in which the Orcadian claimed that Scottish writers should write in English and join the English tradition. MacDiarmid answered Muir by leaving him out of his *Golden Treasury of Scottish Poetry* (1940). Muir's view of Scotland's cultural condition in 'Scotland 1941', where Burns and Scott are 'sham bards of a sham nation',[25] and 'Scotland's Winter' is certainly pessimistic, yet on the condition-of-Scotland question Muir's diagnosis is not dissimilar to MacDiarmid's.

Muir, who might be described as a Christian existentialist, wrote poetry in English depicting a disunited, fallen world that is only bearable through the memory of Eden's wholeness. Muir also used Greek myth to suggest the fractured, diminished nature of modernity. In 'The Labyrinth', for instance, lived reality is an 'illusion': 'It is a world, perhaps; but there's another'.[26] Place recurs in Muir's poetry – *Journeys and Places* (1937), *The Narrow Place* (1943) – usually with symbolical, mythical or religious connotations. Muir's vision can be apocalyptic, as in 'The Horses', but this poem is also imbued with a planetary, ecological awareness. He may have disagreed with MacDiarmid's direction, but, as Margery Palmer McCulloch states, Muir's poetry 'fulfilled the Scottish Renaissance aim of taking Scottish literature back into the mainstream of European culture'.[27]

Concerns regarding dialect and, on a larger scale, a growing awareness of political disunity and the threat of war in Europe are also prevalent in Gaelic poetry of this period. The friendship and shared creative admiration between MacDiarmid and Sorley MacLean (Somhairle MacGill-Eain, 1911–1996) has been well documented,[28] highlighting most clearly the interaction between the Scottish Renaissance and modern Scottish Gaelic, but, before the emergence of MacLean as a poetic force in Scottish Gaelic literature, MacDiarmid also encouraged earlier Gaelic poets such as Barra-born Donald Sinclair (Dòmhnall Mac na Ceàrdaich, 1885–1932), who later moved to Edinburgh. Sinclair mixed with the Edinburgh literati and was involved in the Gaelic movement in Edinburgh. Sinclair's concern for reviving and maintaining a modern Gaelic literature is emphasised by MacDiarmid, who writes that he had 'conversations of absorbing interest with him on Scottish and Irish politics, on the disintegration of the Gaelic into dialects and on the problems of synthesis that exist also in regard to the Scots vernacular, and the necessity in both of a resurrection of great amounts of "dead vocabulary".[29] The themes of reviving language and literature are typically MacDiarmidian, but were ideas being explored by Gaelic poets too. In Sinclair's 'Slighe nan Seann Seun' (*'The Way of the Old Spells'*) a sense of foreboding can be detected, perhaps hinting at the horrors of the First World War and the subsequent political situation in Europe – 'An iongnadh an iarmailt shiar bhith nochd fo shnuadh / 'S ur n-àrosan an cian bhith laist' le lias bith-bhuan?' (*'Is it a surprise that the western sky tonight is in gloom / And your far-off palaces lit up with glow eternal?'*).[30] There is also an underlying sense of threat in the storm imagery of Domhnall Mac an t-Saoir's (Donald MacIntyre, 1889–1964) 'Aeòlus agus am Balg' (*'Æolus and the Bellows'*), which was partly inspired by Sinclair's 'Là nan Seachd Sìon' (*'The Day of the Seven Elements'*) and which, given the timescale of its composition (1920–38), Ronald Black has suggested may be a prophetic allegory on the rise of Mussolini and Hitler.[31] The description of the storm in the poem is followed by a highlighting of fascist ideology – 'Cuim' a dh'fhanainn air mo chrìochan?' (*'Why should I stay within my bounds?'*)[32] – and shows that the concerns of a modern Gaelic poet were stretching far beyond the Gàidhealtachd, although the personification of the landscape as a living entity, mirroring the feeling of the people who lived on it, was often a primary device in showing this sense of unsettlement.

On a narrower scale, Mac an t-Saoir's later poem 'Òran na Cloiche' (*'The Song of the Stone'*) celebrates the removal of the Stone of Destiny from England in 1950, imbuing the stone with the hopes of a rising 'Gaelic' sense of Scottish nationalism, and hinting at a nationalist vein in Gaelic poetry that was to go further in the 1950s and beyond. During the 1938 National Mod, when Mac an t-Saoir won the Bardic Crown for 'Aeòlus agus am Balg', one of the judges hailed it as 'the Gaelic poem of the century'.[33] This view was somewhat premature. The modernist poems of the 'Famous Five' of twentieth-century Gaelic poetry – Sorley MacLean, George Campbell Hay (Deòrsa mac Iain Dheòrsa, 1915–1984), Ruaraidh MacThòmais (Derick Thomson, 1921–2012), Iain Crichton Smith (Iain Mac a' Ghobhainn, 1928–1998) and Dòmhnall MacAmhlaigh (Donald MacAulay, b. 1930) – had still to emerge during the same period as the second wave of the Scottish Renaissance, but this comment does go some way in indicating the drive for more ambitious Gaelic poems, both in terms of content and style.

Several poets who were influenced by MacDiarmid formed the second wave of the Scottish Renaissance from the 1930s to the 1950s. These include William Soutar (1898–1943), who wrote in English and Scots. Soutar's *Seeds in the Wind* (1933), Scots poems for children, was written with the conviction that 'if the Doric is to come back alive, it will come first on a cock-horse'.[34] Robert Garioch (1909–1981) and the New Zealand-born Sydney Goodsir Smith (1915–1975) were poets of Edinburgh, heirs of Robert Fergusson, and at home in neoclassical mode and the vernacular. John Speirs rated Smith's *Under the Eildon Tree* (1948) the 'one notable piece in Scots' since MacDiarmid's *Drunk Man*.[35] Garioch published his first pamphlet, *Seventeen Poems for Sixpence* (1940), with Sorley MacLean. His 'Saxteen Edinburgh Sonnets' has a similar streetwise and comical cynicism to Tom Leonard's *Six Glasgow Poems* (1969), while 'The Wire' is a moving account of his experiences as a Second World War prisoner of war. Folklorist and Gramsci translator Hamish Henderson (1919–2002) wrote *Elegies for the Dead in Cyrenaica* (1948) about the desert campaigns in North Africa. Less directly, the war influenced the emergence of the New Apocalypse movement. Central were J. F. Hendry (1912–1986), co-editor of *The New Apocalypse* anthology (1939), and G. S. Fraser (1915–1980). On the fringes of this group were Ruthven Todd (1914–1978), editor of Blake and proponent of the surrealists, and the Glasgow poet Maurice Lindsay (1918–2009), editor of *Modern Scottish Poetry* (1946). Norman MacCaig (1910–1996) renounced his early New Apocalypticism to write lucid poems that, according to Christopher Whyte, 'exhibit a wry playfulness which can effectively mask their preoccupation with [...] how we can know and conceive our manner of being'.[36]

The similar social and political experiences of poets writing in Scots and English and those who were composing in Gaelic up to the late 1930s go some way to disproving the notion that the appearance of the symbolist and modernist work of Sorley MacLean and George Campbell Hay came out of nowhere. Rather, MacLean and Hay harnessed an innovative tradition, one which existed both within and outside their Gaelic world view and that had already been gathering strength for some years. What makes MacLean and Hay so significant to their own generation and the next was the energy and sense of purpose that comes from poets who were 'between' worlds. Both were university-trained and spent time away from their local communities. Their interest ranged from the bardic and the song tradition of Gaelic poetry to the modernist poets Pound, Eliot, MacDiarmid and Yeats. Their exposure to different European traditions and their growing friendships with writers of the Scottish Renaissance allowed them to develop a stronger sense of their identities as Gaelic poets, and a clear view of themselves as voices of a tradition which they were well aware they were altering irrevocably. This self-awareness is one of the most modern aspects of their work and places them firmly in a different category to the Gaelic poetry that had gone before. Perhaps the most overtly self-conscious poetry to emerge during this period was MacLean's *Dàin do Eimhir*, which consisted of sixty poems addressed to 'Eimhir' who, in Irish myth, was the wife of the great heroic figure Cù Chulainn. However, while use of 'Eimhir' as an image manages to connect to a real and imagined Gaelic tradition, shared by Ireland and Scotland, Eimhir acts as a symbol of the Muse for MacLean in these poems and also operates as a smokescreen for the real women who inspired them. Among the poems in this collection are some of the most symbolic of twentieth-century Gaelic poetry, for example, Dàin XXIX 'Coin is Madaidhean-allaidh' ('*Dogs and Wolves*')[37] in which MacLean's unwritten poems chase 'beauty' across the eternal landscape. Other poems in the collection address more political concerns such as the Spanish Civil War and the rise of fascism (for instance, Dàin IV).[38] MacLean was a communist and his social concerns come through clearly in other poems such as 'Ban-Ghàidheal' ('*Highland Woman*'), 'Calbharaigh' ('*Calvary*')[39] and his long poem 'An Cuilithionn' ('*The Cuillin*'), which could be compared to MacDiarmid's *Drunk Man*, exploring the multifaceted symbol of the mountain against the backdrop of the history of oppression and suffering of the masses. Despite an emphasis on collective history, the image of the individual hero is always evident and 'An Cuilithionn' finishes on a curiously personal tone for a poem described as a communist 'rant' by the poet himself:

> Cò seo, cò seo oidhche 'n spioraid?
> Chan eil ach tannasg lom cridhe,
> manadh leis fhèin a' falbh a' smaointinn

> *Who is this, who is this in the night of the spirit? / It is only the naked ghost of a heart, / a spectre going alone in thought.*[40]

Some of MacLean's and Hay's most ambitious work in the early 1940s, while known to their own literary circle, took much longer to be published and obtain a readership; sections of Hay's magnum opus 'Mochtàr is Dùghall' were not published until 1982, but it is significant that rather than appearing dated, much of the poetry deals with a sense of cultural and linguistic identity, which is still relevant in the present time. Perhaps partly due to his linguistic abilities and his work in the Education Corps in Italy, Algeria and Greece during the Second World War, Hay was able to see links between Gaelic identity and other cultures. Thus in 'Mochtàr is Dùghall' the futility of war is shown by the ending of noble cultures previously embodied by a Gael and an Arab – 'crìoch dhà shaoghal' (*'the end of two worlds'*).[41] In 'Bisearta' the Tunisian predicament of being trapped in Allied–German crossfire in the North African campaign is treated by Hay as a situation in which evil infects humanity by moving within the body itself – 'An t-Olc 'na chridhe 's 'na chuisle' (*'Evil as a pulse / and a heart'*)[42] – and the landscape is viewed as a pawn in a game in which the native inhabitants have no real part. While Hay's identity as a Gael stretches to a broader vision of Europe, Ruaraidh MacThòmais's vision as a modern poet is more firmly based within the rural–urban divide within his own sense of self, as a Gael from Lewis whose experience also encompasses life in Glasgow. Although mostly belonging to a slightly later period, his first poetry collection, *An Dealbh Briste / The Broken Picture* was published in 1951; 'Nam Dhachaigh Eadar Dhà Dhùthaich' (*'In My House Between Two Countries'*) most overtly captures the physical, linguistic and emotional experience of being separated from homeland.

The poetry of this period, in all three languages, depicts a wide range of engagement with Scotland and its political and cultural state, often with the ambitious aim of inciting cultural rebirth in a historically turbulent era. While the development of the poetry in Gaelic, Scots and English does not always precisely correspond in its periodicity, it is clear that there are points of connection and common interest between poets operating in all three languages at this time, often brought about by a shared cultural and political vision. Poets experimented with multiple linguistic registers, drawn from different regional backgrounds and portraying rural and urban experience, to explore how modernity transformed what it meant to be an individual, and how Scotland confronted and contributed to the changes of modernity.

CHAPTER NINE

Contemporary Poetry (1950–)

Attila Dósa and Michelle Macleod

While Scottish modernism has been described as 'inter-national' in the previous chapter, a progressively self-confident transnationalism alongside a self-reflexive hybridisation of the speech forms and cultures of home has characterised poetry since the war. Dialogic engagement with different literatures and languages within and outwith Scotland identifies a number of poets, from Edwin Morgan to Kathleen Jamie, whose works investigate man as both a socially determined individual and a spiritual being independent of political borders: Matt McGuire and Colin Nicholson, in fact, refer to a sense of freedom in contemporary Scottish poetry.[1] The literary and linguistic intersections can be traced out with the help of Deleuze and Guattari's concept of a 'minor literature' – 'not the literature of a minor language but the literature a minority makes in a major language'[2] – which, striving to find a voice in an idiom at once familiar and strange, operates in the twofold paradigm of deterritorialisation and political commitment in order to construct a literature that holds collective value.

The second wave of the Scottish Renaissance is barely more than a label of convenience, which embraces a clutch of divergent talents coming into maturity in the 1950s. This includes Norman MacCaig (1910–1996), whose *Riding Lights* (1955) presents philosophical contemplations of lucid and compact images from North-West Highland farm life, as in 'Summer Farm': 'I lie, not thinking, in the cool, soft grass, / Afraid of where a thought might take me'. Looking back, the closest equivalent to these metaphysical poems may be found in William Drummond's medieval Scots poems, though neither is their strange negativity too far from Edwin Muir's near-contemporary existentialist mindset. Looking forward, poems like 'Smuggler' and 'Patriot' reveal a lyric integrity combined with humane pacifism which Douglas Dunn later takes as his own. MacCaig's ancestry comes from the island of

Harris on his mother's side and his 'spiritual fulcrum' can be found in Assynt.[3] But he is also a poet of Edinburgh, where he enjoyed the companionship of other writers prominent in the 1950s, including Sydney Goodsir Smith (1915–1975), Tom Scott (1918–1995), Sorley MacLean (Somhairle MacGill-Eain, 1911–1996) and Robert Garioch (1909–1981). And though not a native Gaelic speaker and always suspicious of politics (he was a conscientious objector during the war), he records a tragic observation of diminishing ancestral Gaelic culture, as in 'Loch Sionoscaig': 'Yet clear the footprint in the puddle sand / That slowly filled / And rounded out and smoothed and disappeared'.

Greenock-born W. S. Graham (1918–1986) also looks at philosophical problems of perception (through language rather than image) in 'Seven Letters' (*The Nightfishing*, 1955): 'The great verbs of the sea / Come down on us in a roar. / What shall I answer for?' Graham's scrutiny of how language is encouraged to take on meaning looks ahead (partly via his friend Edwin Morgan's work) to the interest of a 1990s cluster of then-young poets, called Informationists. The handling of the past, the position of the 'I' perceiving itself while perceiving the 'non-I', and the long dramatic monologues with a foreign inflection (in *Malcolm Mooney's Land*, 1970) may be an unacknowledged and as yet unexplored micro-line of continuity between Graham and Frank Kuppner (b. 1951).

Muir's disciple and later friend George Mackay Brown (1921–1996) came from Orkney and returned to live there. In *Loaves and Fishes* (1959) and *Fishermen with Ploughs* (1971) his negotiations of identity and temporality depend on exploiting timeless symbols of pagan and Christian rituals in an ambition to resist progress, 'a rootless utilitarian faith, without beauty or mystery'.[4] He describes quotidian details of fishing and farming life in a language that is contemporary, minimalist, and archaic, biblical, at the same time.

Both the thematic and the formal concerns in Brown's epic attempt to confront inevitable modernity in the name of organic communities beyond the northernmost shores of Britain differ from those of prolific English-Gaelic poet Iain Crichton Smith (Iain Mac a' Ghobhainn, 1928–1998). Brought up on the Isle of Lewis, he looks at historical-economic exploitations of the land and its people in 'The Clearances' or 'Shall Gaelic Die?' But he as often speaks about less pleasing aspects of living on geographical, linguistic and cultural peripheries (in 'The Law and the Grace') as he is nostalgic about the decline of Gaeldom: 'sometimes I hear graves singing / their Gaelic song to the dingos'.[5] His existence on the boundary leaves him searching for meaning because in spite of his effort in 'A' dol dhachaigh' ('*Going Home*'),⁶ it is impossible for him to feel settled and at peace.

Throughout the last century there has been a continued weakening of Gaelic culture: traditional communities have changed and have less clearly defined borders, with Gaelic being spoken almost as much in the Central Belt as it is in its heartland Highland and island areas. The resulting hybridisation of culture is deliberated upon by a number of Gaelic poets of this era: for some this represents loss, while for others it is an indication of the procurement of Gaelic as badge of whole-Scottish identity.

Of the Gaelic poets of the period under consideration here, George Campbell Hay (Deòrsa mac Iain Dheòrsa, 1915–1984) posits that Scotland is better off for having two cultures, yet this proposition is made as if it is a controversial one, as in 'Ceithir Gaothan na h-Albann' ('*The Four Winds of Scotland*'): 'is i Alba nan Gall 's nan Gàidheal is gaire, is blàths, is beatha dhomh' ('*it is Scotland, Highland and Lowland, that is laughter and warmth and life for me*'). Any perceived challenge in this sentiment at the time of writing is now gone, as evidenced by its inclusion on the Canongate Wall of the Scottish Parliament.

If this proposition was controversial in the first half of the twentieth century, it becomes less so, perhaps, especially with the increased number of non-native Gaelic speakers writing in the language. Such writers include Meg Bateman (b. 1959), Fearghas MacFhionnlaigh (b. 1948), Christopher Whyte (b. 1952), Rody Gorman (b. 1960) and Niall O'Gallagher (b. 1981). Their presence in the literary landscape challenges the old order: currently there is very little poetry being written by native speakers under the age of sixty. As the youngest of those mentioned here, O'Gallagher is part of a society where there is now a well-developed Gaelic network where second-language speakers are able to use the language of their choice with relative frequency and with acceptance: he concedes that while his language choice might be puzzling to some, for him it is an instrument of communication which best suits his 'new' craft as poet.⁷ So confident is he in his linguistic choice that he rejects the common practice of publishing with facing translations. Whyte has said that for him the practice of self-translation is without pleasure or value and 'almost a question of voiding the poem of its content, which may, indeed, be the language in which it was written'.⁸ Neither O'Gallagher or Whyte labour over their right to compose in Gaelic, neither do they spend time considering the state of the language; however, Whyte does concede, in the envoi to the wonderfully crafted long poem 'Bho Leabhar-Latha Maria

Malibran' ('*From the Diary of Maria Malibran*') (first published in 1996), that 'Gaelic' poetry readers might prefer to read about things more 'Gaelic', such as abandoned crofting tools and waning traditions.

Throughout the verse of this era the issue of identity is one which is repeatedly addressed by Gaelic poets, especially so by Ruaraidh MacThòmais (Derick Thomson, 1921–2012), one of the most prolific modern Gaelic poets, whose output spanned more than half a century and included seven volumes and one collected works. In his earlier works Gaelic language and culture is shown as suppressed, for example in 'Anns a' Bhalbh Mhadainn' (literally '*In the Mute Morning*', but in his own translation '*Sheep*'),[9] where the sheep smothered in the snowdrift are representative of the oppressed Gaelic language and culture. MacThòmais does not restrict himself to talking in general terms about how the linguistic and cultural situation is changing. He has a number of poems which show how becoming part of greater Scottish (and intellectual) society affected him: he agonises over how he is at times torn between two cultures and two languages. His final collection clearly shows a second stage to this denouement of hybridisation. For him the process has changed Gaelic culture and language too much: and while hybridisation may assist in keeping Gaelic language alive, it is a language that is very far removed from the one that he grew up with and one that holds little appeal for him.

Silke Stroh discusses the 'colonising and de-colonising implications' of 'the increasing proportion of participants in Gaelic culture who come from non-Gaelic backgrounds'.[10] Referencing Glaser's anthropological-linguistic work,[11] Stroh notes that this can be liberating in that it shows people are freer to shape their own identities, but she also notes that 'where hybrid identities veer too strongly towards the anglophone/non-Gaelic side, or too strongly towards the temporary or merely symbolic, there is a danger that Gaelicness will be reduced to the equivalent of a hobby or interest group'.[12] This is clearly expressed in MacThòmais's 'Dh'fhalbh siud is thàinig seo' ('*That went and this came*'), which refers to the linguistically superior Gaelic rooted in community and history (MacThòmais uses the word 'dualchas', roughly '*heritage*' in English, but very emotively loaded) which is then replaced by the inauthentic Gaelic on road-signs and in translated school texts and on television. He is almost in opposition to the viewpoint put forward by Bateman, who defends wholeheartedly the contribution and merit of the second-language speaker in the aptly named 'Cànain' ('*Language*').[13]

James Thomson's and John Davidson's proto-modernist concerns with the city continue to thrive in 1960s and 1970s in poetry in Scots and English. MacDiarmid's modernist foregrounding of a metaphysical marriage of the local and the international as a site of formal-thematic intersections inspires not only Edwin Morgan, who wrote essays on MacDiarmid,[14] but also (if only with a different outcome) Glasgow Group writers like Tom Leonard, who abhors MacDiarmid's prescriptivism. In contrast to what is perceived as MacDiarmid's rural 'backofbeyondism',[15] urban life becomes the new religion. Avant-garde experiments are affected by American speech rhythms, while the impact of Soviet ideology remains powerful for many of these admittedly socialist-republican poets.

OBE, Scots Makar and Glasgow's Laureate, Edwin Morgan's (1920–2010) urban cosmopolitism has been described as 'undoubtedly Scottish, but without the baggage of previous generations'.[16] While recent critical takes on Scotland's literary place in the world tend to highlight Scottish cultural export,[17] Morgan pays at least as much attention to import, making use of a variety of diatopic transactions, including translation, absorption, adaptation, influence and dialogue. He adds European poets such as Montale and Mayakovsky to the post-war American context of the Glasgow Renaissance. He is regarded as the best English-language translator of Hungarian modernist poet Attila József (whose effect on Morgan's urban lyric cannot be overestimated), and formal strategies in *Themes on a Variation* (1988) twin with that of fellow language wizard Sándor Weöres. In *From Glasgow to Saturn* (1973) or *Cathures* (2002) urban environment is more than a mere setting, while in earlier poems North African desert landscapes (as in MacLean or Campbell Hay) also gain symbolic-cultural resonances – foreshadowing later interests in ecosystems among Fife poets John Burnside, Kathleen Jamie and Don Paterson. Mixed aesthetic effects and class sympathies in urban stories told through images in Morgan's *Instamatic Poems* (1972) are not entirely alien to photographic documentaries of city life in Douglas Dunn's *Terry Street* (1969), *The Happier Life* (1972) and *Love or Nothing* (1974).

The reciprocal metamorphosis of linguistic codes in Morgan's outwardly science fiction poem 'First Men on Mercury' has been read allegorically in terms of Scotland's changing political voice in the Union. Indeed, it was a long haul from the 1979 referendum to 1999, when Scotland partially regained its say. During those years, lyrical synopses of history such as Dunn's *St Kilda's Parliament* (1981) and Morgan's *Sonnets from Scotland* (1984) affirmed the need for peaceful but unrelenting resistance to political-cultural homogenisation. For understandable reasons, small and oppressed nations tend to have an esteem for their writers. It is a case in point that Morgan's poem 'For the Opening of the Scottish Parliament' was read at the opening ceremony in 2004 and the Canongate Wall façade of the parliamentary complex is decorated with literary quotations.

The range of Tom Leonard's (b. 1944) experiment covers concrete poetry, poster poems and sound poetry in a radical project that looks into the nature of and attacks cultural prejudices and complacencies. Deleuze and Guattari argue that in a minor literature 'every individual matter is immediately plugged into the political'.[18] Indeed, the personal and the political intersect on all levels in Leonard's work. In *Six Glasgow Poems* (1969) and *Intimate Voices* (1984), Leonard's influences include William Carlos Williams's minutely observed colloquialisms as well as the Whitmanesque rhetoric of radical Beat poets like Allen Ginsberg. While he regards voice as fundamentally human and hence intimate,[19] he is also interested in how speech, accent, dialect and utterance are tied to large-scale discrimination in society and culture across the ages – see for example his *Radical Renfrew* (1990) anthology. Like other poets of working-class origin such as Dunn (whom Leonard regards as 'cultured' rather than 'barbarian'[20]), Leonard, too, holds on to his oppositional-republican world view. But while Dunn has intimate links with the countryside (coming from a then semi-rural area of Renfrewshire and living now in rural Fife), Leonard is a city man who wages a literary war against authority in cursed urban idioms: 'this / is me tokn yir / right way a / spelling. this / is my trooth. / yooz doant no / thi trooth / yirsellz cawz / yi canny talk / right' ('Unrelated Incidents').

Looking back on the last two or three decades within the period in discussion gives too short a perspective to set off trends and movements or to separate the lasting from the momentary in terms of poetic achievement. There has been a remarkable output of creative talent in such a great diversity of tones and voices that recent poetry in Scotland has been compared to a 'crowded pool' of individual talents.[21] It is possible, though, to identify loose groupings or to point out tendencies, but these might be so nebulous and fast-changing that the danger of such tags is that of becoming obsolete before long.

While poets like Leonard or Dunn have expressed their impatience with MacDiarmid's linguistic prescriptivism, the lexicological aspect of MacDiarmid's work proved seminal to a group of young language experimenters in the 1980s–1990s. Robert Crawford (b. 1959) and W. N. Herbert

(b. 1961) have seen language as an assemblage rather than a given, sacred entity that should not be tampered with.[22] Herbert likes 'the idea that organic models might not fully describe language, so that the artificial, the resurrected and the galvanised [...] all have a role to play in the specific construct of the poem',[23] whereas Crawford lays increasing emphasis on the roots of language in history and personal experience in *Talkies* (1992) and *The Tip of My Tongue* (2003). Both of them are Oxonians with PhDs written on modernists (Crawford on Eliot and Herbert on MacDiarmid) and both see poetry as a site of intersection for different languages, periods, territories, cultures and realities. Scouring dictionaries, like MacDiarmid did, their aims have included stretching the possibilities of verbalisation. They handle the verbal reality of poetry in a postmodern way, which is intimately playful as well as intellectually challenging.

Crossings between text and art characterise the work of another postmodernist experimenter, Richard Price (b. 1966), who has collaborated with visual artists like Chan Ky-Yut. Price has associated himself with avant-garde magazines just as Ian Hamilton Finlay (1925–2006) did before him, whose *Poor.Old.Tired.Horse* (1962–68) was an influential visual-poetry magazine of the period. Considered as a founder of the concrete poetry movement, Finlay had a profound interest in classical philosophy and languages, and 'recognised the power of language and art to shape our perceptions of the world'.[24] 'Expressed in stone and wood',[25] his work goes beyond the printed page, and marries a 'certain formalist purity' with 'an insistent polemical edge'.[26] Though forms of expression such as concrete poetry and conceptual art still enjoy global interest and Dunn himself has collaborated with visual artists, he omitted such poems by Finlay, Morgan or Leonard from his definitive Faber anthology of 1992.

The most challenging postmodernist poetic expression is possibly that by literary recluse Frank Kuppner (b. 1951). But it would be wrong to call him an experimenter, because he has a consistent lyric intellect which has followed a consistent route beneath the surface of diverse generic and thematic experiments. Though he has treated the label with a touch of irony in a recent interview,[27] he may be labelled an 'existentialist'. His quatrain series – inherited from partly Chinese poetry and partly Omar Khayyám and used extensively in *A Bad Day for the Sung Dynasty* (1984) or *The Intelligent Observation of Naked Women* (1987) – unsettle settled beliefs in categories such as perception, time and even quantity, whilst braving existentialist fears of resulting uncertainty. As Watson notes, the hilarious and parodying (e.g. of Ezra Pound) side coexists with a 'Zen stillness' in his poetry of (often mock) facts.[28] Moreover, a large slice of Kuppner's work is inspired by photographs (similarly to Dunn) and exhibits an elegiac tone. Kuppner's discovery of his native Glasgow parallels Ron Butlin's (b. 1949) discovery of his native Edinburgh: changes in particular locations make both poets reflect on spatial, linguistic and temporal alienation – a theme that crops up also in Dunn, whom, though, no critic would term 'postmodernist'.

Kuppner's interest in astronomy offers superficial links with Morgan's science fiction poems. Morgan's space-age optimism is not any more shared and fears of nuclear fallout have been replaced by other fears. But his passion for scientific technology and his curiosity of how systems create, (fail to) transmit and transform meaning perhaps inspired Robert Crawford, who was Morgan's student at Glasgow University. Crawford, fellow Glaswegian David Kinloch (b. 1959), and other friends such as Herbert, Price, Peter McCarey (b. 1956) and Alan Riach (b. 1957) are gathered under the term 'Informationists'. It is a term coined and defined by Price in his introduction to *Contraflow on the Super Highway* (1994), which he co-edited with Herbert: 'the information they make available in their poetry includes rather than necessarily opposes media news because part of their *raison d'etre* is to digest and transmit as many different types of data as they can'.[29] Though never representing a proper school, Informationists have shared a common interest in 'transnational electronic systems of communication'[30] and in how electronic and print media create platforms for encyclopaedic knowledge and what can be done with it locally whilst 'maintain[ing] a connection between the language or languages of home and the often liberating expansiveness of "Elsewhere"'.[31]

'How many people live today in a language that is not their own?' – the work of recent Scottish poets calls attention to the political-linguistic (self-)alienation pinpointed in Deleuze and Guattari's rhetorical question.[32] Brittany-based Kenneth White (b. 1936) concentrates less on language 'in terms of inter-human communication', arguing that you 'have to have some awareness of non-human and cosmic language too', while categorically rejecting idealist philosophy.[33] Writing in two languages (French and English), his 'waybooks' (records of physical journeys and spiritual itineraries) provide an answer to another question from the two French critics: 'How to become the *nomad* and the *immigrant* and the gypsy of our own language?'[34] These keywords set up a good paradigm for us to enter White's 'white world'. Though it takes in a politically and linguistically bound geopoetics or 'an exploration of the cultures of the world, as well as of its physical spaces',[35] White's world is an escape from city, nation, consumerism and market-based economy to an 'open world' of nomadic routes, rivers and territories. Escaping from and returning to Scotland has been a formative experience for generations of Scottish poets from the Middle Ages to most recent times, but some contemporaries like Ian Bamforth (b. 1959), Carol Ann Duffy (see her *Other Country*, 1990, and *Mean Time*, 1993), Jackie Kay (b. 1961), Roddy Lumsden (b. 1966), McCarey, Price, Robin Robertson (b. 1955) and of course White himself have not returned – a phenomenon which has further contributed to the hybridisation of cultures and languages within and outside Scotland.

The Gaelic poets of the last century are aware of the fluid nature of their cultural surroundings. Aonghas MacNeacail's (b. 1942) recent collection *Laoidh an donais òig* (*Hymn to a young demon*, 2007) is very political: he displays a distrust of politicians and mocks current manifestos and political debate,[36] and continues to question the moral correctness of actions in the past. And while Gaelic poetry has become truly national and international in terms of content – Peter MacKay has said of MacNeacail, for example, that his 'poetry is awash with influences, acknowledged and silent, and tends to position itself within various cultures and religions'[37] – there are still examples which reflect local issues or negotiate between the environments. Murchadh MacPhàrlain (Murdo MacFarlane, 1901–1982) in 'Is mise guth nan Innse Gall' ('*I am the voice of the Hebrides*')[38] is self-aware of his position as local interpreter of national issues, and the sharply observed commentary of Dòmhnall MacAmhlaigh (Donald MacAulay, b. 1930) on man's idiosyncrasies works equally well situated in a house in Bernera (Lewis) or Turkey.

As Gaelic poetry becomes more Scottish and international, an interesting feature of publishing over the last few decades has been the dual Gaelic–Irish publications with Gaelic poetry being translated into Irish, e.g.: Rody Gorman, Maoilios Caimbeul (Myles Campbell, b. 1944), Meg Bateman and Màiri NicGumaraid (Montgommery, b. 1955) all have dual-language, single-authored publications, and in addition to this there have also been bilingual anthologies. While this is in no doubt due to the interests of one particular publisher, Coiscéim, it gives this Scottish poetry an additional readership with potential for inter-cultural dialogue.

Non-urban perspectives have been associated with backward-looking sentimentalism in Scots-English poetry, and were vigorously criticised by MacDiarmid, but later given a new resonance by MacCaig. Douglas Dunn (b. 1942) has poems about cities (Glasgow and Hull) but his return to Tayside has opened up new ways of seeing and new vistas. Dunn prefers Douglas Young's rich botanical sensibility to MacDiarmid's and Morgan's lithospheric poetics. His *Northlight* (1988) and *Dante's Drum-kit* (1993) paint large-scale estuarial panoramas while in *The Year's Afternoon* (2000) miniature wonders of gardening prompt his Horatian withdrawal from public issues. Dunn's influence on younger generations is half hidden but nevertheless multifarious – even a poet of such different sensibility as Herbert has acknowledged surprising debts to Dunn in his attempts at 'construct[ing] a location, a creatively satisfying landscape'.[39]

Poetry has begun to stir again in North-East Fife after a long hiatus following Robert Fergusson's graduation from St Andrews University in 1768. During Dunn's professorship there in the 1990s, a loose grouping of poets became interested in the creative consequences of occupying places in a given ecosystem. John Burnside (b. 1955), Crawford, Kathleen Jamie (b. 1961) and Don Paterson (b. 1963) link environmental responsiveness with Catholic, Gnostic, Calvinist, Buddhist and other forms of transcendentalism, while their search for a coexistence of culture and ecology results in lyrical poems that have less and less direct political reference.

Interest in nature, habitat and spirit, however, does not mean turning back on topical (political or gender) issues. As for politics, several poets of the middle generation (young in the 1990s) took an active part in the run-up to the 1997 referendum. Crawford's 'Scotland' ('Semiconductor country …') is both a response to MacDiarmid's 'Scotland, Small?' and an end-of-the-millennium love-song to the country, whereas Jamie re-examined devolutionist claims in a critical-satirical vein in *The Queen of Sheba* (1994). Much of such sentiment is gathered in *Dream State* (1994), edited by Glaswegian Donny O'Rourke (b. 1959), who states that 'a fully authentic culture requires a fully authentic politics; and a fully authentic politics requires a state'.[40]

As for gender politics, age-old antagonisms between the sexes were given subtle reconsideration in Dunn's *Elegies* (1985). A lyrical revision of male–female gender roles and identities is undertaken in Crawford's *Masculinity* (1996), whereas Carol Ann Duffy (b. 1955) takes a satirical stand in *The World's Wife* (1999) and *Feminine Gospels* (2002). Reflections on motherhood can be found in Bateman's tender yet frank verse in *Aotromachd agus dàin eile / Lightness and other poems* (1997) and in Jamie's *Jizzen* (1999), which goes perhaps as deep in human, historical and cultural consciousness as *The Grimm Sisters* (1981) and *Dreaming Frankenstein* (1984) a little earlier by Liz Lochhead (b. 1947), appointed Scots Makar after Morgan's death in 2011. Such works by 'elder sisters' inspired books like *Slattern* (1995) and *Newborn* (2004) by Kate Clanchy

(b. 1965), who, contrary to her Glasgow birth and Edinburgh upbringing, has sought to insist she is not a Scottish poet. Same-sex relationships have been shown from a male viewpoint by Morgan, Kinloch and Christopher Whyte, and from a female viewpoint in *Other Lovers* (1993) by Jackie Kay.

Defining a period which includes two national referenda on decentralisation and another that aimed to open the possibility of achieving independence, this chapter has provided an overview of over six decades. These were key decades of cultural change in Scotland, which have translated into an increasing vernacularisation of poetic voices and an attendant resurgence in political-cultural confidence. This period finds poets in rejection of stereotypical conceptions of Scottishness, insisting on greater representation for the voices which comprise a polyphonic and multicultural series of Scotlands. However, the geographical and linguistic expansion of poetry in Scots and English is in stark contrast with the changing sociolinguistic context for Gaelic, where approximately half of all native speakers live outside Gaelic-speaking communities and when these Gaelic-speaking communities themselves continue to be eroded.

PART 2: POETIC FORMS

CHAPTER TEN

The Form of Scottish Gaelic Poetry

William Gillies

Scottish Gaelic (ScG) poetry, as described here, was composed in the Highlands and islands, mostly between the sixteenth and twentieth centuries, and collected between the eighteenth and twentieth centuries. It shares many features with Irish Gaelic poetry composed during the same period. Some Gaelic poetry was composed in 'Classical Gaelic', the literary dialect shared by Ireland and Scotland between the twelfth and seventeenth centuries.

Much of ScG poetry was composed to be sung or chanted. Rhythm, metrical structure and melody produced an amalgam of music and words. Rhythm and metrical structure may also be viewed in conjunction with rhyme and other forms of ornament as forming a verbal poetic package. Describing that verbal package is the prime aim of this chapter; but musical considerations frequently need to be borne in mind.

The following descriptive account groups ScG poetry into seven structural types – six vernacular and one 'Classical'. It is tentative and provisional, since the study of Gaelic metrics is in its infancy, most scholars over the years having accepted the shaky premise that the vernacular poetry derives historically from the Classical.[1]

The 'building blocks' of ScG poetry are rhythm, metrical structure (including phrase, line and verse) and ornament (especially rhyme).

Rhythm[2]

ScG (like English) is a stress-timed language. That is, natural spoken utterances in ScG have an innately rhythmical character, in which the main stresses tend to occur at regular intervals, and varying numbers of unstressed syllables fill the spaces between roughly isochronous stresses. Poetry can intensify the regularity, building up aural expectations by regulating the occurrence of stressed and unstressed syllables. The rhythm of (1), which would be

u −uu −uu −uu −

in unmarked speech, is actually the first line of a song:

(1) Tha 'mis' a' dol 'dhachaidh aig 'deireadh a' 'bhòids'

In (2) the spoken rhythm would be −uu − ˆu −u −uu −, but the stress-timed rhythm assigns the same duration to feet with −uu as to feet with −u:

(2) 'Eilean mo 'ghaoil, is 'caomh leam 'eilean mo 'ghràidh

In a sense one has to 'stretch' or 'shrink' syllables to accommodate the words to the musical pulse or 'beat'. There is thus a little more time for the segment [*gaoil, is*], allowing additional duration to the key word *gaoil* or a little pause at the sense-break between *gaoil* and *is*. Likewise, there is additional time to dwell on the emotionally loaded *caomh*. In musical terms one could express the rhythm as:

♩♪♪ | ♩.♪ | ♩.♪ | ♩♪♪ | ♩.

Not all Gaelic poetic types are subject to a regular beat, especially the older ones. And even those where we intuit a regular rhythm may manifest something more subtle: a continuous negotiation between, on the one hand, speech-rhythm and sense and, on the other hand, the metrical-musical pulse.

While it is useful to think of stresses (as demarcating the 'feet' of poetry) and lines, the unit which forms the real basis of ScG poetry is the phrase. A phrase contains two or three stresses. Sometimes it is co-extensive with a written line of verse; but longer lines break (often with sense-breaks corresponding to phrase junctures) into shorter phrasal units. The following verse (3) contains eight phrases which can be printed as eight short, one-phrase lines or as four long, two-phrase lines, as here:

(3) An 'ataireachd 'bhuan, | cluinn 'fuaim na 'h-ataireachd 'àird';
    tha 'torann a' 'chuain | mar 'chualas 'leam-s' e 'nam 'phàist;

gun 'mhùthadh gun 'truas, | a' 'sluaistreadh 'gaineamh na 'tràgh'd,
an 'ataireachd 'bhuan, | cluinn 'fuaim na 'h-ataireachd 'àird'.

Like (2), this composition has a –◡(◡) rhythm, coinciding pretty closely with natural speech rhythm. Each long line contains a two-stress phrase followed by a three-stress phrase:

[◡ '–◡◡ '–(◡)] [◡ '–◡(◡) '–◡◡ –(◡)]

Each phrase has an anacrusis or 'up-beat' before the first stress, and there is room for the last stress to be lengthened and/or followed by a short pause corresponding to a sense-break.

Metrical Structure[3]

In metrical terms, Gaelic poetry is organised in sequences of similar or contrasting units, each containing two or more stresses. These are the lines of ScG poetry, insofar as 'lines' is appropriate in an oral context. Such lines occur in sequences of one or more (very often two, four or eight), which are demarcated both formally (see 'Rhyme' below) and by major sense-breaks. These are the verses or stanzas of ScG poetry.

Rhyme[4]

Rhyme occurs in all types of Gaelic verse. Gaelic rhyme falls almost always on stressed vowels, and is almost always a simple vowel rhyme, without concern for identity of consonants following the rhyming vowel. Thus *mòr* can rhyme with *lòn*, *cladach* with *bragail*. Gaelic distinguishes long and short vowels, however, and vowel length does count for rhyming purposes: *mòr* does not rhyme with *cor*, nor does *lòn* rhyme with *con*. Over recent centuries ScG has been lengthening originally short vowels before certain consonantal sounds (some 'doubled' consonants and some consonant clusters). This process results in new long vowels (e.g. *àrd*, earlier *ard*) which are usually written with an accent, and new diphthongs (e.g. *mall* /maul/, earlier /mal:/) which are usually written without an accent. Because this is a still ongoing process, it is most helpful to think in terms of long versus short *syllables* (i.e. V:C and VC: are long, VC is short, VC^{1}C^2 may be long or short depending on which consonants are involved). Within the sphere of long syllables, Gaelic poets tend to rhyme long vowels with long vowels (*òr* with *ròn* and *àrd* with *bàrd*) and diphthongs with diphthongs (*am* with *rann*). Some other Gaelic consonant clusters result not in lengthening, but in epenthesis (as in Scots *film*, *worm*), e.g. *dearg*, *gorm*. Stressed syllables containing these clusters count as long, and the poets tend to rhyme these with each other (*gorm* with *borb*). Occasionally we meet with 'cross-over' rhymes between different types of long syllable (e.g. *bàn* with *balg* or *caoidh* with *tinn*), but never between long and short syllables (i.e. *corr/còrr* with *cor*).

Rhyme is deployed in two ways, which we may term 'bridging' and 'binding'. Bridging rhymes are 'short-range', between consecutive or near-consecutive stressed syllables; they create continuity by 'bridging' the sense-gap between successive phrases:

(4) Eilean mo *ghaoil*, | is *caomh* leam eilean mo ghràidh

(5) An ataireachd *bhuan*, | cluinn *fuaim* na h-ataireachd àird'

Binding rhymes are 'long-range', and occur at corresponding points (i.e. on the final stressed syllables) of successive phrases or lines. They serve to indicate the conclusion of a phrase or line, and bundle it with the preceding or following ones.

(6) An t-Eilean Muileach, | an t-eilean *àgh*mhor,
an t-eilean grianach | mun iadh an *sàile*,
eilean buadhmhor | nam fuarbheann *àrda*,
nan coilltean uaine | 's nan cluaintean *fàs*ail.

Rhymes occur on stressed syllables and give prominence to the syllable in question. In (7) the poet has abandoned normal speech rhythm (which would have given *cha 'dèan mi* or *cha dean mi 'ceum*) in order to give special assertive force to *mì*, rhyming with *buill*:

(7) Tha mi 'cràiteach '*tinn* | 's tha mi '*sgìth*, làn 'dochair,
'ceangail air mo '*bhuill*, | cha dean '*mì* ceum 'coiseachd.[5]

Bridging and binding rhymes are regularly deployed together; as well as the marked rhymes, (7) also has line-end rhymes between *dochair* and *coiseachd*, while (6) also has line-internal rhymes in lines *b–d*, between *grian(ach)* and *iadh*, etc.[6] Editors of ScG poetry often indicate the rhyme-schemes of Gaelic poems (i.e. the vowels of the stressed syllables), which is a helpful guide to their phrase structure, especially in complex examples. Example (6) might appear as follows:[7]

⏑ x ⏑ (i) ⏑ ⏑ (i) ⏑ à ⏑
⏑ x ⏑ ia ⏑ ⏑ ia ⏑ à ⏑
(⏑) x ⏑ ua ⏑ ⏑ ua ⏑ à ⏑
⏑ x ⏑ ua ⏑ ⏑ ua ⏑ à ⏑

Alliteration

Alliteration between the initial sounds of successive stressed words is integral to the aural effect of Type VII poems (i.e. in Classical Gaelic verse). In other types it occurs intermittently.[8] Gaelic alliteration ignores the presence or absence of lenition (i.e. *c* alliterates with *ch* and so on), except in the case of *fh*, which is simply ignored (e.g. *uaigh fhuar*) and *sh*, which is deemed to be a different sound from *s*. In Gaelic poetry any vowel can alliterate with any other vowel (e.g. *òran èibhinn*).

Scottish Gaelic Metrical Types

ScG poets and song-makers have combined the above elements to create various types of poetic structure. The following account places simple types before more complex ones; in the present state of knowledge this is intended to be descriptive rather than explanatory. It is certainly not exhaustive.

Type I

These songs contain sequences of one-phrase lines of equal length, held together solely by end rhyme:

(8) Alasdair, a laoigh mo *chèille*,
    cò chunnaic no dh'fhàg thu 'n *Èirinn*?
    Dh'fhàg thu na mìltean 's na *ceud*an […][9]

In this song the groups of lines, or 'verses', contain between six and eleven lines. Each has end rhyme (/e:/ in the quoted lines) on the penultimate syllable. The rhyme usually changes with each new verse. Internal rhyme occurs occasionally, but is not part of the metrical structure:

(9) Ceann-*feadhna greadhn*ach gun ghiorraig.[10]

In songs of this type, lines usually contain two to four stressed syllables; in (8) there are three (i.e. ʹAlasdair, a ʹlaoigh mo ʹchèille). End rhymes are typically on disyllables (–⌣) as in (8), though monosyllabic and trisyllabic cadences (i.e. – or –⌣⌣) are also found.[11]

Although verses like these were usually printed as 'paragraphs' of text in the early collections, in performance each line of text usually counted as a verse, since it formed the message-bearing part of a sung verse in which the verbal text alternated with lines of vocables.[12] Often the textually meaningful line was melodically the least distinctive part of a verse, in which line *a* could be text and lines *b–d* vocables. In many songs the textual lines were sung in pairs, in a 'rolling' sequence of (1+2), (2+3), etc.; again, the verse could consist of alternating textual and vocable parts in various patterns.

These songs are old, most examples dating from the sixteenth and seventeenth centuries. Many surviving specimens owe their survival to their being sung as work-songs for the waulking of the cloth (*luadhadh a' chlò*). This entailed a faster tempo and a heavy, regularised rhythm which could result (unusually for Gaelic) in unstressed syllables receiving stress when they coincided with the 'beat':

(10) ʹBha stiùir ʹòir oirr' ʹs ʹdà chrann ʹairgid
     's ʹcupaill ʹde shìo- ʹda na ʹGailmhinn [...][13]

Type II
These songs contain sequences of couplets, each couplet being held together by an internal or bridging rhyme, and linked to the other couplets in the sequence by a recurrent end rhyme:

(11) Bha Griogair mòr *ruadh* ann,
     làmh *chruaidh* air chùl *claidh*imh;

     agus Griogair mòr *meadh*rach,
     ceann-*feadh*na ar luchd-*taigh*e ...[14]

The internal rhyme usually changes from couplet to couplet; the end rhyme may be repeated throughout, but often gives way to another end rhyme, as in Type I, where a new sequence of couplets introduces a sense-break or mood-change.

Like Type I, these songs include sixteenth-century examples, and some were sung as *òrain luadhaidh*; but they also continued productive until recent times.¹⁵ Couplets of text were often supplemented by vocables (regularly omitted in the early collections). In many songs two couplets were sung in the 'rolling' pattern noticed for Type I, with or without vocables. The vocables themselves tend to be more 'meaningful' in Type II songs, e.g. containing recognisable words which give a 'mood signature' to the song, and in some cases give way to a fully meaningful chorus.

Type II couplets most commonly contain 2+2 stresses with an (*xa|ab*) rhyme-scheme (cf. (*xaab*) in (6) above). Their lines have a more open-textured feel than Type I lines, and this sometimes allows secondary stresses to develop, as in (12):

>   (12) Is 'gheibh sibh "sgioba 'eile a "Èirinn
>   o 'Iarl' "Anntram nan '*steud* "rìomhach.¹⁶

Type III

This type consists of metrically self-contained four-line verses (or quatrains). This very common structure deploys the metrical building blocks in various ways, including (13) quatrains with Type I-like end rhymes:

>   (13) An cuala sibh an tionndadh *duin*eil
>   thug an camp bha an Cille *Chuim*ein?
>   Is fad chaidh ainm air an *iom*airt:
>   thug iad as an nàimhdean *iom*ain.¹⁷

Examples of this type can be found with internal rhyme: cf. (6) above. Another sort (14) contains two more clearly marked couplets, each containing bridging and binding rhymes as in Type II:

>   (14) Nam biodh dà fhear dheug d'a *chinn*eadh
>   is mo *Ghrio*gair air an *ceann*,
>   cha bhiodh mo shùil a' sileadh *dheur*
>   no mo leanabh *fèin* gun *dàimh*.¹⁸

Amongst other patterns, (15) combines characteristics of Types I and II in an *aaab* pattern in which the first couplet contains the binding rhyme of Type I and the last couplet the bridging rhyme of Type II:

>   (15) Thoir soraidh gu Iain *Mannt*ach uam,
>   rag-mheàirleach nan each *breannd*alach;

> gur tric a thug am *meàirl*each ud
> *meann* a-mach on chrò.[19]

The verses of Type III songs are mostly self-sufficient units musically as well as metrically. However, many had a refrain of words, vocables or a combination of both, either contained within the verse or external to it, while others repeated part of each verse in performance.[20] Type III was an extremely productive song metre from the eighteenth century to the present, but there are also examples from the earlier period. As with Types I and II the number of stresses per line can vary; longer lines are more likely to contain internal rhymes, though all are one-phrase lines in musical terms. Line cadences include $-\cup\cup$ and $-$, as well as the commonest $-\cup$. A special form resembling the 'Limerick' is found (16), in which the third line becomes two half-lines with binding rhyme:

> (16) Tha mulad, tha gruaim orm, tha *bròn*,
> on dh'imich mo chàirdean air *folbh*,
> on chaidh iad air *astar*
> gun chinnt mu'n teachd *dhach*aidh,
> tha m'inntinn fo *airt*neal gu *leòr*.[21]

Type IV

A high proportion of seventeenth- and eighteenth-century ScG poetry is composed in eight-line verses; strictly speaking, this is what the term *amhran* (or *òran*) connotes. It is organised in four couplets held together by bridging rhymes and linked by a binding rhyme.

> (17) 'S i seo an 'aimsir an '*dearb*har
> an '*tair*geanachd '*dhùinn*:
> is bras 'meanmnach fir '*Alb*ann
> fo'n '*arm*aibh air '*thùs*;
> an uair 'dh'èireas gach '*treun*-laoch
> 'nan '*èid*eadh glan '*ùr*,
> le rùn 'feirge agus '*gaisge*
> gu '*seirbh*is a' '*chrùin*.[22]

Formulaically the rhyme-scheme of such songs can be rendered as 4(*xaab*). In (17) the poet has intensified the aural experience by bringing the first stressed vowel ('x') into the rhyme-scheme, giving 4(*aaab*); but this is not usual in *amhrain*, and is not maintained throughout the present poem, in which the first verse receives extra embellishment like an illuminated capital.

Type IV couplets come in various rhythms and can also contain more than the 'default' of four stresses per couplet. (18) contains five:

>   (18) Gura 'mòr mo chuid '*mhul*aid
>   bhith 'g 'amharc na '*guin*' a-ta 'm '*thìr* [...][23]

In the hands of the more 'literary' eighteenth-century poets, more ambitious and elaborate structures appear:

>   (19) 'Se 'Coir' a' "<u>Cheath</u>aich | nan '<u>aigh</u>ean "*siùbhlach* |
>   an 'coire "<u>rùn</u>ach | as '<u>ùr</u>ar "*fonn* [...]

In (19) the (*xaab*) rhyme-scheme of each four-phrase couplet (italicised and with primary stresses marked "'") is replicated within each two-phrase line (underlined and with secondary stresses marked "'").[24] In musical terms, most Type IV songs have an AABA phrase structure, and this can be reflected at the metrical level, i.e. the third couplet can differ structurally from the others, as in the 'Limerick' example (16).[25]

These songs can have a coda or refrain outside the structure of the verse; e.g. each verse of Uilleam MacDhun-lèibhe's 'Fios thun a' Bhàird' concludes with the couplet *Mar a fhuair 's a chunnaic mise | thoir am fios seo thun a' Bhàird*, which is then followed by the two-couplet refrain:

>   (20) Thoir am fios seo thun a' Bhàird,
>   thoir am fios seo thun a' Bhàird,
>   Mar a fhuair 's a chunnaic mise,
>   thoir am fios seo thun a' Bhàird.[26]

In this case the poem was made to fit a Scots song ('When the Kye Comes Hame', which has this 'AABA + BA' structure as sung); and the same is doubtless true of many other *amhrain*. But in some cases the 'coda' is simply a repetition of the final line or couplet, or of a thematically evocative phrase; and in others it consists of native vocables.[27] These may reflect a choral response to a verse sung by a soloist in earlier times. While the words of most *amhrain* fall easily into a –◡◡ or a –◡ rhythm, a small number of exemplary *amhrain* are sung in a distinctly non-rhythmical way, and this too may be a survival of an earlier mode of delivery.[28]

Type V
The simplest form of this category consists of seven-stress verses built around binding rhymes at both line and verse level:

> (21) Fuil 'rìoghail nam '*buadh*
> bhith 'ga 'dìobairt san '*uair*,
> is mac 'dìolain le '*s̲hluagh* ag '*èi*righ.[29]

The /ua/ rhyme is specific to this verse but the final /eː/ rhyme continues throughout the poem. The verse-structure may accordingly be represented as (*xa xa xab*). In this example *rìoghail*, *dìobairt* and *dìolain* also rhyme; but the extra rhyme is not achieved in every verse, nor does it feature in most Type V poems. In performance, the individual verses of songs like this are often sung twice or in pairs (especially in the 'rolling' pattern of (1 + 2), (2 + 3), etc.), in which case the two halves of the sung verse may have related but contrasting melodies.

Type V(A)
The basic (*xa xa xab*) pattern of Type V can be developed in two distinct ways. In (22) groups of four such seven-stress 'verses' are combined to create large *amhran*-like stanzas:

> (22) 'Chunna mi '*fèin* | 'aisling, 's cha '*bhreug*,
> 'dh'fhàg sin mo '*chrè* '*brò*nach:
> 'fear mar ri '*tè*, | a' 'pògadh a '*beul*,
> a' 'brìodal an '*dèidh* '*pò*saidh;
> 'dh'ùraich mo '*mhiann*, | 'dh'athraigh mo '*chiall*,
> 'ghuil mi gu '*dian* '*dòi*meach;
> gach 'cuisle agus '*fèith* | o 'ìochdar mo '*chlèibh*',
> 'thug iad gu '*leum* '*còm*hla.

An eight-stress extension is also found, with the shape (*xa xa xa ab*). Each verse in (23) contains two such four-phrase structures:

> (23) A' 'Chlach a bha mo '*sheanmhair*
> 's mo 'sheanair oirre '*seanchas*
> air 'tilleadh mar a '*dh'fhalbh* i –
> mo '*ghalgh*ad a' 'Chlach!
> 'S gur 'coma leam i 'n 'Cearrara,

an 'Calasraid no 'n '*Calbh*aidh,
cho 'fad 's a tha i 'n '*Alb*ainn
nan '*garbh*laichean '*cas*.³⁰

Another variation of Type V(A) shows lines of just five stresses (*xa xab*). In (24) each verse contains four five-stress lines like the following:

(24) A '*Chaitrìona* Nic '*Mhath*ain,
's ann leam bu 'mhiannach gach '*math* a
bhith 'n '*dàn* dhut!³¹

Type V(B)

The (*xa xa xab*) sound-pattern which is basic to Type V was also developed in a different direction: here the verses expand to include several additional (*xa*) phrases before the terminative (*xab*). Sometimes the number of (*xa*) phrases is constant within a poem;³² but it is characteristic and distinctive of this type that the number of (*xa*) phrases often varies from verse to verse within the poem.

(25) Mo 'bheud 's mo '*chràdh*
mar 'dhèirich '*dhà*
'n fhear 'ghleusta '*ghràidh*
bha 'treun san '*spàirn*
is nach 'faicear gu '*bràth* an '*Rath*arsair.³³

In (25) the verses contain between five lines (as here) and eight. In performance the closing line of each verse is repeated, with a contrasting but related melody, at the beginning of the following verse. More generally, in songs of this sort, the long terminating line was musically fixed and acted as the 'anchor' of the song. Where the number of preceding lines varied, the musical contour of the verse changed, and singers had to manipulate the melody so as to arrive finally at the fixed line.³⁴

Type VI

This type of verse, when printed, consists of quatrains made up of two couplets, each containing a four-stress line followed by a two-stress line:

(26) 'Triallaidh 'mì lem' 'dhuanaig 'ullaimh
gu 'rìgh '*Ghaoidh*eal,

'aig am 'bì am 'baile 'dùmhail
  'sona 'saidhbhir.³⁵

Lines end on disyllabic words, and Type VI poems have a bouncy –‿
rhythm in general. The density of rhyming is modest, but alternative
aural enrichment can be provided by alliteration, as in *sona saidhbhir* in
line *d*. An extreme example from the same poem is:

(27) 'Loingeas 'leathann 'làidir 'luchdmhor
  'dealbhach 'd*ìo*nach
  'sleamhain 'slios-rèidh 'ro-luath 'ràmhach
  'dair-chruaidh 'd*ì*reach.³⁶

Usually found in quatrains of praise poetry, this verse form is also
associated with the satirical output of the *crosan* ('lampooner'). In 'Cros-
(dh)anachd Fhir nan Druimeannan' clusters of six to eight couplets occur;
the four-stress segments tend to be semantically self-contained, and
their two-stress complements feel semi-detached, amplifying or subverting
the sense of the preceding statement.³⁷

Type VII
Gaelic manuscripts from the eighteenth century or earlier contain the
poetry (technically known as *dán*) of the professional court poets, treated
here as a single type. They used 'Classical Gaelic', as taught in bardic
schools, and their basis was syllabic rather than accentual.³⁸ This meant
that the number and positioning of stressed syllables in a line was variable
except at line-ends, where the cadence had a fixed rhythm (– or –‿ or
–‿‿) depending on the poet's chosen metre. This poetry had minutely
prescribed rules for syllable-count and for ornamentation, which included
rhyme and alliteration.³⁹

(28) 'M'anam do 'scar 'riom-sa a-'réir,
  'calann 'ghlan dob 'ionnsa i n-'*uaigh*;
  'rugadh 'bruinne 'maordha 'mín
  is 'aonbhla 'lín 'uime '*uainn*.⁴⁰

In the metre of (28), known as *rannaigheacht mhór*, each line contains
seven syllables ending with a monosyllable. The final words of lines *b*
and *d* rhyme according to strict rules which govern vowel length and
quality, and likewise the consonants following the stressed vowel, which

are divided into phonetically based classes. The final words of lines *a* and *c* assonate with the main *bd* rhyme, and there are internal rhymes between *anam* and *calann*, *scar* and *ghlan*, *riom-sa* and *ionnsa* in the first couplet, and between *bruinne* and *uime*, *maordha* and *aonbhla*, *mín* and *lín* in the second. Each line contains alliteration (*riom-sa ~ réir, ionnsa ~ uaigh, maordha ~ mín, uime ~ uainn*). This poetry was declaimed or chanted with harp accompaniment; but how the words and music were actually combined is uncertain.[41]

In addition to the strict-metre poetry (*dàn dìreach*) used by the professional poets (*filidhean*) when composing official poetry for patrons, a more relaxed version of *dàn* was used by them for informal subjects, by other classes of literati and by trainee and amateur poets. Before its demise, some rapprochement took place between the 'Classical' tradition and that of vernacular poetry, whereby the essential syllabic irregularity of Classical *dán* was eroded by a tendency to stabilise the position of the main stresses and the rhyming words:

> (29) 'Creag mo "*chridhe*-s' a' 'Chreag "*Mhòr*,
> 's 'ionmhainn an "*lòn* 'tha f'a "*ceann*,
> 's 'anns' an "*lag* 'tha air a "*cùl*
> na 'machair is "*mùr* nan "*Gall*.[42]

A long-standing use of informal *dán* metre was as the vehicle for the narrative poems about Fionn Mac Cumhaill and his warriors (*laoidhean na Fèinne*), attributed to Oisein, the Gaelic progenitor of Macpherson's 'Ossian'.

> (30) 'Gleann 'Síodh an 'gleann-so rem '*thaoibh*,
> a 'mbinn '*faoidh* 'éan agus '*lon*;
> 'minic 'rithidis an '*Fhian*
> ar an 'srath-so i '*ndiadh* a '*gcon*.[43]

These heroic ballads go back, in something like their latest form, at least to the twelfth century. The recitative manner in which they were performed in recent times may be relevant to the question of how Classical poetry was delivered.[44]

Historical Development and External Influences

All of Types I–VII were in existence by the seventeenth century. Though the Gaelic manuscript tradition devoted itself almost exclusively to syllabic poetry (Type VII), there is enough evidence for Types I–VI in earlier times to assure us that these forms were not simply (as some nineteenth- and twentieth-century scholars supposed) post-Classical derivatives from syllabic metres. Where syllabic and accentual versions of the same metre exist (e.g. Type VI), it is at least conceivable that the syllabic form was the secondary growth. The evidence for early composition in accentual metres is both direct – e.g. occasional specimens in collections of syllabic poetry, quotations in literary tales, citations in metrical tracts – and indirect, where significant parallels between ScG and Irish vernacular poetry point to a common origin at a time prior to the emergence of two distinct literary cultures.

While ultimate origins for Gaelic poetic forms have been sought in Celtic or even Indo-European antiquity, the only major importations we are aware of in historical times are (1) the syllabic tradition itself, probably adapted from or influenced by Latin hymn-metres in the Early Christian period,[45] and (2) the *amhran*, whose 'European'-looking AABA musical structure appears to have come into the Gaelic tradition(s) in the post-Norman period.[46]

Over the last three centuries, poetic forms based on four-line and eight-line stanzas have tended to squeeze out the others, especially in the Southern Highlands and Inner Hebrides, and Types I and V(B) have ceased to be productive, though surviving marginally in the oral tradition of the Outer Hebrides. Named Lowland melodies have been associated with Gaelic compositions from the Jacobite period onwards, and the practice continues to the present day (we do not know how far back it reaches before the late seventeenth century).

Metrical experiment is unusual before the twentieth century. The most obvious innovations – connected with the adoption of Lowland Scots song-forms and the ground-and-variations structure of *pìobaireachd* – affected overall form rather than the basics of phrase and rhythm. The translators of the Metrical Psalms in the seventeenth century, Dùghall Bochanan (Dugald Buchanan) adapting Isaac Watts's hymns in the eighteenth and Eoghann MacLachlainn (Ewen MacLachlan) adapting Homer in the nineteenth all utilised the 'building blocks' of Gaelic verse as far as they could. The more 'literary' of the twentieth-century traditional bards, including most notably Domhnall Mac an t-Saoir (Donald MacIntyre, 'Bàrd Phàislig'), have continued to employ Types II–V(A) with confidence.

The traditional nature and the relatively dense aural enrichment of Gaelic poetry (especially by comparison with English poetry) made its form suspect in the eyes of twentieth-century intellectual poets influenced by modernist ideas about originality, the individual author, and the purposes of art. Of the Renaissance writers, Ruaraidh MacThòmais (Derick Thomson) and Iain Crichton Smith were quickest to reject the traditional poetic forms in favour of free verse; on the other hand, Sorley MacLean's approach was more subtly innovative – to draw freely on the organisational and representational arts of the traditional poetry, while steering clear of rhythmic monotony – while George Campbell Hay leaned further towards imitating the traditional forms. Both approaches have their adherents among contemporary Gaelic poets. A few composers of traditional *bàrdachd* survive today; and echoes of the traditional art can be detected in the lyrics of some Gaelic popular song-writers.

[Since this paper was written, I have offered some remarks on the metrical structure of Duncan Ban Macintyre's *Moladh Beinn Dòbhrain* (note 21) in 'Some developments in eighteenth-century Gaelic poetry', in Anders Ahlqvist and Pamela O'Neill (eds), *Language and Power in the Celtic World* (Sydney, NSW, 2011: University of Sydney), pp. 61–95; and Colm Ó Baoill's *Màiri nighean Alasdair Ruaidh: Song-maker of Skye and Berneray* (Glasgow, 2014: Scottish Gaelic Texts Society) has superseded James Carmichael Watson's edition of the same poetess (note 33).]

CHAPTER ELEVEN

Scots Poetic Forms

J. Derrick McClure

The range and variety of verse forms which have emerged in the corpus of Scots poetry during its long history is enormous. In the Stewart period, poets such as William Dunbar, Alexander Scott and Alexander Montgomerie experimented with an abundance of metres and stanzas; and by the end of the period James VI, in his poetic manual 'Ane Schort Treatise conteining some Reulis and Cautelis to be observit and eschwit in Scottis poesie', could remark with justice that 'new formes are daylie inuentit according to the Poets pleasour'.[1] Later, the song-collections of Allan Ramsay and Robert Burns likewise show a kaleidoscopic diversity of metres and stanza forms. Amid all this plenty, however, certain forms recur, over centuries in some cases: the example which will spring immediately to mind is the Burns stanza; but it is far from the only one. In this chapter, a few of the poetic forms which have contributed to the distinctiveness of Scots literature will be examined and discussed.

Fittingly, the poem which opens the pageant of literature in the Lowland Scots tongue is couched in a verse form which at once established Scots poetry as an integral part of the European scene. John Barbour's *Bruce* (c. 1375), an epic commemoration of Robert Bruce and his success in defending Scotland against English aggression, is written in a continuous sequence of rhymed octosyllabic couplets. This verse form was long established in both French and English literature and had, by the late fourteenth century, come to be associated with historical chronicles and other extended narratives: important examples are Wace's *Roman de Brut* (c. 1155) and Robert Mannyng's *Chronicle of England* (c. 1338). There is no reason to imagine that the Scots branch of the octosyllabic couplet tradition sprang fully armed, so to speak, from the head of Barbour: his skill in handling the form, remarkable by any standards, would be astonishing if he had not had some native as well as foreign models on which to base his work; but since none of them is extant we may fairly take the *Bruce* as setting the pattern for a series of poems lasting until the eighteenth century.

> Quhen þis wes said þat er said I
> Þe Scottis-men commounaly
> Knelyt all doune to God to pray
> And a schort prayer þar maid þai
> To God to help þaim in þat fycht,
> And quhen þe Inglis king had sycht
> Off þaim kneland he said in hy,
> '3one folk knelis to ask mercy'.
> Schyr Ingrahame said, '3e say suth now,
> Þai ask mercy bot nane at 3ow,
> For þair trespas to God þai cry.
> I tell 3ow a thing sekyrly,
> Þat 3one men will all wyn or de,
> For doute of dede þai sall nocht fle'.[2]

It is important to understand that in this period the verse form should not be described as 'iambic tetrameter' or by any term from that taxonomy. In the first line of the quoted extract all odd-numbered syllables are unstressed and all even-numbered stressed; but this is merely fortuitous: it is true of some lines but not others, and is not in any sense a prescription. The reasons for the deliberate adoption in English and Scots of verse structures based on fixed patterns of stressed and unstressed syllables (iambs, trochees, dactyls, anapaests, etc.),[3] and the stages by which this took place, are issues far beyond the scope of this short chapter; but it must be borne in mind that this development was at best only incipient in Barbour's time: the requirement was that each line should contain eight syllables, and in such lines unstressed and stressed syllables quite often simply happened to alternate.

The octosyllabic couplet form is the vehicle for other early works of Scots poetry, important examples being the anonymous *Legends of the Saints* (c. 1400) and Andrew of Wyntoun's *Orygynale Cronikil of Scotland* (c. 1420), the latter a major source of historical information. Its use diminished, however, as the Stewart period continued. James I and Henryson made no use of the form, and Dunbar employed it only rarely and, notably, not for narrative but for satire and diatribe. In 'Complane

I wald, wist I quham til' (c. 1507), as often in Dunbar, his verbal exuberance pushes the metrical form to its limits:

> Stuffettis, strekouris and stafische strummellis,
> Wyld haschbaldis, haggarbaldis and hummellis,
> Druncartis, dysouris, dyowris, drewellis,
> Misgydit memberis off the devillis […][4]

David Lyndsay restored the form to its original use in *Squyer Meldrum* (1547), the by then decidedly old-fashioned metre wittily underlining the joke of a mock-heroic epic written about a contemporary figure.

With the Vernacular Revival and the deliberate use by Allan Ramsay and others of verse forms associated with the great achievements of the past, the octosyllabic couplet sequence enjoyed a new lease of life. To cite only a few of the finest examples, Ramsay's 'The Monk and the Miller's Wife' (1724) employs the form to relate a farcical tale with fitting gusto; in Fergusson's 'Auld Reekie' (1773) the swiftly tripping octosyllabics add to the liveliness of our tour through the city; and the verse form reaches its apotheosis in 'Tam o' Shanter' (1791), where Burns's rhyming ingenuity, lexical fecundity and narrative brilliance combine in a demonstration of verbal artistry unsurpassed in Scottish literature.

> The wind blew as 'twad blawn its last,
> The rattlin' showers rose on the blast,
> The speedy gleams the darkness swallow'd,
> Loud, deep, and lang, the thunder bellow'd:
> That night, a child might understand,
> The Deil had business on his hand.[5]

The partial eclipse of the octosyllabic couplet for extended narrative poems is due in part to the much greater flexibility of the form which arose somewhat later: the decasyllabic couplet. The first major Scots poem to be couched in this form is Hary's *Wallace* (1477); and the epic credentials thus established made it the natural choice for Gavin Douglas's translation of Virgil's *Aeneid* (1513) and for most (not all) of his Prologues to the successive books. The crystallisation of the decasyllabic line into that staple of English poetry, the iambic pentameter, is visible from a comparison of Hary's free-and-easy metrics[6] with the much greater regularity of Douglas's (although this is, of course, a generalisation – Hary can, when he chooses, write decasyllabics which are flawlessly iambic and Douglas can and often does depart from the iambic pentameter prescription for effect):

Hary: Horssyt archaris schot fast and wald nocht spar.
          Of Wallace men thai woundyt twa ful sar.
          In Ir he grew quhen that he saw thaim bleid.
          Him self retornde and on thaim sone he ʒeid,
          Xvi with him that worthi was in wer,
          Off the formast rycht freschly doun thai ber.
          At that retorn xv in field war slayne.
          The laiff fled fast to thair power agayne.[7]

Douglas: Quhen he bewailit had on this maneir,
          This wofull corps he bad do lift on beir
          And with him send a thousand men in hy,
          Walit of every rowt and cumpany,
          For to convoy and do him falowschip
          At his last honour and funerale wirschip,
          And to be present at the lamentyng
          Of hys fadir, to confort his murnyng [...][8]

Like the octosyllabic, the decasyllabic couplet was restored to active use in the Vernacular Revival period, now predominantly in the field of pastoral poetry. Allan Ramsay's play *The Gentle Shepherd* (1725) is the seminal text here, inspiring as direct imitations Alexander Ross's *Helenore, or The Fortunate Shepherdess* (a narrative poem: 1768) and Andrew Shirrefs' *Jamie and Bess* (like its model, a drama: 1790).[9] Fergusson's 'Eclogues', a term which he applies both to poetry in the pastoral vein, satires such as 'The Ghaists: a Kirk-yard Eclogue' and humorous verses such as 'A Drink Eclogue' (all published 1773), likewise demonstrate the versatility of the decasyllabic couplet.

The first important poem in Scots to be written in stanzas instead of a continuous sequence of rhymed lines is James I's *The Kingis Quair* (c. 1424);[10] and the adoption of the new (to Scotland) verse form, coupled with a richer vocabulary and a more elegant poetic style than Barbour's utilitarian register, marks an important new stage in the literary development of the language. James's poem is in stanzas of seven decasyllabic lines ('my buk in lynis sevin', he calls it in the penultimate line of the poem), with the fixed rhyme-scheme *ababbcc*. Chaucer had used the stanza, most notably in *Troilus and Criseyde* and some of the Canterbury

Tales: it is from its adoption by James, however, that it takes its familiar name of Rhyme Royal.

> Heigh in the hevynnis figure circulere
> The rody sterres twynklit as the fyre;
> And in Aquary Cinthia[11] the clere
> Rynsid hir tressis like the goldin wyre,
> That late tofore in faire and fresche atyre
> Through Capricorn heved hir hornis bright.
> North northward approchit the myd-night.

This stately verse form became highly productive for a time in Scots poetry. It was Henryson's staple, used in his *Morall Fabillis*, *The Testament of Cresseid* and *Orpheus and Eurydice*[12] (c. 1480–1500: Henryson's poems cannot be dated exactly). Dunbar chose it for his pageant-poem 'The Thrissil and the Rois' (1503) and some lesser works (but he preferred eight-line stanzas for his poems in decasyllabic lines, and in the memorable case of *The Goldyn Targe* (c. 1485)[13] adopted the nine-line stanza, rhyming *aabaabbab*, which Chaucer had used for *Anelida and Arcite*). (Interestingly, both Henryson and Hary use nine-line stanzas as self-contained passages for a character's lament in poems written in different metres.) Lyndsay applies it didactically in *The Dreme* (1528), in a tone of dignified lamentation in 'The Deploratioun of the Deith of Quene Magdalene' (1537) and satirically in *The Testament of the Papyngo* (1538). Indeed, it endured as part of the common poetic stock-in-trade throughout the Stewart period: a late and little-known example is 'Ane Breif Commendatioun of Uprichtness' by a Protestant minister named John Davidson, published in 1573, a ponderous work in which every stanza ends with the word *uprichtnes*.

Though the octosyllabic and decasyllabic couplets, and the Rhyme Royal stanza, earn their place as Scots poetic forms by their unassailable status as the vehicles of some of the greatest and most iconic poems in Scottish literature, their use is far from unique to Scotland: it is doubtful if any verse form exists of which this is strictly true. On the other hand, several forms can claim to be 'Scottish' in a more decisive sense: in that they have been more extensively exploited and developed in Scotland than outwith it, and have often been used specifically because of their acquired Scottish ring. An interesting case is a stanza based on a principle unrelated to the familiar French-derived technique of syllable-counting. The native Germanic verse form, namely lines with four stresses, two or three (but not all four) of the stressed syllables being marked by alliteration, and neither any specified number of unstressed syllables nor any set arrangements of stressed and unstressed, survived in Scots until well into the Stewart era. In the Old English period poems uniformly consisted simply of sequences of lines in this form, with no divisions;[14] and this lasted almost till the end of the Middle English period, the most notable late example being William Langland's *Piers Plowman* (c. 1360–1400). In Scotland the story of the alliterative line is markedly different. The implication of this as the conventional name of the line is that it shows alliteration instead of end-rhyme – the latter, like syllable-counting, being an importation from French. This consideration, as we will see shortly, does not generally apply in the history of the line in Scots poetry. Only one major poem, Dunbar's *The Tretis of the Tua Mariit Wemen and the Wedo* (c. 1507), is written as a long unbroken sequence of unrhymed alliterative lines.[15] By a distinctively Scottish innovation, alliteration came to be combined with end rhyme in a stanza form of nine four-stress lines followed by four two-stress lines, the rhyming pattern being *ababababcdddc*. The following stanza from the first Scottish exemplar of the form, Richard Holland's *The Buke of the Howlat* (c. 1450), illustrates the pattern:

> This rich river doun ran, but resting or ruve,
> Through ane forest on fold, that farly was fair;
> All the braeis of the brym bare branches abuve,
> And birds blythest of ble on blossoms bare,
> The land lown was and lee, with liking and luve,
> And for to lend by that laik thocht me levar,
> Because that thir hartes in herdis couth huve,
> Pransand and prunyeand, be pair and be pair.
> Thus sat I in solace, sekerly and sure,
>   Content of the fair firth,
>   Meikle mair of the mirth,
>   And blithe of the birth
>   That the grund bure.

Easily observable is that whereas in OE verse alliteration occurs on a maximum of *three* syllables, no such restriction applies here: it may readily be found on all four and on one or more of the unstressed syllables as well. (This applies in English as well as Scots verse of this kind in the post-OE periods.) *The Buke of the Howlat* is one of three major (in scale and quality) poems in this form, and the only one with an identifiable author: the others are *Rauf Coilyear* (c. 1475) and *Golagros and Gawane* (c. 1475).[16] Besides these important works, all dating from the middle or the third quarter of the fifteenth century, the stanza appears in a number of shorter poems, the most accomplished being the Prologue to the Eighth Book of Gavin Douglas's *Eneados* (Douglas's only use of the form).

Despite its popularity in the Middle Scots period, this stanza form had effectively dropped out of use by 1603. James VI had termed it 'tumbling verse' and pronounced it suitable for 'flyting or inuectives',[17] and thus it was used by some of his court poets; but by then it had become regularised in a manner which destroyed its inherent nature: the unprescribed sequencing of stressed and unstressed syllables had given way to straightforward and consistent anapaests. The technique of the old four-beat line had been lost, that is; and no attempt was ever made to revive it.

By contrast, three more highly distinctive verse forms which arose in the Stewart period remained in active use until the nineteenth and (in two of the three cases) the twentieth centuries, and are still readily available in the twenty-first. Two of them are commonly known by the names of poems which exemplify them: the 'Christis Kirk' stanza and the 'Helicon' stanza. The first of these makes its appearance in Scottish poetry with poems belonging to a European tradition of poetry on the theme of rustic revelry and brawls, 'Peblis [Peebles] to the Play' (c. 1430–50) and 'Christis Kirk on the Green' (c. 1490–1510):

> Was never in Scotland hard nor seen
> Sic dancing nor deray,
> Nother at Falkland on the grene
> Nor Peblis at the play,
> As was of Wowaris, as I wene,
> At Chryst kirk on ane day,
> Thare come our Kitteis weschin clene,
> In thair new kirtillis of gray,
>   Full gay,
> At Chrystis kirk of the grene.[18]

The formal characteristics of this stanza are easily recognisable: eight lines of alternating tetrameter and trimeter, rhyming *abababab*, followed by a one-stress 'bob' and a refrain line, repeated either exactly or with slight variations in every stanza. The 'bob' does not normally rhyme with anything, though this particular stanza is an exception.

'Peblis' and 'Christis Kirk', particularly the latter, set a fashion for poems of rambunctious physical comedy, abounding in words from the less dignified register of Scots (derogatory expressions and words relating to noise and violence). This is associated in those two poems with a high degree of technical skill in maintaining the tricky metre and, especially in the case of 'Christis Kirk', combining it with abundant alliteration. 'Christis Kirk' was frequently reprinted throughout the sixteenth and seventeenth centuries, and was taken up by Allan Ramsay in the early eighteenth: his 1721 volume of poems includes not only the original 'Christis Kirk' but two additional cantos by Ramsay himself, continuing the series of vignettes of fun and fisticuffs with a skill fully worthy of the original:

> Was ne'er in Scotland heard or seen
> Sic banqueting and drinkin,
> Sic revelling and battles keen,
> Sic dancing and sic jinkin,
> And unko wark that fell at e'en,
> Whan lasses were haff winkin,
> They lost their feet and baith their een,
> And maidenheads gae'd linkin
>   Aff a' that day.

Observable is that the sequence of bob and refrain line which characterised the early poems in this form has gone, the structure being simplified to a single two-beat line usually ending in ' […] that day' (but once it is 'wi' usquebae', an effective comic detail).

The 'Christis Kirk' stanza proved conducive to exuberant poetic invention for many more years. After Ramsay the next major poet to make use of it was the Reverend John Skinner, whose 'The Christmas Bawing [football match] of Monymusk' (1739) has the distinction of launching the north-east dialect on its illustrious poetic career. This *juvenilium* appears to have caused the learned and much-respected Skinner some embarrassment in later life; yet it is an outstanding specimen of the genre and remains popular in the north-east to this day.[19]

> Like bumbees bizzing frae a bike,
> Whan herds their riggings tirr,[20]
> The swankies lap thro' mire and slike,

> Wow! As their heads did birr:
> They yowph'd the ba' frae dike to dike,
> Wi' unco speed and virr,
> Some baith their shoulders up did fyke,
> For blythness some did flirr
>   Their teeth that day.

Fergusson and Burns produced some of their finest satiric poems in the stanza ('Hallow Fair', 'Leith Races': c. 1773, 'The Holy Fair', 'The Ordination': c. 1785; perhaps Burns's finest is 'Hallowe'en', c. 1785). Both of them discard the abababab rhyme sequence for *ababcdcd*, but retain the metrical structure and the '[...] that day' refrain.

A second and even more complex stanza form which proved highly productive in Scots poetry of the Renaissance and beyond takes its name from a song (the tune is extant), which opens thus:

> Declair, ye bankis of Helicon,
> Parnassus hillis and dalis ilk one,
> And fountain Caballine,
> Gif ony of your Muses all,
> Or nymphes may be peregall
> Unto my lady sheen?
> Or if the ladies that did lave
> Their bodies by your brim
> So seemly were or yit so suave,
> So beautiful or trim?
> Contemple, exemple
> Tak be her proper port,
> Gif ony sa bonnie
> Amang you did resort.[21]

This anonymous song inspired several poets to take up the daunting challenge of its difficult metre.[22] Robert Maitland's graceful 'Ane Ballat of the Creation of the World' (c. 1560) is described in the Bannatyne Manuscript as 'maid to the tune of the bankis of helecon'. The most remarkable example, however, is undoubtedly *The Cherrie and the Slae* (first published 1597) by Alexander Montgomerie, a long and intellectually demanding poem in the tradition, long out of fashion by James VI's time, of allegorical debate initiated in the early thirteenth century by Guillaume de Lorris's *Roman de la Rose*, engaging in its narrative flow and often beautiful in its imagery, which maintains the stanza faultlessly through over one hundred verses.[23] Once again, the form was brought back into use in the Vernacular Revival period. Allan Ramsay took it up for *The Vision* (1724), a long poem in a deliberately archaic style. Burns used it occasionally, though with unerring skill when he did: his 'Epistle to Davie' (1786) is one of the best-known examples; another is the opening stanzas of *Love and Liberty* (1785). It continued sporadically throughout the nineteenth century, being notably popular in Ayrshire among Burns's contemporaries and immediate successors: no modern poets, however, have seemed keen to venture into such metrically tricky territory.

The same cannot be said of the last verse form to be discussed – the last and perhaps the most iconically Scottish of them all. Among the works of the sixteenth-century poet Alexander Scott, metrically one of the most enterprising and versatile of Scottish poets, is a fairly inconspicuous seven-stanza poem 'On Patience in Love' (c. 1540–60), which begins:

> That ever I loved, alas therefor!
> This is to be pynit with painis sore,
> Thirlit through every vein and bore,
>   Without offence;
> Christ send remeid, I say no more,
>   Bot patience.

Each verse ends with either 'bot patience' or 'with patience'. This stanza form originated in Provence; and this, its first recorded appearance in Scotland, gives no hint of the glorious future in store for it. Nor, indeed, did its first re-emergence nearly a century later:

> Kilbarchan now may say alas!
> For she hath lost her game and grace:
> Both Trixie and the Maiden-trace [names of pipe tunes]
>   But what remeed;
> For no man can supply his place
>   Hab Simpson's dead.

This poem (c. 1640), with the elaborate title 'The Life and Death of the Piper of Kilbarchan, or The Epitaph of Habbie Simpson / Who on his Dron bore bonny Flags / He made his Cheeks as red as Crimson / And babbed when he blew his Bags', is by Robert Sempill of Beltrees, a Renfrewshire laird, and his only attested composition. It is scarcely a great poem, though attractive and touching in its combination of light-hearted mockery of the old piper and genuine regret at the loss of his contribution to merriment in the town.[24] But it inspired a series of imitation mock-elegies, including an anonymous[25] one on Habbie Simpson's nephew Sanny Briggs, butler to the Laird of Kilbarchan: four in all were included in James Watson's *Choice Collection* of 1704, a central text in the eighteenth-century recovery of Scottish poetry. Once again, however, it is Allan Ramsay who can take the credit for restoring the stanza form to dynamic life.[26] In 1712 he produced his first poem, 'Elegy on Maggy Johnston' (landlady of an Edinburgh ale-house), which opens:

> Auld Reeky! Mourn in sable hue,
> Let fouth of tears dreep like May dew.
> To braw Tippony bid adieu,
>   Which we, with greed,
> Bended as fast as she cou'd brew.
>   But ah! She's dead.

At intervals thereafter, Ramsay wrote mock-elegies on other more or less disreputable Edinburgh characters, including them in his *Poems* of 1721. 'Maggy Johnston' departed from its predecessors in that only some of the verse-final lines end with some variation on the 'But now he's dead' formula; and the stanza form was freed for other purposes than mock-elegies by William Hamilton of Gilbertfield, who sent Ramsay a laudatory 'epistle' in verse – to which Ramsay enthusiastically responded, initiating the practice of epistles written by poets to their *confrères* which lasted throughout the eighteenth century. Fergusson took up the form: in some instances (e.g. 'Elegy, on the Death of Scots Music' and 'Braid Claith') he followed the Habbie precedent of using an identical or slightly varied line as the refrain for every verse, but more often he disregarded it; and in such cases he exploited more consistently than Ramsay the expressive potential of the short lines, particularly when combined with tricky rhymes:

> Sing then, how, on the Fourth of June,
> Our bells screed aff a loyal tune,
> Our antient castle shoots at noon,
>   Wi' flag-staff buskit,

> Frae which the soldier blades come down
>   To cock their musket.
>
> O! then we needna gie a plack
> For dand'ring mountebank or quack,
> Wha o' their drogs sae bauldly crack,
>   And spred sic notions,
> As gar their feckless patients tak
>   Their stinkin potions.
>
> On einings cauld wi' glee we'd trudge
> To heat our shins in Johnny's lodge;
> The de'il ane thought his bum to budge
>   Wi' siller on us:
> To claw het pints we'd never grudge
>   O' *molationis*.[27]

And it goes without saying that Burns, unfitting as it is that the stanza should be called after him as if he had invented it or been the only important poet to use it, raised its status still further by utilising it in such masterworks as 'The Vision', 'Holy Willie's Prayer', 'Address to the Deil', 'Epistle to James Lapraik', and many others familiar to every reader.

The Habbie stanza continued in active life throughout the nineteenth century: Robert Louis Stevenson's landmark collection *Underwoods* (1887) is introduced by an argumentatively forceful, lexically rich and prosodically flawless poem in this form on the viability of the Scots tongue. And as a final reflection, it is worth noting than in the great twentieth-century 'Scottish Renaissance', a period of sustained achievement to match any in Scotland's earlier literary history, some of the traditional verse forms have demonstrated their unimpaired viability in the context of modern poetry. Robert Garioch's 'Christis Kirk' pastiche 'Embra to the Ploy' is fully worth of its predecessors, as is the same poet's 'The Cannie Hen' in octosyllabic couplets; George Campbell Hay takes up Dunbar's use of octosyllabics for argument in 'Kailyard and Renaissance'; and the unquenchable Habbie stanza appears in, for example, Tom Scott's 'A Wee Cock o the Midden', Garioch's 'To Robert Fergusson' and Douglas Young's short but memorable 'Fife Equinox'. The unfailing ingenuity with which successive generations of poets have exploited the expressive potential of traditional verse forms is one of the factors in the continuity of literature in the Scots tongue.

CHAPTER TWELVE

The Ballad in Scots and English

Suzanne Gilbert

Attempting to capture the evocative power of the traditional Scottish ballad, Willa Muir (1890–1970) wrote, 'Behind the words and the tune lie spaces of silences in which one feels the presence of mysteries.'[1] The lyrical ambiguity of 'spaces of silence' and 'presence of mysteries' in Muir's description reflects the paradoxes at the heart of this form. Ballads have aptly been called 'awkward things' and 'debateable lands' that open up hermeneutic possibilities;[2] as David Buchan acknowledges, 'Few literary genres give so much pleasure to so many kinds of people and yet pose such refractory problems for the scholar and critic.'[3] This chapter will address the 'ballad enigma'[4] by first surveying its attraction over time, and then examining the relationship between content and form in the ballad with its intense focus on the dramatic situation, uniquely structured movement, and remarkable economy of language. Particular attention will be drawn to the ballad's psychologically charged way of telling a story. The chapter will consider forces that have shaped the ballad as we know it today, and touch on the diasporic reach and influence of this most popular of poetries.

The traditional ballad in various combinations of Scots and English (the heroic ballads of Scottish Gaelic culture constitute a distinctly different form that is not considered in this chapter and is recently discussed elsewhere by Anja Gunderloch)[5] developed over centuries into one of the most distinctive forms of Scottish poetry, endorsed enthusiastically by critics from the Renaissance onwards; eighteenth- and nineteenth-century antiquarians; twentieth-century writers, literary critics and folk revivalists; and innumerable poets and singers. While ballads' roots are medieval, during the eighteenth century Scotland's treasure attracted particular interest. Indeed, after the 1707 Union between Scotland and England, Scottish ballads became especially prized, and collectors swarmed to gather the best they could find. Their efforts resulted in a string of anthologies, among them the anonymously edited *Collection of Old Ballads* (1723–25), Allan Ramsay's *Tea-Table Miscellany* (1723–40), David Herd's *Ancient and Modern Scots Songs* (1769, 1776) and James Johnson's *Scots Musical Museum* (1787–1803), for which Robert Burns exhaustively compiled ballads and songs. The English collector Thomas Percy relied heavily on Scottish material for the hugely influential *Reliques of Ancient English Poetry* (1765). Nineteenth-century collections such as Walter Scott's *Minstrelsy of the Scottish Border* (1802–03), William Motherwell's *Minstrelsy, Ancient and Modern* (1827) and many others fuelled the Scottish drive for ballads throughout the next century, which fed into the American scholar Francis J. Child's monumental *The English and Scottish Popular Ballads* (1882–98).[6]

Agendas have varied widely, but most editors have rationalised their fascination by making a case for preserving ballads. English collectors such as Percy assigned authorship to minstrels from Britain's ancient past as a way of explaining this intriguing poetry. Scottish editors staked personal and national claims to the material. As Maureen McLane observes, they were 'able to align themselves with their reciter-informants: like their informants – whether peasants or gentlemen, dairymaids or ladies – they had absorbed ballads in childhood. Ballads were their inheritance, they insisted, before they were their objects of study'.[7] Further, Scottish collectors felt compelled to preserve a part of culture they believed threatened by extinction within the newly established Britain. Walter Scott (1771–1832) and Robert Jamieson (1780–1844) 'were well aware, indeed excruciatingly self-conscious, of the possibility that they were witnessing and perhaps hastening the death of the tradition and ballads they published' – in their notes and introductions they 'penned epitaphs and eulogies'.[8] Some collectors gathered ballads from manuscripts and correspondence, while others also ventured into the field. Scott claimed he was 'obliged to draw his materials chiefly from oral tradition', from itinerant musicians and storytellers, from 'shepherds [...] and aged persons in the recesses of the Border mountains';[9] however, he also made extensive use of Herd's collection and ballads communicated by Alexander Fraser Tytler, transcribed from Anna Gordon Brown (1747–1810), a renowned source of ballads for all subsequent collections. Scott understood ballads' significance for preserving Scottish identity, observing in the notes and the 'occasional Dissertations' of the *Minstrelsy* that he 'may contribute somewhat to the history of my native country, the peculiar features of whose manners and character are daily melting and dissolving into those of her sister and ally'.[10] That drive for cultural preservation was given new impetus in the twentieth-century Folk Revival that once again highlighted Scotland's unique contributions.

It was the ballad's early life in oral tradition, perpetuated by little-known singers and reciters, that shaped the form as we know it today. But the ballad was also moulded by its various interactions with print. Recognising the popular appeal of these *auld sangs*, publishers included ballads among the miscellany of pieces for broadsides and chapbooks, roughly printed on cheap paper for mass distribution well into the nineteenth century. Broadside ballads were famously described by Child as 'veritable dung-hills, in which, only after a great deal of sickening grubbing, one finds a very moderate jewel',[11] a view that perpetuated the long-standing (and ultimately flawed) critical division between the so-called 'pure' traditional ballad of oral tradition and the broadside ballad with its topical content and tabloid style. The distinction breaks down, however, when in chapbooks and broadsides may be found traditional titles such as 'The Bonny Earl of Murray', 'The Old Scots Ballad of Andrew Lammie, or, Mill of Tifty's Annie', 'The Bonny House of Airly', 'Young Beichan' and 'Bonny Barbara Allan'.[12] The relationship between orality and print is one of 'mutual exchange rather than [...] a one-way street leading from tradition to print, or from print to tradition'.[13]

Unquestionably, however, ballads' poetic qualities came to be associated with those most traditional (that is, supposedly oral). Ideas of what this means were mediated by ballad collectors and editors in the eighteenth and nineteenth centuries, and then reified and expanded by diverse interpreters in the twentieth century: folklorists, performers and nationalists emerging during the Folk Revival; writers associated with the modern Scottish Renaissance; and theorists of practical (or 'New') criticism. Collectors' practice of presenting ballads without music obscured their origins in oral tradition and emphasised their literariness, their peculiar relationship between content and form. While Scottish literature embraces the ballad as a kind of poetry, it is properly considered a hybrid genre, a 'narrative song' that tells a story in a distinctive, unique way. Definitions of ballads have varied greatly over centuries; 'narrative song' is at the core of the most currently accepted constructions.

Striking features make traditional ballads easy to recognise. A ballad focuses intently on a crucial moment, engaging with grand subjects at the level of personal relationships to reveal a powerful 'emotional core', a basic human reaction to a dramatic situation.[14] This kind of drama lies at the heart of the most popular ballad subjects. The dramatic consequences are usually dire.[15] Whether capturing the lawless exploits of sixteenth-century Border raiders or relating a cold-blooded murder, ballads frequently thrive on passion or violence at the most personal level. Nearly half of Child's 305 ballads are stories of love or of violence caused by love; sixty deal with violent incidents, forays and feats of arms.[16] M. J. C. Hodgart identifies in Child's ballads of romance and tragedy a 'central type' turning on a single situation 'of jealousy, abduction, and revenge'.[17] A political murder in 1592 sparked a public outcry that spawned both 'The Bonnie Earl o' Moray', lamenting the loss of a beloved 'braw gallant', and 'Willie Macintosh', depicting the consequent retaliation against Moray's killer, the Earl of Huntly:

> As I came in by Fiddich-side,
> In a May morning,
> I met Willie Mackintosh,
> An hour before the dawning.
>
> 'Turn again, turn again,
> Turn again, I bid ye;
> If ye burn Auchindown,
> Huntly he will head ye'.
>
> 'Head me, hang me,
> That sall never fear me;
> I'll burn Auchindowne
> Before the life leaves me'. (183B)[18]

A few terse stanzas gut-wrenchingly dramatise the thirst for revenge.

Obsessive love, too, produces the most horrific outcomes, for example Willie's murder of his own bride, who out of jealousy has killed his true love, 'Fair Annie' (73B). Indeed, violent family conflict underpins a substantial number of ballads. In 'Bonnie Susie Cleland' and 'The Bonnie Earl of Livingstone', daughters are executed when they refuse to marry according to their fathers' wishes. Sibling rivalry abounds, as in 'The Twa Sisters', where a jealous woman murders her sister only for her crime to be revealed by a talking harp fashioned from the breastbone of the victim. Disturbingly recurrent are narratives of infanticide. Mary Hamilton confesses from the gallows, '[H]ad I not slain mine own sweet babe, / This death I wadna dee' (173A). A 'cruel mother' reveals that she has 'taen out her little pen-knife, / And twinnd the sweet babe o its life', after which she has 'howket a grave by the light o the moon, / And there she's buried her sweet babe in' (20B). Incestuous relations lead to inevitable tragedy, as in 'Sheath and Knife', where 'the king's dochter gaes wi child to her brither' and, along with the baby, is killed by him (16A), or, as in 'The Bonny Hind', where she takes her own life. In a frequent motif, a lover wastes away from unrequited love, as does Sir John Graeme, who falls 'sick, and very, very sick' [...] a' for Barbara Allan' (84A) and dies two stanzas later.

A popular vein of balladry turns on interaction between humans and supernatural beings, among them the capricious Scottish fairy. In 'Thomas the Rhymer', the fairy queen abducts 'True Thomas' – the thirteenth-century Thomas of Ercildoune (Earlston) – and whisks him away on her horse to 'fair Elfland', where he is held for seven years before being allowed to return to his 'ain countrie', having gained the 'tongue that can never lie' (37): his poetic and prophetic vision. In 'Tam Lin', a ballad particular to Scotland, the plucky Janet must rescue the father of her unborn child by defying the fairy queen, who transforms Tam into a series of monstrous creatures. In ballads the devil appears either as a seductive, deceptive 'daemon lover' or as the 'fause knight' who must be combatted through wit. And then there are the dangers of overreaching, of challenging the natural order, as in 'The Wife of Usher's Well', where a woman wishes that her dead sons be returned to her 'in earthly flesh and blood'; they come as revenants with hats made 'o the birk' (79). Supernatural occurrences in folksong are 'pure matter of fact, not in the least to be questioned'.[19]

With ballads' inherent, traditional-narrative structures and their emphasis on human drama, they may seem detached from history; as Alan Bold has argued, 'a good ballad has a poetic independence unthreatened by historical fact'.[20] And yet many bear the marks of origins centuries before the first version appeared in print. One of the most famous, 'Sir Patrick Spens', is often associated with the 1290 mission to bring the Norwegian princess Margaret to Scotland. The ballad's focus, however, is not on the mission's purpose, references to which are few and ambiguous; rather, the narrative is driven by the human consequences of pivotal decisions. The Scottish king queries his court, 'O whar will I get guid sailor, / To sail this schip of mine?' on such a treacherous journey, and he is advised by an old knight to send Sir Patrick, 'the best sailor / That sails upon the se' (58A). The king issues the order. Exemplifying the social critique that often underpins a ballad narrative, 'Sir Patrick Spens' turns on the consequences of a ruler's negligence in sending the ship to sea 'at this time o the year', setting in motion a chain of events that ends in devastating loss of life. The group of ballads that emerged following the Earl of Moray's murder in 1592 reveal the persuasive strength of popular response. While such ballads have shed the details that would contextualise any commentary or protest, their power to move public opinion has long been acknowledged. In 1703, the Scottish patriot Andrew Fletcher of Saltoun wrote that he knew 'a very wise man' who believed that 'if a man were permitted to make all the ballads, he need not care who should make the laws of a nation'.[21] A century later the *Encyclopaedia Britannica* (1797) confirms Fletcher's assessment, defining 'ballad' as 'a kind of song, adapted to the capacity of the lower class of people; who, being mightily taken with this species of poetry, are thereby not a little influenced in the conduct of their lives'. The encyclopaedia, however, finds this influence worrying: 'Hence we find, that seditious and designing men never fail to spread ballads among the people, with a view to gain them over to their side.'[22]

Like all art, ballads respond to their cultural situations; as Willa Muir observes, 'the first Ballad-makers simply took whatever was "in the air" and sang it into new shape'.[23] This 'shape' is crucial to the ballad as a whole, as its attributes make possible a particular method of storytelling. This is evident even in the absence of tunes that became detached from texts in the process of collection and publication. The ballad stanza of a large portion of ballads developed in the late Middle Ages[24] is arguably the most recognised form in poetry, usually represented as a quatrain of alternating iambic tetrameter and trimeter lines rhymed *abcb*, sometimes appearing as a couplet with seven stresses per line. This 'common measure' is prevalent in nursery rhymes and hymns, but unlike those forms the ballad stanza drives a narrative. Another common structure is represented as a tetrameter quatrain: four lines of four stresses each. In both cases the narrative pace is measured by the metre, which cradles the textual content of the narrative, but also restricts its movement. When a ballad is sung, this balance is obvious: melody both moves and controls the expression. Bertrand H. Bronson, the twentieth-century musicologist who compiled the tunes for Child's ballads, argues that the 'formal gravity' of ballads, which 'lends characteristic dignity and an effect of ceremonial behaviour to even the most trivial, violent, or abandoned expression of emotion', comes from the music, 'the result of pouring everything in turn into a small, arbitrary mold [*sic*] of sound, with regular divisions, each of which holds so much and no more, and which must be successively refilled at the same temporal pace'.[25]

Oral tradition, by nature, is plural: a ballad's variation occurs in transmission from one singer to another and in response to differences in geographical context. Child originally included all the variants he could find of any ballad he deemed worthy (for example, eighteen of 'Sir Patrick Spens' and twenty-eight of 'Mary Hamilton') and added new ones as he encountered them to the appendices of subsequent volumes. But, as monumental as Child's work is, no ballad's story ends with his collection. In 2003, for example, Mike Yates recorded a variant of 'Mary Hamilton' sung by George Macpherson on the Isle of Skye.[26] The ballad form has its own economy which balances variation and stability, and any one ballad is composed of all its variants, developed over time and across regions.

A ballad narrative covers a lot of ground very quickly, evident from its beginning – like an epic – *in medias res*, at a crucial moment of conflict. We meet Willie Macintosh on his way to avenge Moray's death. We encounter Janet of 'Tam Lin' at the height of her dangerous predicament: alone, pregnant, and gearing up to rescue her fairy-kidnapped lover. In keeping with the dramatic mode, ballads often progress through dialogue, for example in the question-and-answer exchange between Lord Randal and his mother:

> 'O I fear you are poisoned, Lord Randal, my son!
> I fear you are poisoned, my handsome young man!'
> 'O yes, I am poisoned; mother, mak my bed soon,
> For I'm sick at the heart and I fain wad lie down'. (12A)

The pace throughout is controlled by the stanza and metre, as well as by the gaps both between and within stanzas. This 'leaping and lingering' movement has the effect of cinematic cutting from scene to scene, as in the abrupt shift from king's court to Sir Patrick Spens reading the letter containing the king's fateful orders, all within a single stanza:[27]

> The king has written a braid letter,
> And signd it wi his hand,
> And sent it to Sir Patrick Spence,
> Was walking on the sand. (58A)

The gaps contribute to a device observed by ballad enthusiasts over centuries: sparseness of detail and narrative lacunae require readers or listeners to supply the emotional content, to fill in the blanks themselves. Ballad actions are explicit and unequivocally presented, motives often absent or unclear; 'Lord Randal' has been poisoned and is dying, seemingly by his sweetheart's hand, but there is no explanation as to why. Hence, many interpretations are possible.

Feeding on emotional subject matter, but with a matter-of-fact tone, the ballad employs an unmistakeable economy of language. The narrative voice is straightforward, describing actions and events, with passion reserved for expression in a character's voice. Muriel Spark remarked on the 'steel and bite' of ballad language, the way it is enhanced by the use of Scots employed with scalpel-like precision and at times a dark, ironic sense of humour.[28] In 'The Twa Corbies' – a variant of 'The Three Ravens' (26) – the narrative of a murdered knight, who perhaps has been betrayed with his lady's knowledge or collusion, is the subject of a macabre conversation between two crows making their dinner plans:

> 'Ye'll sit on his white hause-bane,
> And I'll pike out his bonny blue een;
> Wi ae lock o his gowden hair
> We'll theek our nest when it grows bare.'

Apparently simple, reliant more on nouns and verbs than on adjectives, ballad diction is also heavily coded and psychologically charged. Formulaic phrases – even entire stanzas – recur, deployed at particular moments in the narrative. In *Commonplace and Creativity*, Flemming Andersen identifies and elaborates on some of the most common. 'Sewing at her silken seam / Kaiming doun her yellow hair' bears a supra-narrative message of 'temptation and (subconscious) erotic longing', while 'Playin at the ba' signals a forthcoming love affair, adultery or abduction with sexual intent. 'She hadna pu'd a flower, a flower' serves as prelude to sexual assault; 'She lookit over her father's castle wa' presages violent confrontation, frequently ending in death; and 'O mother, mother, make my bed' marks the revelation that the character's death is inevitable.[29] These commonplaces were heavily criticised by many early ballad collectors; Scott, for example, attributed them to a fault, even laziness, in the reciters' memories. William Motherwell (1797–1835), however, recognised that such formulaic structures were crucial to the ballad's method: they are 'ingenious devices, no doubt suggested by the wisdom and experience of many ages, whereby oral poetry is more firmly imprinted on the memory' and in the absence of letters, the only efficacious means of preserving and transmitting it to after times'.[30] A distinctive tautology, sometimes introduced in a refrain but more commonly appearing as 'incremental repetition', controls the revelation; Lord Randal's mother asks him a series of questions ('O where ha you been Lord Randal my son?', 'An what met ye there [...]?', 'And what did she give you [...]?' and so on), each slightly different from the one preceding; the son's answers cryptically, incrementally, provide enough information to arrive at the conclusion that his lover has poisoned him.

The precision of ballad dynamics captured the attention of various interests in the twentieth century. The Folk Revival was crucial for countering the long-held belief that ballads were part of a quaint but unrecoverable cultural past, and they became central to a reawakened nationalism. The songs and stories whose sources had long been lost were again being heard on the lips of performers such as the inimitable Jeannie Robertson (1908–1975), Betsy Whyte (1919–1988), Willie Scott (1897–1989) and many others. Scotland's participation in the Folk Revival brought to international attention the survival of some of its most loved and admired ballads. After over a century of collectors pronouncing the death of ballads, the 'discovery' of a living tradition in the middle of the twentieth century – just under the noses of the academic establishment – resulted in a fascinating conjunction of forward-looking modernism and cultural revival of traditional song and storytelling. Hamish Henderson, as a ballad-collector but also an intellectual and literary figure, embodied this conjunction. And despite Hugh MacDiarmid's vexed relationship with the Folk Revival,[31] his early lyrics reflect serious engagement with traditional song. The ballad was adopted and adapted by a wide range of writers, particularly poets such as Willa Muir, Marion Angus, Violet Jacob and, more recently, Liz Lochhead and Kathleen Jamie. Jacob and Angus unabashedly drew on ballads for their poetry in Scots. But fiction-writers and dramatists (for example, Spark and Lochhead) have also been inspired to fill the tantalising gaps in ballad narratives. Further, David Greig's *The Strange Undoing of Prudencia Hart* (2011), which has been successfully toured internationally, not only uses ballad forms in its dialogue and has a heroine who is actually a ballad scholar, but is clearly a modern version of 'Tam Lin'.

From another quarter, literary critics and poet-critics adopted the ballad as an example of best poetic practice, following on from the early twentieth-century emphasis on concrete imagery, language and dramatic technique. The ballad's attributes exemplified emerging poetry theories, and were employed by some of the most influential voices of the day, including the editors of *Understanding Poetry* (1938), Cleanth Brooks and Robert Penn Warren. Steve Newman notes that ten ballads feature at the beginning of the book, and four are subjected to the close scrutiny that was to become known as the New Criticism: 'Only Shakespeare is accorded more poems, and no named author, not even Shakespeare, elicits more than two close readings.'[32] It is the intrinsic dramatic and concrete qualities of ballads, Newman argues, that drew Brooks and Warren to the ballad as a 'chosen vehicle' for introducing students to good poetry.[33] *Understanding Poetry* provided the foundation for a poetic and critical framework that altered how poetry was read and taught, which reverberates still in the emphasis on close-reading practices. Anthologies of poetry have followed Brooks and Warren's lead in categorising ballads as a species of poetry,[34] with the added effect of distancing text from tune. Few students of literature today know that ballads are songs, much less know their melodies.

Scotland's ballads travelled throughout the world during periods of colonial expansion, in the memories of singers and through miscellanies, broadsides and newspapers. With ballads' intrinsic balance of stability and variation, they easily adapted to new environments. Their appeal was not restricted to an ethnic or geographic group; white colonists and slaves in the pre-Civil War United States, for example, circulated ballads of their own. Many variants took root in the Appalachian Mountains of the eastern United States, and were transcribed by a series of collectors, among the most prominent John Jacob Niles, Cecil Sharp, Maud Karpeles and Alan Lomax. This music combined with other influences, especially African ones, to form the basis of American country music. One such well-travelled ballad is 'Bonny Barbara Allan' (84), which has appeared in many contexts and is still being recorded by singers in both folk and country genres. Evidence of its popularity in seventeenth-century theatres and drawing rooms may be found in Samuel Pepys's diary for 1666.[35] In the eighteenth century it appeared in Allan Ramsay's *Tea-Table Miscellany* (1740) as well as in other collections, and in the nineteenth century was current in both oral and print traditions. A popular 1855 Glasgow broadside included 'Barbara Allan the Cruel', described as a 'comic version'.[36] The ballad was popular in the twentieth-century Folk Revival, in both Britain and abroad, as evidenced by the sixteen variants that Sharp and Karpeles transcribed over the course of their Appalachian fieldwork.[37] Emmy Lou Harris recorded a country version for the soundtrack of the film *Songcatcher* (2000), directed by Maggie Greenwald.

Tracing ballads follows a movement not only from oral tradition to print, but from various kinds of oral expression to various forms of media: not a simple movement from one geographical space to another, but a complicated back-and-forth movement that helped to shape new literatures and forms of cultural expression. This dynamic is prominent in the forms produced by Caribbean adaptations of Scottish ballads,[38] where the losses – and cultural gains – result from the translocation of traditional songs, as Robert Burns put it, 'across th' Atlantic roar'. Social anthropologist Isabel Hofmeyr observes that the production of oral tradition 'thrives on fragments, and [...] its producers are like bricoleurs who go to work with material originally intended for another purpose'.[39] The traditional ballad's stable yet flexible form has allowed its more striking and valued attributes to survive, reinforced by admiration from all levels of society. Its poetic quality and cultural capital render the ballad undiminished as an art form.

PART 3: TOPICS AND THEMES

CHAPTER THIRTEEN

Nature, Landscape and Rural Life

Louisa Gairn

Although Scottish poetry abounds in vivid representations of the natural world, twentieth-century Scottish poets have sometimes been reluctant to consider their work as 'nature poetry', wary of negative associations with pastoral myth-making or escapism. Scottish literary criticism has also sometimes been distrustful of works foregrounding rural themes, keen to resist the 'kailyard' denial of modern urban life, or Romantic stereotyping of the Scottish landscape which ignores real, and often painful, human histories. However, in recent years, growing awareness of ecological issues has led to a reconceptualisation of poetry's role in making sense of our contested identity as part of the wider natural world – the recognition that we are, as Burns wrote, 'earth-born companion[s], / An' fellow-mortal[s]' ('To a Mouse, on Turning Her Up in Her Nest with the Plough'). Rather than some aesthetic exercise in escapism, Scottish poetry focusing on the natural world is increasingly valued for its relevance to ecological thought. This is the view suggested by John Burnside, that ecology and poetry are complementary disciplines, making 'a science of belonging, a discipline by which we may both describe and celebrate [...] the world, and so become worthy participants in a natural history'.[1]

Questions about our relationship with the world of nature are explored in some of the most characteristic works of the medieval makars, drawing human, animal and environment into a web of meaning and inter-relationship. In works like Robert Holland's *Buke of the Howlat* (c. 1448), or William Dunbar's 'The Thrissil and the Rois' (1503), nature is conceived of as a 'keekin'-glass' which reflects aspects of ourselves, or as the Europe-wide theological concept of 'the book of Nature', where an understanding of divine order can be gleaned by 'reading' nature through observation and interpretation. Such concepts also feed into Robert Henryson's (c. 1450–c. 1505) adaptation of the 'beast fable' genre, where animals are instructive surrogates for human shortcomings – although, as Antony Hasler argues, Henryson's *Morall Fabillis* (c. 1480) depart from convention by presenting beasts as 'logicians' rather than mere analogues of vice or folly, questioning the validity of interpreting nature along anthropocentric lines.[2] Pastoral is another of the great classical 'nature' genres transformed by the makars. Henryson's 'Robene and Makyne' (c. 1470) is the earliest extant pastoral poem in either English or Scots, an innovative work which draws on native ballad traditions as well as Old French *pastourelle* and the classical Eclogue.[3] Further pastoral experimentation is found in Gavin Douglas's *Eneados* (1513), a translation of Virgil's *Aeneid* featuring strikingly realistic landscape descriptions rendered in alliterative Scots. Particularly remarkable is Douglas's vivid portrayal of winter and its effects on both landscape and people, a harsh season where 'Ryveris ran reid on spait with watir broune' and the mountain peaks are 'slekit with snaw ourheildis'.[4]

The medieval makars' pastoral innovations helped to inspire Allan Ramsay's (1686–1758) later interpretation of the genre. Largely responsible for the eighteenth-century 'rediscovery' of Henryson and Dunbar through his inclusion of their works in *The Ever Green* (1724–27), Ramsay rejected the idealised pastoral then promoted by the London Augustan poet Alexander Pope. It was absurd, Ramsay suggested, for a 'Northern Poet' to look for his pastoral materials in mythological Italy or Greece. Instead, he urged Scottish writers to emulate the medieval makars, where:

> The Poetry is the product of their own Country, not pilfered and spoiled in the transportation from abroad: their images are native, and their landskips domestick; copied from those fields and meadows we every day behold. The morning rises (in the Poet's description) as she does in the Scottish horizon. [...] The groves rise in our own valleys; the rivers flow from our own fountains, and the winds blow upon our own hills.[5]

Given Ramsay's Jacobite and anti-Union sympathies, this resistance to the Augustan idealisation of landscape might be read as having a certain geopolitical significance, encouraging a sense of Scottish environmental distinctiveness following the Union of 1707. Although, as Susan Manning argues, Ramsay's Scottish version of pastoral 'set (Scots) poetic language off on a track towards bucolic rusticity and the kailyard', his contribution is significant in emphasising greater realism and fidelity to local landscapes and identity.[6] Ramsay's own pastoral verse, *The Gentle Shepherd* (1725), was, however, also partly inspired by English pastoral. In featuring the landscape of the Pentland hills south of Edinburgh, as well as colloquial Scots dialogue and vernacular songs, Ramsay drew influences from John Gay's *The Shepherd's Week* (1714), whose landscape was similarly peopled with local rustics speaking colloquial English.[7]

Perhaps the most important British pastoral work of the early eighteenth century was written by another Scot, James Thomson (1700–1748). Born in Roxburghshire, Thomson studied in Edinburgh before moving to London, where he became acquainted with Pope and other writers of the Augustan school. Although influenced by Pope's neo-classical pastoral, Thomson's masterpiece, *The Seasons* (1726–30), departs from Augustan convention in its scale and detail, presenting a panorama of the British landscape and its human and animal inhabitants, with natural phenomena the central focus. In its drive to survey, describe and catalogue nature, *The Seasons* reads somewhat like a poetic treatise on natural history – reflecting georgic didacticism but also aligned with the newly developing perspectives of biological and agricultural sciences such as Carl Linnaeus's *Systema Naturae* (1735). However, if *The Seasons* at times projects an Enlightenment confidence in the potential for human industry to tap the bountiful natural resources of the British Isles, some sections also evince a seemingly contradictory distrust of the 'thoughtless insolence of power' exerted by humans over the natural environment, as in Thomson's reaction to the destruction of a beehive:

> O Man! tyrannic lord! how long, how long
> Shall prostrate Nature groan beneath your rage,
> Awaiting Renovation?[8] ('Autumn', ll. 1189–91)

Drawing moral lessons from observations of animal species is also a feature of Pope's work, and originates with Virgil, whose *Georgics* featured bees as an example of industriousness. However, Thomson moves towards Romanticism in his critique of the 'barbarity' of exploiting creatures for sport or thoughtlessly destroying their habitat – indeed, as the ecocritic Lawrence Buell notes, *The Seasons* is perhaps the first major work in English to foreground the mistreatment of animals in this way.[9] One sequence, describing the frantic rush of a hunted deer through woodlands and across rivers, seems designed to arouse a proto-Romantic sense of sympathy in its depiction of the 'weak, harmless, flying creature' (l. 424) pursued by 'murderous cry' (l. 433). Such episodes take place in a landscape which Thomson himself presents as 'romantic', including an early portrait of sublime Highland terrain, whose 'airy mountains' (l. 879) and 'huge forests, / Incult, robust, and tall' (ll. 881–82), are laid out in panorama for the reader/spectator to contemplate. As Gerard Carruthers points out, Thomson's celebration of wild landscape was innovative, predating the Burkean sublime, and placing an aesthetic value on land often viewed as barbarous or marginal.[10]

Thomson's influence is visible in much eighteenth-century landscape poetry, including that of the Gaelic writers Alasdair mac Mhaighstir Alasdair (Alexander MacDonald, c. 1698–1770) and Duncan Ban Macintyre (Donnchadh Bàn Mac an t-Saoir, 1724–1812), now recognised as two of Scotland's most significant nature poets.[11] However, while MacDonald's seasonal poems 'Oran a' Gheamhraidh' (*'Song of Winter'*) and 'Oran an t-Samhraidh' (*'Song of Summer'*) draw on Augustan pastoral, they also innovate within a long Gaelic tradition of nature description stretching back to the ninth century, which included works on the seasons, landscapes and individual animals, as well as other poetic genres featuring natural imagery, such as aristocratic praise poetry.[12] MacDonald's seasonal poems demonstrate this literary heritage as well as a deft and knowledgeable handling of the characteristics of animals, landscape and weather, building up what Derick Thomson calls a 'composite picture' of each season, but also delighting in details, such as the remarkable portrait of a salmon in 'Summer'.[13] Such descriptive intensity is also reflected in Macintyre's 'Mòladh Beinn Dobhrain' (*'The Praise of Ben Dorain'*, 1768), which takes an obvious sensorial delight in the landscape and its wildlife, celebrating the physical beauty of the deer as well as the bodily experience of hunting and exploring the mountain – a capacity for descriptive realism valued by twentieth-century Gaelic poets as a vigorous alternative to Romanticism.[14] However, in depicting a landscape largely devoid of human presence, '*Ben Dorain*' may also encode a political critique; as a deer forester in the service of the Duke of Argyll, Macintyre would have been well aware of the incipient eviction of crofters from Highland estates in favour of game and sheep.[15] Indeed, in 'Oran nam Balgairean' (*'Song to the Foxes'*), the poet voices the consequences of such changes for both people and wildlife, stressing the interconnection between the two: 'Na bailtean is na h-àirighean / Am faighte blàths is faoileachd, / Gun taighean ach na làraichean, / Gun àiteach air na raointean' (*'The townships and the shielings / where once dwelt warmth and kindness – / no houses but the tumbled stones, / no ploughing of the meadows'*); while 'Earba bheag na dùslainn, / Cha dùisgear i le blaodhan' (*'the small doe of the greenwood / Will not be waked with calling'*).[16] Macintyre sides with the foxes, the force of wild nature and predator of livestock, as antidote to, or revenge upon, the actions of the landlords. As Robert Crawford suggests, Macintyre's poetry speaks of an ecological sensibility based on the poet's own personal and professional experience, reflecting an interconnected ecosystem of land, animals and people, and meditating on the consequences of its destruction.[17]

Such 'agrarian capitalism' was not limited to the Highlands and islands of Scotland; modern land management practices were also applied throughout the Lowlands, often focusing on the consolidation of farming land and the eviction of smallholders.[18] The theory and practice of modern farming techniques were key to Scottish Enlightenment thought, promoted by Adam Smith and developed as a science by figures like James Hutton in Edinburgh, the founder of modern geology who also worked on experimental agriculture at his family's farm in Berwickshire, and William Wilkie, the St Andrews professor whose improvements to his own farm were memorialised by his former student, the poet Robert Fergusson (1750–1774). In 'An Eclogue, To the Memory of Dr William Wilkie', drawing on Ramsay's pastoral model in featuring local characters and vernacular Scots, Fergusson praises Wilkie's achievements as a modern farmer as much as his scientific abilities in deciphering the 'mystic ferlies' and 'secret workings' of Nature. Where once 'the thristles an' the dockans' had 'wag[ged] their taps upo' the green', Wilkie's land improvements ensured that 'now his bonny riggs delight the view, / An' thrivin hedges drink the caller dew'; the modernised farming land provides a fitting epitaph for Wilkie's synthesis of countryside and scientific knowledge.[19]

Robert Burns's poetry also demonstrates this intermingling of Enlightenment thought, farming concerns and pastoral literary traditions. As a struggling tenant farmer, Burns (1759–1796) expresses very acutely the precariousness of rural life, including the often unjust relationship between landowners and rural workers – what Crawford calls 'the politics of economic uncertainty and ecological calamity'.[20] Indeed, the supposed 'naturalness' or 'wildness' of the poetry, promoted by Burns himself as emerging from an uneducated rustic sphere, belies much more complex political and philosophical commentaries about nature and society by a sophisticated writer who was well read in Enlightenment philosophy as well as modern agricultural theory. Some of that material, particularly Adam Smith's *Theory of Moral Sentiments* (1759), with its emphasis on imaginative sympathy – 'fellow-feeling with the sorrow of others' – is evident in Burns's treatment of land politics.[21] Like Henryson, Burns adapts the beast fable to debate moral issues, as in 'The Twa Dogs', which satirises landowners' casual exploitation of rural workers: the 'laird gets in his racked rents' (l. 51) regardless of the 'Poor tenant-bodies, scant o' cash' (l. 95). Engaging with the wider British and Irish debate over absentee landlords and their mismanagement of the rural environment, he criticises the gentry who 'waste / sae mony a braw estate' through neglect when their greater involvement 'wad for ev'ry ane be better, / The laird, the tenant, an' the cotter' (ll. 172–78). Significantly, Burns made one of the earliest Lowland poetic critiques of exploitative Highland land management, criticising the tactics aristocratic landlords used to prevent a desperate mass emigration of crofters to Canada following the introduction of sheep farming on Highland estates.[22] In 'Address of Beelzebub', the Devil praises the lairds' efforts to 'cowe the rebel generation' of crofters, noting how 'your factors, greives, trustees, an' bailies [...] lay aside a' tender mercies'. Thus, while Burns's portraits of rural life in poems like 'The Cotter's Saturday Night' have sometimes been considered as the source of later redundant 'kailyard' nostalgia, other poems undermine the possibility of rural escapism, instead emphasising the vulnerability of dwelling in an environment under threat. Perhaps most memorably, 'To a Mouse' might be considered an early 'ecopoem' in paralleling the plight of human and animal as subject to the destructive force of 'Man's dominion' and the loss of 'Nature's Social Union' – a phrase Pope used to describe prelapsarian harmony in his *Essay on Man* (1734).[23] However, instead of finding a reassuring order as in Pope's view of nature, Burns finds only fragility and uncertainty, perhaps thinking of his own family and the recent death of his brother John.[24] Indeed, perhaps, as Nigel Leask argues, the situation also serves as a metaphor for a wider eco-political reality; like the destruction of the mouse's home, the Lowland clearances of cotters result from the very land improvements tenant farmers like Burns were carrying out during this era.[25]

Spurred by the agricultural and industrial revolutions, this fear of deracination pulses through Scottish poetry from the mid-eighteenth century onwards, including James Macpherson's *Poems of Ossian* (1765). Capitalising on the vogue for primitivism then gaining ground in Europe (Rousseau's *Discourse on Inequality* appeared in 1754), and despite the bitter controversy over their authenticity, the poems proved internationally influential, helping to establish European and North American landscape aesthetics of the 'Sublime'.[26] Although Macpherson (1736–1796) has been criticised for faking Gaelic culture and mythologising the Highlands as an empty wilderness, the Ossian poems can also be read more sympathetically as an attempt to mitigate the loss of place, culture and identity in Highland society following the Culloden defeat.[27] This sense of the vulnerability of dwelling and identity also extends to the historical canvas of Walter Scott's (1771–1832) narrative poems such as *The Lay of the Last Minstrel* (1802), where alterations in the landscape parallel our collective forgetting of the past. The minstrel embodies Scott's urge to conserve and communicate the history of human inhabitation in the Borders landscape, compelled to 'tell – / Of ancient deeds, so long forgot [...] Of forests, now laid waste and bare' (Canto IV). Scott's resistance to the threat of Scotland's loss of identity is evident from his collecting of songs and ballads from the oral tradition, published in *Minstrelsy of the Scottish Border* (1802–03). Scott, too, has been criticised for mythologising the Scottish landscape; he was, however, also concerned with the bond between land and memory, the landscape inscribed with the stories of people's lives and livelihoods. In *The Lay*, Scott sets out a case for poetry's ability to defend identity and reinforce belonging within particular environments. When the last poet dies, the minstrel predicts, the landscape itself will mourn the loss of its stories: 'the stream, the wood, the gale / Is vocal with the plaintive wail / Of those, who, else forgotten long, / Liv'd in the poet's faithful song' (V. ii. 3–6). Here, landscape and human life are bonded by history, and poetry's role is to communicate this truth.

Lament for a fading way of life perhaps inevitably invites nostalgia, and in the later nineteenth century this found expression in Kailyard portraits of Lowland rural communities (provoking vigorous counter-reactions such as John Davidson's 1891 anti-kailyard poem 'Ayrshire Jock'), as well as pathetic fallacy-laden versions of Celtic identity. Drawing inspiration from W. B. Yeats's efforts towards an Irish renaissance, the Scottish 'Celtic Twilight' movement centred around the poet Fiona Macleod / William Sharp, and was promoted by the polymath biologist, geographer and cultural theorist Patrick Geddes and his short-lived periodical *The Evergreen* (1895–96). Despite Geddes's hopes for a 'Scots renascence' based on a renewed 'Literature of Locality', Celtic Twilight poetry largely ignored the situation of real Gaelic-speaking Highlanders still struggling against the very real threat of displacement from their ancestral lands.[28] By contrast, for Highland crofting communities, poetry became a vital political tool in voicing resistance to the Highland Clearances. Gaelic poets during this period allied themselves with Lowland resistance to land enclosure, such as the Scottish Rights of Way movement, critiquing the metropolitan view of the Highlands as an empty playground for sportsmen and hunters.[29] Although landowners have revoked the people's ancestral right of access to the land, warns one poem, the local community intend to resist this: 'Siùbhlaidh sinn na cos-cheuman / Mar bhios ar feum a' toirt oirnn' (*We will walk in the rights of way, / just as our needs require us to do*'), but 'An reachd a bh' againn cha trèig sinn, / 'S cha leig sinn eug i dhar deòin, / Dh'aindeoin bagradh a shèidear' ('*We will not forsake the law that we had, [...] in spite of whatever threat is breathed against us*').[30]

Parallel to the voicing of geopolitical resistance, Gaelic poetry of this time has been read as demonstrating a change in perspective from the descriptive cataloguing of external nature to a contemplation of internal emotions provoked by landscape and memory.[31] This partly autobiographical stance can be traced in poems by Màiri Nic a' Phearsain (Mary MacPherson, known as Màiri Mhòr nan Òran/Big Mary of the Songs, c. 1821–1898), the Bard of the Highland Land League, whose poetry agitated on behalf of Highland crofters during the Crofters' War of 1882–86 and beyond. Her work shifts in register from the morale-boosting 'Brosnachadh nan Gàidheal' ('*Incitement of the Gaels*') to more intimate personal reflection in poems like 'Soraidh leis an Nollaig ùir' ('*Farewell to the New Christmas*'), where she relates her experience of coming home to her family's ruined croft. The poem commemorates the dead, 'luchd mo rùin, / A tha 'n diugh 'san ùir 'nan suain' ('*the dear-loved folk / Earthed now in their eternal sleep*'), but significantly does not give up hope of a return to life and vigour, symbolised by drinking from her family's well: 'na clachan mar a chuir a làmh, / Air am fàgail dhomh mar dhuais [...] Dh'òl mi làn mo bhois de'n bhùrn, / 'S rinn e m'ùrachadh 'san uair' ('*the stones whereon he laid his hands, / are left a legacy to me [...] but there I cupped my hand and drank, / and felt my being made anew*').[32] Nic a' Phearsain skilfully parallels her own emotional transformation, making contact with the land, stones and water her family once possessed, with the hoped-for renewal of the Gaelic crofting community – a poetic smeddum far removed from the studied melancholy of the Celtic Twilight.

By the turn of the twentieth century, Scottish society had shifted decisively towards an urban population. Sensing that the nostalgia of the Celtic Twilight and Kailyard represented 'largely phoney' values, Hugh MacDiarmid (C. M. Grieve, 1892–1978) and the writers associated with the Scottish Renaissance movement of the 1920s and 1930s sought a form of poetry which could more accurately reflect modern experience.[33] However, somewhat paradoxically, such modernist aspirations were often expressed through works which took countryside experience and natural landscapes as their focal point, or by writers who came from small towns, islands or farmlands – a provincial or 'village' modernism which has also been noted in Irish writing.³⁴ Rural language was also an important part of modernist experimentation. Marion Angus and Violet Jacob, both originating in north-east Scotland, had published poems in Scots which combined rural settings and ballad traditions with an atmosphere of psychological unease. Similarly, MacDiarmid's early Scots lyrics in *Sangschaw* (1925) and *Penny Wheep* (1926) have been called 'kailyard-expressionist pieces', endeavouring to fuse together archaic, often obsolete, rural words, rural settings and characters, with a modernistic challenge to traditional values.³⁵ In attempting to adapt 'an essentially rustic tongue to the very much more complex requirements of our urban civilisation', MacDiarmid argued that these old Scots words, evolved in the context of countryside life and experience, represented an 'unutilized mass of observation'.³⁶

This link between observational power and poetic language is key to a developing Scottish ecopoetics throughout the twentieth century, and also seems to motivate MacDiarmid's move towards a 'poetry of facts' in his later work, with the poet's role conceived as that of a keen-eyed observer and synthesiser of knowledge, much like a scientist or naturalist. MacDiarmid's argument that Scottish authors lack 'a real knowledge of nature' in *Scottish Scene* (1934) seems intended to counterpoint his own poetry's virtuosic display of expertise in natural history and even the new science of ecology.³⁷ Exemplary naturalists are pressed into service: the archetypal figure of the Scottish autodidact appears in MacDiarmid's portrait of an amateur naturalist ('Tam o' the Wilds and the Many-Faced Mystery'), who has 'the seein' eye frae which naething could hide', while later MacDiarmid pays tribute to the wealth of knowledge displayed in 'The Praise of Ben Dorain', linking Duncan Ban Macintyre's poetic skills with field notes by the ecologist Frank Fraser Darling. However, for MacDiarmid the biodiverse landscape of Scotland is also a potent source for national symbolism. In *Dìreadh I*, listing the innumerable flora and fauna of a hillside ecosystem, the poet draws a symbol of cultural flourishing, survival and regeneration: 'Our multiform, our infinite Scotland'.

If the idea of the attentive poet-naturalist represents one strand of modern Scottish ecopoetry, another is the attempt to understand the meaning of 'dwelling' or 'belonging' in the context of an increasingly urban and technologically minded society. This is perhaps the defining theme in the work of Edwin Muir (1887–1959), the son of Orkney tenant farmers whose move to Glasgow resulted in terrible personal tragedy with the death of his parents and two siblings. Muir experienced this as a violent deracination, an expulsion from the 'Eden' of his childhood. His poetry sets this experience against the backdrop of international war and industrialisation, considering the implications of modern life's dissociation from the world of nature. Muir's post-apocalyptic vision of possible reconnection with nature in his poem 'The Horses' (1956) reflects his conviction that 'At the heart of civilisation is the byre, the barn, and the midden', and that to forget our dependence on the natural world, and our heritage there, is a dangerous mistake. Muir's apparent turn away from modernity in favour of a mythic pastoral was emphatically rejected by later Scottish poets such as Edwin Morgan, finding the vision described in 'The Horses' to be 'more insulting than comforting to man's restless and aspiring brain'.[38] However, Muir's poetry aligns with later twentieth-century international environmentalism in calling attention to how modern technology 'isolates us from the natural world in a way which is new to mankind', and seeking to recuperate our 'long-lost archaic companionship' with nature.[39]

Similar concerns can be traced in the work of the great twentieth-century Gaelic poet Sorley MacLean (Somhairle MacGill-Eain, 1911–1996). Perhaps most famously, MacLean's 'Hallaig' is a sensuous contemplation of the enduring bond between environment and community. The poem can be read as a lament for the cleared settlement of Raasay, the loss of people and place, but at the same time it asserts a sense of belonging, however vulnerable to time and environmental change. While the advance of the birch wood might seem to erase the evidence of human settlement, gradually obscuring once-cultivated land, MacLean's poem transforms the trees into a kind of animistic presence rather than merely a symbol of loss: the 'daughters and sons' of Raasay are the wood itself. MacLean has been described as a 'post-pastoral' poet, adapting the conventions of both English pastoral and Gaelic praise poetry in poems like 'The Cuillin' to contemplate global problems, invoking his local landscape as a symbol of resistance against European fascism, or in 'Screapadal', paralleling the Highland Clearances with the contemporary threat of nuclear war.[40] Conscious of continuing the tradition of Gaelic landscape poetry by writers like Duncan Ban Macintyre and Màiri Nic a' Phearsain, MacLean rejected the 'weak sentimentality' of Romanticism in the English tradition in contrast to Gaelic poetry's 'realisation of dynamic nature'.[41] Indeed, from the mid-twentieth century onwards, Scottish poets demonstrate an increasing uneasiness about our desire to find human meaning and memory in the natural world, expressing doubt about the truth of 'reading' the landscape in symbolic or anthropocentric terms. This issue is confronted by Iain Crichton Smith (1928–1998) in 'Deer on the High Hills' (1962), contemplating poetry's access to the truth about the external world it represents or perhaps exploits:

> Are rivers stories, and are plains their prose?
> Are fountains poetry? And are rainbows the
> wistful smiles upon a dying face?
> Such symbols freeze upon my desolate lips!

Similar concerns motivate Kenneth White's (b. 1936) theory of 'geopoetics' as expressing 'a contact between the human mind and the things, the lines, the rhythms of the earth', and his call for a reconnection with the natural world that does not depend upon history or anthropocentrism.[42] Instead, envisaging 'the end of history as a primal reference', White's poetry considers how to 'speak from within' the world of nature, and the difficulty of finding the 'necessary words'.[43]

This quest for poetic truth characterises the work of a younger generation of Scottish poets, in poetry which demonstrates a conscious turn towards ecology and 'green' philosophy. Kathleen Jamie (b. 1962) has suggested part of poetry's role is as a 'line of defence' against the loss of our environmental and cultural heritage, asserting that the priority for contemporary Scottish writers is 'the world which is more-than-human, which is beyond the human. I believe that's where our problems actually lie.'[44] John Burnside (b. 1955), too, takes an explicitly ecopoetic stance in his poetry, while writing about green politics and philosophy in his prose. We need to learn to value nature for its own sake, Burnside suggests, but we also need to be aware of our failings in this regard: 'We may be prepared to stand and wonder [...] but we are just as likely to dissect, or genetically modify, or patent the natural world as we are to revere it.'[45] For Burnside, the concept of nature is not limited to the aesthetically pleasing or culturally resonant, but the world that we encounter in our daily lives in cities and suburbs, on the margins or borderlines of nature. As such, his poetry in collections such as *The Light Trap* (2002) often calls attention to the sense of the liminal, the encounter with the animal 'other' leading to an imaginative acceptance of our own status as part of nature, a different self 'who walks alone and barefoot in the woods', at home amongst a family of deer, 'knowing the chasm between / one presence and the next as nothing more / than something learned, like memory, or song' ('Deer', *The Light Trap*). Jamie, too, sets out to negotiate the borderline between nature and human, questioning the limits of poetic representation in 'Skeins o' Geese' (*Mr and Mrs Scotland Are Dead: Poems, 1980–1994*, 2002), asking 'Whit dae birds write on the dusk? / A word nivir spoken nor read', or 'The Dipper' (*The Tree House*, 2004), where a bird's song cannot be replicated in words: 'it isn't mine to give'. However, Jamie remains convinced that poetry can help us to overcome the supposed dualistic divide between human and nature, as 'a sort of connective tissue where myself meets the world' achieved by careful observation.[46] This ecologically minded outlook is an important presence in Scottish poetry, set within the context of societal as well as environmental change. Continuing a rich tradition of poetic observation and encounters with the natural world, Scottish poets remain attuned to cross-currents in international science and philosophy of nature, contemplating, as Jamie writes, 'a way to live / on this damp ambiguous earth' ('Alder', *The Tree House*).

CHAPTER FOURTEEN

Nation and Home

Carla Sassi and Silke Stroh

'Nation' and 'home' point respectively towards distinct ideas of community that are grounded in history/culture and in domestic/affective values; they also share notions of common identity, sense of belonging, and even security. Furthermore, both concepts are shaped, and in their turn shape, a community's 'imagination'[1] of itself, finding their most effective and complex expression in literary utterances. Writers have the ability both to investigate the deeper truths of national/ist sentiment and to shape dialogic 'textual communities'. Genres such as elegy and epic poetry often voice the collective emotions and perceptions of a community struck by grief, calamity or war; panegyrics and satire, by taking centre-stage key contemporary events and characters, contribute towards a sense of living identity; lyrical poems about daily practices, familiar objects or places can powerfully embody a community's most intimate emotional life; by singing national anthems and songs (rebel and protest songs in particular, as the following chapter illustrates), members of a community can both perform and internalise/emotionalise their shared identity. Poems – and their authors – can become powerful national icons themselves – even in relation to nationally un-distinctive subjects, as is the case with Burns's 'A Red Red Rose', centred on an almost 'universal' flower and symbol, which has nonetheless become one of Scotland's possibly most iconic poems. While simplified readings of poems may indeed produce a 'banal nationalist imagination'[2] (the process of iconification undergone by some of Burns's poems provides a case in point), poetry's malleable and contingent nature points towards a complex and fluid idea of national identity – an idea that continually shifts between and across the historical and the domestic, the cultural and affective aspects of identity.

The aim of the present chapter is not that of reconstructing an organic and consistent development of the Scottish nation through an overview of its poetic production across several centuries, but rather to chart (albeit far from exhaustively) the different 'textual communities' that, at different times and from different, even conflicting stances (ideological, linguistic and geopolitical), have created and promoted ideas of nation and home within the boundaries of present-day Scotland.

One of the most celebrated early Scots poems, John Barbour's *The Bruce*, stands out as a stunning redefinition of Scottishness in the fourteenth century. Even though centred on Robert I ('The Bruce'), it includes different social classes and both genders: prophecies by women, for example, such as St Margaret (ll. X. 741–60) and the Arran woman (ll. IV. 646–67), play a central role in Bruce's triumph. Also, by proclaiming to be both a 'truthful story' and a 'romance', the poem provides an early example of those constructions of nationhood – grounded both in history and myth – that will become established in Europe between the eighteenth and the nineteenth centuries. Unsurprisingly, its powerfully 'ethnosymbolic'[3] construction of a 'national' historical event will indeed develop into the 'quintessential myth of Scottish distinctiveness'[4] of the modern age.

Arguably, the Scottish Wars of Independence (1296–1357) were central in shaping the identities of both the Scottish and the English nations: in this period a literature of political antagonism – satirical texts, political songs – juxtaposed the two countries starkly, and yet represented a lively dialogue across shifting borders.[5] Celebration of military triumphs against the English, of manly courage and heroism also characterise *The Wallace* by 'Blind' Hary (c. 1488), eulogising the Scottish 'freedom fighter' who had lived a century and a half earlier. National identity is here presented as inherited from one's ancestors, and anti-English sentiments are as lively as in *The Bruce*. *The Wallace*, very much like *The Bruce*, would kindle the imagination of Scottish nationalists in the eighteenth and nineteenth centuries.

Not all poems between the fourteenth and fifteenth centuries celebrate conflict equally enthusiastically: Robert Baston, the English Carmelite friar and poet who, in the fifteenth century, was sent to the Battle of Bannockburn to immortalise England's hoped-for victory, was captured by the Scots and forced to write a poem on its defeat instead. His 'Metrum de Praelio apud Bannockburn' ('*The Poem of the Battle of Bannockburn*')[6] is more an indictment of the cruelty of war than a celebration of a victory the author cannot obviously bring himself to rejoice in. In the sixteenth century, William Dunbar's 'The Thrissil and the Rois' (1503), a complex allegory composed to mark the wedding of King James IV of Scotland to Princess Margaret Tudor of England, also breaks with the tradition of anti-English sentiment, and admonishes the king to be faithful to his bride, the 'fresche Rois, of colour reid and quhyt' (l. 44).

National politics feature less prominently in the Gaelic segment of medieval and Renaissance Scottish poetry – although the practical involvement of the Gaelic world in national matters was strong. Often, poets focus on smaller units like clans or individual leaders. Various panegyrics praise a leader's prowess in war without identifying specific wars, causes or enemies. Where references to wider Scottish national politics and society do appear, they are often vague and rather brief. Another focus for a wider, (quasi-)'national' orientation is a pan-Gaelic framework which includes Ireland and sometimes seems to portray the latter as an alternative (ancestral and cultural) 'motherland'. Sometimes there are also suggestions of Irish political alliances, but secession from Scotland and the creation of a new pan-Gaelic state is not envisaged; essential belonging to the Scottish polity is not questioned, and there were cultural differences between Scottish and Irish Gaels, too. The proportion of Scottish and Irish orientations varies between clans (or septs) and over time (e.g. based on political expediencies). Examples of pan-Gaelic orientations include 'Mairg thréigeas inn, a Amhlaoibh' (*'Woe to him who neglects me, Amhlaoibh'*, c. 1217) by the Irish-born founder of the MacMhuirich bardic dynasty, Muireadhach Albanach Ó Dálaigh, and 'Fíor mo mholadh ar MhacDomhnaill' (*'True my praising of MacDonald'*, c. 1450), probably by a later MacMhuirich. A combination of pan-Gaelic and pan-Scottish orientations appears in another MacMhuirich poem, 'Alba gan díon a ndiaidh Ailín' (*'Scotland is defenceless after Ailean'*, c. 1513).

Borders also run across the territory of the modern Scottish nation. Despite the complexity of Gaelic loyalties, Lowland texts increasingly denigrated Gaeldom as an internal Other: Richard Holland in his *Buke of the Howlat* (c. 1448), like his predecessors, stresses the importance of loyalty to the Scottish monarchy but also voices Lowland prejudice against the Gaelic language. Along similar lines, William Dunbar (c. 1460–1513) voices his contempt of Gaelic in 'The Flyting of Dunbar and Kennedy' (ll. 49, 56), even though this is somehow counterbalanced, within the text, by Kennedy's celebration of the myth of Scota and of the Irish origin of the Scots (ll. 344–32). Poetry in Gaelic does not really respond to Lowland hostility until later. There is some reference to political conflict (the Scottish Crown's attempt to abolish the MacDonald Lordship of the Isles, a major Gaelic power base) in

Giolla Coluim mac an Ollaimh's 'Ní h-eibhneas gan Chlainn Domhnaill' (*'There is no joy without Clan Donald'*, c. 1500), but allusively rather than explicitly. Moreover, the poem simultaneously asserts political loyalty and makes no reference to cultural antagonism. The anonymous early sixteenth-century fragment 'Ar sliocht Gaodhal ó ghort Gréag' (*'The Gaels from the land of Greece'*), which exhorts the Earl of Argyll to lead Gaelic resistance against hostile outsiders, is sometimes interpreted as another poem about Highland/Lowland hostilities. But it is not clear whether the outsiders really are Lowlanders: the now dominant view on the poem considers the outsiders to be English, suggesting that the poem requests Scottish Gaelic support for anti-English resistance in Ireland, and/or for the Scottish Crown's military campaign against England that culminated at Flodden.[7]

Satire has a strong presence in the sixteenth century. Many of Dunbar's poems provide a sharp critique – at times good-natured, more often scornful and derisive – of contemporary Scottish society, while in Robert Wedderburn's *Complaynt of Scotland* (1550) Dame Scotia – one of the earliest representations of the Scottish nation as a woman – hears the complaints of her three sons, the 'Thrie Estaits' of Scottish society, thus turning the reader's attention from the 'external' threat posed by England (the poem also lingers on the differences that divide the two nations) to Scotland's internal strife. David Lyndsay's (c. 1490–c. 1555) work conveys a more bitter satirical vision, castigating both Church and court, than either Dunbar's or Wedderburn's, culminating in his *Ane Dialog Betwix Experience and ane Courteour* (1555). A serious meditation over the troubled condition of Scotland in the sixteenth century characterises also the poetry of Sir Richard Maitland (1496–1586), whose role as collector of Scottish poetry represents in itself a lasting 'nation-building' project. Among the few women poets of this period, Christian Lindsay (*fl.* 1580s) engages in political and social matters. Regional rather than national loyalties are negotiated in the humorous Gaelic *spaidsearachd* genre, a kind of flyting where two female speakers dispraise each other's clans or home regions (including the inhabitants) while extolling their own. Examples (both anonymous) include 'A' Ghriadach Dhonn' (*'The Brownhaired Girl-child'*, c. 1550) and 'An spaidsearachd Bharrach' (*'The Barra Saunter'*, c. 1620).

In other kinds of Gaelic poetry, the seventeenth century saw a shift in the relative proportion of Gaelic/local and national orientations, which continued into the eighteenth century. Irish connections gradually weakened, pan-Gaelic references focused more on Scottish Gaeldom, and national (Scottish and British) themes became more prominent. Partly, the homogenising drive of the modern nation-state became a focus of critique: poetry increasingly responded to cultural, economic and political marginalisation of Gaeldom by the English-speaking mainstream. Cathal MacMhuirich's 'Saoth liom do chor, a Cholla' ('*I grieve for your condition, Colla*', c. 1623–24)[8] criticises the encroachment of central government authority upon formerly more autonomous Gaelic lands. His 'Do ísligh onóir Gaoidheal' ('*The honour of the Gael is lowered*', 1649)[9] laments not only the death of an individual chief, but also the general decline of Gaeldom's status in Scotland. But there are also Gaelic poems which identify with the nation-state, welcome influences from anglophone culture, and adopt pan-Scottish or pan-British political causes shared across ethnic lines.

Anglophone seventeenth-century poetry has remained for a long time relatively uncharted, possibly more for its elusive quality in terms of a narrowly defined Scottishness than for its aesthetic quality. Anglophone poets either do not engage so openly with political and social themes as in the previous centuries or, if they do, their loyalties align with the political and religious factions that divide Britain across national borders in Cromwellian and Restoration times. William Drummond of Hawthornden (1585–1649) chose to write in English and to mould his delicate verses on Petrarch's model – and yet his keen interest in Scottish history (his *History of Scotland during the Reigns of the Five Jameses* was published in 1655) signals, rather than a detachment from his native country, a complex refashioning of national identity as Anglo-Scottish. James Graham, 1st Marquis of Montrose (1612–1650), a soldier and a poet, signed the National Covenant, but subsequently switched his loyalty to King Charles I, and was eventually executed on the gibbet as a Royalist. About thirteen extant poems are attributed to him, among which are the passionate 'On the death of Charles I' and 'Written on the eve of his execution'. In Gaelic poetry, national concerns are strongest in Iain Lom (John MacDonald). 'Cumha Morair Hunndaidh' ('*Lament for the Marquis of Huntly*', 1649) zooms out from the forfeited Huntly estates to the Royalists of the entire nation, all awaiting the return of their king. The poem implores Charles II to take action. 'Cumha Mhontròis' ('*A Lament for Montrose*', 1651) deplores Charles's powerlessness and Scotland's fate under the Cromwellian occupation. The Restoration is marked in 'Crùnadh an dara Rìgh Teàrlach' ('*The Crowning of King Charles II*', 1660). But sub-national loyalties did not disappear. Even poems about national events frequently interpret them through a local, clan-based or Gaelic lens, as in Iain Lom's 'Là Inbhir Lòchaidh' ('*The Battle of Inverlochy*', 1645).

Elizabeth Melville, Lady Culross (c. 1578–c. 1640) should also be mentioned here, as a poet who defined her nation devotionally: her homiletic *Ane Godlie Dreame*, a dream vision poem of a soul's progress, first printed in Scots in 1603, was widely read and loved throughout the seventeenth century (in its anglicised version), and it is still mentioned in discussions of early Scottish Presbyterianism.

Most women poets of the pre-modern age, being largely illiterate or undereducated, voiced their art anonymously, contributing to the development of one of Scotland's most important poetic traditions – ballads and songs (see chapter 12). In the eighteenth century, however (and in Gaelic partly already in the seventeenth), women became more visible. Some composed along similar lines as male poets did: Màiri nighean Alasdair Ruaidh (Mary MacLeod, c. 1615–1707) produced works that are closely akin to the 'male' tradition of official clan panegyrics. Mairghread nighean Lachlainn (c. 1660–post-1749) and Sìleas na Ceapaich (Sìleas MacDonald, 1660s–c. 1729) also tackled supposedly 'male' themes from the public affairs of clan society and national politics. Other women produced a different kind of poetry which gradually defined new areas and shades of national or regional identity and feeling. Jean Elliott's (1727–1805) lyrics in the ballad 'The Flowers of the Forest', commemorating the army of James IV slain with their king at Flodden in 1513, touchingly voices the grief of women at the loss of their men. Susanna Blamire (1747–1794), Scottish by adoption, writes in Scots a memorable portrait of an émigré ('The Nabob') returning to his homeland after thirty years and looking at it through the lens of nostalgia. Janet Little's (1759–1813) only book, *The Poetical Works of Janet Little, the Scotch Milkmaid* (1792), goes a long way to challenge the gendered discourse of the nation, by inscribing herself and working-class women in the national imagined community. In 'Given to a Lady Who Asked Me to Write a Poem', for example, she compares herself to the national Bard, Robert Burns; in 'Verses Written on a Foreigner's Visiting the Grave of a Swiss Gentleman' she engages with a most predictable national icon (William Wallace), and yet 'refuses to adopt one single national perspective'.[10]

The Union of Parliaments (1707) and the two Jacobite risings of 1715 and 1745 mark a dramatic reconfiguration of the imagination of the Scottish nation, both as stateless and politically assimilated to Britain, and as deeply proud and protective of its distinct heritage and cultural identity. Sìleas na Ceapaich combined Jacobitism with a Scottish nationalist perspective. Her 'Do Rìgh Seumas' ('*To King James*', c. 1714/1715) punningly compares the Union to a poisoned onion, employs the 'bought and sold for English gold' theme, and demands a Scottish rebellion. Mairghread nighean Lachlainn is less passionate about national politics. She mainly focuses on the clan, contrasting the MacLeans' proud history with their current low fortunes, but asserting that a sense of community survives. Usually, pan-Gaelic and national frameworks feature only as far as they affect the clan. Her support for Jacobitism seems perfunctory, a matter of clan loyalty, but her heart may not be in it. Representative poems include 'Òran' ('*Song*', c. 1704), 'Do dh'Ailein MacGilleathain' ('*To Alan Maclean*', 1722), 'Do Shir Eachann, Mac Gilleathain' ('*To Sir Hector Maclean*', c. 1750), and 'Gaoir nam ban Muileach' ('*The wailing of the Mull women*', c. 1716). The latter even hints a reproach to Jacobitism for the misfortunes it has brought on the clan. One of the most passionate Jacobite poets was Alasdair mac Mhaighstir Alasdair (Alexander MacDonald, c. 1698–1770). His patriotism veers between wider British identifications hinted in 'Òran a rinneadh 'sa bhliadhna 1746' ('*A song composed in the year 1746*') to the Scottish nationalism of 'Fuigheall' ('*Fragment*', post-1745), which mentions Jacobitism in the same breath with Bannockburn. He also defends the Gaelic language and culture against Lowland and English hostility, for instance in 'Moladh an ùghdair don t-seann chànain Ghàidhlig' ('*The author's praise of the old Gaelic language*'), 'Am breacan uallach' ('*The proud plaid*', c. 1747) and 'Fuigheall eile' ('*Another fragment*', post-1746). While defending tradition, he is also a great innovator, and open to Lowland and Classical influences, as in his songs to the seasons (early 1740s) and 'Guidhe no ùrnaigh an ùghdair don cheòlraidh' ('*The author's prayer to the muses*').

James Macpherson (1736–1796) exemplifies possibly better than anyone else the double pull of assimilation and distinctiveness, establishing himself – like Robert Burns and, in the nineteenth century, Sir Walter Scott – as a most formidable myth-maker and reinventor of Scottish nationhood. His 'prosaic' *Poems of Ossian* (1760–73), by both looking backwards to a mythical and self-contained past, and (implicitly) forward to a progressive British future, fascinatingly bridges Gaelic and Lowland-Scottish/English cultures, the (real or supposed) ancient epic traditions and the themes of modernity. In the same century, Robert Burns's (1759–1796) polyphonic corpus of poetry assembles a veritable encyclopaedia of rural Scottish life and culture. In recording and memorialising ordinary daily details – characters, food, familiar landscapes – as well as in engaging with historical events as much as with folklore, he builds the national space both as universally applicable across culture and history, and as culturally and historically specific. A demotic strain also appears in some Gaelic panegyrics: Alasdair mac Mhaighstir Alasdair's 'Birlinn Chlann Raghnaill' (*'Clanranald's galley'*, post-1750) and Duncan Ban Macintyre's (Donnchadh Bàn Mac an t-Saoir, 1724–1812) 'Rainn gearradh-arm' (*'Verses on arms'*) recognise the contribution of clan commoners (sailors and farmers) to their leaders' success. The eighteenth century also produced one of the earliest known Gaelic poets to compose a sizeable corpus in the *bàrd baile* ('village poet') tradition: Iain mac Fhearchair (John MacCodrum, 1693–1779). Such poetry focuses on people from the local community (rural or urban) and events immediately concerning them, but can also become more widely known.

In the nineteenth century, Scotland's popular traditions and 'romantic' past loom large in the work of James Hogg (1770–1835) and Sir Walter Scott (1771–1832). Both collectors of ballads and songs, poets and novelists, they share many interests, but are divided by an antagonistic ideological and class perspective. Scott's collection of ballads, *The Minstrelsy of the Scottish Border* (1802), implies an editor/collector that records tradition as an outsider, while Hogg, of a labouring-class background, in *The Mountain Bard* (1807) positions himself firmly as an insider – the Bard himself. Along similar lines, Scott's *Marmion* (1808), set during the battle of Flodden Field, focuses on chivalric themes and aristocratic characters; in Hogg's *The Queen's Wake* (1813), the aristocratic tradition represented by Mary Stuart's jewel-encrusted harp is counterbalanced by the 'Caledonian Harp', standing for the voice of the people, symbolically won by the 'Bard of Ettrick' (Hogg himself) in the bardic contest. The two perspectives stand for two approaches to Scottish nationhood that clash and intersect throughout the nineteenth and great part of the twentieth centuries. It is, however, Scott's vision (to whose complexity the present discussion cannot do justice) that gains the upper hand in the nineteenth century – his immensely popular poems, such as the *Lay of the Last Minstrel* (1805) or *The Lady of the Lake* (1810), contribute towards the reification of Scotland as the Land of Romance in the UK as much as across the world.

Romantic images of native traditions also influenced Gaelic poets like Iain MacGhillEathain (John MacLean, 1787–1848).[11] His 'Òran molaidh do Alasdair MacDhòmhnuill, Tighearna Ghlinne-Garadh' (*'Praise-song to Alexander MacDonnell of Glengarry'*, c. 1815) praises this epitome of Romantic chieftainly self-fashioning for wearing Highland dress and listening to pipe music. Here and elsewhere, the poet also subscribes to the ideal of the picturesque Highland soldier as a valiant stalwart of British national interests – for example, see 'Marbh-rann do Chòirneal Iain Camshron' (*'Elegy for Colonel John Cameron'*) and 'Do Thighearna Òg Cholla, an uair a cheannaich e Bheinn Mhór ann am Muile' (*'To the Young Laird of Coll, when he Bought Benmore in Mull'*). However, his 'Cumha' (*'Lament'*) for Donnchadh MacAonghais (pre-1816) questions whether British military glory is worth the sacrifices.

MacGhillEathain's emigration to Nova Scotia in 1819 fuelled further reflections on nation and belonging. 'Òran do dh' Ameireaga' (*'Song to America'*) and 'Am mealladh' (*'The deception/disappointment'*) foreground initial hardships, alienation and homesickness. Later poems show an increasing reconciliation to diasporic life: comfort and cultural continuity are provided by community events, proud ethnic memories, affirmations of transoceanic sympathies, print media, moral reflections on vexation as an inevitable part of human existence, and the progress of colonial 'cultivation' – see 'Am bàl Gàidhealach' (*'The Gaelic gathering'*, 1826), 'Òran do Alasdair MacDhòmhnuill, Tighearna Ghlinne-Garadh, an déidh a bhàis' (*'Song to Alexander MacDonnell of Glengarry, after his death'*, 1828), 'Seann Albainn agus Albainn Ùr' (*'Old Scotia and Nova Scotia'*), 'Craobhsgaoileadh an t-soisgeil san tìr seo' (*'The propagation of the Gospel in this country'*, c. 1830) and 'Òran don *Chuairtear*' (*'A Song to the Traveller'*, c. 1842).[12]

Diasporic life (this time of formerly rural Gaels in Scottish cities) also looms large in the poems of Màiri Nic a' Phearsain (Mary MacPherson, known as Màiri Mhòr nan Òran/Big Mary of the Songs, c. 1821–1898). She likewise veers between nostalgia and a celebration of diasporic cultural survival, e.g. in 'Fàgail Eilean a' Cheò' (*'Leaving the Isle of Mist'*), 'Deoch-slàinte Gàidheil Ghrianaig' (*'A Toast to the Gaels of Greenock'*) and 'Camanachd Ghlaschu' (*'The Glasgow Shinty Match'*, 1876).

Poets also addressed the Highland Clearances which threatened the social community in the rural homelands, and supported the land rights movement which aimed to redress those wrongs. Examples include Màiri Mhòr's 'Ceatharnaich Bheàrnaraigh' (*'The Bernera Heroes'*, 1874), 'Fàistneachd agus beannachd do na Gàidheil' (*'Prophecy and blessing to the Gaels'*, 1880s), and her election propaganda piece 'Brosnachadh nan Gaidheal' (*'Incitement of the Gaels'*, 1885), which links the defence of traditional ethnic lifestyles to the emerging mass democracy that transformed the nation-state.

The twentieth century marks yet another fracture in the imagination of the Scottish nation, and opens up one of the most fascinating, kaleidoscopic and controversial chapters in Scotland's literary history. The Scottish Renaissance in particular marks the beginning of a wider and more militant engagement of poets with the idea of Scotland that will continue up to the present day. Among these, Edwin Muir (1887–1959) and Hugh MacDiarmid (1892–1978), who, even though from a markedly different ideological stance (Muir rejected the possibility of an independent contemporary Scottish culture, while MacDiarmid's work focused on asserting and valorising such independence), revisioned Scottishness by looking at the nation's past and its myths and reconceptualised its *lieux de mémoire*. MacDiarmid's *A Drunk Man Looks at the Thistle* (1926) stands out as a stunning modern/ist reinvention of Scots and Scottishness, while Muir's poems also convey a vision of national significance, if only indirect, nostalgic and retrospective (as in 'The Mythical Journey', or 'Scotland 1941'). The pivotal role of Sorley MacLean (Somhairle MacGill-Eain, 1911–1996) in modern Gaelic poetry has often been likened to MacDiarmid's significance for Scottish poetry in English and Scots. Here as well, Scottish traditions are revisited and reconceptualised in a radically innovative manner which at the same time stresses its openness to international alignments and influences. MacLean's long poem 'An Cuilithionn' (*'The Cuillin'*, 1939) – which is actually inspired by MacDiarmid – reviews a vast array of Gaelic, Scottish, British and international social and cultural phenomena (past, present and future) through the common lens of class inequality and revolutionary socialism. MacLean's international outlook does not, however, undermine his concern with the preservation of local cultural specificities. This is evident in his anxiety about language death – a theme shared by various other Gaelic poets. In 'Tha na beanntan gun bhruidhinn' (*'The mountains are speechless'*), MacLean asserts the centrality of language to a sense of belonging, warning that the country's landscape and history will become unintelligible if Gaelic is allowed to disappear.

The number of women poets that joined in the national debate in this century is remarkable: from Violet Jacob (1863–1946) and Marion Angus (1865–1946) to Nan Shepherd (1893–1981) and Helen Cruickshank (1886–1975), they brought in a new dimension, often ironic, ecocritical and regional, domestic and irreverent in respect to patriarchal ideas of nationhood.

The openly revolutionary socialism which permeates certain works by MacDiarmid and MacLean is not the only form of internationalism that complicates attitudes to nationhood. Another is the kind of cosmopolitanism that informs Christopher Whyte's (Crìsdean MacIlleBhàin,

b. 1952) poems. While he, too, is sensitive to class (e.g. in 'An Glaschu, sa Ghearran fhuar'/'*In Glasgow, in the February Cold*', late 1980s), his left-wing sympathies are less pervasive, and his international outlook seems equally owed to his highly international life: he has lived in Italy and Hungary, and his collections *Uirsgeul/Myth* (1991), *An tràth duilich* (*The Difficult Time*, 2002) and *Bho leabhar-latha Maria Malibran/From the Diary of Maria Malibran* (2009) contain a high density of continental European settings, subjects and references.

The debates surrounding the referenda about devolution in 1979 and 1997 and about independence in 2014 marked a growing militancy of poets within widening demands for autonomy – a 'poethical' approach that has revolutionised politics by establishing alternative discursive arenas (more visibly so in the recent, imaginative and passionate referendum campaign).[13] The nationalist debates of the 1970s are strongly reflected in Ruaraidh MacThòmais's (Derick Thomson, 1921–2012) poetry collection *Saorsa agus an Iolaire* (*Freedom and the Eagle*, 1977). His disappointment with the failed 1979 referendum is voiced in 'Rabaidean' ('*Rabbits*') and '1707–1979' (*Creachadh na clàrsaich/Plundering the Harp*, 1982). The resurgence of the 1990s is reflected in his collection *Meall Garbh/The Rugged Mountain* (1995) and in the work of Anna (Anne) Frater (b. 1967), a student and, poetically, a follower of MacThòmais. Her collection *Fon t-Slige/Under the Shell* (1995) contains various nationalist poems. Another relevant poem is Frater's 'Semaphore', published in Donny O'Rourke's evocatively titled anthology *Dream State* (second edition, 2002 [1994]). Among the most original voices, Edwin Morgan (1920–2010), Scotland's first official Makar (the National Poet for Scotland), foregrounds his cosmopolitan and fluid vision of Scotland, as in *From Glasgow to Saturn* (1973) and *Sonnets from Scotland* (1984). His successor, Liz Lochhead (b. 1947), appointed in 2011, has brought humane wit and a subtle feminist perspective to the Makar's role – her poems (collected in 2003 in *The Colour of Black and White: Poems 1984–2003*), as much as her plays, engage with the contemporary, showing a deep commitment to the ideals of social justice and equity. More recently, Robert Crawford's (b. 1959) collection *Testament* (2014) has combined lyrics of love, family and inheritance with a passionate engagement with the themes of nationhood and independence.

Not all those who love and identify with the Scottish nation, however, want to see it as an independent state. The 2014 referendum campaign was characterised by a passionate debate that involved deeper emotions than those usually at stake in political confrontations. These, along with the complex relationship that binds England to Scotland, have been memorably voiced by Scottish poet Carol Ann Duffy (b. 1955), the first woman to hold the post of Poet Laureate, in 'September 2014', a poem published in the *Guardian* on the day after the referendum: 'A thistle can draw blood, / so can a rose, / growing together / where the river flows, shared currency, / across a border it can never know […]'.[14]

The independence debate continues. Hence, further poetic engagements with this issue (on both sides) are likely to follow – adding new facets to the complex story of nation and home in Scottish literature.

CHAPTER FIFTEEN

Protest and Politics

Wilson McLeod and Alan Riach

Protest and politics are the provenance of certain forms of poetry, some explicitly engaged as contagious public rhetoric, intended to help bring about action, some more implicit in their political engagement. Scottish poetry is rich in poetic traditions of protest, exemplified in work with specific local and personal reference, or more general reference to national identity and language, and, at least since the 1970s, to the imperatives of feminism. Yet nuanced poems engaging political preference, written in protest but unemphatic, are significant aspects of this story. Arguably the most politically passionate American poet of the twentieth century, Edward Dorn, once said that the modern world was characterised by the search for an adequate exclamation, but the anger, political authority and strength of protest in his work was sustained not by shouting, but rather through commitment, intensity, and a subversive wit and sense of humour that might help bring down the worst excesses of tyranny.[1] The humanist journalist Christopher Hitchens once wrote: '[t]he people who must never have power are the humourless. To impossible certainties of rectitude they ally tedium and uniformity.'[2] This chapter highlights some of the poems of explicit protest and political engagement precipitated by historical developments, while acknowledging that all poetry is intrinsically opposed to tedium, humourlessness and desensitisation.

The earliest most explicit political poems of protest arise from the Scottish Wars of Independence (c. 1296–c. 1357): *The Bruce* (c. 1375) by John Barbour (c. 1320–1395) and *The Wallace* (c. 1477) by 'Blind' Hary (c. 1440–1492). The poems were written within two hundred years of the events, and were major contributions to a defining theme in Scottish myth, history and literature: that of freedom from oppression.

There is, perhaps surprisingly, little Gaelic poetry from before the seventeenth century that deals with 'the matter of Scotland' or with specific political questions of national significance. In part this is because the learned poets of the classical period (c. 1200–c. 1650) were often focused on Ireland rather than Scotland.³ The most important and most studied text is the so-called 'Flodden poem' in the Book of the Dean of Lismore, probably composed for the Earl of Argyll on the eve of the battle of Flodden in 1513, which appears to urge vigorous national resistance against the encroaching English. But there are serious difficulties of interpretation, and the poem is very much an outlier rather than a representative text of a well-developed strand in the Gaelic literary tradition.⁴

The humanitarian impulse is magnified and eloquent in *Ane Satyre of the Thrie Estaitis* (1552–54) by David Lyndsay (c. 1490–c. 1555), where John the Common-weill engages the allegory and justifies the impulse for reformation. The corrupt authority of nobility, merchants and Church is confronted by the figures representing those outside the governmental system – the rest of us – demanding fair and equal treatment. This is a key theme, present implicitly even in William Dunbar's poem in celebration of the marriage of King James IV and Margaret Tudor in 1503, 'The Thrissil and the Rois' ['*The Thistle and the Rose*'], when Dame Nature advises the Lion, King of Beasts, to do law 'elyk [alike] to aips and unicornes'.⁵ A central myth of egalitarianism is emphasised here, even in the hierarchical structure of the court.

After the Wars of Independence and the Reformation, in the centuries before and after the Union of the Crowns in 1603, the most significant political poetry was deeply coded, negotiating religious loyalties in the political arena. Alexander Montgomerie (c. 1555–1597) was embroiled in the transition from the reigns of Mary, Queen of Scots and Elizabeth I of England, through to that of James VI of Scotland and I of the United Kingdom. As a Catholic supporter of Mary, Montgomerie carefully embedded messages in the political and religious allegory of his long poem *The Cherrie and the Slae* (1597). His older contemporary George Buchanan (1506–1582) was one of the most significant literary and political figures of the sixteenth century, poet, playwright, historian, intellectual humanist scholar, teacher of the great French essayist Michel de Montaigne, Mary, Queen of Scots and later of her son, later James VI and I. A native Gaelic-speaker from near lower Loch Lomond, he was deeply impressed that the Gaels had held on to their language and culture for more than two thousand years. A Catholic who committed himself to the Reformation and joined the Reformed Protestant Church in the 1560s, he published *De Jure Regni apud Scotos* in 1579. Here Buchanan says that all political power resides in the people, and that it is lawful and necessary to resist kings if they become tyrants; he was basing his argument at least partly on his understanding of the clan system. There were numerous attempts to suppress this work in the century following its publication.

The violence of the border ballads and a sense of Christian piety informed the short and violent life of James Graham, Marquis of Montrose (1612–1650). A Royalist soldier and strategist who fought for Charles I against the Covenanters, Charles ordered him in 1646 to desist and he went into exile in France. Proclaiming his loyalty to Charles II on his accession in 1649, he returned to Scotland, became his captain-general, and was betrayed, captured and hanged. His poems arise from the heights and depths of his political career and religious belief as in 'Lines written on the eve of his execution':

> Let them bestow on every airth a limb,
> Then open all my veins, that I may swim
> To thee, my Maker, in that crimson lake,
> [...]
> Lord, since thou knowest where all these atoms are,
> I'm hopeful thou'lt recover once my dust,
> And confident thou'lt raise me with the just.

Charles's cause and Montrose's campaign found widespread support in Gaeldom. From the 1640s Gaelic poetry became deeply engaged with national and international politics, increasingly so following the ejection of James VII in 1688 and the subsequent Jacobite risings. While by no means all Gaels supported the Royalist and Jacobite cause, the great bulk of the surviving literature is unquestionably Royalist or Jacobite in sympathy. Much of the poetry is strongly ideological, built on the principle of the divine right of kings and the importance of loyalty to the just monarch. The installation of the Hanoverian monarchs was a particular affront, as expressed forcefully by Alasdair mac Mhaighstir Alasdair (Alexander MacDonald, 1698–1770) in his 'Òran a rinneadh sa bhliadhna 1746' ('*A song composed in the year 1746*'):

> O! 's caol an teud, a Dheòrs',
> Air na sheinn thu gu trì rìoghachdaibh;
> Gur meallt' an t-achd le 'n chleòc
> Iad thusa nad rìgh oirnn;
> Tha leth-cheud pears' us còrr

> As faisge fuil us tagraichean
> Na thusa san Roinn Eòrp' [...]

O, thin's the string, King George, / On which thou'st harped to win three realms; / And false the Act [of Succession] which clad / Thee with the kingship over us; / Full fifty folk and more / Have better claims, and truer blood / Than thou, in Europe's continent [...][6]

Although in the Gaelic context Jacobitism developed as an expression of the relatively powerless against the powerful, it was by no means a progressive ideology. Clan panegyric, rooted in the medieval tradition but coming into flower in vernacular Scottish Gaelic in the seventeenth century,[7] was also profoundly conservative, justifying and celebrating a rigidly hierarchical social order.

If the Union of Crowns generated relatively little poetry of direct protest, the Union of the Parliaments in 1707 has been a source of political engagement and poetic protest ever since. Among the most vehement denunciations of the 'parcel o' rogues' who voted the Treaty through is Iain Lom's (John MacDonald, c. 1624–c. 1710) 'Òran an aghaidh an Aonaidh' ('*A song against the Union*'), which attacks the key proponents of Union in turn, concluding with a ferocious threat against the Earl of Seaforth:

> Ach nam faighinn mo raghainn
> Is dearbh gu leaghainn an t-òr dhuit,
> A-staigh air faochaig do chlaiginn
> Gus an cas e do bhòtainn.

But if I had my way, / truly I would melt gold for you, / and inject it into the shell of your skull / until it would reach your boots.[8]

'Rule Britannia' (1740) was written by James Thomson (1700–1748), thirty-three years after the Union and twenty-five years after the 1715 Jacobite rising, and in the context of Hanoverian court politics which sought to support the Union under the model 'Patriot King', Frederick, Prince of Wales, who was opposed to his father George II.[9] 'The Tears of Scotland' (1746) by Tobias Smollett (1721–1771) is a bitter lament written in the aftermath of Culloden.[10] Jean Elliot (1727–1805), in her version of 'The Flowers of the Forest' (1756), was ostensibly setting words to a traditional tune associated with the Battle of Flodden (1513), which marked the disastrous end of James IV's Renaissance court.[11] However, the context clearly makes the lament keenly appropriate for the post-Culloden era.

Robert Fergusson (1750–1774), in 'Lines, to the Principal and Professors of the University of St Andrews, on their superb Treat to Dr Johnson' (1773), responded to establishment sycophants and Johnson's denigration of Scots with a menu including haggis, sheep's head, four black trotters, white and black puddings and oatcakes. In 'To Dr Samuel Johnson. Food for a New Edition of his Dictionary' (1773), Fergusson satirises Johnson's Latinate style and questions his understanding of Scotland, addressing him as: 'Great Pedagogue!' coming from 'Thames's banks to Scoticanian shores, / Where Lochlomondian liquids undulize'. Fergusson wishes 'blackest execrations' on Edinburgh for welcoming Johnson and advises the Englishman to 'hie you home, / And be a malcontent, that naked hinds, / On lentils fed, could make your kingdom quake, / And tremulate Old England libertized!'

Johnson's visit to Scotland was in the aftermath of Culloden, and the demolition of Highland culture and the sorrow at its passing were figured in stark political poems. One of the century's most vigorous satires is 'Òran don Ollamh MacIain' ('*A song to Dr Johnson*') by Seumas Mac an t-Saoir (1727–1799).[12] Mac an t-Saoir's poem takes as its premise Johnson's abuse of hospitality: after enjoying his accommodation among the people of Scotland, he returns to England to spread slander and lies about them. Mac an t-Saoir erupts into fireworks of abuse:

> Gur tu an losgann sleamhainn tàrrbhuidh,
> 'S tu màigein tàirrngneach nan dìgean,
> Gur tu dearc-luachrach a' chàthair
> Ri snag 's ri màgaran mìltich;
> 'S tu bratag sgreataidh an fhàsaich,
> 'S tu 'n t-seilcheag ghrànda, bhog, litheach […]

You're the slimy yellow-bellied toad, / You're the sluggish crawler of ditches, / You're the lizard of the swamp / Which creeps and slithers through sweet-grass, / You're the ugly wasteland caterpillar, / You're the foul, soft, slimy snail […][13]

This is a poem whose vividness deserves to be far more widely known.

By the end of the century, Robert Burns (1759–1796) had written not only to condemn the Union as a betrayal brought about by 'A Parcel of Rogues' (1791) but also to incite 'patriotic fire' in 'Scots Wha Ha'e' (1793), composed after reading William Hamilton of Gilbertfield's (1665–1751) 1722 version of Hary's *The Wallace*. However, Burns also wrote in protest against the threat of French invasion of the United Kingdom in 'Does haughty Gaul invasion threat?' (1795). He was hedging his bets.

Much political poetry expressed regret for what had happened in tones of nostalgia, lament and exile, but in the later nineteenth century a new tone was heard, demanding change. Industrialising Scotland altered the nation's character. The rate of urbanisation in Scotland, the rising number of emigrants leaving the country in the early nineteenth century, and the increasing concentration of the population in the cities, particularly in Glasgow, had a deep legacy. Thomas Campbell (1777–1844), one of the most popular poets of his era, in 'Lines on Revisiting a Scottish River', laments so-called progress as industrial effluvia has turned the rippling beauty of the Clyde into a seething, polluted mess: 'And call they this Improvement?' Campbell's Clyde is now a place where 'Nature's face is banish'd and estranged' and the riverbanks are 'cover'd o'er' with 'sooty exhalations' where 'brick-lanes smoke, and clanking engines gleam' in the effort 'To gorge a few with Trade's precarious prize [...]'.[14]

Similar abhorrences are expressed in the poetry of Elizabeth Hamilton (1758–1816), William Thom (1799–1848) and Marion Bernstein (1846–1906). Tom Leonard's ground-breaking anthology *Radical Renfrew* (1990)[15] drew attention to a vast amount of neglected poetry of nineteenth-century industrial Scotland and crucial ways of reading it, including consideration of emigrant poets like John Barr (1812–1892), who went from Paisley to New Zealand to sing the praises of a non-industrialised social order in which capitalist economics might be developed without tyranny and the agonies of class discrimination. Other poets – particularly women writing between 1850 and 1900 – reflect and protest about the social conditions of industrialised Scotland. Janet Hamilton (1795–1873) writes in 'Oor Location' of 'the whisky-shop and pawn' and the 'ruination' characteristic in cities of men 'fechtin', drinkin''. Jessie Russell (1850–1923) in 'Woman's Rights versus Woman's Wrongs' is magnificently unforgiving in her feminist priorities. Many wives are beaten by husbands who never suffer due punishment: 'a life for a life, and the murderer's hung, and we think not the law inhuman, / Then why not the lash for the man who kicks or strikes a defenceless woman?'

The poetry of James Young Geddes (1850–1913) allows that industry might have a strange beauty but it is charged with moral force at the civic hypocrisies evident in industrial Dundee. 'The New Jerusalem' ('Machineries / Are there whose vast pulsations tear and thrash / the groaning air') and 'The New Inferno' (full of 'harsh dissonance') are characteristic (*The New Jerusalem and Other Verses*, 1879), while 'Glendale & Co. (After Walt Whitman)' (in *The Spectre Clock of Alyth and Other Selections*, 1886) begins with the great American poet's sense of social justice, and employs Whitman's long line, chanting a litany of bitter indignation to describe a firm that has 'grown from small beginnings' to something now hellish that 'dominates the town': 'Lit up at night, the discs flare like angry eyes in watchful supervision, impressing on the minds of the workers the necessity of improving the hours and minutes purchased by Glendale & Co.'. The bitterness of the poem escalates in Blakean indignation. Geddes is Scotland's most radical political poet between Burns and MacDiarmid.

Both John Davidson (1857–1909) and James ('B. V.') Thomson (1834–1882) were significant influences on MacDiarmid and T. S. Eliot. Thomson's visionary poem *The City of Dreadful Night* (1880) is a phantasmagorical nocturnal journey through a nightmare city of sleepwalking, enervated, alienated individuals. For Thomson, injustice is not curable in economic terms though the moral authority of his poem might charge us to address social and remediable economic causes of alienation. John Davidson, in his Nietzschean, pessimistic *Testaments* – 'The Testament of a Vivisector' is perhaps the most repellent poem of the century and 'The Testament of a Man Forbid' begins characteristically, 'Mankind has cast me out' – views political developments with fearful disdain. Writing in the working-class voice of the wage-slave in 'Thirty Bob a Week', he inhabits the world of the industrial worker:

> It's a naked child against a hungry wolf;
>   It's playing bowls upon a splitting wreck;
> It's walking on a string across a gulf
>   With millstones fore-and-aft about your neck;
> But the thing is daily done by many and many a one;
>   And we fall, face forward, fighting, on the deck.

Hopelessness also characterises many of the poems of Robert Buchanan (1841–1901), whose city-poems 'London' and 'Vanity Fair' teem with people and appeal to a popular readership, though their subject is alienation. Desolation, loneliness and elemental, inhuman nature are most powerful in 'Sonnets Written by Loch Coruisk, Isle of Skye'. 'We

Are Fatherless' ends with Nietschean finality: 'There is no God – in vain we plead and call, / In vain with weary eyes we search and guess – / Like children in an empty house [...]'. The protest here is metaphysical and spiritual, more than political.

Although tens of thousands of Gaelic-speaking Highlanders migrated to Lowland cities following the Industrial Revolution, the urban experience is relatively little explored in Gaelic literature. Depictions of the city are generally stereotypical; the urban environment is presented as dirty, loud and culturally barren, and the topic is often little more than a foil for praise of the distant homeland, a mood generally summarised under the term *cianalas*, referring to a mix of homesickness and nostalgia.[16] Occasionally urban poetry attempts to deal with urban difficulties in a humorous manner, notably in the work of Iain MacPhaidein (John MacFadyen, 1850–1935). Only in the twentieth century do Gaelic poets begin to present serious critiques of urban poverty and degradation, in such works as Aonghas Moireasdan's (Angus Morrison) 'Dun Èideann' ('*Edinburgh*') and Sorley MacLean's (Somhairle MacGill-Eain) 'Calbharaigh' ('*Calvary*').

The dominant political issue in nineteenth-century Gaelic poetry, and beyond, was the land question. Much poetry of the Clearances was backward-looking and lacking in political bite; for Sorley MacLean, 'the Highlanders' resistance, political and moral, was [...] very weak', and the poetry of the period reflects 'this impotence'.[17] But there are outstanding exceptions, especially in the work of Uilleam MacDhun-lèibhe (William Livingstone, 1808–1870) and Iain Mac a' Ghobhainn (John Smith, 1848–1880), and from the 1870s on there is a powerful corpus of songs of resistance arising out of the Land Agitation, most notably the work of Màiri Nic a' Phearsain (Mary MacPherson, c. 1821–1898). Even so, there is no real voice of radicalism in this material: the poets tend to work within the confines of Christian teaching or British imperial ideology, or to misallocate the blame to Lowland shepherds or 'Sasannaich'.

A vast international readership born of the diaspora of Scots exiled after the Jacobite risings and the Clearances continued to yearn for images and icons of Scotland that would offer pastoral consolations. The worst excesses of such images indulge sentimentalism to the point of fatality, but emotionally piercing laments and songs of reminiscence and cianalas, such as 'An t-Eilean Muileach' ('*The Isle of Mull*') by Dùghall MacPhàil (1818–1887) or 'The Wild Geese' by Marion Angus (1865–1946), might also have sustained a feeling for the need of redress as well as reaffirming identity.

Scottish poets with immediate experience of the First World War included Roderick Watson Kerr (1893–1960), who, when his poems were first published, during the war, was immediately compared with Siegfried Sassoon, and Joseph Lee (1875–1949), who saw battle in France, writing and drawing pictures from the trenches before he was taken prisoner. There is a taut, bitterly ironic quality to 'The Green Grass': 'The grass grows green on the long, long tracks / That I shall never tread – / Why are we dead?' The earliest poems of Ewart Alan MacKintosh (1893–1917) were heroic glorifications of war but quickly he recognised the horror and waste he was witnessing, and began writing anguished, bitter parodies and Brechtian deflations. 'Departure of the 4th Camerons' begins: 'The pipes in the street were playing bravely / The marching lads went by [...]', but in 'Recruiting' he writes: 'Go and help to swell the names / In the casualty lists. / Help to make a column's stuff / For the blasted journalists'. Charles Murray (1864–1941), in 'Dockens Afore His Peers', a desperately moving, challenging and unsentimental monologue spoken by a soldier at an exemption tribunal, uses the Scots voice to develop the sense of helplessness, human resilience and utter vulnerability in a dramatic monologue with theatrical resonance. One of the most unforgettable poems of protest at war is by Charles Hamilton Sorley (1895–1915), who was killed in the Battle of Loos: 'When you see millions of the mouthless dead / Across your dreams in pale battalions go, / Say not soft things [...]'.

The most impressive Gaelic poet of the First World War was Iain Rothach (John Munro, 1889–1918), whose death in the trenches deprived Gaelic literature of an important modern voice. But Rothach's poetry evokes contemplative serenity rather than anger or condemnation, and some other Gaelic verse from the war was resolutely imperial in tone, celebrating the achievements of the Highland regiments and accepting without question the assertions and assumptions of their political and military leaders. This poetry of empire is an important strand in Gaelic poetry from the mid-eighteenth century onwards,[18] and reminds us that assimilation rather than resistance was the most common political response of Scottish Gaeldom to political and social transformations.

In the immediate aftermath of the First World War, Hugh MacDiarmid (1892–1978) initiated the Scottish Literary Renaissance, a movement both cultural and political, intrinsic with violent protest against the Victorian conventions of Scoto-British mediocrity and self-suppression. The politics of the movement were both nationalist, determined to break down the British Empire and re-establish Scotland as a nation-state, and also socialist, opposed to class division, social hierarchy and exploitation of the working class. Read in this light, even MacDiarmid's early lyrics in Scots are infused with political protest. Far more explicit political protest poems were to come. In the 1930s, MacDiarmid's *Three Hymns to Lenin* emphatically endorsed hopes of a communist revolution delivering a better way of life for all, while 'In the Children's Hospital' and 'At the Cenotaph' comment on royal condescension and on militarism. In the former, a princess visiting a hospital patronises a legless boy, whom MacDiarmid addresses: 'Would the sound of your sticks on the floor / Thundered in her skull for evermore!' The latter condemns: 'Keep going to your wars, you fools, as of yore. / I'm the civilisation you're fighting for!' Against these, MacDiarmid asserts values of human companionship, culture and diversity, identity, languages and arts, in 'Lament for the Great Music' and 'In Talk with Duncan Ban MacIntyre' as well as the most searching of all his philosophical enquiries, 'On a Raised Beach', a profound protest against nihilism and despair, a long and difficult journey through a wasteland of human effort and negligible achievement – human values measured against geological time – to reach a point of affirmation.

After the Second World War, Hamish Henderson (1909–2002) published not only *Elegies for the Dead in Cyrenaica* (1948), a sequence of poems in deep protest against war's indiscriminate waste of life, but also a number of ballads and songs that quickly passed into anonymous familiarity, sung by soldiers without reference to their author. His most popular songs, 'The John MacLean March' and 'Freedom, Come-All-Ye', embody political affirmation of self-determination and protest against racism, social injustice and British imperialism, continuing in the popular repertoire of many singers. Major poets coming to prominence after the war were connected by their experience of that war, often in North Africa, and in varying degrees their protest and political poems arose from that experience: Robert Garioch (1909–1981), Sorley MacLean (1911–1996), George Campbell Hay (1915–1984), G. S. Fraser (1915–1980) and Edwin Morgan (1920–2010). The older generation lived on, and Edwin Muir (1887–1959), in 'The Good Town', describes the insidious circumstance of the creeping chill that turns a community of neighbourly, courteous people into a barren dystopia of prejudice, hostility and ultimately murderous anti-humanity: 'This was the good town once'.

In Scotland, protest was more often found in specific reference to local and linguistic matters. In 'Two Thieves' and 'Aunt Julia', the intense and boiling anger of Norman MacCaig (1910–1996) is built up through restraint, quiet repetition and implicit judgement upon absentee landowners and the imperialism that eradicated the Gaelic language from generations of people – a situation still needing redress. In 'A Man in Assynt', MacCaig describes a specific area of north-west Scotland across millennia, wondering whether the tide will ever turn and people come back to the depopulated landscape. That the crofters of this area have bought their land and repossessed it since the poem was written reminds us that change is indeed possible.[19]

Poetic commentary on contemporary political events in the second half of the twentieth century included poems and popular songs in English, Scots and Gaelic protesting against the presence of nuclear submarines on the Clyde and the rocket range in South Uist, or celebrating the repossession of the Stone of Scone from Westminster. 'Chairlies' by Andrew Tannahill (1900–1986) satirises various figures in history, from Prince Chairlie of Windsor to Chairlie Marx and Chairlie Magne. Equally politicised engagements with language are in 'Unrelated Incidents' by Tom Leonard (b. 1944), where Glasgow working-class speech is the medium through which sophisticated protest is made against class-based assumptions about linguistic authority. This ethos of protest is extended in Leonard's essays in *Reports from the Present* (1995). The political spirit of resistance, while it addressed issues made urgent by contemporary pressure, also reaffirmed its continuity with a longer tradition, in poems such as 'On John MacLean' by Edwin Morgan: 'We are out for life / And all that life can give us! / is what he said, that's what he said'.

For Gaelic poets, the language question has loomed large at least since the eighteenth century, when the threat to the language's survival became an important theme in Gaelic verse.[20] In the twentieth century, the poetic response was more diverse and variegated, sometimes oblique, notably in Iain Crichton Smith's (Iain Mac a' Ghobhainn, 1928–1998) 'Mas e Gàidhlig an cànan' ('*If Gaelic is the language*'):

> Mas e Gàidhlig an cànan
> a bh' ac' ann an Eden,
> an e sin fhèin as coireach
> gu bheil an cionta gar lìonadh
> 's gu bheil sinn cho mollaicht'
> 's nach fhaic sinn le fìrinn
> air Leòdhas beag corrach
> ròsan no frìthean?

If Gaelic is the language / that they spoke in Eden / is that itself the reason / that we're full of guilt / and that we're so accursed / that we can't see with truth / on little rugged Lewis / roses or deer-forests?[21]

Increasingly in the 1970s and 1980s, the voices of women began to be heard more clearly and more self-confidently in Scottish poetry. *Memo for Spring* (1972), the first collection by Liz Lochhead (b. 1947), arose modestly from her own personal experience but altered the scope of Scottish poetry profoundly, and was followed by such militant assertions as the declamatory 'Mirror's Song' and poetic plays such as *Mary Queen of Scots Got Her Head Chopped Off* (1987) and her version of Euripides' *Medea* (2001), with its central portrait of the self-determined, vulnerable, murderous wife and mother. Kathleen Jamie (b. 1962) deepened and developed the poetic authority of women in such work as 'The Queen of Sheba', the manifesto-poem of the authority of women's self-worth, and her tender, fiercely challenging 'nature writing', including the poem 'Crossing the Loch', which insists on the significance of border-crossing, liminality, and the importance of the space where things change. In the explicitly and sometimes flippantly feminist *The World's Wife* by Carol Ann Duffy (b. 1955), in the collection *Held* by Elizabeth Burns (b. 1957) and throughout the work of Jackie Kay (b. 1961), there are poems of subtle, nuanced expression which nevertheless have much to say as protests against the conventions of a society of patriarchal authority, social class-based hierarchy and national subordination in a United Kingdom. They are all vital political engagements with the contemporary. Yet the role of women poets in Gaelic has been rather different. Although new voices emerged in the same period, notably Catrìona NicGumaraid (b. 1947), Màiri NicGumaraid (b. 1955) and Meg Bateman (b. 1959) with their own powerful voices, it could be argued that women were less prominent in the canon of twentieth-century Gaelic verse than was the case in earlier centuries.

Late twentieth- and early twenty-first-century protest and political poetry is evident also in polemics and popular songs. Craig and Charlie Reid (both b. 1962), the popular duo the Proclaimers, through the Thatcher years of industrial closedown of steelworks and social devastation, sang memorably, 'I can't understand why you let someone else rule your land / Cap in hand!' The novelist Alan Bissett (b. 1975), in his poem 'Vote Britain!: My Contribution to the Debate on Scottish Independence' (2012), delivered an attack on the assumptions of unionist preference. The YouTube performance of the poem[22] reached over 66,000 viewers, signifying the continuing adaptation of poets to the opportunities of the new media. As an exemplary polemical poem, it may well, like other poems discussed in this chapter, be read long after its contemporary occasion.

CHAPTER SIXTEEN

Love and Erotic Poetry

Peter Mackay

How do I love thee? Let me count the ways. There is a common tendency when dealing with love poetry, as with love, to itemise, taxonomise or dissect. Take two anthologies of Scottish poetry from the 1970s, for example. Antonia Fraser's 1975 *Scottish Love Poems* identifies twenty-one distinct groupings: 'Celebrations of Love'; 'Wooings'; 'First Love'; 'Longing and Waiting'; 'Encounters'; 'Romantics'; 'Unromantics'; 'Marriages'; 'The Nature of Love'; 'Obsessions'; 'Warnings'; 'Laments'; 'Unrequited Love'; 'Fainthearts'; 'Doomed Love'; 'Farewells'; 'Love Lost'; 'Love in Abeyance'; 'Change and Paradox'; 'Old Loves' and 'Enduring Love'.[1] Meanwhile, Thomas Crawford's 1976 *Love, Labour and Liberty: The Eighteenth-century Scottish Lyric* distinguishes – in its treatments of love lyrics alone – between 'The Gentle Passion', 'Love Longing', 'The Kiss', 'Sensual Love', 'The Brutal Male', 'The Consequences', 'Sodom', 'The Plaintive Strain', 'The Cult of Sentiment', 'Parting and Jilting', 'Young Girls Singing', 'Tales', 'Dialogues', 'Pastoral', 'Highland and Lowland', 'Love's Comedy', 'The Marriage Yoke', 'Love and Money', 'Love and Drink' and – ominously – 'Love and the Kirk'.[2] If there is a superabundance of types or moods of love in these anthologies, there is also a sense that love itself is an immutable, ahistorical category – an unchanging, eternal subject matter for poetry, a series of (seemingly) inevitable moments stretching from initial desire to loss. But there is also a hint – in Crawford's collection at least – at a changing social and political milieu: the inclusion of a 'Sodom' category was not inevitable in a country where homosexuality would remain illegal until 1980 (in England and Wales it had been legalised in 1967). This chapter will examine how the theme of love has been developed in Scottish love poetry through changing social and generic circumstances. It will focus primarily on poetry that is erotic, amatory or bawdy (despite the fact that bawdry has tended to be separated from erotic poetry and critically undervalued, in part simply because it does not take love too seriously[3]), on constraints and restraints that have been placed on love poetry, and on the extent to which love poetry has been used as an escape from, challenge to or joyous explosion of existing social orders, despite the heteronormative (and often misogynistic) critical environment which has traditionally framed love poetry.

To a large extent, love poetry exists in an ongoing dialectic with control, whether that be political, religious or ethical. The manuscript collected by George Bannatyne in the sixteenth century, for example, exists in quite a different context from the taxonomies of Fraser and Crawford. Bannatyne divided his selection of (mainly) Scottish poems and ballads into five categories: 'Ballatis of Theologie', 'Very Singular Ballatis, full of Wisdom and Moralitie etc.', 'Ballatis Mirry, and Uther Solatius Consaittis, Set Furth Be Divers Ancient Poyettis', 'Ballatis of Luve Devydit in Four Pairtis' and 'Fabillis'; the four 'partis' of love ballads are 'Songis Of Luve', 'Contemptis Of Luve and Evill Wemen', 'Contempis Of Evill Fals Vicius Men' and 'Ballatis Detesting Of Luve And Lichery'.[4] These categories suggest a generally negative approach to love and love poetry (especially to 'lechery' and the social 'evils' of love). One thing that is not included within the realm of love poetry is political or patriotic passion. This is perhaps unsurprising – politics and poetry as a whole were a dangerous combination. As James VI would later write in 'Ane Schort Treatise conteining some Reulis and Cautelis to be observit and eschwit in Scottis poesie', 'materis of commoun weill, or other sic grave sene subiectis [...] are to grave materis for a Poet to mell in'.[5] James did not proscribe love poetry, but did try to control and limit it, to temper the power of the erotic in the political realm. In part this was a recognition that for centuries Scottish love poetry had been located precisely at the seat of power and the 'commoun weill'.

The earliest extant Scottish love poetry – excluding Gaelic verse – comes from the royal courts, or their attendant aristocratic spheres, and is explicitly implicated in the institutions and self-reflections of the court and aristocracy, with their intrigues, secrecies and instabilities. The amatory and the political are, in this poetry, almost inextricable;[6] the flesh-and-blood body of a beloved stands in for or simply is the body politic; and desire is at least in part a desire for power.[7] *The Kingis Quair* (c. 1424), for example, generally ascribed to James I and apparently based on the adolescent king's experience of love while in exile in England, explores the convergence of the sovereign's sexual desire and manner of government. As Sally Mapstone comments, the poem 'is expressed from a reflective vantage-point that equates success in love with acquisition of wisdom, and [...] with attainment of kingly self-government' and, as such, 'puts the amatory into an ethical context'.[8] *The Kingis Quair* clearly works within the medieval genre of advisory writing directed at monarchs and nobility, texts such as the pseudo-Aristotelian *Secretum Secretorum*, translated from Arabic to Latin in the mid-twelfth century, and Giles of Rome's *De Regimine Principum*;[9] it has a particular edge, however, since it is the king himself who gives advice. With its reworking of Chaucer and Gower as well as continental models, and 'its subjectivity, structural complexity, choice of the theme of love, and elevated style', the *Kingis Quair* was also a forerunner of and possible spur for an extraordinary flourishing of poetry – and especially courtly love poetry – in Scotland in the fifteenth and sixteenth centuries.[10]

Robert Henryson's *Testament of Cresseid*, the masterpiece of Middle Scots verse, also focuses on (love) poetry as a means of control. Picking up where Chaucer's *Troilus and Criseyde* had left off, Henryson's poem outlines how Cresseid 'offended against the code of love'[11] by betraying Troilus, blasphemed against Venus and Cupid and succumbs to prostitution, leprosy and death; her end is held to be a warning to other women: 'Now, worthie wemen, in this ballet schort, / [...] I monische and exhort, / Ming not your lufe with fals deceptioun'.[12] Where in *The Kingis Quair* it was the control of the king's or prince's libido that was important, in Henryson's poem it is the condemnation and control of female *cupiditas*. As such the poem can be seen to respond to the medieval genre of the *querelle des femmes*, 'the philosophical, cultural and rhetorical debate about the nature of Woman in which there was a resurgence of interest in the mid sixteenth century';[13] and the misogyny of *The Testament of Cresseid*, with its stress on the punishment and abjection of 'aberrant' female sexuality, has led to repeated feminist criticisms of the text, and especially the idea of Cresseid having any agency, 'whether in a legal, moral or spiritual capacity'.[14] Henryson's misogyny is no worse than that of his contemporary, William Dunbar – a master of the bawdy and of sexual puns – or of much of the discourse of the medieval world. For example, the Book of the Dean of Lismore (1512–42), the repository of much of the oldest extant Scottish Gaelic poetry, features a 'Catalogue of Unfaithful Women' among other satirical reactions to dominant courtly love images and symbols.[15]

The Book of the Dean gathers together some of the earliest surviving Gaelic love poetry, work which belongs not to the continental courtly love tradition (or not to that tradition alone) but to the Classical Gaelic tradition shared between Ireland and Scotland. The poems of Muireadhach Albanach Ó Dálaigh, for example, include many traditional motifs of beauty derived from nature; his elegy for Maol Mheadha, his wife, for example, compares her to the whitethorn, the hazel flower and the hazel nut, and praises her 'ivory-white' breast, 'branching hair' and elegant fingers. These are all images which retained currency, without attaining the status of cliché, until the twentieth century (when Gaelic poetry started to place a greater value on innovation rather than generic modulation); in Ó Dálaigh's time they were already codified images of female beauty suitable for religious poetry as well as the elegiac or romantic.[16] Gaelic engagements with the continental *amour courtois*, meanwhile, often exploit – like Scottish poems in Scots and English – the ambiguities of the genre, overturning its conventions in a quasi-Goliardic manner. The work of Iseabail Ní Mheic Cailéin, from the late fifteenth or early sixteenth century (and also preserved in the Book of the Dean of Lismore), by turns faithfully replicates the mores of the *amour courtois* and inverts them outrageously.[17] On the one hand are poems such as the verses beginning 'Atá fleasgach ar mo thí' (*'There's a young man in pursuit of me'*) and 'Is mairg dá ngalar an grádh' (*'Woe to the one whose sickness is love'*), which present standard courtly tropes such as unfulfilled desire, distance from the beloved, and love as a sickness. On the other is the raucous poem in praise of a priest's penis, beginning 'Éistibh, a luchd an tighe-se' (*'Listen, people of this house'*); this poem is particularly important as it provides a female, aristocratic and bodily inversion of a tradition that would generally see a lower-class male poet praising a socially superior woman in ethereal, spiritual and unsustainable idealistic terms.[18]

The poetic expression of female desire also played an important part in the downfall of Mary, Queen of Scots. The 'casket sonnets', 'twelve love poems associated with the queen's name',[19] were discovered in 1567, shortly after the death of Mary's husband, Darnley; in these sonnets, written in French, female sexual desire is portrayed as a dangerous, unreliable force – particularly in a sovereign. The sonnets apparently show the queen willing to give up her kingdom to the rapacious, murderous Bothwell – 'Entre ses mains & en son plein pouvoir / Je metz mon filz, mon honneur, & ma vie, / mon pais, mes subjectz, mon ame / assubiectie est tout à luy' ('In his handis and in his full power, / I put my sonne, my honour, and my lyf, / My contry, my subiects, my soule al subdewit, / To him, and has none vther will')[20] – and so were obviously a potent weapon to those who wished to see her deposed. In the controversy surrounding the casket sonnets, the 'advice to princes' combines with the *querelle des femmes* in a distrust of – and desire to control – female sexuality. As Sarah Dunnigan persuasively argues, the role the sonnets played in the crisis that engulfed his mother's reign shaped James VI's proscriptions against political poetry, despite the fact that love poetry paradoxically remained central to the life of James's own court, both in James's own poetry – notably the ambiguously homoerotic *Ane Metaphoricall Invention of a Tragedie called Phoenix* – and in the work of the poets gathered at his Scottish court, especially Alexander Montgomerie and John Stewart of Baldynneis, in which James took on the role of Cupid or Apollo.[21]

Alongside the courtly and aristocratic love poetry discussed above, there was also a healthy – and often quite distinct – tradition of folk love ballads, preserved through oral tradition, and collected from the late eighteenth century onwards. In Gaelic the ballads composed between the fifteenth and eighteenth centuries offer some of the most emotionally arresting verse in the language. Many of the love songs of this period – sometimes extempore, sometimes the accompaniment to a communal activity such as waulking tweed or rowing – have a spare directness which combines a sense of loss with a brutal (and occasionally fantastical) precision as to how that loss occurred. The eighteenth-century song 'Ailein Duinn' ('*O Brownhaired Allan*'), attributed to Anna Chaimbeul (Ann Campbell) of Scalpay, is a late example: it laments the loss of the singer's beloved Allan, who has been lost at sea and is presumed torn apart by whales. Loss, in this song, is a matter of consumption: using a traditional motif, the singer wishes to drink 'chan ann de dh'fhìon dearg na Spàineadh – / A dh'fhuil do chuim, do chlèibh 's do bhràghad' ('*not of the red wine of Spain – / Of the blood of your body, your chest and your breast*'), and then desires to be 'sa bhall am bheil thus', Ailein, / Ged a b'ann san liadhaig fheamann / No am broinn na muice mara' ('*in the spot where you are, Allan, / Even if that's in the seaweed tangles / Or in the belly of the whale*').[22] There are codified images of beautiful bodies in the songs of this period, with no shortage of 'cìochan corrach' ('*peaked breasts*') and sides as white as 'canach an t-slèibhe' ('*bog cotton*'); but – as in 'Ailein Duinn' – there is also a tendency for bodies (especially the bodies of male loved ones or family members) to endure great violence. Heads fester on stakes, teeth are smashed on rocks, blood is spilt on stones and – in the case of a drowned woman – her body is eaten by eels, her breast milk mingling with mud; these attacks on the body are, to some degree, inversions of the images of strength and solidity central to panegyric poetry.[23] The zenith of this anti-corporeal trend is perhaps the work of Uilleam Ros (William Ross), rightly the most celebrated Gaelic love poet of the eighteenth century, and the closest in spirit to English-language Romantic (or Gothic) love poetry; Ros's unrequited love is itself figured as a parasite on his body (in an extreme version of the notion of love as a disease): 'Tha durrag air ghur ann am' chàil' / A dh'fhiosraich do chàch mo rùn' (*A maggot has hatched in my frame / That has told my tale to all*).[24]

Vernacular folk ballads – as gathered by Allan Ramsay and other collectors in the eighteenth century – made use of a wide range of linguistic registers, an 'array of voices', in R. D. S. Jack's words, 'from Latinate English through English and Anglo-Scots to […] Scots' and ranged from religious love songs to the bawdy, carnivalesque tradition that dated back to the fifteenth-century 'Christis Kirk on the Green'.[25] The linguistic and tonal exuberance of this tradition provided the context and raw material for Scotland's greatest love poet. Robert Burns's love poetry is astonishing for its scope and quality: stretching from the tender 'Red, Red Rose' or 'Rigs of Barley', through the playful 'Coming Thro' the Rye' and 'Green Grow the Rashes, O', to the politically charged bawdry of 'Why Should Na Poor Folk Mowe' (and indeed the earthier versions of 'Coming Thro' the Rye' and 'Green Grow the Rashes, O' published after Burns's death in *The Merry Muses of Caledonia* (1800)). Very often Burns was working with established tunes, poetic forms and images available from the folk tradition; as such some have gone so far to question how far we can call Burns the 'author' of 'A Red, Red Rose', since the images are all to be found in previous songs.[26] But in this song – as in one of Burns's early masterpieces, the cantata 'Love and Liberty', which responds to various poems collected in Allan Ramsay's *Tea-Table Miscellany* (1723–37), such as 'The Happy Beggars' or 'The Merry Beggars'[27] – the conventional imagery is not as important as the heightened, more formally impressive use to which Burns puts that material. Burns could not be accused of subsuming the erotic to the political; many of his lyrics are vibrant evocations of the many moods of love – pleasure, reminiscence, loss, dalliance and so on – for love's own sake. But when there is a political edge to Burns's love poetry it is extremely potent, and at least implicitly attacks the hierarchical nature of the society in which he was writing, as the focus on the love-lives of an illegal underclass in 'Love and Liberty' or indeed all of 'Why Should Na Poor Folk Mowe', with its naming of European monarchs, and its chorus in which sex offers recompense for social inequity – 'The great folk hae siller, and houses and lands / Poor bodies hae naething but mowe'.[28]

The success of Burns's love poetry cast a shadow far into the nineteenth century; less through his radical association of love and liberty, however, than in a sanitised, sentimental version of his vernacular verse, suited to the narrow palate of a 'polite' Victorian reading public. Publications such as the *Whistle-Binkie* anthologies dominated the poetic landscape, with, as Edwin Morgan argues, their 'tightly packed, assiduously produced, biographically annotated, and constantly revised anthologies, in which you would be hard put to find a dozen really good poems, but which seemed so innocuously comic and sentimental, [and] were carefully devised as instruments of social control' aspiring to 'exhibit, to cherish, and to preserve all the tenderness, the refinement, and the genius of the national muse, without the coarseness and licentiousness by which it had been debased'.[29] William Kennedy's 'First Love' is described in the anthology as an 'exquisite ballad [... perhaps] the most finished piece published in modern times', and gives a taste of what was extremely popular verse, with its anachronistic English – using 'Thou', 'hath' and 'think'st' – ballad form and melodrama: 'no knight more faithfully / Ere wore his lady's glove, / Than I within my breast have borne / A first, an only love'.[30] There is a case to be made that the love poems by female writers of this period, such as Joanna Baillie or Carolina Oliphant, Lady Nairne, 'were rarely the soft, gentle pastoral lyrics which were so common of the male song writers of the period', as Kirsteen McCue notes, but were more likely to be 'excited, rhythmic, more physical love lyrics'[31] that expressed 'not an *affected* feeling of things, but real, earnest, genuine feeling'.[32] But even then, any immediacy of feeling was often hidden or nullified by stultifying adherence to generic images or simple rhythmic forms, such as the rhyming couplets of Baillie's poem of unrequited stalking, 'A Proud Lover's Farewell to his Mistress': 'I've track'd thy footsteps o'er the green, / And shared thy rambles oft unseen; / I've linger'd near thee night and day, / When thou has thought me far away!'[33]

Similar limitations are to be found in nineteenth-century Gaelic verse. Much Gaelic love poetry of the period was suffocated by sentimentality, vapidity and vagueness. There was a common sentimentalisation of love and the land; the loss of one or other (or both) encouraged the century's dominant mode, a sub-Romantic 'cianalas' – a sense of longing or home-sickness – that appealed in particular to the growing urban readership for Gaelic literature. 'Seo nam shìneadh air an t-sliabh' ('*Here on the Moor as I Recline*') – by Iain MacLachlainn (Dr John MacLachlan) – strikes a characteristically teary note: 'Seo nam shìneadh air an t-sliabh, / 'S mi ri iargain na bheil bhuam' ('*Here on the moor as I recline, / I pine for her who is not with me*').[34] One of the main achievements of the greatest Gaelic poet of the twentieth century was to reinvigorate love poetry in the language, through a pained exploration of the relationship of love, violence, guilt and political ardour. The 1930s love sequence 'Dàin do

Eimhir' by Sorley MacLean (Somhairle MacGill-Eain) bypassed the example of the Twilight-era folklorists to engage directly with the medieval courtly love tradition (as filtered through centuries of Gaelic literature) in the context of contemporary poetry, philosophy and politics from across Europe. Much of the power of MacLean's own 'Dàin do Eimhir' comes – as in Hugh MacDiarmid's early lyrics – from the tension between a universal perspective *sub specie aeternitatis* and emotion as it is lived and experienced on the human scale, as here in 'Dàn L': 'Chan eil anns a' bhròn ach neoni / 's chan eil anns a' ghaol ach bruan / fa chomhair nan reul a' sgaoileadh / 's an saoghal a' dol 'na chuairt' (*'Grief is only a nothing / and love is only a crumb / in the face of the stars extending / and the Earth going round'*)[35]. The 'Dàin do Eimhir', reworking the *amour courtois* tradition, cycle through many different tensions that ultimately render the poet's beloved necessarily unattainable: the conflict between love and political commitment – the belief that if the poet does not fight in the Spanish Civil War he is not worthy of Eimhir's love, but, if he does fight, then he will die and never experience her love; a seeming contradiction between giving love now or writing love for eternity; the sense that if the poet's desire attains its object then it will destroy her, like a pack of wolves chasing its prey; or the disjunction between poetic artifice and felt emotion, which leads MacLean to desire to lop off 'le faobhar-rinn gach àilleachd / a chuir do bhòidhche 'nam bhàrdachd' (*'with sharp blade every grace / that your beauty put in my verse'*).[36]

The sensuousness, torment and gusto of the 'Dàin do Eimhir' have been hugely influential for many subsequent Gaelic poets (and indeed non-Gaelic poets – Sydney Goodsir Smith's *Under the Eildon Tree* (1948), a sequence of Scots poems about 'luve's arcane delirium',[37] was written while he shared a house with MacLean). Aonghas MacNeacail, Meg Bateman, Rody Gorman and Kevin MacNeil – among others – have, following MacLean, written love poetry which marries traditional motifs and elements from different cultures, including North American, European and Chinese literature and philosophy. Christopher Whyte (Crìsdean MacIlleBhàin), meanwhile, also heavily influenced by MacLean (and a fine editor of MacLean's work), has used Gaelic poetry as a way of presenting homosexual love and desire. His critical work – especially his queer readings of Scottish literature – has also opened up tempting approaches to previous Gaelic love poetry. In songs, for example, whose creators are unknown and that employ stock images of masculine or feminine beauty – thighs like oak-trunks, skin as white as bog-cotton – how sure can we always be that it is a heterosexual voice speaking?

Such questions are apposite in late twentieth-century Scottish poetry where the normative nature of heterosexual desire and love has been utterly exploded. The importance of Edwin Morgan in that process is hard to overstate. Morgan did not publicly come out until 1990, almost forty years after the publication of his first collection, and as Whyte has commented, throughout his career Morgan's love poetry was built upon a 'doubleness' or an 'extra space' in which ambiguity rules and the possibility of multiple readings persists.[38] This is certainly true of many poems in Morgan's *The Second Life* (1968): 'One Cigarette', for example, where the poet's lover has already departed the scene, or 'Strawberries', where the gender of the lover is carefully avoided. In these poems there is a combination of joyous celebration with dark foreboding – the storm that is presaged at the end of 'Strawberries' or the violence threatened in 'Glasgow Green'. For Morgan, this combination of the 'romantic and the realistic' came to some extent from a positive 'repression', from the sense that 'it's very hard to imagine a thoroughly joyful art that comes out of no tension',[39] a tension imagined in 'Glasgow Green' as being between two worlds, two lives, that of 'married love' and a 'sea of desire' whose 'waves break here, in this park, / splashing the flesh as it trembles / like driftwood through the dark'.[40]

Perhaps because of the weight of the traditions of love poetry, and the *jouissance*[41] possible in unsettling these weighty traditions, much of the best contemporary Scottish love poetry – like Morgan's – has been written from homosexual, lesbian or feminist perspectives. The work of Liz Lochhead introduced a striking feminist voice into Scottish love poetry, a voice that – as in the poem 'Smuggler' from *Dreaming Frankenstein* (1984) – ambiguously 'explains it [love] another way'.[42] This process of 'explaining it another way' has continued through the work of Carol Ann Duffy and Jackie Kay. In Duffy's love poetry, there is – as in Lochhead's – an undermining of the masculine power politics that pervade the genre, and in particular an attack on the male lover's gaze. In 'Oppenheim's Cup and Saucer', from *Standing Female Nude* (1985), for example, the element of reflection in a lesbian encounter is central: 'As she undressed me, her breasts were a mirror / and there were mirrors in the bed. She said Place / your legs around my neck, that's right. Yes'.[43] This is unsentimental, active love poetry – romantic and realistic, one might say – and completely removed from the assumption of heterosexual normality involved in much love poetry and, indeed, in the taxonomies of love poetry discussed earlier; crucially, by overturning the male lover's gaze some space is opened up in which love poetry is not controlled and circumscribed.

In general, what recent Scottish love poetry has shown is the possibility of the genre to provide joyous excess, of being able to return to the most clichéd of themes – erotic or romantic love, obsession and loss – and still find a fresh, startling, and more than true image, as in 'Swim', the fourth section of the title sequence of Jackie Kay's 1993 collection *Other Lovers*:

> So, at the end of a perfect rainbow
> you have upped and left, and I
> have taken to swimming a hundred
> lengths of breast-stroke per day.
> This is the way of love.
> Even swimming, I am obsessed
> with the way your feet arc
> when stroked, your legs,
> the long length of them,
> how I could have you all worked
> up in seconds. My fingers
> doing the butterfly, you saying,
> *Don't stop Don't stop Don't stop.*[44]

CHAPTER SEVENTEEN

Faith and Religion

Meg Bateman and James McGonigal

This chapter deals with traces and erasures in a most perplexing area of human life: the awkward seriousness of faith, past and present, and its otherness. It describes poets writing within the context of a post-Reformation Scotland that was in many ways distrustful of the life of the senses upon which religious liturgy, music and also poetry depend. It records other poets speaking out of a more ancient and oral pre-Christian Gaelic culture deeply at odds with the Church powers that had mainly supplanted it – and also the paradox that most Gaelic communities came to embrace the new Protestantism, and to be defined, indeed, by a strictly Calvinistic cast of mind. Finally we consider contemporary Scottish poetry composed in a 'postmodern' and 'post-religious' age, where religion nevertheless seems oddly resilient, with global and ethnic conflicts often defined along religious lines.

Scotland has its own long record of spiritual warfare, iconoclasm and bloodshed. The Scots word 'thrawn' ('uncompromising') is often used almost admiringly of people likely to follow their own path of commitment. Perhaps this stubborn streak is what has kept religious differences at the centre of Scottish cultural life for centuries, and has left across the landscape evidence of the cost of many divergences of faith. There are the mysteriously carved Pictish stones, the many ruined abbeys and ancient empty churches and Celtic crosses with weather-worn carvings. And there are the many extant Churches (albeit with declining congregations in the main) whose denominations record frequent schisms and quarrels from the sixteenth-century Reformation onwards – Protestant or Calvinistic values of individual interpretation of Scripture and justification by faith seemed almost to foster divergence.

Unexpected resonances from a spiritual, sometimes pre-Christian, past are also part of Scottish literature's depiction of forces that belong in the domain of religion: the human response to the superhuman; to the sublime or numinous power of a presence beyond this world yet sensed within the world. This may be perceived as an evil presence. In the Gaelic tradition, the pre-Christian gods and earth goddesses have become euhemerised as heroes or fairies, and demonised as ogresses or monsters. Colin Manlove describes how often in Scottish writings the supernatural suddenly bursts through into mundane reality, an individual apparition of disruptive force, forcing itself into normality and changing it remorselessly.[1] The figure of Gil-Martin in James Hogg's *The Private Memoirs and Confessions of a Justified Sinner* (1824) is perhaps the best known of such figures in prose. In poetry, we might cite the supernatural beings that haunt the earlier Border ballads, or their recognisable descendants in the early twentieth-century poems of Marion Angus (1866–1946); but poetry's most vivid example is surely the sudden apparition of light and devilish music from within the abandoned kirk in Robert Burns's 'Tam o' Shanter' (1791). Even ruined churches of the old religion in beautiful remote places, some abandoned maybe centuries before the Reformation, can shock the dozy consciousness awake. Such a sense of an immanent spiritual presence within the landscape persists in contemporary Scottish poetry, although poets of the present generation might hesitate to call their commitment to modern ecological values a 'faith'.

Tracing such poetic motifs across time is certainly possible through poetry, even where the paths of faith have so often been distressingly at odds. Poems counter the convenient political denial of previous faith, since their imagistic compression, symbolism and patterns of sound are deliberate devices of memory and commemoration. In them we can follow the continuities and bifurcations of Scotland's troubled relationship with religion – its people's 'courage beyond the point and obdurate pride' (to use Edwin Muir's description in 'Scotland 1941') that has left a landscape, both physical and cultural, of attempted erasures for poets of succeeding generations to address. Poetry can be a sounding board, then, for ancestors who built those ruins that can yet be made to speak.

It is possible to do little more here than to chart a trajectory of Scotland's poetry of faith. This begins in religious literature with the monastic and missionary Church of Columba and his Irish monks in the sixth century, which countered in poetry the heroic oral traditions of the pre-Christian faith it aimed to supplant. Within a Christian Scotland, the layered signification of the medieval makars, Henryson (c. 1424–c. 1506) and Dunbar (c. 1456–c. 1513), was created out of a European and Catholic (there was no other) philosophical perspective. This in turn was overthrown by the thoroughgoing Calvinistic reshaping of society at the Reformation, releasing vernacular and individualistic energies from Bible reading, preaching and communal singing of translated Psalms. Such revolutionary impetus gradually became formalised across society, and eventually as oppressive for many as the regime it replaced – and thus, in its turn, open to challenge not only through Enlightenment ideas but through poetic satire and simple human song and wit. Meanwhile, in the Gaelic world, the military and legal crushing of a culture following two failed Jacobite risings was no light matter: here an evangelical creed of rebirth and redemption offered an alternative to the heroic ideal, and a strong identification with reformed religion.

The Victorian age brought new challenges, not only to religious faith but also to poets. For how was poetry to encompass the vastness of technological development, the attendant shifts of population from the land to new conurbations, and the ambiguities of imperial conquest, emigration and administration in which many Scots took part? Hamish Whyte's Glasgow anthology *Mungo's Tongues* (1993) records the perceptions of Janet Hamilton (1795–1873), Alexander Smith (1829–1867) and James Macfarlan (1832–1862) of human life within that fiery industrial world. Gaelic poets such as Neil Macleod (1843–1913) engaged with the temperance movement and music hall to write cautionary and edifying songs for the Lowland Gaelic diaspora. Later, and making his uncertain way as a literary journalist in London, James Thomson (1834–1882) would explore the depths of alienation in urban mass society in *The City of Dreadful Night* (1874), as Faith, Hope and Love die one by one, and God too is dead. His nightmarish dark creation made an immediate impression, and looks forward both to the surrealists and to T. S. Eliot's *The Waste Land*. Eliot was also affected by another expatriate London Scot, John Davidson (1857–1909), a journalist and early modernist with a sharp sense of the beauty and squalor of the city. Alert to intellectual currents of contemporary scientific thinking, Davidson's poetry would be an acknowledged influence on a later visionary poetry of ideas from Hugh MacDiarmid (1892–1978), who memorably describes this father-figure's suicide in 'Of John Davidson' as 'A bullet hole in a great scene's beauty, / God through the wrong end of a telescope'.

Such uprooting of artistic talent from Scotland to England and overseas was part of a wider dispersal and mixing of cultures, as famine and clearances in the Highlands and Ireland drove people off the land and into industry or emigration, complicating religious and ethnic identities not only in the Lowlands of Scotland but also in the Americas, Asia, Australia and New Zealand. At home, economic migration made Scottish and Irish

Gaelic and Catholic voices and values present again to Protestant central Scotland, often disturbingly so, and very gradually cultural hegemonies were altered, particularly through state education. At the same time, disruption in the Church of Scotland saw the secession of a radical Free Church which considered that the established Church had lost its integrity through collusion with landowners and the politically powerful. (In the twentieth century, a Scottish radicalism would become a feature of the most significant poetry – more political than spiritual, to be sure, yet typical of a cultural tendency to carry ideas to their logical conclusions.) During this nineteenth-century cultural disruption, ancient Gaelic spiritual perspectives were gathered, if occasionally sweetened, in the folkloric expeditions of Alexander Carmichael (1832–1912), whose *Carmina Gadelica*, published in six volumes between 1900 and 1971, preserved prayers, charms and blessings that would continue to influence 'Celtic spirituality' into the present age. The political land-reform songs of Màiri Nic a' Phearsain (Mary MacPherson, c. 1821–1898) add poignancy to her more personal 'Soraidh leis an Nollaig ùir' ('*Farewell to the New Christmas*'), recalling traditional practices from her experience of deracinated city life.

However, the interpenetration of modes of language and thought from different faith communities would enrich Scottish poetry in remarkable ways, often working against the grain of false sentiment and bigotry. The twentieth century saw a burgeoning of poetry in all three main Scottish languages, a second renaissance where the first had been stalled by the conflicts of sixteenth-century Reformation. Modern poets were drawn to confront revolutionary changes in politics, technology, warfare, social attitudes, philosophy, linguistics, the urban environment, and scientific investigation of the minutest particles of life and deepest reaches of the universe. Religion could not be treated simply, yet perhaps the nuance of poetry in a range of tones and forms became one vehicle through which the mystery, origins and ultimate purposes of life could be explored. Thus in the anthologies, meditational or even devout poetry by Edwin Muir (1887–1959) or George Mackay Brown (1921–1996) can be found side by side with poems by Hugh MacDiarmid, Sorley MacLean (Somhairle MacGill-Eain, 1911–1996) and Iain Crichton Smith (Iain Mac a' Ghobhainn, 1928–1998) confronting Church belief, or with avant-garde 're-writings' of Christianity by Edwin Morgan (1920–2010) and Tom Leonard (b. 1944), or with the agnostic yet palpably religious perception of John Burnside (b. 1955) or Carol Ann Duffy (b. 1955):

'Some days, though we cannot pray, a prayer / utters itself' ('Prayer', *Meantime*, 1993).

Considering such a vexatious chronology, it may be helpful to look at a few abiding themes in particular works over time, and to draw contrasts or continuities between poets and languages not normally partnered. The first of these may be termed 'cosmic piety'.

A distinguishing feature of some Gaelic poetry is the use of nature as a gateway to religious feeling. Monasticism, following the Egyptian model, had come to Scotland with St Columba. While the monks of late antiquity had sought seclusion in the desert, Gaelic monks looked for deserted islands off the Atlantic shore. Poetry expounding the ascetic ideal, such as 'Columba's Island Paradise',[2] speaks of the spiritual benefit of looking at nature as the work of the Creator. While this practice of *peregrinatio pro Christo* came from Egypt, the admiration of the cosmos and attention to nature probably came from the pre-Christian faith of the Gaels, that, so far as one can tell, looked on nature as the principal Other with which human society had to reach accord if it was to prosper. In the neoplatonic theology of the ninth-century Irishman John Scotus Eriugena, Creation is part of the emanation of God, in which He is profoundly present. The idea of the immanence of God in Creation can be seen in the prayers preserved in *Carmina Gadelica*: Christ is on hand to help Columba with his horse in 'An Stringlein' (*'In Strangles'*); the saints and the Godhead stand by to heal us of sin in 'Cuirim Fianais' (*'I Send Witness'*) and to bring us peace and protection in our daily lives in 'Achan Chadail' (*'Sleep Invocation'*). We are in loving communion with them and should undertake every task in their name, and because God is present in the Creation his sign can shield us, as in 'Mugron's Cross'. Fearghas MacFhionnlaigh's twentieth-century poem 'Laoidh nach eil do Lenin' (*'A Hymn which is not to Lenin'*) resonates with this same cosmic piety: 'cailèideascop-Dhia / beò-dhathan dian-loisgeach [...]' (*'kaleidoscope-God / conflagration of living colours [...]'*).

'Altus Prosator', often attributed to St Columba and translated as 'The Maker on High' (1997) by Edwin Morgan, has appeared as the earliest Scottish poem in two significant post-millennial anthologies, *The New Penguin Book of Scottish Verse* (2000) and *Scottish Religious Poetry: An Anthology* (2000). The relentless drive of its internally rhymed Latin and its sublime perspective on Creation, Paradise and the Fall seem designed to drown out the heroic verse of unrecorded times. This blending of ideology and piety within a cosmic perspective may remind us of

MacDiarmid's later fusion of universal and local, for instance in 'The Eemis Stane', where the earth is a lichened and mysteriously lettered stone, or in 'The Innumerable Christ', with the crucified figure hung between the cosmic and human worlds, on a distant planet.

Evangelisation is no simple process. Whether new preaching aims at the conversion of pagan kingdoms, or at reformation of religious hierarchies grown distant from the concerns of ordinary people, the changes that follow will be disruptive. Contrary poetic voices have long been heard across a Scottish cultural landscape frequently in flux. William Dunbar is the sublime yet earthy poet of diverse attitudes and forms: from 'Surrexit Dominus de Sepulchro', his great poem of Christ's resurrection, to the dark morality of 'The Dance of the Seven Deidly Synnis' or 'Lament for the Makaris', we are drawn into the medieval awareness of death, and the centrality of ancestral remembrance through words and sacred imagery, where prayer runs parallel to the elegiac mode. This mode persisted in Gaelic poetry with the natural world being seen, rather than as a fount of beauty, as the vale of tears through which we journey in exile; or worse, this world's distractions, in league with the Devil, seek to waylay us from reaching our true home, as for example in Athairne MacEoghain's 'Is Mairg Do-ní Uaille as Óige' ('*Woe to the One who takes Pride in Youth*', c. 1600).

The 'roads to Reformation' (in Michael Lynch's phrase) were many and intersecting, and involved economic and political forces as well as theological dissent, too complex for brief summary.[3] Reform offered ideological gains but also losses, as a traditionally immanent or incarnational God, often intimately linked with local pieties, became in the new creed an unknowable transcendent force of obscure and unchangeable motivation. The attractiveness of earlier morality, as in Henryson's fable 'The Preiching of the Swallow' (c. 1480), where folk wisdom is allied to religious reflection, now tended to darken in the intensity of Reformation, with its Calvinistic theology of an elect minority destined for heaven, the rest being damned and therefore not to be prayed for. Moreover, the Reformed Church condemned as 'vanity' all literature other than Scripture. In his preface to his Gaelic translation of John Knox's *Book of Common Order*, Bishop Carswell rails against poets who would disseminate stories of Fenian heroes rather than use their skills to spread the Gospel.[4]

Protestant poetry was still drawn to cosmological witness to God's majesty, as in the reformer George Buchanan's Latin 'Elegy on John Calvin' (1590): 'you are beyond the stars, you nudge / God'.[5] Yet the popular demotic ballad rhythms of the Scots hymns of *The Gude and Godlie Ballatis* (1567) evoke a positive Reformation culture of grounded worship. Biblical translation extended the poetic range, as in 'For the Baptiste' and 'For the Magdalene' by William Drummond of Hawthornden (1585–1649). The impact of Bible rhetoric is seen also in 'Job. Chapter III Paraphrased' by Robert Fergusson (1750–1774); and the strength of family religion and Bible-reading is sincerely expressed by Robert Burns in 'The Cotter's Saturday Night' (1785). It has also been suggested that translation of the Protestant Bible into Scottish Gaelic (in 1767 and 1801) to propagate the Reformed faith had the unforeseen effect of enhancing the Gaels' linguistic identity through their exposure to scriptural rhetoric.

In the twentieth century, MacDiarmid's vision ranged widely through philosophical, political or geological destiny, as in 'On a Raised Beach'. Edwin Muir's perspectives on time, myth and history deepen the significance of 'One Foot in Eden', or 'The Horses', gathering past into present; but Edwin Morgan preferred a more radical focus on the future, with sublime exploration of space and time in 'From the Domain of Arnheim' or 'Sonnets from Scotland'. Sorley MacLean's view of time and nature in such poems as 'Coilltean Ratharsair' (*'The Woods of Raasay'*), 'Hallaig' and 'Uamh an Òir' (*'The Cave of Gold'*) evokes, for some readers, a pre-Christian Gaelic vision. In these poems time is essentially circular, and nature an alternately succouring and destructive force.

Mariology, pantheism and the place of women are other features that can seem thematically interlinked in Scottish poetry. In the Reformed religion, male authority, with biblical justification, simplified or relegated women's role in spirituality, in contrast with the honoured place of Mary or Brighid in Gaelic poetry, and in earlier ornate Scots verse such as Dunbar's 'Ane Ballat of Our Lady'. In the thirteenth century, Muireadhach Albanach depicted the Virgin as an all-powerful figure in 'Éistidh riomsa, a Mhuire Mhór' (*'O Great Mary, Listen to Me'*). She is queen of heaven, presiding over a drinking hall filled by her kinsmen, whose admission she has engineered as co-redemptrix. Perhaps this view of women owes something to, besides contemporary and European views of Mary, the various goddesses who had represented nature to the pre-Christian Gaels.[6]

Plain-spoken Protestant tendencies created difficulties for poets. Alexander Montgomerie (c. 1555–1597), a gifted Catholic in the Protestant court of James VI, seems caught between ideologies. His late allegory 'The Cherry and the Slae' explores his own emotional development, and perhaps also religious ideologies in competition, with the accessible but sour new sloe bush set against the attractive yet distant cherry tree.

Working in uncertain times, Montgomerie wrote Psalm translations acceptable to the reformers before being finally outlawed. Swept away with the ancient liturgies were most sacramental signs of spiritual linkage between divine and human life. However, ongoing emotional engagement remained possible, whether through hymn writing or later, as with Marion Angus (1866–1946) and Violet Jacob (1863–1946), in a female spirituality touched by landscape, memory, the supernatural and Scots language. A sense of immanence is present in Muir's 'The Annunciation', and more widely in George Mackay Brown's reverential response to Orkney's history; and even, occasionally, in the lucid poetry that Norman MacCaig created from his annual holidays in Highland Assynt ('Zen Calvinism' was his own ironic self-description of a faith), or in the sophisticated perceptions of Muriel Spark's early poetry (see *Collected Poems*, 1967). Among current poets, John Burnside's contemplative 'Annunciations' (*Common Knowledge*, 1991) and Carol Ann Duffy's 'The Virgin Punishing the Infant' (*Selling Manhattan*, 1987), while not in the least pious, reflect the rich iconography of Catholic childhood.

A contrary strand invites distrust for the world and a turning from it. There is a link between medieval poems of contempt for the world and the evangelical poetry that rose during the 'awakenings' of the eighteenth century. Attempting to wean the Gaels from the 'tribalism' that had determined their allegiance in the Jacobite wars, poets such as Dùghall Bochanan (1716–1768) redefined the hero as a Christian, who, instead of conquering others, conquered his own desires. In his 'Là a' Bhreitheanais' ('*Day of Judgement*'), the anticipated destruction of the world, 'crupaidh an lasair e r'a chèil' / mar bheilleig air na h-èibhlibh beò' ('*wrinkled up by that red flame / like birch-tree bark in living fire*'), is a greater incentive towards religion than its beauty had formerly been. The 'natural state' was by definition bad, yet while the world and the body are corrupt, there is great joy to be had in contemplating the justified soul in eternal life with Christ – expressed by Iain Gobha (John Morison, 1780–1852), the Harris blacksmith, as the rebirth of a new man from the old corrupt one. The joy of an intensely personal, rather than sacramental, relationship with Christ is conveyed in ecstatic, even erotic, terms in the 'Luinneag' ('*Song*') of Anna NicEalair (*fl.* c. 1800), as it is still celebrated by Catrìona NicDhòmhnaill (b. 1925) in 'Mo Chalman' ('*My Dove*'), Christ's love song to man.

Such an evangelical emphasis on social and personal life, and the public shaming of those accused of (mainly sexual) misdemeanours, produced a counter-movement of anti-clericalism and, in poetry, anti-clerical satire. Of course, such writing is also found in pre-Reformation times, in the Book of the Dean of Lismore (c. 1500), poking fun equally at lecherous priests and at the gloom of the holy. But regular preaching of a perfectionist morality, and encouragement to keep close observation on the moral failings of others (as well as oneself), fostered a satirical view of any hypocrisy in the moralisers, as in Burns's 'Holy Willie's Prayer', and in his 'The Holy Fair', which mocks religion's appropriation of local festivals, each preacher's performance being rated merely as entertainment by an earthy audience. In genteel Victorian society, the mockery can be relatively gentle, as in 'Let Us All Be Unhappy on Sunday' by Charles, Lord Neaves (1800–1876), or John Davidson's cleric 'The Rev Habakkuk McGruther of Cape Wrath, in 1879', who accepts some changes to strict doctrine but pleads: '[...] leave us / For Scotland's use, in Heaven's name, Hell'. Later, Robert Garioch's Scots translations of Giuseppe Belli's sonnets from nineteenth-century Roman dialect (first published in *Selected Poems*, 1966) give a new twist to anti-Catholic satire, written now from the inside. In twentieth-century Gaelic poetry, a history of cultural suffering adds a keener edge to Sorley MacLean's 'Ban-Ghàidheal' ('*A Highland Woman*') and 'Tìodhlacadh sa Chlachan' ('*Funeral in the Clachan*'), or Iain Crichton Smith's 'A' Chailleach' ('*Old Woman*') and his Puritan poems, or Ruaraidh MacThòmais's (Derick Thomson, 1921–2012) 'Àirc a' Choimhcheangail' ('*The Ark of the Covenant*') and 'Srath Nabhair' ('*Strathnaver*'), for in these that suffering is partially condoned by the Church as the wages of sin.

Intellectual and artistic revolt against a narrow preaching culture meant that poets also created a ready strand of 'cosmic impiety', subverting traditional religious imagery. George Gordon, Lord Byron (1788–1824) creates a cynical 'Vision of Judgement' involving a poetic rival. MacDiarmid in 'Prayer for a Second Flood' and 'An Apprentice Angel', or Morgan in 'Message Clear' and 'The Fifth Gospel', both create free-ranging and radical rewritings of the Protestantism in which they were raised: 'Give nothing to Caesar, for nothing is Caesar's'. Am Puilean (Aonghas Caimbeul or Angus Campbell, 1903–1982) wickedly drinks a toast to the Devil, in 'Am Fear Nach Ainmich Mi' ('*The One I Shall Not Name*'), for his disproportionate concern with the sinning of the Gaels. Poems such as 'Leòdhas as t-Samhradh' ('*Lewis in Summer*') by Ruaraidh MacThòmais, and 'Soisgeul 1955' ('*Gospel 1955*') and 'Fèin-Fhìreantachd' ('*Selfrighteousness*') by Dòmhnall MacAmhlaigh (b. 1930), display a more subtle form of anticlericalism which simultaneously recognises the deleterious effect of a world-denying religion on a people's happiness and the integral part played by the church in Lewis culture.

The concept of the elect, and indeed of predestination, was inimical to modern humanism and left-wing politics. George Campbell Hay (Deòrsa mac Iain Dheòrsa, 1915–1984) expresses the alternative view in 'Prìosan da Fhèin an Duine?' ('*Locked in the Human Cage?*'), that mankind and the world are fine if allowed to flourish. Social justice has become a key feature of both Scottish politics and poetry, as radical socialist politics replaced pietistic acceptance for many modern poets. As early as the eighteenth century, the Gaelic poet Rob Donn (1714–1778) had urged on his neighbours not so much the individual rebirth of the Evangelicals, as the rational society of the Moderates, as in 'Marbhrann do Chloinn Fhir Taigh Ruspainn' ('*The Rispond Misers*'). Sorley MacLean in 'Calbharaigh' or '*My Een are Nae on Calvary*' (as translated into Scots by Douglas Young) finds that the limited life-chances of the poor in 'shitten back-lands in Glesca toun' forbid easy Christian consolation and demand a political response.

A number of poets from the next generation were 'sons of the manse', and Alastair Reid (1926–2014), Robin Fulton (b. 1937) and Stewart Conn (b. 1936) have all written movingly about their fathers' qualities, and their own search for alternative meaning. Among younger poets from a Nonconformist or 'brethren' upbringing, the emotional residue of early strictness has marked the poetry of Iain Bamforth (b. 1959), Don Patterson (b. 1963) and Helen Lamb (b. 1956). Medicine, teaching and mentoring have offered another sort of social commitment. Alan Spence (b. 1947) and Gerry Loose (b. 1948), and the Gaelic poets Kevin MacNeil (b. 1972) and Rody Gorman (b. 1960), have been drawn towards Buddhist meditation and Japanese forms that refresh our appreciation of nature and the present. Traditional Christianity is seen variously as an instrument and as an enemy of social justice. Rob A. MacKenzie (b. 1964), a Church of Scotland minister, satirises the ethical hollowness of financiers in *Fleck and the Bank* (2012), while Christopher Whyte (b. 1952) has consistently rejected Church dogma as a source of ongoing gay prejudice.

Our stewardship of the planet, whose exploitation formerly found biblical legitimisation in Adam's God-given dominion over the earth, has become another issue of justice. 'Celtic Christianity' is sometimes thought to carry a different emphasis, in the ecological tone of some early texts that value the world and its creatures more as God's creation than as man's resource. Pelagius, a Roman thinker born in Britain or Ireland

and active around AD 400, has been brought into this late twentieth-century nexus of aspiration and commitment, notably in his thesis that human beings have it in their own power to avoid sin and achieve righteousness. Theologically, such magnification of the will seemed heretically to downplay the power of God's grace. That appears part of the attraction for Edwin Morgan in 'Pelagius', revealing a strong identification with Pelagian attitudes as the poem boldly returns him to Glasgow to speak out for life's 'amazing, but only human, grace' (*Cathures*, 2002). John Scotus Eriugena, mentioned above, is another ancient philosopher cited in ecological debate. A Christian neoplatonist, he developed a cosmology with Nature as the first principle, the totality of all things – including both God and Creation. His teaching too was later condemned. Such ancient 'Celtic' theologies, owing something to pagan Greek and possibly pre-Christian Celtic attitudes, are being mined again in current discussions and are part of the context of contemporary Scottish poetry. Exploring human relationship with nature, Kenneth White (b. 1936) has made use of 'geo-poetic' wanderings, as have Alec Finlay (b. 1966) and Ken Cockburn (b. 1960) nearer home, while Kathleen Jamie (b. 1962), visiting North Atlantic islands, is one of several ecologically aware poets expressing closeness to and responsibility for natural environments under pressure, as in her *The Overhaul* and essay collection *Sightlines* (both 2012). John Burnside has been the most prolific, drawn increasingly to Nordic and Arctic landscapes: see, for example, *The Light Trap* (2002). His early poetry used traditional Catholic imagery in ways that some readers found religious, whereas he saw himself as trying to remake that iconography, and as being more interested in politics and Gnosticism than established religion.[7] Nevertheless, his poetry has retrieved a liminal sense of ancestral presences, and of spiritual engagement with this world through which we live, that echoes anciently Scottish matters and genres of faith.

CHAPTER EIGHTEEN

Scottish Poetry as World Poetry

Paul Barnaby

Scottish poetry might be viewed as belonging to world poetry from a number of perspectives. One might cite its internationalist outlook and readiness to import formal innovation, or stress the universality or global historical relevance of its subject matter. One might, conversely, privilege that which is quintessentially national, assuring Scotland a unique voice on the world stage. This chapter, however, defines world poetry as work which travels beyond its source-culture to achieve an active presence in other literary systems. It will focus on six Scottish poets who have vitally influenced the development of world writing: George Buchanan, James Thomson, James Macpherson, Robert Burns, Sir Walter Scott and Lord Byron. It will chart their creative impact on the non-anglophone world (with particular emphasis on Europe), but will also briefly consider why other major figures in the Scottish canon – the makars, the Vernacular-Revivalists, the post-MacDiarmid Lallans poets – have largely failed to cross international borders. It will conclude with a brief look at the resurgence of global interest in Scottish writing from the 1970s onwards.

George Buchanan

For a pre-Union global audience, Scottish literature was synonymous with neo-Latin writing. Only three pre-eighteenth-century vernacular translations of Scots-language verse are known: a Danish version of Sir David Lyndsay's *Ane Dialog Betwix Experience and ane Courteour* (1591) and French and Dutch versions of James VI's *Lepanto* (1591 and 1593). Dunbar and Henryson appeared in Latin alone, in Buchanan's free adaptation of 'This hinder nycht befoir the dawing cleir' in his *Somnium* (c. 1535) and Sir Francis Kynaston's translation of the *Testament of Cresseid* (c. 1640). Otherwise, Barbour, Dunbar, Henryson and

James I remained untranslated until the nineteenth century.[1] This need not be surprising. The Danish and French translations of Lyndsay and James VI stemmed directly from diplomatic ties with Scotland's closest pre-Union allies. Lyndsay played a prominent role in Scoto-Danish relations and James VI's French translator Du Bartas was Henry of Navarre's ambassador to the Scottish court in 1587.[2] Given the limited physical diffusion of Scots texts, political ties (and Scottish residence) were probably essential for translation. Perhaps too, in the case of Barbour or 'Blind' Hary, a literature's foundational texts, programmatically affirming a language's ability to support an autonomous tradition, may be too culture-specific to attract translators until that literature gains international prestige through the success of writers whose innovations have more immediate universal resonance. The focus of later makars on adapting and reworking canonical European texts may also have rendered their own innovations opaque to non-Scots readers. One should remember, though, that English literature from Chaucer to Shakespeare was almost equally little known abroad before the eighteenth century. The adoption of English by the Castalians and their successors won them no greater international audience than their Scots predecessors.[3]

Such was George Buchanan's fame, conversely, that his publisher Henri Estienne could uncontroversially present him as 'poetarum sæculi sui facile princeps' ('*easily the prince of contemporary poets*').[4] His reputation rested largely on the ground-breaking tragedies *Jephthes* and *Baptistes*. Besides numerous reprints of the original, *Jephthes* was translated into French (seven times between 1566 and 1613), German (four times between 1571 and 1604), Italian (1583, 1587), Polish (1587), Hungarian (1590) and Dutch (1656). It taught European dramatists to fuse Christian themes with Euripidean tragic form and to seek analogous situations in Scripture and antiquity.[5] Its five-act structure, strict observation of Aristotelean unities, and use of a chorus for moral commentary provided a blueprint for pre-Racinian dramatists in France, such as Théodore de Bèze, Robert Garnier, Jean de La Péruse, Marc-Antoine Muret, Jacques Grévin and Jean de La Taille. In Portugal too, *Jephthes* was a conspicuous model for the first major vernacular tragedy, António Ferreira's *Castro* (1567).[6] *Baptistes*, with its anti-absolutist exploration of religious and political persecution, had greater impact in Protestant Europe. In particular, Jeremias de Decker's 1654 Dutch translation framed it as a defence of the right to resist a tyrannous monarchy.[7] Read in conjunction with Buchanan's theories of elective kingship in *De Iure Regni apud Scotos*, it also proved influential in the North German states.[8]

Buchanan was equally celebrated for his Psalm paraphrases, published (singly or with other works) in over one hundred editions and set to music by Jean Servin (1579) and Statius Olthof (1585). Conceived, perhaps, as a means of healing religious strife,[9] they were imitated by both neo-Latinists like the Portuguese Ludovicus Crucius and vernacular writers such as Jan Kochanowski (Poland) and Jan van Hout (Netherlands). Van Hout also translated *Franciscanus*, Buchanan's satire against Cardinal Beaton (1566),[10] as did the French poet Florent Chréstien (1567). Buchanan's satires attracted writers of the stature of Joachim du Bellay in France and Martin Opitz in Germany. Du Bellay inserted a translation of 'Quam misera sit conditio docentium literas humaniores Lutetiæ' into the fourth book of his *Aeneid* (1552),[11] and Opitz translated two satirical epigrams in his *Florilegium variorum epigrammatum* (1644).[12] Buchanan's *Silva*, conversely, was an influential mode for pastoral poets, including the German neo-Latinist Nathan Chyträus.[13] It is perhaps Buchanan's sheer formal and thematic versatility and inexhaustible experimentation that most impressed European readers. Equally important was a power of empathy that brought new depth to the representation of character and feeling.[14]

James Thomson

Buchanan was widely acclaimed as the father of a school of Scottish neo-Latinists including Mark Alexander Boyd, George Crichton, Thomas Dempster and Andrew Melville, celebrated in the popular anthology *Deliciæ poetarum scotorum hujus ævi illustrum* (Amsterdam, 1637).[15] Seventeenth- and early eighteenth-century verse in Scots, however, remained unknown abroad. Neither Allan Ramsay nor, later, Robert Fergusson were translated before the late twentieth century, their verse perhaps too polished for post-Herderian lovers of *Volkspoesie*.[16]

The first post-Union writer to exert significant international influence was James Thomson. *The Seasons* was first translated into German (1745), followed by French (1759), Dutch (1765), Italian (1793), Russian (1798), Spanish (1801), Swedish (1811), Czech and Hebrew (1842). Its first European admirers were struck less by Thomson's descriptive skills than by his moral and philosophical digressions. Nicolas-Germain Léonard and Jacques Delille in France imitated his meditations on eternal life and conjugal happiness, while, in Germany, Friedrich von Hagedorn and Friedrich Gottlieb Klopstock echoed his patriotism and celebration of friendship and country living.[17] Subsequently, however, European

Sentimentalism stressed the portrayal of nature as divine revelation and the depiction of the individual in communion with the natural world. Rousseau's influence brought greater focus on Thomson's contrast between 'natural' village-life and corrupt city-life, while *The Poems of Ossian* and Edward Young's *Night Thoughts* directed readers to Thomson's depiction of solitary, desolate, uncultivated spaces. At the same time, the poem's narrative episodes (Lavinia and Palemon, Damon and Musidora) profoundly marked the European verse tale, leading writers like Salomon Gessner in Switzerland to turn from satire to idyll and to blend narrative with description.[18]

Among other writers marked by *The Seasons* are Ewald Christian von Kleist, Friedrich Schiller and the young Goethe (Germany), Jean-François de Saint-Lambert, Louis Jean Pierre Fontanes and André Chénier (France), Nikolai Karamzin and Vasily Zhukovsky (Russia), Ippolito Pindemonte (Italy), Julian Ursyn Niemcewicz (Poland), Henrik Wergeland (Norway) and Almeida Garrett (Portugal). Its creative reception extends well beyond the 'pre-Romantic' eighteenth century. In Portugal, Spain and Eastern Europe, *The Seasons* was a nineteenth-century discovery, and Romantic readings stressed its lyrical, subjective character.[19] Far from being a polite phenomenon swept away by *The Poems of Ossian*, its reception largely coincided with the cult of Macpherson's bard. Where Ossian, however, remains central to international perceptions of Scottishness, Thomson was seldom viewed as a Scot. His generic neoclassical landscapes eschewed Scottish colour, and he was widely associated with English Sentimentalists like Thomas Gray and Edward Young.

The Poems of Ossian

The first Ossianic fragments were translated in the 1760s by some of France's leading Enlightenment thinkers: Denis Diderot, Anne-Robert-Jacques Turgot and Jean-Baptiste-Antoine Suard. The complete *Poems of Ossian* were subsequently translated in Austria (1768–69), Italy (1773), France (1777), Denmark (1790–91), Russia (1792), Sweden (1794), Hungary (1815), Poland (1838), Norway (1854) and Spain (1880). Many readers, however, first encountered Ossian in Goethe's *The Sorrows of Young Werther* (1774), which included translated extracts from 'The Songs of Selma' and 'Berrathon'.

Macpherson's Ossian was initially acclaimed as a lyricist, possessed of a directness, naivety and figurative boldness proper to primitive peoples. Johann Gottfried Herder in his 'Auszug aus einem Briefwechsel über Oßian und die Lieder alter Völker' (1773) proposed Ossian as the model for a spontaneous, Sentimental verse which cast off Classical restraint. For Herder, northern Europeans retained sufficient native vigour to foster a genuine *Volkspoesie* expressive of national character. Stress on the national element gradually led to the perception of Ossian as an epic rather than lyric poet. His Celtic heroes, the common ancestors of the northern peoples, were the architects of a culture more vital than that of the over-refined south. The 'Homer of the North' inspired a bardic school hymning the heroic deeds of the national past, initially strongest in Germany and Scandinavia, but soon extending to central and eastern Europe.

Equally influential was a pantheistic vision, in which no personal God existed, and no redemption besides the 'joy of grief' derived from mourning past glories. Macpherson created a taste for landscapes wilder and more sublime than Thomson's, with which his heroes lived in intimate fusion. Formally, a fusion of genres (lyric, hymn, elegy, epic narrative, dramatic dialogue), perceived as primitive and instinctive, helped liberate European poetry from rigid compartmentalisation.

The Poems of Ossian gave particular stimulus to German literature, shaping the work of Klopstock, Goethe, Schiller, Gottfried August Bürger, Ludwig Tieck and Friedrich von Hölderlin. Elsewhere, Ossianic elements are found in François René de Chateaubriand, Alphonse de Lamartine, Alfred de Musset and Alfred de Vigny (France); Vincenzo Monti, Ugo Foscolo and Giacomo Leopardi (Italy); Juan Meléndez Valdés, Cristóbal de Beña, Angel de Saavedra, duque de Rivas, and José de Espronceda (Spain); Almeida Garrett and Alexandre Herculano (Portugal); Karamzin, Zhukovsky, Pushkin and Lermontov (Russia); Adam Mickiewicz and Niemcewicz (Poland); Karel Hynek Mácha and František Palacký (Bohemia); Mihály Vörösmarty and Sándor Petőfi (Hungary); Bengt Lidner, Thomas Thorild and Esaias Tegnér (Sweden); Johan Ludvig Runeberg and Aleksis Kivi (Finland); Adam Oehlenschläger (Denmark); Jacob van Lennep (Netherlands); and Philippe Sirice Bridel (Switzerland).[20]

As these names suggest, Ossian's impact far outreached the eighteenth century and was arguably richest in the 1820s, the heyday of European Romanticism. Macpherson is the father of Romantic nationalism, offering hope that each nation harboured a tradition to rival the Greek and creating the myth of the moral superiority and greater cultural antiquity of subjugated peoples. His influence extended beyond Europe to Latin America, where he was translated by the exiled Cuban nationalist

José María Heredia. Too often treated as a brief and baffling European infatuation, *The Poems of Ossian* revolutionised world literature. As Peter McCarey has argued, they destroyed the assumption that culture came from Greece, civilisation from Rome and religion from Jerusalem. Macpherson rejected the authority of Classical history, asserting the value of his own, and ultimately undermining Eurocentrism.[21]

Considering the spur that Macpherson gave to the study of Celtic languages, it is simplistic to blame him for obscuring genuine Gaelic verse. Nevertheless, the association of Gaelic culture with antiquity and primitivism may have discouraged exploration of the living tradition. No translation from Gaelic into a non-Celtic language (other than English or Latin) appeared before 1972.[22] When Herder argued that 'cultivated' Scotland had produced nothing to match the 'primitive' Ossian, he also discouraged exploration of its Scots and English traditions.

Herder, however, spearheaded the international discovery of traditional Scots ballads, including fourteen (found in Percy's *Reliques of Ancient English Poetry*) in his anthology *Volkslieder* (1778). Further Scots ballads were translated by Johann Joachim Eschenburg (1777), Johann Jakob Bodmer (1780), Friedrich Heinrich Bothe (1795), Ludwig Gotthard Kosegarten (1800), Leo von Seckendorf (1807–08) and Wilhelm Grimm (1813).[23] A contemporaneous vogue for 'Scotch song' saw texts set by Beethoven, Weber and Haydn. Even when written by living poets such as Burns, these were published without the author's name, cementing the idea that Scots verse was essentially popular, ancient and anonymous.[24]

Sir Walter Scott

Scott's *Minstrelsy of the Scottish Border* (1802), translated into German (1817), French (1826) and Italian (c. 1830), gave renewed impetus to international exploration of Scots balladry.[25] Scott's text of the 'The Twa Corbies' prompted imitations by Pushkin (1829), Hans Christian Anderson (1832) and Theodor Fontane (1861). János Arany's Scott-derived version of 'Sir Patrick Spens' (1853) is considered a masterpiece of Hungarian literature in its own right.[26] Other ballads were translated into Dutch (Willem Bilderdijk and J. J. L. ten Kate), Swedish (Arvid August Afzelius and Erik Gustaf Geijer), Danish (Knud Lyne Rahbek), Czech (František Doucha), Finnish (Runeberg) and Norwegian (Wergeland). The *Minstrelsy* equally moved poets like Almeida Garrett (Portugal), Rahbek (Denmark) and Manuel Milá i Fontanals (Catalonia) to collect ballads and folksongs and to propose them as the foundation for a regenerated national literature.

Although overshadowed by his novels, Scott's own poetry significantly informed European Romanticism. Initially, his ballad imitations proved most influential, particularly 'The Eve of St John', translated or adapted by Zhukovsky (Russia), van Lennep and Nicolaas Beets (Netherlands) and Antoine Fontaney (France). Other popular models were 'Lochinvar', 'The Fire-King' and 'Rosabelle' (notably translated by Karolina Pavlova, Russia's greatest nineteenth-century woman poet). Other writers fired by Scott to imitate their native ballad tradition include I. I. Kozlov (Russia), Mickiewicz (Poland), Fontane (Germany) and the Czech František Ladislav Čelakovský.[27]

Attention soon turned, however, to Scott's poetic romances, which, for many, bridged a gap between Ossianic epic and folk balladry. By 1830, they had been translated into French, German, Italian, Spanish, Russian, Polish, Czech, Danish and Swedish. They led narrative poets to draw on national history, allude to folklore rather than classical mythology, and evoke a precisely documented time and place. *Marmion* influenced Kozlov's *Chernets* (1825), Pushkin's *Poltava* (1828), Lermontov's *Izmail-Bei* (1832)[28] and Almeida Garrett's *Adosinda* (1828).[29] *The Lady of the Lake* informed Pushkin's *Boris Godunov* (1831) and Mácha's Czech epic *Máj* (1836).[30] The *Lay of the Last Minstrel*'s embedding of imitation ballads within a narrative frame is mirrored in Almeida Garrett's Portuguese national epic *Camões* (1825).[31] It can be difficult, however, to separate the impact of Scott's verse and prose. It is the novels, for example, that lay behind poems like Mickiewicz's *Konrad Wallenrod* (Poland, 1828) and *Pan Tadeusz* (1834), Tommaso Grossi's *I Lombardi alla prima crociata* (Italy, 1826) and Rivas's *El moro expósito* (Spain, 1833).[32]

Lord Byron

It can be equally difficult to detach Scott's influence from Byron's. Many Romantic verse epics placed a brooding Byronic hero against a Scott-derived historical and geographical backdrop. Their unparalleled joint impact on nineteenth-century verse is perennially underestimated by anglophone critics for whom the Romantic impulse is essentially lyrical. Where, for many Europeans, Scott embodied the national bard, Byron, however, was seldom perceived as a Scot.[33] If noted at all, his Scottish roots merely accentuated his outsider status in English society. He was nonetheless consistently placed, alongside Scott, in a 'northern' Romantic tradition descending from Ossian.

For an international readership, Byron was quintessentially the poet of freedom. He showed that the poet could be a man of action, inspiring the writer-politicians of the Latin American wars of independence (Andrés Bello, José María Heredia), the 1848 revolutions in Europe (Giuseppe Mazzini, József Eötvös, Lamartine, Arany, Mickiewicz) and democratic movements like the Russian Decembrists, whose leader Kondraty Ryleyev carried a volume of Byron to the scaffold.[34] Political exiles or refugees (Almeida Garrett, Mickiewicz, Giorgi Eristavi, Espronceda, Pushkin, Lermontov) equally found solace in Byron's evocation of the pain of banishment. For a post-Napoleonic generation which saw revolutionary idealism doused by the *ancien régime*, the Byronic hero potently embodied the crisis of all values. Byron further challenged the established order in rejecting both Christian and rationalist beliefs for a vision of cosmic injustice where irony is our only defence. Here Byron's influence extends well beyond Romanticism. As Richard A. Cardwell has argued, his heroes' metaphysical revolt fed into surrealism, the theatre of the absurd, and existentialism.[35]

Formally, many European poets imitated Byron's technique of merging the experiences of narrator and character, and balancing self-dramatisation with detached observation of the protagonist's follies. Many too adapted a structure based on the inner conflicts of an itinerant hero, rather than a carefully plotted narrative. Here, Byron's Oriental Tales proved the most significant model, but the digressive, satirical manner of *Don Juan* informs works like Almeida Garrett's *Dona Branca* (1826), Pushkin's *Eugene Onegin* (1833) and Musset's *Namouna* (1832).[36]

Other writers marked by Byron include Heinrich Heine and Annette von Droste-Hülshoff (Germany), Franz Grillparzer and Nikolaus Lenau (Austria), Vigny and Victor Hugo (France), Giovanni Berchet and Francesco Domenico Guerrazzi (Italy), Gustavo Adolfo Bécquer (Spain), Frederik Paludan-Müller (Denmark), Tegnér (Sweden), Wergeland (Norway), Yevgeny Baratynsky and Kozlov (Russia), Juliusz Słowacki (Poland), Vörösmarty (Hungary) and Mácha (Bohemia). In Germany, Goethe translated extracts from *Manfred* (1817), *Don Juan* (1819) and *English Bards and Scotch Reviewers* (1821) and cast Byron as Euphorion in *Faust II* (1832), where he symbolises an ideal marriage between northern Romanticism and southern Classicism. For most international readers, however, Byron remained the Romantic *par excellence*.

Robert Burns

Burns is considered here as his reception post-dates that of Scott and Byron. Only two poems were translated in Burns's lifetime and, although known to Goethe by the early 1800s,[37] he was translated into only five languages before 1850.[38] Several factors may explain initial international indifference. As we have seen, the eighteenth-century cult of *Volkspoesie* privileged the ancient and anonymous, the bard or the minstrel. Burns's work may have seemed too close to contemporary popular song, particularly in neoclassical cultures like France, Italy and Spain. Potential translators may also have been disconcerted by his heteroglossia and fusion of high and low culture. Perhaps, above all, Burn's political, religious and sexual audacity seemed incompatible with the naivety demanded of a folk poet. Reception was also delayed by the suspension of literary traffic between Britain and mainland Europe during the Napoleonic Wars (which also explains the late discovery of Scott's narrative poems and may have contributed to the longevity of Thomson and Ossian).

Robert Crawford has identified Burns as Europe's first 'bard of liberty, fraternity, and equality',[39] yet he was unacknowledged as such for almost half a century after his death. Burns's first European readers, in 1820s France, Germany and Italy, perceived an essentially pastoral poet of exquisite, untutored sensitivity. They followed early British readings in neglecting his virtuosity, deep knowledge of the Scots and English poetic traditions, and alertness to international developments. Translators chose poems which could be cast as celebrations of the domestic affections or the timeless simplicity of country life. Even this conservative Burns, however, influenced a poet of the stature of Leopardi, whose 'A Silvia' (1828) and 'Il sabato del villaggio' (1829) echo 'To Mary in Heaven' and 'The Cotter's Saturday Night' respectively.[40]

The political Burns emerged only in 1840s Germany via the translations of Ferdinand Freiligrath, who paired Burns with Byron as poets of democracy. Burns was subsequently translated by some of the most significant figures in Europe's emerging literatures, including the Czech Doucha (1852), Croat Stanko Vraz (1854), Hungarian Arany (1873) and Ukrainian Ivan Franko (1896). Their versions coupled patriotism and political radicalism, and provided a model for reclaiming a marginalised language and folk tradition. Elsewhere, in the Netherlands, Scandinavia, Switzerland and parts of Germany, translators offered a less progressive Burns, stressing his hostility to metropolitan modernity, and presenting a rural idyll where the soul of the nation was preserved (or where an organic society was threatened by industrial capitalism).[41]

Outside Europe, Burns was the first Scottish poet to be translated in Japan (1892), and subsequently appeared in Arabic, Chinese, Korean and Panjabi. His verse was sung by the Young Bengal movement ('Honest Poverty') and the Chinese resistance under Japanese occupation ('My Heart's in the Highlands'). While Western European interest waned, the post-1945 period saw massive translation in Communist Europe, including versions in fifteen languages of the Soviet Union, alongside Albanian, Bulgarian, Czech, Slovak, Hungarian, Polish, Romanian, Serbian, Croatian and Slovenian. Although an 'official' poet, presented as Marx's favourite writer, Burns enjoyed genuine popular success, selling over 600,000 volumes in Russia alone. Recent editions in France, Germany, Norway, the Netherlands, Spain and Portugal suggest that a broader European Burns revival is underway.[42]

Twentieth-Century and Beyond

Burns remains much the most translated Scottish poet but has seldom prompted a wider exploration of Scottish writing.[43] Whether as 'heaven-taught ploughman' or class spokesman, he is often presented as a figure unrooted in a specific literary culture. His extensive late nineteenth-century reception triggered little interest in contemporary Scottish writing. Between Scott's death (1832) and the 1960s,[44] only one volume by a living Scottish poet appeared in translation: Horatius Bonar's *Hymns of Faith and Hope* (Basel, 1872). This is perhaps foreseeable in the case of Scottish Victorian poets, few of whom achieved critical or commercial prominence outside their homeland. Perhaps more surprisingly, given its quest to restore Scotland to the European mainstream, the Renaissance movement of the 1920s and 1930s failed to reverse the trend.

French critic Denis Saurat's much-cited 1924 article introducing 'le groupe de la Renaissance écossaise' was essentially an isolated response.[45] Only one other MacDiarmid lyric was translated before 1945: D. S. Mirsky's Russian version of 'The Seamless Garment' (1937).[46] Outside Communist Europe, MacDiarmid remained practically untranslated until the 1960s. Besides individual poems by Douglas Young and Lillias Forbes Scott (1950), no other Scots-language poet was translated before 1970.[47] Perhaps to audiences ignorant of the sub-Burnsian Victoriana against which it rebelled, the Renaissance seemed merely to echo earlier cultural revivals, or, in absorbing European influences, to renovate rather than innovate. Above all, however, it suffered from prevailing conceptions of modernism as a central, metropolitan and cosmopolitan phenomenon which rejected the local and vernacular.[48] Renaissance focus on national identity automatically excluded it from a modernist canon built around literal or metaphorical exiles like Joyce or Kafka.[49]

Modernist critics and translators more readily embraced Edwin Muir, stressing his interest in psychoanalysis, his alienation from both Scottish and English literary traditions, and his vision of modern man as an exile from Eden, threatened by industrialisation and totalitarianism (and, later, nuclear warfare).[50] When Western European translators finally turned to MacDiarmid, they portrayed a similarly isolated figure: not the spokesman for a thriving movement but an iconoclastic individualist.[51]

Given the unprecedented role played by academic criticism in the diffusion of modernism, Renaissance poets were clearly further hindered by the lack of institutional backing for Scottish literature. The resurgence of interest in Scottish writing post-1970 is unquestionably linked to the emergence of Scottish studies as an academic discipline and the promotional energies of the Scottish Arts Council, the Association for Scottish Literary Studies and Scottish Poetry Library. The 1970s saw the first translated anthologies of Scottish poetry since the mid-nineteenth century: in Italy (1976), Iran (1977) and Georgia (1979). Further anthologies followed in West Germany (1982), Wales (1986: the first translated anthology of Scottish Gaelic verse) and Israel (1988). From the 1990s onwards, though, Scottish poetry has achieved an international profile unparalleled since Scott's day, matched (and possibly prompted) by extensive translation of Scottish fiction and drama. Anthologies have appeared in France (1991, 2005), Italy (1992, 1997), Croatia (1993: the first non-Celtic anthology of Scottish Gaelic verse), Hungary (1995, 1998, 2004, 2007), Belgium (1998), the Czech Republic (2001), China (2002), Finland (2003, 2006), Austria (2006), Brazil (2007), Russia (2007) and Germany (2011).

At the same time, a growing number of volumes are devoted to individual Scottish poets, including Kenneth White (Basque Country, Bulgaria, France, Germany, Italy, Spain, Switzerland, Venezuela), Douglas Dunn (Armenia, France, Germany, Italy, Norway, Spain, Slovakia), George Mackay Brown (Germany, Iceland, Poland, Switzerland), Edwin Morgan (Brazil, Greece, Italy, Poland), John Burnside (Catalonia, France, Germany), Jackie Kay (Germany, Italy, Poland), Carol Ann Duffy (Austria, Slovakia), Robin Fulton (Germany, Sweden), Frank Kuppner (Denmark,

Norway), Norman MacCaig (Italy, Poland), William Neill (Denmark, Italy), Don Paterson (Germany, Netherlands), Ron Butlin (Spain), Kate Clanchy (Italy), Robert Crawford (Norway), Christine De Luca (France), Duncan Glen (Italy), W. S. Graham (Netherlands), Alexander Hutchison (Italian), Kathleen Jamie (Germany), Liz Lochhead (Poland), Richard Price (Brazil), Robin Robertson (Italy), Iain Crichton Smith (Germany), William Soutar (Austria), Muriel Spark (France) and Christopher Whyte (Catalonia).

There is no space here for detailed analysis, but anthologists of modern Scottish verse have broadly moved from stressing the integrity of an embattled national tradition (whether mono- or trilingual), to presenting Scottish writing as a hybrid and heteroglot phenomenon, regionally, ethnically and sexually diverse. Translators of individual Scottish poets seldom cite Scottish literary predecessors, more frequently identifying a 'Scottishness of the mind', characterised by an openness to global influences and a sympathy for the 'other' perceived as lacking in contemporary English verse.[52]

Contemporary Scottish writing is increasingly presented as an emerging, postcolonial literature that resists a dominant culture via the appropriation and creolisation of its forms and language. Reluctance to chart continuity with a literary past is striking in two areas. Firstly, the legacy of the interwar Renaissance is restricted to MacDiarmid's 'synthetic English' with Lallans writing largely marginalised. Yet new approaches to modernism stress how, outside major metropolitan centres, it often involved experimentation within a traditional framework and the quest for a national style.[53] Scottish writing hitherto judged too local or vernacular might then be reclaimed for modernism, permitting a more nuanced exploration of relations between modernist and postmodernist constructions of Scottish identity. Secondly, contemporary Scottish poetry is seldom linked to the post-Union writers – Thomson, Macpherson, Scott, Byron – who changed the face of world literature. Yet these writers might be seen as pre-empting postcolonial appropriations of the language and literary tradition of a dominant culture in order to revolutionise its categories and values. George Buchanan too wrestled a global language into new shapes. Drawing such parallels might permit an integrated picture of Scottish poetry to emerge, albeit one that is internationally visible less as a continuous self-sustaining tradition than via a perpetual polemical relationship with a cultural centre.

CHAPTER NINETEEN

The Literary Environment

Robyn Marsack

Writing poetry may be a solitary act, but reaching an audience has always involved a complex and changing network of what might broadly be called 'institutions', which may in fact be another solitary person – typesetter, independent bookseller, magazine editor – or long-established newspapers, publishers, cultural organisations. In order to thread our way among these in Scotland, we will imagine a late twentieth-century poet – let us call her Kate Stevenson, and imagine she was born in the early 1960s – and follow the progress of her first two books.

Kate has attended university, probably a Scottish one, and let us say that she spent her four years studying history and English. She may well have been the first person in her family to go to university. Until the mid-1960s there were just four universities in Scotland, all ancient foundations (St Andrews, 1413; Glasgow, 1451; Aberdeen, 1495; Edinburgh, 1583); in Glasgow and Edinburgh, as argued by Robert Crawford, the 'invention' of the academic subject of English literature developed from the teaching of rhetoric and belles lettres in the eighteenth century.[1]

Unless she attended the University of Glasgow, Kate would not have come across 'Scottish Literature' as a separate subject rather than as a subset of English literature courses: a Department of Scottish Literature was set up in Glasgow only in 1971. At primary school she would have encountered the poems of Robert Burns, no matter what part of the country she lived in; she may have been encouraged to learn some poems off by heart for the annual competitions run by the local Burns Club, part of the World Federation of Burns Clubs founded in 1885 (Paisley claims to have the oldest formally constituted Burns Club in the world, from 1805, while the Dalry Burns Club boasts that it has the longest unbroken record of Burns Suppers, from 1825). She heard some of the Scottish ballads and, at secondary school, was given poems by some contemporary Scottish poets to study for her public examinations: 'In the Snack-bar' (1968) by Edwin Morgan, for example, and Norman MacCaig's 'Assisi' (1964) or 'Summer Farm' (1953). By 2012, she might have children at secondary school who will be affected by the decision to make a question on a Scottish text a mandatory part of the Higher English examination (taken when pupils are about sixteen, and a qualifying examination for Scottish universities), a decision that has been the subject of a strong lobby for many years, but also a cause of protest by some teachers.[2] Certainly Kate did not come across many female Scottish writers before her university days, and was probably familiar with only a handful of poets.

At university, though, she had the opportunity to hear and talk to contemporary poets, as the first writer-in-residence posts were being established. There had been informal creative writing groups in the past, such as Stephen Mulrine's at Glasgow School of Art, which Liz Lochhead attended in the later 1960s, and Philip Hobsbaum's Glasgow group in the early 1970s. With support from the Scottish Arts Council, Sorley MacLean became the first writer in residence at the University of Edinburgh in 1975; Alasdair Gray was writer in residence at Glasgow University from 1977 to 1979, and by 2010 the Scottish Arts Council had supported over 100 such residencies, gradually widening out from the more traditional university bases to work with local authorities through libraries and community settings, including prisons.[3] Kate's contemporary, Roddy Lumsden, describes beginning to write poetry at seventeen in St Andrews, continuing at Edinburgh University, where 'writers-in-residence sanded [him] down and encouraged [him] to keep on'.[4]

This was one way in which would-be writers met established writers, before creative writing was offered as a degree course. It was not an option available to students in Scotland in the 1970s, although the first creative writing course for postgraduates in the UK was set up at the University of East Anglia in 1961. The opportunities are very different in the twenty-first century: 'Ninety-four British universities now offer a range of postgraduate degrees in creative writing and in any one year there are usually more than 10,000 short-term creative writing courses or classes on offer in the UK.'[5] St Andrews began creative writing courses in the early 1990s, established by Douglas Dunn, and in 2012 its M.Litt. in Creative Writing could be taken in poetry or fiction, the programme being headed by Don Paterson. Kathleen Jamie, who had taught at St Andrews alongside John Burnside and Robert Crawford, became Professor of Creative Writing at Stirling in 2011, to establish new postgraduate opportunities there. In fact, undergraduates at the University of Stirling had been able to offer a creative (rather than critical) dissertation in their final year since the 1970s: Norman MacCaig was Reader in Poetry at Stirling from 1970 to 1978, and would talk to students about their own writing.[6] He had previously held the post of Fellow in Creative Writing at the University of Edinburgh from 1967 to 1969; although initially very suspicious of the notion of teaching people to write poetry, he later said:

> I thought that if the young person, the student, has poetry in him or her, to offer them help is like offering a propeller to a bird. [...] Two things happened. One was, because they had a sympathetic guy to talk to, they started writing more. The other thing was, since they knew I was going to go through it, niggling away, they wrote far more self-critically, and they improved to an extraordinary degree. I would think I saved them a few years in reaching the stage they did.[7]

Once Kate had shown some of her poems to an established poet, and been encouraged, her next step was to send some to a literary magazine. Of course this need not have been a Scottish magazine: *London Magazine*, *Poetry Review*, *PN Review*, *The Rialto*[8] – to name just a few magazines that have lasted – were all open to submissions; she hesitated to send poems to the more august weekly *Times Literary Supplement* and the newish *London Review of Books* (founded 1979), although the latter was hospitable to Scottish poets of her generation.[9]

Nevertheless, Scotland has its own strong tradition of literary magazines; some long-lasting and some more fugitive but influential. In the 1980s, Kate could have found a fairly wide range of magazines in the larger bookshops, which is next to impossible these days because of centralised ordering and the reduced number of bookshops in general. Her contemporary James Robertson – poet, novelist and publisher – remembers working in the first Waterstones bookshop to open outside London, in Edinburgh's George Street.

> It was an exciting place to be, with readings and launches happening two or three times a week. Through these I met some of the old guard of Scottish poetry, men like Norman MacCaig, Sorley MacLean and Iain Crichton Smith. [...] In 1989 I transferred to Waterstone's Union Street branch in Glasgow. I had been having poems published in those literary magazines, like *Chapman* and *Cencrastus*, that played so important a part in revitalising Scottish cultural life in the 1980s.[10]

Between 1960 and 1975, it is reckoned that thirteen new little magazines devoted to poetry, or with a strong poetry component, were published in Edinburgh alone, and another nine in Glasgow. These ranged from fairly short-lived titles such as Ian Hamilton Finlay's internationalist, avant-garde *Poor.Old.Tired.Horse* (1962–67) and Bob Tait's *Scottish International*, with Robert Garioch and Edwin Morgan as co-editors (1968–74), to those with greater staying power, such as Duncan Glen's *Akros*, which moved with its editor from Bishopbriggs (near Glasgow) to Preston and then Nottingham, with fifty-one issues from 1965 to 1983. Glen was a fervent admirer and friend of Hugh MacDiarmid, but through his magazine also encouraged a broad range of younger poets. He himself wrote poetry, sometimes in Scots and sometimes in English, and the space for writing in Scots was enlarged by *Scotia Review*, from Caithness, founded and edited by David Morrison from 1970 until 2004, when he handed it on. *Gallimaufray* was published irregularly from the University of Dundee between 1974 and 1993 (twenty issues), and included work by poets Tracey Herd, Kathleen Jamie and Sean O'Brien.

New Edinburgh Review took its title from the great nineteenth-century magazine edited from 1803 to 1829 by Francis Jeffrey, 'the most influential magazine and arbiter of literary taste in Britain and Europe', famous for its attacks on Wordsworth, Scott's *Marmion* and Byron's early poems.'[11] By the time it closed in 1929, it had no such power. The title was optimistically revived in 1969, with a succession of editors including James Campbell and Allan Massie, and wound down in 1984. It appeared again in 1985, this time as the *Edinburgh Review*, and is edited at the time of writing by the poet Alan Gillis from the Department of English at Edinburgh University, succeeding Brian McCabe. Its cast is more literary, less philosophical and political than it was in the 1980s under the editorship of Peter Kravitz; the first decade of the magazine in particular championed Glasgow-based writers and new fiction by writers such as James Kelman and Alasdair Gray. It also featured rediscovered authors, and its special number on W. S. Graham in 1986, for example, was influential in bringing the poet to the notice of a number of younger writers and readers.

Summing up the period 1960 to 1975 in their magnificent bibliography, David Miller and Richard Price remark:

> People in over four hundred places up and down the country – nearly 80 per cent of the whole survey of this period – published small numbers of magazines (between one and four titles each). Many of their locations

were small towns or villages. From Aberdeen to Zennor, a radically decentralised form of publication had arrived.¹²

Chapman was founded in 1970, and Joy Hendry became its sole editor in 1976, a position she has held ever since. Its name comes from the itinerant sellers of chapbooks and ballads who feature in the opening line of Burns's 'Tam o' Shanter', and indicates its democratic intentions. Writing on the *Chapman* website, Hendry recalls the atmosphere in which it was founded:

> When the magazine was founded, there was almost no interest in Scottish writing in the UK, Europe and the world at large – and most conspicuously in Scotland. [...] There seemed no prospect of any decent literary infrastructure. Lacking a Parliament of any kind, there seemed no way to stem, for example, the strong tide flowing against our indigenous languages, Scots and Gaelic, which were generally derided as inherently inferior, even primitive, as languages per se (sometimes by writers themselves); both of them thoroughly deserved to die out, and, with them, the cultures they underpinned.¹³

Yet, of course, there were other magazines publishing Scottish writers: *Cencrastus*, published and edited by Raymond Ross for twenty of its years, was founded in 1979 and ran to 2005, taking its title from MacDiarmid's long poem *To Circumjack Cencrastus*. The poem's concerns with the loss of Scottish identity, its cultural consequences and the consequences for its three languages were shared by the magazine's editors.

Kate was not writing in Scots or Gaelic, which precluded sending her work to *Lallans* or *Gairm*, the former founded in 1973 and edited for the next ten years by J. K. Annand, who defined his editorial policy in the following manner: 'Our pages sall be open til scrievers in local dialects, as weill as thaim that ettle to scrieve in what is taen for a "standard" or "literary" Scots.'¹⁴ Because he found that Scots prose had fewer publishing outlets than poetry, he discouraged poetry submissions at first, but later relented. Published twice yearly under the aegis of the Scots Language Society, it was latterly edited by John Law until his untimely death in 2010. *Gairm*, founded and edited by the distinguished Gaelic poet and scholar Ruaraidh MacThòmais (Derick Thomson), ran from 1952 to 2004, over 200 issues containing work by the foremost Gaelic poets of the day.

From 1984, Kate would have been able to locate a good range of magazines at the Scottish Poetry Library in Edinburgh, founded by

Tessa Ransford, editor of *Lines Review* from 1988 until its last number in March 1998. The magazine began as a broadsheet, edited by Alan Riddell during the Edinburgh Festival in 1952; the second number was produced by the printer-publisher Callum MacDonald in 1953; as managing editor he worked with a succession of editors and finally with Tessa Ransford, whom he married in 1989. Like the Scottish Poetry Library, *Lines* was keen to present Scottish poetry in an international context.

Contemporary poets, too, were founding their own publications: *Verse*, begun in 1984, was edited by poets David Kinloch and Robert Crawford, both graduates of Glasgow University and doctoral students at Balliol College, Oxford, where they were joined in the venture by an American, Henry Hart, and later by Richard Price. They were committed to 'an international approach and to maintaining a Scottish accent'. Reflecting on the progress of the magazine as the original editors relinquished their posts (*Verse* is now published from the University of Richmond, Virginia), Robert Crawford noted that they

> were unable to attract as much first-rate poetry by women as we would have wished [...] never achieved a circulation of over 1,000 copies per issue; usually we hung round the 800 mark, selling almost exclusively to subscribers. [...] The conversations with Simon Armitage, John Burnside, W. N. Herbert, Kathleen Jamie, Angela McSeveney, and Don Paterson [...] are in each case the first really substantial interviews to be offered. [...] *Verse* played some part in fostering a new generation of Scottish poets.[15]

Jamie remarked in her interview that 'in '89 I had one of the most exciting and creative periods of my life [...]. But I shoved the results in a drawer. I stopped publishing because I was scunnered with the small magazines. Waiting nine months for a wee slip of paper saying "Not quite". Or getting no reply at all from the likes of *Edinburgh Review!*'[16] Meanwhile, Price and Herbert had started *Gairfish* (Dundonian Scots for 'dolphin'), a project noted in a substantial interview in the Glasgow *Herald* (29 July 1989), in which Glasgow-centric notions of Scottish culture were dismissed by Price: it certainly wasn't 'the superficialities of the Glasgow City of Culture 1990 campaign', or the Garden Festival, which was 'simply tacky' and not a 'legitimate expression of Scottish culture'.[17] The magazine was to be trilingual in Scots, Gaelic and English, and concerned with Scottish identity but not exclusively. Inspired by MacDiarmid's energy and invention, they were not bound by his ideology: 'We recognise a certain Scottish culture and are interested in the nationalist debate. But we are not out to make martyrs of Scotland.' For its five years (1990–95), *Gairfish* 'self-consciously took its aesthetic bearings from the high Scottish modernism of the interwar years. It published what it only half-jokingly called the "McAvant-Garde", including Tom Leonard. Frank Kuppner, Tom McGrath and Peter Manson [...]'[18] Kuppner, Kinloch, Price and Peter McCarey went on to be published by the Manchester-based Carcanet Press, which also brought back into print much of MacDiarmid's work in prose and poetry.

As *Gairfish* stopped, *Southfields*, edited by Price and Raymond Friel, began in 1995, and so did *The Dark Horse*, edited by poet and critic Gerry Cambridge as a Scottish-American poetry magazine, with an emphasis on new poetry using traditional forms (still being published, sometimes with and sometimes without arts council support), and *Markings: New Writing and Art from Dumfries and Galloway*, edited by John Hudson (ceased in 2010), followed shortly afterwards by poet, publisher and bookseller Sally Evans's A4 broadsheet *Poetry Scotland* (1997–).

Kate gets her first poems published in *New Writing Scotland*, which has been going since 1983. Produced annually under the aegis of the Association for Scottish Literary Studies (established in 1970 and currently based at the University of Glasgow), its editors change every three years and, until recently, have considered submissions anonymously, so Kate appears with both well-known and other new writers. She has some poems published in *Verse* as well, and starts to take part in readings. Informally, she is encouraged by Edwin Morgan, not only by his example but by his commenting on her poems in draft – he was a great enabler and supporter of the younger generations.

Public readings, of course, had long been a feature of Scottish literary life, but their increased number was part of a wider trend in the UK from the 1960s onwards. Liz Lochhead's first real public reading was at 'Poem '72', just before *Memo for Spring* (1972) was published, as the support act for Norman MacCaig: ten minutes to his half-hour in an enormous poetry festival with lots of simultaneous events.[19] In 1974, writer and playwright Tom McGrath founded the Third Eye Centre in Glasgow, a focus for the city's counterculture with performers such as Allen Ginsberg coming up and Edwin Morgan as a regular.[20] In 1983 the Edinburgh Book Festival began in Charlotte Square, an August fortnight to focus on books while the city was in the grip of the International Festival, set up in 1947 as part of the post-war cultural effort at reconnecting the UK with Europe and beyond. At first it was biennial, and held about 30 author events, but in 1997 it became an annual event and is now the largest book festival of its kind, with about 800 authors appearing over the fortnight in a constant stream of simultaneous events. The poetry content is a small section of all this activity, but poetry has a festival all of its own in St Andrews. The StAnza Festival was planned in 1997 by its founders, three St Andrews-based poets, Brian Johnstone, Anna Crowe and Gavin Bowd, the first two of whom are still involved in the organisation. The first festival took place in 1998, launching on National Poetry Day in October; since 2003 it has taken place in March.

By 2012 there were forty book festivals in Scotland, from Wordplay in Shetland (2001–) to the Ullapool Festival (2005–) with a special focus on Gaelic, to the Wigtown Book Festival in Galloway (1998–) in Scotland's officially designated book town. And there are reading opportunities in almost every city and town throughout the year, from bookshop launches to events at public libraries to gatherings in pubs and other venues. In fact, Kate could probably participate in a reading three or four nights a week if she lived in the Central Belt: the Shore Poets in Edinburgh have been going since 1991, when Brian Johnstone and Roz Brackenbury began organising readings at Leith's Shore Gallery (they describe themselves as 'an informal but durable collective who have been providing a platform for new poets to read alongside more established names'[21]), and St Mungo's Mirrorball was founded by Jim Carruth in 2005 as a network of Glasgow-based poets, actively supporting those who are up-and-coming. There is also a growing and lively culture of poetry in performance, with elements of music and film. Kate did not have such a range to choose from when she set out.

The publishing of poetry in Scotland has a long history: Walter Chapman in 1507 obtained royal patents to set up Scotland's first printing press in the Cowgate in Edinburgh, and the first book produced there was a selection of poems by Robert Henryson and William Dunbar in 1509. When Kate gets to the stage of putting a collection together, she wonders which publishers she might approach. A selection is offered by *Dream State, the New Scottish Poets*, edited by Daniel O'Rourke and published by Polygon in 1994. A representative gathering of Scottish poets under forty, it allows readers to take stock of this new generation, beginning with Carol Ann Duffy (b. 1955) and closing with Anne Frater (b. 1967). Of the twenty-five poets, eight were published by English presses – Jackie Kay, W. N. Herbert and Kathleen Jamie all had new collections from Bloodaxe; three had collections from Edinburgh-based Polygon.

Kathleen Jamie, with a pamphlet and two collections already published, remarked:

> It's easy to be a big fish in a small pond. On the other hand it saddens me that no Scottish publisher has approached me, and asked if I was interested in doing a book for them (the English have). No Scottish magazine has asked me for an interview until today – I've done them for English mags and American students. An Australian university wrote out of the blue, could they buy my manuscripts? No Scottish institution has done that. [...] Then folks moan at you for going south. This isn't a money problem; that comes in afterwards, this is a problem of attitude. The SAC [Scottish Arts Council] is very good at supporting writers, myself included, but something is missing, some other structure. [...] What I'd really like, what I long for, is a proper review, a critical essay.[22]

By the twenty-first century, most Scottish poetry publishing was receiving some support from the Scottish Arts Council.[23] In 2009 it was supporting nine literary magazines, including *Northwords Now*, freely distributed, and the quarterly *Scottish Review of Books*, established in 2004 and available free within the *Herald* as well as by subscription – providing longer and more considered reviews than are available in the confined and reduced books pages of the quality newspapers. *Gutter*, the poetry and fiction magazine published by Freight (Glasgow), is a welcome addition, however the reviewing and critical culture remains underdeveloped. By 2012 there were few Scottish publishers with a poetry list: Luath (Edinburgh, established in 1981), Polygon (Edinburgh, late 1960s), Two Ravens (Isle of Lewis, 2006). Canongate, founded in 1973 and refinanced by Hugh Andrew and the current managing director Jamie Byng in 1994, has published a little poetry in the past and some in the Canongate Classics list; Edinburgh University Press also used to publish poetry, for example the elegantly designed and significant collection by Edwin Morgan, *The Second Life* (1968), but now rarely does so. For a while, with the encouragement of its publisher Martin Spencer, EUP's paperback list Polygon (originating from the Edinburgh University Students' Publication Board, and editorially independent) published an important range of poetry and fiction by new writers, but after Spencer's untimely death in 1990, Edinburgh University Press gradually changed its structure. In 2002 the imprint was bought by Hugh Andrew, whose Birlinn publishing company now includes several previously independent imprints, and Polygon once again publishes poetry, although fewer titles than in its radical heyday.

Kate is lucky, then, to get her first collection published by Polygon, with a launch at Waterstones in Edinburgh and also at John Smith's in Glasgow – a bookseller founded in 1751 and still in existence, although now only on university campuses throughout the UK, and no longer at St Vincent Street in the heart of Glasgow, where it was such an institution for so long.[24] The book does well, but she feels that it did not get much noticed or distributed beyond Scotland. Nevertheless, on the strength of its modest success she is able to apply to the Scottish Arts Council for a writer's bursary to work on her second collection. Like most poets, she cannot make a living entirely through her writing, though it gives her some opportunities: as the new century developed, so did some important sources of support. In 1998 the Scottish Book Trust – formerly Book Trust Scotland, founded in 1960 as the Scottish office of the National Book League – had become independent of its English parent, much like the Arts Council, and as part of its remit to 'inspire readers and writers' it funds 'Live Literature', a programme that subsidises writers' visits to schools and libraries in particular. Kate being a communicative poet, who enjoys reading her work and encouraging others to write, earns some money through school and community visits. She has also been to Moniack Mhor as a guest reader, invited by two poets who were teaching an adult writing course there. Moniack is the Scottish writing centre near Inverness, which in 1993 became part of the Arvon Foundation's group of such houses for residential courses run by writers. Happily, one of the poets at Moniack is also an editor with Picador, launched in 1972 and now an imprint of PanMacmillan, with a prestigious poetry list including several Scottish poets. Invited to submit her next collection to Picador, Kate feels that it will provide better distribution and marketing than the (temporarily) lapsed Polygon, and moves to the new publisher.

We shall leave her with her second collection just published, and shortlisted for a Scottish Arts Council Book Award. She knows that if she takes a long time to produce a new collection, but meanwhile has a small selection of poems including a few translations she would like to air, she could offer those to one of the pamphlet publishers such as Mariscat or Happenstance that have been flourishing in Scotland for some years now (thirty in Mariscat's case), and that the pamphlet will be produced elegantly.[25]

Kate is living in a literary landscape that has changed enormously since she set out. The Scottish Poetry Library, which had a couple of staff and 300 books in 1984, now has over 40,000 items in its collection, eight staff and makes over 4,000 loans a year, has over 20,000 Twitter followers and thousands of visitors to its website.[26] The web is the first place most people will go to find out about Kate, and many of them will buy her next book online. Her contemporaries and younger poets are publishing in online journals, and creating their own audiences through contributing to or initiating blogs. There are formal and informal poetry reading groups all over Scotland. The Scottish Arts Council was replaced by Creative Scotland in 2010, with changed funding structures. Her contemporaries have won many of the UK's most prestigious poetry prizes: the T. S. Eliot, the Forward, the Whitbread/Costa. Having lived in the atmosphere of the failed 1979 referendum, in 2015 she now lives in a country that has a devolved 'Scottish government', and where the Scottish National Party, which MacDiarmid fought for and against, held an independence referendum in 2014 in which writers' voices were eloquent in the stirring debates. Liz Lochhead is the national poet for Scotland, or Scots Makar; the Poet Laureate of the UK is Carol Ann Duffy, born in Scotland.[27] Kate still carries her notebook with her, and shows her poems to a few trusted readers, before and beyond the whole process begins that brings news of her poems, and then the work itself, to her audience.

Endnotes

Introduction

1   www.scotland.gov.uk/News/Releases/2011/01/19141814.
2   Anne Varty, 'Introduction', in Anne Varty (ed.), *The Edinburgh Companion to Liz Lochhead* (Edinburgh: Edinburgh University Press, 2013), p. 1.
3   Roderick Watson (ed.), *The Poetry of Scotland: Gaelic, Scots, and English, 1380–1980* (Edinburgh: Edinburgh University Press, 1995).
4   Christopher Whyte, *Modern Scottish Poetry* (Edinburgh: Edinburgh University Press, 2004), p. 8.

1: Early Celtic Poetry (to 1500)

1   On this, see Katherine Simms, 'Muireadhach Albanach Ó Dálaigh and the Classical revolution', in Thomas Clancy and Murray Pittock (eds), *The Edinburgh History of Scottish Literature* vol. 1 (Edinburgh: Edinburgh University Press, 2007), pp. 83–90; and for the Ó Dálaigh family in general, her 'Ó Dálaigh Family (*per. c.* 1100–*c.* 1620)', *Oxford Dictionary of National Biography*, ed. Lawrence Goldman, www.oxforddnb.com/view/article/54668. For Muireadhach's poetry and that of his companion, see Thomas Clancy (ed.), *The Triumph Tree: Scotland's Earliest Poetry, AD 550–1350* (Edinburgh: Canongate, 1998), pp. 247–83, and sources there cited, pp. 339–40.
2   For further discussion of this issue, see 'Scottish Literature before Scottish Literature', in Gerard Carruthers and Liam McIlvanney (eds), *The Cambridge Companion to Scottish Literature* (Cambridge: Cambridge University Press, 2012), pp. 13–26.
3   Oliver J. Padel, 'Aneirin and Taliesin: Sceptical Speculations', in Alex Woolf (ed.), *Beyond the Gododdin: Dark Age Scotland in Medieval Wales* (St Andrews: St John's House, 2013), pp. 115–52 (p. 142); this collection of essays is the most recent treatment of the matter. For

editions and earlier commentary, see e.g. Kenneth H. Jackson, *Gododdin: The Oldest Scottish Poem* (Edinburgh: Edinburgh University Press, 1969); A. O. H. Jarman, *Aneirin: Y Gododdin: Britain's Oldest Heroic Poem* (Llandysul: Gomer Press, 1988).

4   Especially John T. Koch, see his *The Gododdin of Aneirin: Text and Context from Dark-Age North Britain* (Cardiff: University of Wales, 1997); and recently, and very coherently, Thomas M. Charles-Edwards, *Wales and the Britons, 350–1064* (Oxford: Oxford University Press, 2012), pp. 365–78.

5   Ifor Williams (ed.), *Canu Aneirin* (Cardiff: University of Wales Press, 1961), §LXXIXB, with slight emendation; translation Joseph P. Clancy in Clancy, *Triumph Tree*, p. 114.

6   Robert Crawford, *Scotland's Books: The Penguin History of Scottish Literature* (London: Penguin, 2007), ch. 1, 'Praise'; see also Thomas Owen Clancy, 'The Poetry of the Court: Praise', in Clancy and Pittock, *Edinburgh History*, vol. 1, pp. 63–71.

7   Ifor Williams (ed.), *The Poems of Taliesin* (Dublin: Dublin Institute for Advanced Studies, 1975), p. 11 (spelling and punctuation slightly adjusted); translation J. P. Clancy, in Clancy, *Triumph Tree*, p. 88.

8   Ifor Williams, *Canu Aneirin*, §LXXXVIIB; translation Joseph P. Clancy in Clancy, *Triumph Tree*, p. 68.

9   Wilson McLeod and Meg Bateman (eds), *Duanaire na Sràcaire/Songbook of the Pillagers: Anthology of Scottish Gaelic Verse to 1600* (Edinburgh: Birlinn, 2007), pp. 68–69; see also Clancy, *Triumph Tree*, pp. 260–62.

10 McLeod and Bateman, *Duanaire na Sràcaire*, pp. 80–91 (pp. 82–83); see also Clancy, *Triumph Tree*, pp. 288–91.

11 Thomas Owen Clancy, 'A Gaelic Polemic Quatrain from the Reign of Alexander I, c. 1113', *Scottish Gaelic Studies* 20 (2000), pp. 88–96 (p. 90); Clancy, *Triumph Tree*, p. 184.

12 See Thomas Owen Clancy and Gilbert Márkus, *Iona: The Earliest Poetry of a Celtic Monastery* (Edinburgh: Edinburgh University Press, 1995), pp. 152–54, for discussion of this term.

13 McLeod and Bateman, *Duanaire na Sràcaire*, pp. 304–07.

14 Maria Tymoczko uses the idea of a photo montage in exploring this technique in one Irish poem, on May Day, in '"Cétamon": Vision in Early Irish Seasonal Poetry', *Éire-Ireland* 18.4 (1983), pp. 17–39.

15 McLeod and Bateman, *Duanaire na Sràcaire*, pp. 28–29. On the bodily imagery here – and the poem in general – see Sìm Innes, 'Cràbhachd do Mhoire Òigh air a' Ghàidhealtachd sna meadhan-aoisean anmoch,

le aire shònraichte do Leabhar Deadhan Lios Mòir', PhD thesis, University of Glasgow, 2010, esp. pp. 129–35.
16 Rudolf Thurneysen, 'Mittelirische Verslehren', *Irische Texte* 3.1 (1891), p. 104, spelling mildly altered; translation, Clancy, *Triumph Tree*, p. 144.
17 For fuller attempts to interrogate this literature, see Clancy, *Triumph Tree*, introduction; Clancy and Pittock, *Edinburgh History* vol. 1, part 1.
18 On which, see especially Martin MacGregor, 'Creation and Compilation: The Book of the Dean of Lismore and Literary Culture in Late-Medieval Gaelic Scotland', pp. 209–18, and William Gillies, 'Gaelic Literature in the Later Middle Ages: The Book of the Dean and Beyond', pp. 219–25, in Clancy and Pittock, *Edinburgh History*, vol. 1.
19 For the first three poems, see Clancy, *Triumph Tree*, pp. 158–63; on the unedited poem, and Mugrón's historical context, see Clancy, 'Iona v. Kells: Succession, Jurisdiction and Politics in the Columban *Familia* in the Later Tenth Century', in Fiona L. Edmonds and Paul Russell (eds), *Tome: Studies in Medieval Celtic History and Law in Honour of Thomas Charles-Edwards* (Woodbridge: Boydell, 2011), pp. 89–101.
20 For the corpus, see Clancy, *Triumph Tree*, pp. 247–83, and notes.
21 See McLeod and Bateman, *Duanaire na Sràcaire*, pp. 168–74; note that the full text of this poem has not yet been edited.
22 See essays cited in note 18; and also Martin MacGregor, 'The View from Fortingall: the Worlds of the Book of the Dean of Lismore', *Scottish Gaelic Studies* 22 (2006), pp. 35–85; and Sìm Innes, 'Gaelic Religious Poetry in Scotland: The Book of the Dean of Lismore', in Tadhg Ó hAnnracháin and Robert Armstrong (eds), *Christianities in the Early Modern Celtic World* (Basingstoke: Palgrave Macmillan, 2014), pp. 111–23.
23 McLeod and Bateman, *Duanaire na Sràcaire*, pp. 174–79.
24 McLeod and Bateman, *Duanaire na Sràcaire*, pp. 198–99; translation Clancy, *Triumph Tree*, p. 316.
25 Clancy, *Triumph Tree*, p. 310.

2: Scots Poetry in the Fourteenth and Fifteenth Centuries

1 Kurt Wittig, *The Scottish Tradition in Literature* (Edinburgh: Oliver and Boyd, 1958), p. 3.
2 Paul J. Ketrick, *The Relationship of Golagros and Gawane to the Old French Perceval* (unpublished doctoral thesis, Catholic University of

America: Washington, 1931); and R. D. S. Jack, 'Arthur's Pilgrimage: A Study of *Golagros and Gawane*', *Studies in Scottish Literature* 12 (1974), pp. 3-20.
3   F. O. Matthiessen, *Translation: An Elizabethan Art* (Boston, Mass.: Harvard University Press, 1931), p. 3.
4   *The Works of Allan Ramsay*, ed. Martin Burns and John W. Oliver, 4 vols, Scottish Text Society (Edinburgh: Blackwell, 1944-62) IV (1962), pp. 10-12.
5   Dante Alighieri, 'Epistle to Can Grande della Scala', in Alastair J. Minnis and A. B. Scott (eds), *Medieval Literary Theory and Criticism: c. 1100-1375* (Oxford: Clarendon Press, 1988), pp. 458-62.
6   Larry D. Benson, *Art and Tradition in Sir Gawain and the Green Knight* (New Brunswick, NJ: Rutgers University Press, 1965), pp. 163, 246.
7   On the relation between pagan gods and Christian Trinity, see Étienne Gilson, *The Spirit of Mediaeval Philosophy*, trans. A. H. C. Downes (Notre Dame: Notre Dame University Press, 1991), chapters 4-10 (p. 191).
8   In relation to artificial ordering, see *Poetria Nova of Geoffrey of Vinsauf*, trans. Margaret F. Nims (Toronto: Pontifical Institute of Mediaeval Studies, 1967), pp. 16-24; *The Didascalicon of Hugh of St Victor*, trans. Jerome Taylor (New York: Columbia University Press, 1961), VI: pp. 145-47.
9   *Didascalicon*, p. 140.
10 See Minnis, *Medieval Literary Theory and Criticism* (Dante, *Convivium*, pp. 394-412; Boccaccio, *Genealogy of the Pagan Gods*, pp. 420-31).
11 R. D. S. Jack, 'Translating Buchanan', in Philip Ford and Roger P. H. Green (eds), *George Buchanan: Poet and Dramatist* (Swansea: Classical Press of Wales, 2009), pp. xxviii, 223-26.
12 *The Letters of Robert Burns*, ed. George Ross Roy, 2nd edn, 2 vols (Oxford: Clarendon, 1985), I: pp. 125, 136.

3: Poetry in Latin

1   I wish to thank Luke Houghton, Jack MacQueen, Gilbert Márkus and Steven Reid for help on various matters.
2   Juvenal, XV.112, 'iam conducendo loquitur de rhetore Thule'; note also Virgil, *Georgics*, I.30, 'tibi [*the future Augustus*] serviat ultima Thule' ('*may farthest Thule serve you*').
3   Thomas Owen Clancy (ed.), *The Triumph Tree: Scotland's Earliest Poetry AD 550-1350* (Edinburgh: Canongate, 1998), pp. 185-86, 317-19.

4   See, for example, Jane Stevenson, 'Altus Prosator', *Celtic* 23 (1999), pp. 326–68.
5   J, U and W, which were not distinct letters for the Romans, are not used.
6   For example, there are eight-syllable lines in Peter G. Walsh (ed.), *One Hundred Latin Hymns: Ambrose to Aquinas* (Cambridge, Mass. and London: Harvard University Press, 2012), pp. 206–25, and sixteen-syllable lines in Thomas Owen Clancy and Gilbert Márkus (eds), *Iona: The Earliest Poetry of a Celtic Monastery* (Edinburgh: Edinburgh University Press, 1995), pp. 44–53.
7   This feature is often called 'Hisperic', a term of limited usefulness.
8   Clancy and Márkus, *Iona*, pp. 89–93, under the poem *Noli Pater*.
9   Clancy, *The Triumph Tree*, p. 45.
10 G. Márkus, '*Adiutor laborantium*: A Poem by Adomnán?', in Jonathan M. Wooding (ed.), *Adomnán of Iona: Theologian, Lawmaker, Peacemaker* (Dublin: Four Courts Press, 2010), pp. 145–61.
11 Clancy and Márkus, *Iona*, pp. 72–80, with commentary at pp. 235–37; for English translations, see Clancy, *The Triumph Tree*, p. 100.
12 Clancy and Márkus, *Iona*, pp. 177–92 and pp. 256–57; Clancy, *The Triumph Tree*, pp. 118–19.
13 See Karolus Strecker (ed.), *Monumenta Germaniae Historica, Poetae Latini Aevi Carolini*, vol. 4. 2 and 3 (Berlin: apud Weidmannos, 1923), pp. 943–62.
14 Thomas O'Loughlin, 'The Library of Iona in the Late Seventh Century', *Eriú* 45 (1994), pp. 33–52.
15 For the Latin, see W. F. Skene, *Historians of Scotland* (Edinburgh: Edmonston and Douglas, 1871), I: pp. 449–51; and for a translation, Clancy, *The Triumph Tree*, pp. 212–14.
16 Greta-Mary Hair and Betty I. Knott (eds), *Vespers, Matins and Lauds for St Kentigern, Patron Saint of Glasgow* (Glasgow: Musica Scotica Trust, 2011).
17 *Scotichronicon by Walter Bower*, gen. ed. D. E. R. Watt, 9 vols (Aberdeen: Aberdeen University Press, 1987–98).
18 'One thousand, thrice one hundred, also to one ten add one four times', *Scotichronicon*, XII.22.
19 J. IJsewijn and D. F. S. Thomson, 'The Latin Poems of Jacobus Follisius or James Foulis of Edinburgh', *Humanistica Lovaniensia* 24 (1975), pp. 102–60.
20 John Durkan, 'The Beginnings of Humanism in Scotland', *Innes Review* 4 (1953), pp. 5–19 (p. 8).

21 D. F. S. Thomson, 'The Latin Epigram in Scotland: The Sixteenth Century', *Phoenix* 11 (1957), pp. 63–78 (p. 65 n. 17).
22 Letter 541 in *Collected Works of Erasmus*, vol. 4 (II.489 Allen).
23 For this *Vita* see I. D. McFarlane, *Buchanan* (London: Duckworth, 1981), pp. 541–43.
24 The words 'authore Georgio Buchanano, Scoto, poetarum nostri saeculi facile principe' adorned the title page of the first complete edition of the Psalm paraphrases.
25 Durkan, 'Beginnings', pp. 11–13.
26 Richard Sharpe, 'Roderick MacLean's *Life* of St Columba of Iona in Latin Verse (1549)', *Innes Review* 42 (1991), pp. 111–32.
27 Buchanan's poems specifically relating to Scots and Scotland are illuminatingly discussed in Jack MacQueen, 'From Rome to Ruddiman: The Scoto-Latin Tradition', in Thomas Owen Clancy and Murray Pittock (eds), *The Edinburgh History of Scottish Literature*, vol. I (Edinburgh: Edinburgh University Press, 2007), pp. 184–208 (pp. 189–93).
28 McFarlane, *Buchanan*, pp. 255–56, with Roger P. H. Green, *George Buchanan: Poetic Paraphrase of the Psalms of David* (Geneva: Droz, 2011), p. 25.
29 Roger P. H. Green, 'George Buchanan, Arthur Johnston, and William Laud', *Scottish Literary Review* 2 (2010), pp. 14–16.
30 McFarlane, *Buchanan*, pp. 445–50.
31 These works are mentioned by James Macqueen, 'Scottish Latin Poetry', in Cairns Craig (ed.), *History of Scottish Literature*, vol. I, ed. R. D. S. Jack (Aberdeen: Aberdeen University Press, 1987–8), pp. 213–25.
32 Green, *Poetic Paraphrase*, p. 88.
33 J. W. L. Adams, 'The Renaissance Poets (2)', in J. Kinsley (ed.), *Scottish Poetry: a Critical Survey* (London: Cassell and Company, 1955), pp. 68–98.
34 Leicester Bradner, *Musae Anglicanae: A History of Anglo-Latin Poetry* (London: Oxford University Press, 1940), pp. 123–200.
35 *Georgii Buchanani Scoti Poemata* (Edinburgh: Andro Hart, 1615).
36 Green, *Poetic Paraphrase*, pp. 89–90.
37 The source is Sir Sydney Smith. See Henry Cockburn, *Memorials of His Time*, ed. Karl F. C. Miller (Chicago: University of Chicago Press, 1974), p. 19.
38 The Glasgow-based research project 'Bridging the Continental Divide; neo-Latin and its cultural role in Jacobean Scotland, as seen in

the *Delitiae Poetarum Scotorum* (1637)', led by Steven Reid with David McOmish as head researcher, was completed in August 2015. See www.dps.gla.ac.uk for developments. Reid has also written a valuable introductory survey, '"Quasi Sybillae Divina Folia": the anatomy of the *Delitiae Poetarum Scotorum*', in Janet Hadley Williams and J. Derrick McClure (eds), *Fresche Fontanis: Studies in the Culture of Medieval and Early Modern Scotland* (Newcastle upon Tyne: Cambridge Scholars Publishing, 2013), pp. 397–414.

39 L. B. T. Houghton, 'Lucan in the Highlands: James Philp's *Grameid* and the Traditions of Ancient Epic', in L. B. T. Houghton and Gesine Manuwald (eds), *Neo-Latin Poetry in the British Isles* (London: Bristol University Press, 2012), pp. 190–207.

40 John and Winifred MacQueen (eds and trans), *Archibald Pitcairne: the Latin Poems* (Assen: Royal van Gorcum, 2009).

4: Poetry in the Languages and Dialects of Northern Scotland

1   Simon Hall, *The History of Orkney Literature* (Edinburgh: John Donald/Birlinn, 2010); Mark Ryan Smith, *The Literature of Shetland* (Lerwick: The Shetland Times, 2014).

2   Old Norse texts are cited from the in-progress multi-volume M. Clunies Ross (gen. ed.), *Skaldic Poetry of the Scandinavian Middle Ages* (Turnhout: Brepols, 2007–), with its up-to-date bibliographies and explanatory notes (abbrev. *SkP*). Stanzas by Arnórr jarlaskáld Þorðarson (ed. Diana Whaley) and Rögnvaldr jarl Kali Kolsson (ed. Judith Jesch) are from vol. II: Kari E. Gade (ed.), *Poetry from the Kings' Sagas 2* (2009), pp. 258 and 592–93 respectively. Bjarni Kolbeinsson's *Jómsvíkingadrápa*, ed. by Emily Lethbridge, appears in vol. I: Diana Whaley (ed.), *Poetry from the Kings' Sagas 1* (2013), pp. 954–97; *Málsháttakvæði* is scheduled to appear in vol. III (2015). All translations of the poetry are my own.

3   See Roberta Frank, 'Marketing Odin's Mead in a Strange Land', in Daniel Donoghue, James Simpson and Nicholas Watson (eds), *The Morton Bloomfield Lectures, 1989–2005*, Medieval Institute Publications (Kalamazoo, MI: Western Michigan University, 2010), pp. 246–70.

4   The contemporary Aberdeen poet Ian Crockatt manages to capture some of the sound effects, colour and imaginative reach of this stanza: 'Who else hoards such yellow / hair, bright lady – fair as / your milk-mild shoulders, / where milled barley-gold falls? / Chuck the cowled hawk, harry / him with sweets. Crimsoner / of eagles' claws, I covet / cool downpours of silk; yours', in *Crimsoning the Eagle's Claw:*

The Viking Poems of Rognvaldr Kali Kolsson, Earl of Orkney, trans. Ian Crockatt (Todmorden: Arc Publications, 2014), p. 53.

5   *The Pirate*, in *The Works of Sir Walter Scott: The Waverley Novels* (Boston and New York: Houghton Mifflin, 1913), XXIII: p. 324.
6   William Donaldson, *Popular Literature in Victorian Scotland: Language, Fiction and the Press* (Aberdeen: Aberdeen University Press, 1986).
7   Brian Smith, '"Eels": Strange Masterpiece', *New Shetlander* 230 (2004), pp. 29–31.
8   L. G. Scott, 'Reminiscences of Haldane Burgess', *New Shetlander* 16 (1949), p. 15.
9   Ernest W. Marwick (ed.), *An Anthology of Orkney Verse* (Kirkwall: The Kirkwall Press, 1949), p. 11.
10 G. M. B., 'Culture and Co-operation', *New Shetlander* 7 (1947), p. 20.
11 William Sandison (ed.), *Shetland Verse: Remnants of the Norn* (Shrewsbury: privately published, 1953), pp. viii–ix.
12 Alex Cluness (ed.), *Dialect 04* (Lerwick: Shetland Arts Trust, 2004).

5: The Sixteenth and Seventeenth Centuries

1   Sarah M. Dunnigan, 'Reformation and Renaissance', in Gerard Carruthers and Liam McIlvanney (eds), *The Cambridge Companion to Scottish Literature* (Cambridge: Cambridge University Press, 2012), pp. 41–55 (p. 41).
2   On the relationship between manuscript and print in early modern Scotland, see Denton Fox, 'Manuscripts and Prints of Scots Poetry in the Sixteenth Century', in Adam J. Aitken, Matthew P. McDiarmid and Derick S. Thomson (eds), *Bards and Makars: Scottish Language and Literature: Medieval and Renaissance* (Glasgow: University of Glasgow Press, 1977), pp. 156–71; Priscilla Bawcutt, 'Manuscript Miscellanies in Scotland from the Fifteenth to the Seventeenth Century', in Sally Mapstone (ed.), *Older Scots Literature* (Edinburgh: John Donald, 2005), pp. 189–210.
3   William Ramson, 'On Bannatyne's Editing', in Adam J. Aitken, Matthew P. McDiarmid and Derick S. Thomson (eds), *Bards and Makars: Scottish Language and Literature: Medieval and Renaissance* (Glasgow: University of Glasgow Press, 1977), pp. 172–83 (p. 172).
4   Ramson, 'On Bannatyne's Editing', pp. 180–81.
5   Now the object of a research and digitisation project in the University of Glasgow, available at www.dps.gla.ac.uk.
6   Angus Matheson, 'Poems from a Manuscript of Cathal Mac Muireadhaigh II', *Éigse* 11 (1964), pp. 1–17.

7   William J. Watson (ed.), *Bàrdachd Ghàidhlig: Specimens of Gaelic Poetry 1550–1900*, 3rd edn (Stirling: An Comunn Gaidhealach, 1959), pp. 221–23.
8   Calum Mac Phàrlain, *Làmh-Sgrìobhainn Mhic Rath: Dòrlach Laoidhean do Sgrìobhadh le Donnchadh Mac Rath, 1688* (Dun Dè: Calum S. Mac Leòid, 1923). 'Sgeula leat' is in fact not found in a contemporary manuscript, but in later collections.
9   Colm Ó Baoill and Meg Bateman (eds and trans), *Gàir nan Clàrsach/ The Harp's Cry: An Anthology of 17th Century Gaelic Poetry* (Edinburgh: Birlinn, 1994), pp. 100–05.
10 It is often more commonly linked to his uncle and predecessor as chief of the Sleat MacDonalds, Dòmhnall Gorm Mòr (d. 1617). See Ó Baoill and Bateman, *Gàir nan Clàrsach*, pp. 66–68; Anne Lorne Gillies, *Songs of Gaelic Scotland* (Edinburgh: Birlinn, 2005), pp. 10–14.
11 J. L. Campbell and Francis Collinson (eds and trans), *Hebridean Folksongs*, 3 vols (Oxford: Clarendon Press, 1969–81), II: p. 238; Ó Baoill and Bateman, *Gàir nan Clàrsach*, pp. 66–69.
12 In his *The Scottish Tradition in Literature* (Edinburgh: Oliver and Boyd, 1958) Kurt Wittig entitled the chapter dedicated to Lindsay 'Ebbing' (p. 91).
13 Theo van Heijnsbergen, 'The Love Lyrics of Alexander Scott', *Studies in Scottish Literature* 26 (1991), pp. 366–79 (p. 367).
14 Alasdair A. MacDonald (ed.), *The Gude and Godlie Ballatis*, (Woodbridge: Boydell and Brewer, for the Scottish Text Society, 2015).
15 See Evelyn S. Newlyn, 'The Female Voice in Sixteenth-century Scots Poetry', and Sarah M. Dunnigan, 'Feminising the Early Modern Erotic: Female-voiced Love Lyrics and Mary Queen of Scots', both appearing in Mapstone, *Older Scots Literature*, pp. 283–91, 441–66.
16 Sarah M. Dunnigan, *Eros and Poetry at the Courts of Mary Queen of Scots and James VI* (Basingstoke: Palgrave Macmillan, 2002).
17 William J. Watson (ed.), *Scottish Verse from the Book of the Dean of Lismore* (Edinburgh: The Scottish Gaelic Texts Society, 1937).
18 For exceptions see Alexander MacBain and John Kennedy (eds), *Reliquiae Celticae*, 2 vols (Inverness: Northern Chronicle Office, 1892–94), I: pp. 134–35; Wilson McLeod, *Divided Gaels: Gaelic Cultural Identities in Scotland and Ireland c. 1200–c. 1650* (Oxford: Oxford University Press, 2004), p. 109 n. 5; M. Pía Coira, *By Poetic Authority: The Rhetoric of Panegyric in Gaelic Poetry of Scotland to c. 1700* (Edinburgh: Dunedin, 2012), p. 70.

19　McLeod, *Divided Gaels*, p. 76; Derick S. Thomson, 'Gaelic Learned Orders and Literati', *Scottish Studies* 12 (1968), pp. 57–78 (p. 73).

20　Alison Cathcart, 'The Forgotten '45: Donald Dubh's Rebellion in an Archipelagic Context', *The Scottish Historical Review* 91 (2012), pp. 239–46 (p. 241).

21　Martin MacGregor, 'The Campbells: Lordship, Literature and Liminality', *Textual Cultures* 7 (2012), pp. 121–57. Survival may also be a factor since in 1558 Colin Campbell (Cailean Liath), sixth of Glenorchy, confirmed land in Lorne to a family of *Jocalatores wlgariter Rymouris*, identified as MacEwens, see Derick S. Thomson, 'MacEwen Poets', in Derick S. Thomson (ed.), *The Companion to Gaelic Scotland*, (Glasgow: Gairm, 1994), pp. 170–71.

22　Katherine Simms, 'The Transition from Medieval to Modern in the Poems of Tadhg Dall Ó hUiginn', in Pádraigín Riggs (ed.), *Tadhg Dall Ó hUiginn: His Historical and Literary Context* (London: Irish Texts Society, 2010), pp. 119–34.

23　She married: Colin Campbell (Gilleasbuig Ruadh Òg), fourth Earl of Argyll (d. 1558); An Calbhach Ó Dómhnaill of Tír Conaill (d. 1566); Seaán Ó Néill (Shane Ó Néill) (c. 1530–1567, chief of the Uí Néill of Tír Eoghain); Stewart of Appin. Jane Dawson, *The Politics of Religion in the Age of Mary, Queen of Scots: The Earl of Argyll and the Struggle for Britain and Ireland* (Cambridge: Cambridge University Press, 2004), pp. 129–30; Hans Claude Hamilton (ed.), *Calendar of the State Papers Relating to Ireland, of the reigns of Henry VIII, Edward VI, Mary, and Elizabeth, 1509–1573* (London: Longman, 1860), p. xxvii; John Bannerman and Ronald Black, 'A Sixteenth-Century Gaelic Letter', *Scottish Gaelic Studies* 13 (1978), pp. 56–65 (p. 61).

24　Hamilton, *Calendar of the State Papers*, p. 172; John Bannerman, 'Literacy in the Highlands', in Ian B. Cowan and Duncan Shaw (eds), *The Renaissance and Reformation in Scotland* (Edinburgh: Scottish Academic Press, 1983), pp. 214–35 (p. 223).

25　'John Smyths Advice for the Realme of Ireland', printed by Gerard A. Hayes-McCoy, *Scots Mercenary Forces in Ireland (1565–1603)* (Dublin: Burns Oates & Washbourne, 1937), pp. 346, 116.

26　Eleanor Knott (ed.), *The Bardic Poems of Tadhg Dall Ó hUiginn (1550–1591)*, 2 vols (London: Irish Texts Society, 1922–26), poem 8, l. 40.

27　Damian McManus and Eoghan Ó Raghallaigh (eds), *A Bardic Miscellany: Five Hundred Bardic Poems from Manuscripts in Irish and British Libraries* (Dublin: Dept of Irish, Trinity College, 2010), poem 104.

28 Wilson McLeod and Meg Bateman (eds), *Duanaire na Sracaire: Anthology of Scotland's Gaelic Verse* (Edinburgh: Birlinn, 2007), poem 67.
29 Pat Menzies (ed.), *Òran na Comhachaig le Dòmhnall mac Fhionnlaigh nan Dàn* ([Edinburgh]: The Scottish Gaelic Texts Society, 2012), pp. 76–77.
30 Poems 65 and 66 in McLeod and Bateman, *Duanaire na Sracaire*.
31 Priscilla Bawcutt, 'James VI's Castalian Band: A Modern Myth', *The Scottish Historical Review* 80 (2001), 251–59.
32 David J. Parkinson (ed.), *James VI and I, Literature and Scotland. Tides of Change, 1567–1625* (Leuven: Peeters, 2012).
33 Helena Mennie Shire, *Song, Dance and Poetry of the Court of Scotland under King James VI* (Cambridge: Cambridge University Press, 1969).
34 Jane Rickard, *Authorship and Authority: The Writings of James VI and I* (Manchester: Manchester University Press, 2007).
35 J. Derrick McClure, '"O Phoenix Escossois": James VI as Poet', in Alisoun Gardner-Medwin and Janet Hadley Williams (eds), *A Day Estivall: Essays on the Music, Poetry and History of Scotland and England & Poems Previously Unpublished in Honour of Helena Mennie Shire* (Aberdeen: Aberdeen University Press, 1990), pp. 96–111.
36 J. Derrick McClure, 'Translation and Transcreation in the Castalian Period', *Studies in Scottish Literature* 26 (1991), pp. 185–98.
37 Michael R. G. Spiller, 'The Scottish Court and the Scottish Sonnet at the Union of the Crowns', in Sally Mapstone and Juliette Wood (eds), *The Rose and the Thistle* (East Linton: Tuckwell Press, 1998), pp. 101–15.
38 Sebastiaan Verweij, 'The Manuscripts of William Fowler: A Revaluation of *The Tarantula of Love, A Sonnet Sequence*, and *Of Death*', *Scottish Studies Review* 8.2 (2007), pp. 9–23.
39 David J. Parkinson (ed.), *Poems of Alexander Montgomerie*, 2 vols (Edinburgh: Scottish Text Society, 2000); Roderick J. Lyall, *Alexander Montgomerie: Poetry, Politics, and Cultural Change in Jacobean Scotland* (Tempe: Arizona Center for Medieval and Renaissance Studies, 2005).
40 David J. Parkinson, 'Alexander Montgomerie: Scottish Author', in Mapstone, *Older Scots Literature*, pp. 493–513 (p. 499).
41 Iain Grimble, *Scottish Islands* (London: BBC, 1988), p. 57.
42 *Calendar of the Carew Manuscripts, Preserved in the Archiepiscopal Library at Lambeth*, ed. by J. S. Brewer and William Bullen (London: Longman and Trübner, 1971), V: *1603–1623*, p. 291.

43 Aonghas MacCoinnich, 'Daltachas, Fineachan agus Alba anns an t-siathamh agus san t-seachdamh linn deug', in Gillian Munro and Richard A. V. Cox (eds), *Cànan & Cultar/Language & Culture: Rannsachadh na Gàidhlig 4* (Edinburgh: Dunedin, 2010), pp. 37–53 (p. 45), nn. 35, 37.

44 Domhnall Uilleam Stiùbhart, 'Women and Gender in the Early Modern Western Gàidhealtachd', in Elizabeth Ewan and Maureen M. Meikle (eds), *Women in Scotland c. 1100–c. 1750* (East Linton: Tuckwell Press, 1999), pp. 233–49 (p. 237).

45 Allan Macinnes, 'Gaelic Culture in the Seventeenth Century: Polarization and Assimilation', in Steven G. Ellis and Sarah Barber (eds), *Conquest and Union: Fashioning a British State, 1485–1725* (London: Longman, 1995), pp. 162–94 (p. 163).

46 Matheson, 'Poems', p. 4.

47 J. Carmichael Watson, 'Cathal Mac Muireadhaigh Cecinit', in John Ryan (ed.), *Essays and Studies Presented to Professor Eoin MacNeill* (Dublin: At the Sign of the Three Candles, 1940), pp. 167–79 (p. 171).

48 MacBain and Kennedy, *Reliquiae Celticae*, II: p. 226.

49 James Carney, *The Irish Bardic Poet* (Dublin: Dublin Institute for Advanced Studies, 1967), p. 16.

50 Ronald Black, 'A Manuscript of Cathal Mac Muireadhaigh', *Celtica* 10 (1973), pp. 193–209 (199).

51 Seán Ó Tuama, 'Love in the Medieval Irish Literary Lyric', in *Repossessions: Selected Essays on the Irish Literary Heritage* (Cork: Cork University Press, 1995), pp. 164–95 (p. 173).

52 Thomas Owen Clancy, 'A Fond Farewell to Last Night's Literary Criticism: Reading Niall Mór MacMhuirich', in Gillian Munro and Richard A. V. Cox (eds), *Cànan & Cultar/Language & Culture: Rannsachadh na Gàidhlig 4* (Edinburgh: Dunedin, 2010), pp. 109–25, English translation at p. 116.

53 Wittig, *The Scottish Tradition in Literature*, p. 129.

54 Sarah M. Dunnigan, 'Drummond and the Meaning of Beauty', in Sarah Carpenter and Sarah M. Dunnigan (eds), *'Joyous Sweit Imaginatioun': Essays on Scottish Literature in Honour of R. D. S. Jack* (Amsterdam: Rodopi, 2007), pp. 128–54.

55 David Atkinson, 'William Drummond as a Baroque Poet', *Studies in Scottish Literature* 26 (1991), pp. 394–409.

56 Dunnigan, 'Drummond and the Meaning of Beauty', p. 132.

57 Colm Ó Baoill (ed.), *Mairghread nighean Lachlainn: Songmaker of Mull* (Edinburgh: Scottish Gaelic Texts Society, 2009), pp. 38–39.

58 Derick Thomson, *An Introduction to Gaelic Poetry* (Edinburgh: Edinburgh University Press, 1989), p. 115.
59 See William Gillies, 'Clan Donald Bards and Scholars', in Gillian Munro and Richard A. V. Cox, *Cànan & Cultar*, pp. 91–108.
60 Ó Baoill and Bateman, *Gàir nan Clàrsach*, p. 22.
61 John MacInnes, 'The Panegyric Code in Gaelic Poetry and its Historical Background', *Transactions of the Gaelic Society of Inverness* 50 (1976–78), pp. 435–98; M. Pía Coira, *By Poetic Authority*; Máire Ní Annracháin, 'Metaphor and Metonymy in the Poetry of Màiri nighean Alasdair Ruaidh', in Sharon Arbuthnott and Kaarina Hollo (eds), *Fil súil nglais – A Grey Eye Looks Back: A Festschrift in Honour of Colm Ó Baoill* (Ceann Drochaid: Clann Tuirc, 2007), pp. 163–74.
62 Allan Macinnes, 'Gaelic Culture in the Seventeenth Century', p. 164.
63 Ó Baoill and Bateman, *Gàir nan Clàrsach*, pp. 198–207.

6: The Eighteenth Century

1 Kurt Wittig, *The Scottish Tradition in Literature* (Edinburgh: Oliver & Boyd, 1958); David Craig, *Scottish Literature and the Scottish People 1680–1830* (London: Chatto & Windus, 1961); David Daiches, *The Paradox of Scottish Culture* (London: Oxford University Press, 1964).
2 Ronald Black (ed.), *An Lasair: Anthology of 18th Century Scottish Gaelic Verse* (Edinburgh: Birlinn, 2001), pp. 88–95.
3 William Matheson (ed.), *The Blind Harper: The Songs of Roderick Morison and his Music* (Edinburgh: Scottish Gaelic Texts Society, 1970), pp. 58–73; Black, *An Lasair*, pp. 28–37.
4 Derick Thomson, *An Introduction to Gaelic Poetry* (London: Gollancz, 1974), pp. 127, 135; John MacInnes, 'The Panegyric Code in Gaelic Poetry and its Historical Background', *Transactions of the Gaelic Society of Inverness*, 50 (1976–78), pp. 435–98.
5 John Mackenzie (ed.), *Sar-Obair nam Bard Gaelach: or, The Beauties of Gaelic Poetry* (Glasgow: Macgregor, Polson, 1841), pp. 58–60, 68–75, 94–99, 394, 400; Colm Ó Baoill (ed.), *Bàrdachd Shìlis na Ceapaich: Poems and Songs by Sìleas MacDonald* (Edinburgh: Scottish Gaelic Texts Society, 1972); Colm Ó Baoill (ed.), *Iain Dubh: Orain a Rinn Iain Dubh Mac Iain Mhic Ailein* (Aberdeen: An Clò Gaidhealach, 1994); Black, *An Lasair*, pp. 373–75, 379–82, 388–93, 402–05, 423–25; Colm Ó Baoill (ed.), *Mairghread Nighean Lachlainn, Song-Maker of Mull* (Edinburgh: Scottish Gaelic Texts Society, 2009).

6 Colm Ó Baoill (ed.), *Gàir nan Clàrsach: The Harps' Cry* (Edinburgh: Birlinn, 1994), pp. 206–13; Pat Menzies (ed.), *Òran na Comhachaig* (Edinburgh: Scottish Gaelic Texts Society, 2012).

7 Archibald Pitcairne, *The Assembly*, ed. Terence Tobin (Lafayette, Ind.: Purdue University Press, 1972); see also John MacQueen, *The Enlightenment and Scottish Literature* (Edinburgh: Scottish Academic Press, 1982), pp. 1–6.

8 See Douglas Duncan, *Thomas Ruddiman: A Study in Scottish Scholarship of the Early Eighteenth Century* (Edinburgh: Oliver & Boyd, 1965).

9 The 'Habbie' stanza owes something to the satirical *snéadhbhairdne* metre of Gaelic verse, see Ronald Black, 'The Genius of Cathal MacMhuirich', *Transactions of the Gaelic Society of Inverness* 50 (1976–78), pp. 327–66 (p. 335), and Black, *An Lasair*, p. 408.

10 For this background, see Murray Pittock, *Poetry and Jacobite Politics in Eighteenth-Century Britain and Ireland* (Cambridge: Cambridge University Press, 1994).

11 See Carol McGuirk, 'Augustan Influences on Allan Ramsay', in *Studies in Scottish Literature*, 16 (1981), pp. 97–109.

12 See Gerard Carruthers, *Scottish Literature: A Critical Guide* (Edinburgh: Edinburgh University Press, 2009), pp. 47–53.

13 See Richard Holmes, 'James Arbuckle's *Glota* and the Poetry of Allusion', *Journal for Eighteenth-Century Studies* 35.1 (2012), pp. 85–100; for Ulster Scots poetry more generally, see Frank Ferguson (ed.), *Ulster-Scots Writing: An Anthology* (Dublin: Four Courts Press, 2008).

14 For Thomson in his national context, see Mary Jane Scott, *James Thomson, Anglo-Scot* (Athens, Ga.: University of Georgia Press, 1988); see also Richard Terry (ed.), *James Thomson: Essays for the Tercentenary* (Liverpool: Liverpool University Press, 2000).

15 Ronald Black (ed.), *To the Hebrides: Samuel Johnson's Journey to the Western Islands of Scotland and James Boswell's Journal of a Tour to the Hebrides* (Edinburgh: Birlinn, 2007), p. 503; for Malloch generally, see Sandro Jung, *David Mallet, Anglo-Scot: Poetry, Patronage and Politics in the Age of Union* (Newark, Del.: University of Delaware Press, 2008).

16 Ronald Black, *Mac Mhaighstir Alasdair: The Ardnamurchan Years* (Coll: Society of West Highland & Island Historical Research, 1986), pp. 11, 32–33; Ronald Black, 'Alasdair mac Mhaighstir Alasdair and the New Gaelic Poetry', in Susan Manning (ed.), *The Edinburgh History*

of Scottish Literature, (Edinburgh: Edinburgh University Press, 2007), II: pp. 110–24 (pp. 119–22); Ronald Black and Jane Ridder-Patrick, 'The Date of "Oran a' Gheamhraidh" Revisited', *Scottish Gaelic Studies* 27 (2010), pp. 1–18.

17 A. and A. Macdonald (eds), *The Poems of Alexander MacDonald* (Inverness: Northern Counties, 1924), p. xxxvii; Black, *Ardnamurchan Years*, p. 10.

18 Black, *Ardnamurchan Years*, pp. 5, 7–8; John Lorne Campbell, *A Very Civil People: Hebridean Folk, History and Tradition* (Edinburgh: Birlinn, 2000), pp. 152–59.

19 Alexander Robertson of Struan, *Poems, on Various Subjects and Occasions* (Edinburgh: Charles Alexander, [n.d.]); Neil MacGregor, 'John Roy Stuart, Jacobite Bard of Strathspey', *Transactions of the Gaelic Society of Inverness*, 63 (2002–04), pp. 1–124.

20 Angus MacLeod (ed.), *The Songs of Duncan Ban Macintyre* (Edinburgh: Scottish Gaelic Texts Society, 1952), pp. xxiii–xxiv; Black, *An Lasair*, pp. 437–38.

21 Black, *Ardnamurchan Years*, pp. 19, 37–39; Black, 'Alasdair mac Mhaighstir Alasdair and the New Gaelic Poetry', pp. 114–15, 122–23.

22 John Lorne Campbell (ed.), *Highland Songs of the Forty-Five*, 2nd edn (Edinburgh: Scottish Gaelic Texts Society, 1984), pp. 144–53.

23 Campbell, *A Very Civil People*, pp. 150–59.

24 Black, *An Lasair*, pp. 162–65, 190–93; Campbell, *Highland Songs of the Forty-Five*, pp. 76–77, 128–31, 154–63.

25 National Library of Scotland, Adv. MS 72.2.11.

26 Ronald Black, 'Alexander MacDonald's *Ais-Eiridh*, 1751', *Journal of the Edinburgh Bibliographical Society* 5 (2010), pp. 45–64 (pp. 60–61).

27 Hugh MacDiarmid (ed.), *The Golden Treasury of Scottish Poetry* (London: Macmillan, 1946), pp. 65–85; Black, *An Lasair*, pp. 202–17, 469–75; Black, 'Alasdair mac Mhaighstir Alasdair and the New Gaelic Poetry', pp. 119–22.

28 Mackenzie, *Sar-Obair nam Bard Gaelach*, p. 187; Donald John MacLeod, 'The Poetry of Rob Donn Mackay', *Scottish Gaelic Studies*, 12.1 (1971), pp. 3–21 (p. 3); Black, *An Lasair*, p. 431.

29 Ian Grimble, *The World of Rob Donn* (Edinburgh: Edina Press, 1979); on Pope, see p. 32.

30 Grimble, *The World of Rob Donn*, pp. 71–75.

31 Criticism of many of these writers remains scant, but as a starting point, see Christopher MacLachlan (ed.), *Before Burns: Eighteenth Century Scottish Poetry* (Edinburgh: Canongate, 2002).

32 George Calder (ed.), *Gaelic Songs by William Ross* (Edinburgh: Oliver and Boyd, 1937); John MacDonald (ed.), *Ewen MacLachlan's Gaelic Verse* (Aberdeen: Aberdeen University Press, 1937); Black, *An Lasair*, pp. 500–02, 518–21; William Gillies, '"Merely a Bard"? William Ross and Gaelic Poetry', *Aiste* 1 (2007), pp. 123–69

33 MacDiarmid, *Golden Treasury of Scottish Poetry*, pp. 43–58; MacLeod, *Songs of Duncan Ban Macintyre*, pp. 196–225; Black, *An Lasair*, pp. 490–93.

34 MacLeod, *Songs of Duncan Ban Macintyre*, pp. 86–101, 322–25, 350–57, 396–405.

35 William Matheson (ed.), *The Songs of John MacCodrum* (Edinburgh: Scottish Gaelic Texts Society, 1938), pp. 196–203; Hugh Cheape, 'A Song on the Lowland Shepherds: Popular Reaction to the Highland Clearances', *Scottish Economic and Social History* 15 (1995), pp. 85–100; Donald Meek (ed.), *Tuath is Tighearna: Tenants and Landlords* (Edinburgh: Scottish Gaelic Texts Society, 1995), pp. 47–53, 186–89; Black, *An Lasair*, pp. 286–93, 517–18.

36 Black, *An Lasair*, pp. 481–85.

37 D. E. Meek, 'Buchanan, Dugald', in *Dictionary of Scottish Church History & Theology*, ed. by Nigel M. de S. Cameron *et al.* (Edinburgh: T. & T. Clark, 1993), p. 106. See also Donald Meek, 'Evangelicalism, Ossianism and the Enlightenment: the Many Masks of Dugald Buchanan', in Christopher MacLachlan (ed.), *Crossing the Highland Line* (Glasgow: ASLS, 2009), pp. 97–112.

38 Derick S. Thomson, *The Gaelic Sources of Macpherson's 'Ossian'* (Edinburgh: Oliver & Boyd, 1951).

39 See for example Neil Ross (ed.), *Heroic Poetry from the Book of the Dean of Lismore* (Edinburgh: Scottish Gaelic Texts Society, 1939).

40 Fiona J. Stafford, *The Sublime Savage: A Study of James Macpherson and the Poems of Ossian* (Edinburgh: Edinburgh University Press, 1988), pp. 18–19; James Macpherson, *The Poems of Ossian and Related Works*, ed. Howard Gaskill (Edinburgh: Edinburgh University Press, 1996), p. ix. On 'vermin', see e.g. National Library of Scotland MS 3734, ff. 328v, 586v, 620v, 659v (correspondence of Maj.-Gen. John Campbell of Mamore with the Duke of Cumberland and others, 1745–46).

41 For Fergusson in his intellectual context, see F. W. Freeman, *Robert Fergusson and the Scots-Humanist Compromise* (Edinburgh: Edinburgh University Press, 1984).

42 Black, *An Lasair*, pp. 499–500; Joseph J. Flahive, 'Duncan Campbell: A Scottish-Gaelic Bard in Eighteenth-Century Cork', *Journal of the*

Cork Historical and Archaeological Society 113 (2008), pp. 80–89; Ronald Black, 'Gaelic Secular Publishing', in Stephen W. Brown and Warren McDougall (eds), *The Edinburgh History of the Book in Scotland* (Edinburgh: Edinburgh University Press, 2012), II: pp. 595–612 (pp. 607, 608–09).
43 Black, 'Gaelic Secular Publishing', pp. 605–06.
44 For a multifarious range of recent critical perspectives on Burns, see Nigel Leask, *Robert Burns and Pastoral* (Oxford: Oxford University Press, 2010); Robert Crawford, *The Bard* (London: Jonathan Cape, 2009); Gerard Carruthers (ed.), *The Edinburgh Companion to Robert Burns* (Edinburgh: Edinburgh University Press, 2009); and Liam McIlvanney, *Burns the Radical* (East Linton: Tuckwell, 2002).
45 Charles Macphater, *Dain, is Luinneagan, Robert Burns* (Glasgow: Alex. McLaren, [n.d. 1910?]); Ruairidh MacDhòmhnaill, *Bardachd Raibeirt Burns* (Edinburgh: [n.pub.], 1992).

7: The Nineteenth Century

1 Donald E. Meek (ed.), *Tuath is Tighearna: Tenants and Landlords* (Edinburgh: Scottish Gaelic Texts Society, 1995), pp. 49, 188.
2 A. MacLean Sinclair, *Clàrsach na Coille: A Collection of Gaelic Poetry* (Archibald Sinclair: Glasgow, 1881), p. 143.
3 Margaret McDonell (ed.), *The Emigrant Experience: Songs of Highland Emigrants in North America* (Toronto: University of Toronto Press, 1982).
4 *Teachdaire nan Gaidheal* 7 (1845), pp. 55–56.
5 George Gordon, Lord Byron, *Don Juan*, X.17–19.
6 Penny Fielding, *Scotland and the Fictions of Geography* (Cambridge: Cambridge University Press, 2009), pp. 130–60.
7 Murray Pittock, *Scottish and Irish Romanticism* (Oxford: Oxford University Press, 2008), pp. 19–21.
8 Donald E. Meek, 'Gaelic Printing and Publishing', in Bill Bell (ed.), *The Edinburgh History of the Book in Scotland* (Edinburgh: Edinburgh University Press, 2007), III: *Ambition and Industry*, pp. 232–39.
9 Calum Caimbeul MacPhàil, *Am 'Filidh Lathurnach'* (Glasgow: Gilleasbuig Mac-na-Ceardadh, 1878), p. 33.
10 Iain Mac-Lachain, *Dain agus Orain* (Glasgow: Gilleasbuig Mac-na-Ceardadh, 1869), p. 17.
11 Meek, *Tuath is Tighearna*, pp. 71, 202.
12 Domhnall E. Meek (ed.), *Màiri Mhòr nan Òran: Taghadh de a h-Òrain* (Edinburgh: Scottish Gaelic Texts Society, 1977), p. 110.

13 Ibid., p. 204.
14 Iain MacAonghais, *Duain agus Orain* (Glasgow: Gilleasbuig Mac-na-Ceardadh, 1875), p. 57.
15 Tom Leonard, *Radical Renfrew: Poetry from the French Revolution to the First World War* (Edinburgh: Polygon, 1990).

8: The Poetry of Modernity (1870–1950)

1 Robert Crawford, *Scotland's Books: The Penguin History of Scottish Literature* (London: Penguin, 2007), p. 453.
2 Tom Leonard, *Places of the Mind: The Life and Work of James Thomson ('B.V.')* (London: Jonathan Cape, 1993).
3 James Thomson, *The City of Dreadful Night* (Edinburgh: Canongate, 1993), p. 57.
4 Regenia Gagnier, 'Literary Alternatives to Rational Choice: Historical Psychology and Semi-Detached Marriages', *Occasion: Interdisciplinary Studies in the Humanities* 1 (2009), p. 7, occasion.stanford.edu/node/30.
5 John Davison, 'Thirty Bob a Week', in Robert Crawford and Mick Imlah (eds), *The New Penguin Book of Scottish Verse* (Harmondsworth: Penguin, 2000), p. 381.
6 George Bruce (ed.), *The Scottish Literary Revival: An Anthology of Twentieth-Century Poetry* (London: Collier-Macmillan, 1968), p. 1.
7 Katherine Whyte, *Aig Tigh na Beinne* (Oban and Glasgow: H. MacDonald and Alexander MacLaren, 1911). For a biography of Kenneth Macleod see Ronald Black (ed.), *An Tuil: Anthology of 20th Century Scottish Gaelic Verse* (Edinburgh: Polygon, 1999), pp. 720–22. Duncan Johnston, *Crònan nan Tonn* (Inverness: Dun Eisdein, 1997).
8 Donald E. Meek, '*Sitrich an Eich Iarainn* ("The Neighing of the Iron Horse"): Gaelic Perspectives on Steam Power, Railways and Shipbuilding in the Nineteenth Century', in Wilson McLeod, Abigail Burnyeat, Domhnall Uileam Stiùbhart, Thomas Owen Clancy and Roibeard Ó Maolalaigh (eds), *Bile ós Chrannaibh: A Festschrift for William Gillies* (Ceann Drochaid: Clann Tuirc, 2010), pp. 271–92.
9 Black, *An Tuil*, pp. 726–29.
10 Ibid., pp. 124–31.
11 Ibid., pp. 122–23.
12 Ibid., pp. 96–99.
13 Ibid., pp. 130–31.
14 See Penny Fielding, 'Stevenson's Poetry', in Penny Fielding (ed.), *The Edinburgh Companion to Robert Louis Stevenson* (Edinburgh: Edinburgh University Press, 2010), pp. 102–17.

15 Robert Louis Stevenson, *Underwoods* (London: Chatto and Windus, 1887), pp. xi, xii.
16 Robert Louis Stevenson, *Songs of Travel and Other Verses* (London: Chatto and Windus, 1896), p. 84.
17 Edwin Morgan, 'Scottish Poetry in the Nineteenth Century', in Douglas Gifford (ed.), *The History of Scottish Literature* (Aberdeen: Aberdeen University Press, 1989), III: *Nineteenth Century,* p. 346.
18 Colin Milton, 'Modern Poetry in Scots Before MacDiarmid', in Cairns Craig (ed.), *The History of Scottish Literature* (Aberdeen: Aberdeen University Press, 1987), IV: *Twentieth Century,* p. 16.
19 Lewis Spence, 'Great Tay of the Waves', in Douglas Dunn (ed.), *The Faber Book of Twentieth-Century Scottish Poetry* (London: Faber and Faber, 1993), p. 10.
20 C. M. Grieve, *Albyn, or Scotland and the Future* (1927); repr. in Hugh MacDiarmid, *Albyn: Shorter Books and Monographs*, ed. Alan Riach (Manchester: Carcanet, 1996), p. 4.
21 Ibid., p. 1.
22 Ibid., p. 4.
23 Roger Griffin, *Modernism and Fascism: The Sense of a Beginning under Mussolini and Hitler* (Basingstoke: Palgrave Macmillan, 2007), p. 52.
24 Hugh MacDiarmid, *Complete Poems,* ed. Michael Grieve and W. R. Aitken (Manchester: Carcanet, 1993), I: p. 106.
25 Edwin Muir, 'Scotland 1941', in Dunn, *The Faber Book of Twentieth-Century Scottish Poetry,* p. 23.
26 Edwin Muir, 'The Labyrinth', in Dunn, *The Faber Book of Twentieth-Century Scottish Poetry,* p. 27.
27 Margery Palmer McCulloch, *Edwin Muir: Poet, Critic and Novelist* (Edinburgh: Edinburgh University Press, 1993), p. 118.
28 Susan R. Wilson (ed.), *The Correspondence Between Hugh MacDiarmid and Sorley MacLean* (Edinburgh: Edinburgh University Press, 2010).
29 Hugh MacDiarmid, *At the Sign of the Thistle* (London: Stanley Nott, 1934), pp. 84, 87, quoted in Black, *An Tuil,* p. 737.
30 Black, *An Tuil,* pp. 114–17.
31 Ibid., p. 743.
32 Ibid., pp. 150–53 (excerpt with translation by Black); Bill Innes (trans.), *Aeòlus!: Dòmhnall Ruadh Mac an t-Saoir/Donald MacIntyre, Introduction, Notes and Parallel Translation* (Ochtertyre: Grace Note, 2008).
33 Black, *An Tuil,* p. 743.

34 William Soutar, letter to C. M. Grieve, 1931, quoted in William Soutar, *Poems in Scots and English* (Edinburgh: Scottish Academic Press, 1972), p. 10.
35 John Speirs, *The Scots Literary Tradition: An Essay in Criticism* (London: Faber and Faber, 1962), p. 16.
36 Christopher Whyte, *Modern Scottish Poetry* (Edinburgh: Edinburgh University Press, 2004), p. 103.
37 Christopher Whyte and Emma Dymock (eds), *Caoir Gheal Leumraich/ White Leaping Flame: Sorley MacLean, Collected Poems* (Edinburgh: Polygon, 2011), pp. 132–35.
38 Ibid., pp. 98–101.
39 Ibid., pp. 16–17, 20–21.
40 Ibid., pp. 412–13.
41 Michel Byrne (ed.), *Collected Poems and Songs of George Campbell Hay* (Edinburgh: Edinburgh University Press, 2003), pp. 105–61 (p. 161).
42 Ibid., p. 176.

9: Contemporary Poetry (1950–)

1 Colin Nicholson and Matt McGuire (eds), *The Edinburgh Companion to Contemporary Scottish Poetry* (Edinburgh: Edinburgh University Press, 2009).
2 Gilles Deleuze and Félix Guattari, 'What is a Minor Literature?', trans. by Robert Brinkley, *Mississippi Review* 11.3 (1983), pp. 13–33 (p. 16).
3 Roderick Watson, *The Literature of Scotland* 2 vols (Houndmills: Palgrave Macmillan, 2007), II: *The Twentieth Century*, p. 122.
4 George Mackay Brown, *An Orkney Tapestry* (London: Quartet, 1973), p. 20.
5 Ian Crichton Smith, *The Exiles* (Manchester: Carcanet, 1984), p. 20.
6 Iain Mac a' Ghobhainn, 'A' dol dhachaigh', in Moray Watson (ed.), *Iain Mac a' Ghobhainn: A' Bhàrdachd Ghàidhlig* (Stornoway: Acair, 2013), p. 63.
7 Niall O' Gallagher, *Beatha Ùr* (Inverness: Clàr, 2013).
8 Christopher Whyte, 'Against Self-Translation', *Translation and Literature* 11.1 (2002), pp. 64–71.
9 Ruaraidh MacThòmais, 'Anns a' Bhalbh Mhadainn', in *Eadar Samhradh is Foghar* (Glasgow: Gairm, 1967), p. 38.
10 Silke Stroh, *Uneasy Subjects: Postcolonialism and Scottish Gaelic Poetry* (Amsterdam: Rodopi, 2011), p. 327.

11 Konstanze Glaser, 'Essentialism and relativism in Gaelic and Sorbian Language Revival Discourses', www.poileasaidh.celtscot.ed.ac.uk/seminarwebversion2.html [accessed 13 February 2014].
12 Stroh, *Uneasy Subjects*, p. 327.
13 Meg Bateman, 'Cànain', in *Soirbheas: Fair Wind* (Edinburgh: Polygon, 2007), pp. 22–23.
14 See Edwin Morgan, *Hugh MacDiarmid* (Harlow: Longman for the British Council, 1976) and *Crossing the Border: Essays on Scottish Literature* (Manchester: Carcanet, 1990).
15 Robert Crawford, 'Cosmopolibackofbeyondism', in W. N. Herbert and Matthew Hollis (eds), *Strong Words: Modern Poets on Modern Poetry* (Tarset: Bloodaxe, 2000), pp. 262–64 (p. 264).
16 Watson, *The Literature of Scotland*, p. 206.
17 'Scotland's books belong to the world and the world disproportionately enjoys them. More than twenty thousand works of Scottish literature have been translated into a range of over seventy languages, from Albanian to Yakut. From "Auld Lang Syne" to Sherlock Holmes, the imaginings of Scottish authors are part of international currency. *Treasure Island*, Jekyll and Hyde, Peter Pan are familiar reference points of twenty-first-century culture.' Robert Crawford, *Scotland's Books* (London: Penguin, 2007), p. 1.
18 Deleuze and Guattari, 'What is a Minor Literature?', p. 16.
19 See Tom Leonard, *Intimate Voices: Selected Work, 1965–83* (Newcastle upon Tyne: Galloping Dog Press, 1984; repr. London: Vintage, 1995; and Buckfastleigh: Etruscan Books, 2003).
20 Tom Leonard, 'The Sound of Poetry', in Attila Dósa, *Beyond Identity: New Horizons in Modern Scottish Poetry* (Amsterdam: Rodopi, 2009), pp. 167–88 (p. 185).
21 Douglas Gifford et al., 'Scottish Poetry after 1945', in Douglas Gifford et al. (eds), *Scottish Literature* (Edinburgh: Edinburgh University Press, 2002), pp. 737–93 (p. 780).
22 See their co-written *Sharawaggi*, Crawford's *Scottish Assembly* (both 1990), or Herbert's *Forked Tongue* (1994) and *Cabaret McGonagall* (1996).
23 W. N. Herbert, 'The Poetry Game', in Dósa, *Beyond Identity*, pp. 221–42 (p. 229).
24 Wild Hawthorn Press, *The Archive of Ian Hamilton Finlay*, www.ianhamiltonfinlay.com/ian_hamilton_finlay.html.
25 Gifford et al., 'Scottish Poetry after 1945', p. 752.

26 Wild Hawthorn Press, *The Archive of Ian Hamilton Finlay*.
27 Frank Kuppner, 'The Pragmatism of Profundity', in Dósa, *Beyond Identity*, pp. 189–219 (p. 200).
28 Watson, *The Literature of Scotland*, p. 309.
29 Richard Price, 'Approaching the Informationists', in Richard Price and W. N. Herbert (eds), *Contraflow on the Super Highway: A Primer of Informationist Poetry* (London: Southfield and Gairfish, 1994), reprinted in *Hydrohotel.net: A Richard Price Webspace* www.hydrohotel.net/approach.htm.
30 Gifford et al., 'Scottish Poetry after 1945', p. 782.
31 Crawford, *Scotland's Books*, p. 719.
32 Deleuze and Guattari, 'What is a Minor Literature?', p. 19.
33 Kenneth White, 'A Strategist of Mutation', in Dósa, *Beyond Identity*, pp. 259–79 (p. 261).
34 Deleuze and Guattari, 'What is a Minor Literature?', p. 19. Emphasis added.
35 Kenneth White, 'A Strategist of Mutation', p. 273.
36 Aonghas MacNeacail, *Laoidh an donais òig / Hymn to a young demon* (Edinburgh: Polygon, 2007), pp. 12–15.
37 Peter MacKay, 'Aonghas MacNeacail', in Matt McGuire and Colin Nicholson (eds) *The Edinburgh Companion to Contemporary Scottish Poetry* (Edinburgh: Edinburgh University Press, 2009), pp. 126–40 (p. 128).
38 Murchadh MacPhàrlain, 'Is Mise Guth nan Innse Gall' ('*I Am the Voice of the Hebrides*'), in *An Toinneamh Dìomhair: Na h-Orain aig Murchadh MacPhàrlain Bàrd Mhealaboist* (Stornoway: Stornoway Gazette, 1973), pp. 88–89.
39 W. N. Herbert, 'The Poetry Game', p. 238.
40 Daniel O'Rourke, 'Introduction', in *Dream State: The New Scottish Poets* (Edinburgh: Polygon, 1994), p. xliv.

10: The Form of Scottish Gaelic Poetry

1 See the 'Airs and Metres' (or similar) sections of poetry editions in early volumes of the Scottish Gaelic Texts Society, and the Introduction to William J. Watson, *Bardachd Ghàidhlig*, 3rd edn (Stirling: A. Learmonth, 1959), which was influential during most of the twentieth century. Virginia Blankenhorn's *Irish Song Craft and Metrical Practice since 1600* (Lewiston, NY: Edwin Mellen Press, 2003), which addresses similar issues in Irish vernacular poetry, has assisted the present description in numerous ways.

2   When discussing rhythm I use '–' and '⌣' to denote stressed and unstressed syllables respectively, and '‚' for phrase-breaks. To analyse the rhythm of quoted texts I use '"' to mark a stressed syllable ('"' marks a primary, as opposed to a secondary stress) and '|' to mark a phrase-break.
3   When discussing metrical structure I use '*a*', '*b*', '*c*' etc. to refer to the first, second, third etc. lines of couplets, quatrains etc.
4   When discussing rhyme I use 'V' and 'C' to denote 'any vowel' and 'any consonant' respectively, ':' denotes length and phonetic matter is enclosed between slashes.
5   William Matheson, *The Songs of John MacCodrum* (Edinburgh: Oliver & Boyd, 1938), p. 6.
6   The lack of internal rhyme in line *a* may be more apparent than real, if we admit a variously spelt 'short unrounded vowel' (cf. Blankenhorn, *Irish Song-Craft*, pp. 5 and 334) into ScG metrical phonology; or the repetition of *eilean* may have been felt to supply the necessary aural enrichment. Alternatively, we may recall that the first lines of many ScG songs are metrically irregular – as though the poet or singer has not yet got into his/her stride.
7   Here '*x*' denotes a stressed vowel which does not take part in the rhyme-scheme of the verse. In more abstract terms the rhyme-scheme of all these lines may be represented as (*x a a b*).
8   See e.g. (9); (11) lines *b* and *c*; (23) lines *e* and *f*; (26) lines *c* and *d*; (27) lines *a–d*.
9   Paruig Mac-an-Tuairneir (i.e. Peter Turner), *Comhchruinneacha do dhòrain taghta Ghàidhealach* (Edinburgh: Clo-bhuailte air Son an ùghdair, 1813), p. 186.
10 Verse 3, line *c*.
11 J. L. Campbell and Francis Collinson (eds), *Hebridean Folksongs*, 3 vols (Oxford: Clarendon Press, 1969–81), I: nos. XI and XXXVIII (monosyllabic); no. III (trisyllabic).
12 i.e. 'meaningless refrain syllables', on which see Campbell and Collinson, *Hebridean Folksongs*, I: pp. 227–37; III: pp. 318–23.
13 Campbell and Collinson, *Hebridean Folksongs*, III: no. CII.
14 Watson, *Bardachd Ghàidhlig*, ll. 6405–09.
15 e.g. (published Edinburgh: Scottish Gaelic Texts Society) A. Mackenzie (ed.), *Òrain Iain Luim* (1964), pp. 158–61 (seventeenth century); Campbell and Collinson, *Hebridean Folksongs*, vol. 3, no. CXIII, and A. MacLeod (ed.), *The Songs of Duncan Ban Macintyre* (1952), pp. 132–45 (eighteenth century); D. E. Meek (ed.), *Tuath is Tighearna*

(1995), pp. 57–58, 74–76 (nineteenth century); S. Macmillan (ed.), *Sporan Dhòmhnaill* (1968), pp. 23–24, 59–60 (twentieth century).

16 Campbell and Collinson, *Hebridean Folksongs*, III: ll. 927–28. For further thoughts on these and related matters see R. G. Wentworth, 'An darnacha beum ann an òrain na Gàidhlig', *Scottish Gaelic Studies*, 20 (2000), pp. 117–46.

17 Watson, *Bardachd Ghàidhlig*, ll. 5710–13. For the rhyming of words in -*io*- and -*ui*- here compare the reference to a 'short unrounded vowel' in note 6.

18 Watson, *Bardachd Ghàidhlig*, ll. 6455–58. The end rhyme in lines *bd* between *ceann* and *dàimh* is a 'cross-over rhyme' as described above (p. 97); cf. *bròn* and *folbh* in (16), lines *ab*.

19 Mackenzie, *Òrain Iain Luim*, pp. 60–63. The /o:/ at the end of line *d* recurs at the end of every verse.

20 Thus (14) has a separate refrain, (15) repeats the latter part of each verse, and each verse in *Bùth Dhomh'll 'ic Leòid* (Macmillan, *Sporan Dhòmhnaill*, pp. 160–63), has an extra-metrical coda whose words are part of the verse.

21 Watson, *Bardachd Ghàidhlig*, ll. 3366–70. For the 'Limerick' metre see Colm Ó Baoill, 'The Limerick and Gaelic Song', *Transactions of the Gaelic Society of Inverness*, 58 (1995), pp. 171–96. For 'Limerick'-style pairs of '*xa|xa*' half-lines in more complex alternations with '*xxa*' or '*xaab*' lines, cf. *Moladh Beinn Dòbhrain* (MacLeod, *Songs of Duncan Ban Macintyre*, pp. 196–225) and *Moladh air Pìob mhòir Mhic Cruimein* (Watson, *Bardachd Ghàidhlig*, pp. 104–11).

22 Watson, *Bardachd Ghàidhlig*, ll. 4026–33. In line *h*, *seirbhis* (a loan-word from *service*) should perhaps be *searbhais to rhyme with *gaisge*.

23 Watson, *Bardachd Ghàidhlig*, ll. 2331–32 (rhyme-scheme *xaxab*); cf. *Òran Mòr Mhic Leòid* (id., pp. 161–65).

24 MacLeod, *Songs of Duncan Ban Macintyre*, ll. 2279–80. In linear terms, perhaps more appropriate to the oral-aural context, the phrases unfold as *xa ab xb bc*, i.e. alternating between bridging and binding rhymes.

25 e.g. Sìleas MacDonald and Colm Ó Baoill (ed.), *Bàrdachd Shìlis na Ceapaich* (Edinburgh: Scottish Academic Press for the Scottish Gaelic Texts Society, 1972), pp. 16–19 (*Mo Mhaili bheag ò*) and pp. 44–49 (*Tha mi 'num chadal 's na dùisgibh mi*).

26 Meek, *Tuath is Tighearna*, pp. 69–73.

27 Repeated final couplet (when sung): *An gille dubh ciardhubh* (Anne Lorne Gillies, *The Songs of Gaelic Scotland* (Edinburgh: Birlinn, 2005),

pp. 333–36), in which the final couplet also functions textually as a refrain within the verse. Repeated phrase: *Mo rùn geal òg* (Gillies, *Songs of Gaelic Scotland*, pp. 185–89), in which the final phrase is metrically outside but musically within the verse. Vocables outside the verse: *A Mhic Coinnich bhon tràigh* (Ó Baoill, *Sìleas na Ceapaich*, pp. 32–37).

28 By 'exemplary' I mean 'used as a pattern by later bards'. Examples include *Murt Ghlinne Comhann* by the 'Bàrd Mucanach' (Colm Ó Baoill with Meg Bateman, *Gàir nan clàrsach* (Edinburgh: Birlinn, 1994), pp. 190–99; cf. Matheson, *John MacCodrum*, p. 335), and *Alastair à Gleanna Garadh* (Ó Baoill, *Sìleas na Ceapaich*, pp. 70–75; cf. id., pp. 240–41).

29 Watson, *Bardachd Ghàidhlig*, ll. 2436–38.

30 MacMillan, *Sporan Dhòmhnaill*, pp. 147–52. A three-line refrain of vocables is sung after each verse of this song.

31 MacMillan, *Sporan Dhòmhnaill*, pp. 144–46.

32 Colm Ó Baoill (ed.), *Mairghread nighean Lachlainn* (Edinburgh: Scottish Gaelic Texts Society, 2009), no. VI (four-line verses), no. V (five-line verses), no. X (eight-line verses); cf. Watson, *Bardachd Ghàidhlig*, pp. 141–44, by Niall Mac Mhuirich (eight-line verses).

33 James Carmichael Watson (ed.), *Gaelic Songs of Mary MacLeod* (2nd edn, Edinburgh: Scottish Gaelic Texts Society, 1965), ll. 285–89; cf. Watson, *Bardachd Ghàidhlig*, pp. 205–09, by Eachann Bacach (5–8 lines); id., 189–92, by Iain Lom (5–6 lines); Ó Baoill, *Mairghread nighean Lachlainn*, no. VIII (7–8 lines).

34 See further Virginia Blankenhorn, 'The Rev. William Matheson and the Performance of Scottish Gaelic "Strophic" Verse', *Scottish Studies*, 36 (2013), pp. 15–44. I am grateful to Dr Blankenhorn for letting me see a draft of this paper prior to its publication.

35 Watson, *Bardachd Ghàidhlig*, ll. 6867–70; *saidhbhir* is to be pronounced *saoibhir* (or perhaps *Ghaoidheal* as *Ghàidheal*).

36 Watson, *Bardachd Ghàidhlig*, ll. 6891–94.

37 Iain Dubh's *crosanachd* is printed in John Mackenzie, *Sàr-obair nam bard Gaelach*, 2nd edn (Edinburgh: Maclachlan and Stewart, 1872), p. 74.

38 Accentual poems can be 'syllabic' if the syllable-count in each line is regular; but if their rhythm is fundamental they are to be termed 'syllabically regular accentual poems'. Conversely, lack of regular rhythm does not make a poem 'syllabic' unless the syllable-count of its lines is genuinely fixed.

39 Details in Eleanor Knott, *Irish Syllabic Poetry 1200–1600*, 2nd edn (Dublin: Dublin Institute for Advanced Studies, 1957); Gerard Murphy, *Early Irish Metrics* (Dublin: Royal Irish Academy, 1961); Cáit Ní Dhomhnaill, *Duanaireacht* (Baile Átha Cliath: Oifig an tSoláthair, 1975).

40 Osborn Bergin, *Irish Bardic Poetry*, ed. David Greene and Fergus Kelly (Dublin: Institute for Advanced Studies, 1970), p. 101.

41 Discussion in William Gillies, 'Music and Gaelic Strict-metre Poetry', *Studia Celtica*, 44 (2010), pp. 111–34, and Virginia Blankenhorn, 'Observations on the Performance of Irish Syllabic Verse', id., pp. 135–54.

42 Watson, *Bardachd Ghàidhlig*, ll. 6679–82, in an informal version of *rannaigheacht mhór*; syllables in italics show the main stresses, which display the familiar (*xaab*) rhyme-scheme of accentual verse.

43 Neill Ross (ed.), *Heroic Poetry from the Book of the Dean of Lismore* (Edinburgh: Scottish Gaelic Texts Society, 1939), ll. 905–08.

44 Alan J. Bruford, 'The Singing of Fenian and Similar Lays in Scotland', in Hugh Shields (ed.), *Ballad Research* (Dublin: Folk Music Society of Ireland, 1986), pp. 55–70; John MacInnes, 'Twentieth-century Recordings of Scottish Gaelic Heroic Ballads', in Bo Almqvist, Séamus Ó Catháin and Pádraig Ó Héalaí (eds), *The Heroic Process: Form, Function and Fantasy in Folk Epic* (Dún Laoghaire: Glendale Press, 1987), pp. 101–30.

45 See Murphy, *Early Irish Metrics*; Roibeard Ó Maolalaigh, 'On the Possible Origins of Scottish Gaelic *Iorram* "Rowing Song"', in Michel Byrne, Thomas O. Clancy and Sheila Kidd (eds), *Litreachas agus eachdraidh: Rannsachadh na Gàidhlig 2* (Glasgow: Roinn na Ceiltis Oilthigh Ghlaschu, 2006), pp. 232–88 (pp. 261–72).

46 See Virginia Blankenhorn, 'Verse Structure and Performance in Scottish Gaelic Vernacular Poetry', in C. Ó Baoill and N. McGuire (eds), *Rannsachadh na Gàidhlig 6* (Aberdeen: An Clò Gàidhealach, 2013), pp. 53–92.

11: Scots Poetic Forms

1 *The Poems of James VI of Scotland*, 2 vols, ed. James Craigie (Edinburgh and London: Blackwood for the Scottish Text Society: Third Series, no. 22, 1955), I: p. 82.

2 Book XII, ll. 477–90. *Barbour's Bruce*, 3 vols, ed. Matthew P. McDiarmid and James A. C. Stevenson (Edinburgh: Blackwood for the Scottish

Text Society, 1980–85); the misleading *y* of this edition is here replaced by *þ*.
3   In the classical languages those terms referred to patterns of *long* and *short* syllables, by no means the same thing as stressed and unstressed.
4   *The Poems of William Dunbar*, 2 vols, ed. Priscilla Bawcutt (Glasgow: Association for Scottish Literary Studies, 1998), I: p. 67.
5   *The Canongate Burns*, ed. Andrew Noble and Patrick Scott Hogg (Edinburgh: Canongate, 2001), p. 265.
6   See my 'Blind Hary's Metrics', in Sally Mapstone (ed.), *Older Scots Literature* (Edinburgh: John Donald, 2005), pp. 147–64.
7   *Hary's Wallace*, 2 vols,. ed. Matthew P. McDiarmid (Haddington: Scottish Text Society, 1968–69), I: p. 97
8   *Eneados*, XI.ii, ll. 1–8.
9   Those two are noteworthy as being among the first writings in a strongly marked north-east dialect. The dates are those of their first publication, but both were written somewhat earlier: *Helenore* had circulated locally in manuscript for several years prior to its appearance in print.
10 There is no serious reason to doubt the traditional attribution of the poem. For discussion, see what is still the standard critical edition, *The Kingis Quair of James Stewart*, ed. Matthew McDiarmid (London: Heinemann, 1973).
11 McDiarmid adopts this emendation for the MS *Citherea* (i.e. Venus); but the latter reading makes equally good sense.
12 This does not apply to the *Moralitas* of the last-mentioned poem, which is in decasyllabic couplets. For discussion of the possibility that the *Moralitas* is by another author, see Dietrich Strauss, 'Some Comments on the Moralitas of Robert Henryson's "Orpheus and Eurydice"', *Studies in Scottish Literature* 32.1 (2001), pp. 1–12.
13 See Matthew P. McDiarmid, 'The Early William Dunbar and his Poems', *Scottish Historical Review* 59 (1980), pp. 126–39, for an argument for an early dating of this poem.
14 With some rare exceptions, such as *Deor*, divided into sections marked by the recurrence of the refrain line 'Þæs ofereode, þisses swa mæg' ('*That passed away, so may this*').
15 See my '*The Tua Mariit Wemen and the Wedo*: the final fling of the heroic line', in Janet Hadley Williams and J. Derrick McClure (eds), *Fresshe Fontanys: Studies in the Culture of Mediaeval and Early Modern Scotland* (Newcastle: Cambridge Scholars Publishing, 2013), pp. 127–42.

16 The most recent discussion of this set of poems is my 'The Prosody of the Middle Scots Alliterative Poems', *Florilegium* 25 (2008), pp. 193–216, the notes to which include references to most of the previous studies.
17 Craigie, *Poems of James VI*, p. 81.
18 Allan H. MacLaine (ed.), *The Christis Kirk Tradition* (Glasgow: Association for Scottish Literary Studies, 1996), pp. 10–11. MacLaine's copy-text for the poem is the Bannatyne Manuscript. This well-annotated anthology is an indispensable introduction to the history of the verse form.
19 For the most recent edition see *John Skinner: Collected Poems*, ed. David M. Bertie (Peterhead: Buchan Field Club, 2005); for some discussion of it as a north-east dialect text, see my 'The Beginnings of Doric Poetry', in Janet Cruickshank and Robert McColl Millar (eds), *After the Storm: Papers from the Forum for Research on the Languages of Scotland and Ulster Triennial Meeting, Aberdeen 2012* (Aberdeen: Forum for Research on the Languages of Scotland and Ireland, 2013), pp. 166–86; also online at www.abdn.ac.uk/pfrlsu/volumes/vol4/.
20 The reminiscence of this in 'Tam o' Shanter', ll. 195–96 is probably deliberate: Burns admired Skinner greatly and corresponded with him.
21 The date of the poem is uncertain: it first appears in the Maitland Quarto MS of 1586, but is referred to in the Bannatyne MS of 1568 (see text).
22 For discussion see my '"Declair 3e bankis of Helicon": The Rise and Fall of a Stanza', in Kevin J. McGinley and Nicola Royan (eds), *The Apparelling of Truth* (Newcastle: Cambridge Scholars Publishing, 2010), pp. 266–89.
23 The number is different in the two early versions of the poem.
24 For a discussion of the poem, see Kenneth Buthlay, 'Habbie Simpson', in Adam J. Aitken, Matthew P. McDiarmid and Derick S. Thomson (eds), *Bards and Makars* (Glasgow: University of Glasgow Press, 1977), pp. 214–20.
25 Attributed to Robert Sempill in *The Poems of the Sempills of Beltrees*, ed. James Paterson (Edinburgh: Thomas George Stevenson, 1849) but not at all suggestive of the author of Habbie: more probably by his son Francis Sempill, author of a small set of humorous poems.
26 For some discussion of Ramsay's contribution to the literary development of the Habbie stanza see my 'Language and Genre in Allan

Ramsay's 1721 *Poems*', in Jennifer J. Carter and Joan H. Pittock (eds), *Aberdeen and the Enlightenment* (Aberdeen: Aberdeen University Press, 1987), pp. 261–69.
27 *The King's Birth-day in Edinburgh*, st. 5, *Caller Oysters*, st. 4, *Elegy on John Hogg*, st. 11.

12: The Ballad in Scots and English

1   Willa Muir, *Living with Ballads* (London: The Hogarth Press, 1965), p. 46.
2   Sarah Dunnigan, *Scottish Ballads* (Glasgow: ASLS, 2005), p. 1.
3   David Buchan, *The Ballad and the Folk* (London: Routledge and Kegan Paul, 1972), p. 1.
4   Sigurd Bernhard Hustvedt, *Ballad Books and Ballad Men: Raids and Rescues in Britain, America, and the Scandinavian North since 1800* (Cambridge, MA: Harvard University Press, 1930), p. 4.
5   See Anja Gunderloch, 'The Heroic Ballads of Gaelic Scotland', in Sarah Dunnigan and Suzanne Gilbert (eds), *The Edinburgh Companion to Scottish Traditional Literatures* (Edinburgh: Edinburgh University Press, 2013), pp. 74–84.
6   Francis J. Child, *The English and Scottish Popular Ballads*, 5 vols (New York: Dover, 1965 [1882–98]).
7   Maureen McLane, *Balladeering, Minstrelsy, and the Making of British Romantic Poetry* (Cambridge: Cambridge University Press, 2008), p. 73.
8   Ibid, p. 75.
9   Walter Scott, *Minstrelsy of the Scottish Border*, ed. T. F. Henderson (Edinburgh: Oliver and Boyd, 1932 [1803]), vol. 1, pp. 65, 66.
10 Scott, *Minstrelsy*, p. 70.
11 See Child's letter to Svend Grundtvig (25 August 1872), quoted in Hustvedt, *Ballad Books and Ballad Men*, p. 254.
12 See Suzanne Gilbert, 'William Harvey and the Scottish Chapbooks', *Scottish Studies Review* 5.1 (Spring 2004), pp. 9–18.
13 Joseph Donatelli, '"To Hear with Eyes": Orality, Print Culture, and the Textuality of Ballads', in James Porter and Ellen Sinatra (eds), *Ballads and Boundaries: Narrative Singing in an Intercultural Context* (Los Angeles: UCLA Department of Ethnomusicology and Systematic Musicology, 1995), p. 349.
14 Tristram P. Coffin, 'Mary Hamilton and the Anglo-American Ballad as an Art Form', in MacEdward Leach and Tristram P. Coffin (eds), *The Critics and the Ballad* (Carbondale, Illinois: Southern Illinois UP, 1961), pp. 245–56 (p. 246).

15 As many critics have observed, the majority of ballads address themes of sex and violence, usually conjoined: see, for example, M. J. C. Hodgart, *The Ballads* (London: Hutchinson's University Library, 1950), pp. 134–35; and Patricia Ingham, 'The World of the Ballad', *Review of English Studies* N. S. 8.29 (1957): pp. 22–31 (pp. 28–29). See also Natascha Würzbach and Simone M. Salz, *Motif Index of the Child Corpus: The English and Scottish Popular Ballad* (Berlin: Walter de Gruyter, 1995).
16 Hodgart, *The Ballads*, p. 134.
17 Hodgart, *The Ballads*, p. 15.
18 Ballads are referenced according to the system of classification devised by Francis J. Child for the 305 ballads in *The English and Scottish Popular Ballads*. The number is often followed by a letter indicating the variant of the ballad.
19 Lowry Charles Wimberly, *Folklore in the English and Scottish Ballads* (Chicago, Illinois: University of Chicago Press, 1928), p. 17.
20 Alan Bold, *The Ballad* (London and New York: Methuen, 1979), p. 58.
21 Andrew Fletcher of Saltoun, *Political Works* (Glasgow, 1744), p. 265.
22 *Encyclopaedia Britannica*, 3rd edition (1797).
23 Muir, *Living With Ballads*, p. 97.
24 Emily Lyle, Introduction, *Scottish Ballads* (Edinburgh: Canongate, 1998), p. 9. See also Lyle's discussion of the ballad in Dunnigan and Gilbert (eds), *Scottish Traditional Literatures*, pp. 14–18.
25 Bertrand H. Bronson, *The Traditional Tunes of the Child Ballads*, 4 vols (Princeton, NJ: Princeton University Press, 1959), vol. 1, p. x.
26 Mike Yates, 'Two Problematical Scottish Ballad Texts: "Mary Hamilton" and "The Young, Young Laird o Gilnockie"', *Musical Traditions*, Article MT146 (24 October 2004), www.mustrad.org.uk/articles/prob_bal.htm.
27 This term was coined by Francis B. Gummere in *The Popular Ballad* (Boston: Houghton, 1907; reprinted New York: Dover, 1959), and the concept frequently appears in subsequent analyses of ballad form. Hodgart describes the 'cinematic' qualities of this movement, p. 28.
28 Muriel Spark, *Curriculum Vitae: A Volume of Autobiography* (London: Penguin, 1992), p. 98.
29 See Flemming G. Andersen, *Commonplace and Creativity: The Role of Formulaic Diction in Anglo-Scottish Traditional Balladry* (Denmark: Odense UP, 1985); and Natascha Wurzbach and Simone Salz, *Motif Index of the Child Corpus: The English and Scottish Popular Ballad*, trans. Gayna Walls (Berlin: Walter de Gruyter, 1995).

30 William Motherwell, *Minstrelsy: Ancient and Modern* (Glasgow: John Wylie, 1827), p. xix.
31 See Corey Gibson, 'The Politics of the Modern Scottish Folk Revival', in Dunnigan and Gilbert (eds), *Scottish Traditional Literatures*, pp. 134–43.
32 Steve Newman, *Ballad Collection, Lyric and the Canon: The Call of the Popular from the Restoration to the New Criticism* (Philadelphia: University of Pennsylvania Press, 2007), p. 210.
33 '"The Wife of Usher's Well" is "typical of poetry in general" by giving us a concrete dramatization over abstract statement, and its "structure" is formed by a desire to have the reader experience these concrete details, such as the suspense generated by its leaping and lingering'; see Newman, *Ballad Collection*, p. 210.
34 See, for example, the influential *Norton Anthology of English Literature*, which historically has included ballads in its medieval section, despite their first print appearance in the eighteenth century.
35 On 2 January 1666, referring to a performance by an actress called Mrs Knipp, Pepys noted, 'In perfect pleasure I was to hear her sing, and especially her little Scotch song of Barbary Allen'. *The Diary of Samuel Pepys*, vol. 2, ed. Henry B. Wheatley (London: G. Bell, 1920), p. 126.
36 See this broadside in the University of Glasgow's Special Collections, *Glasgow Broadside Ballads: Cheap Print and Popular Song Culture in Nineteenth-century Scotland*, special.lib.gla.ac.uk/teach/ballads/barbara.html. The heading proclaims, 'It can only be had at the Poet's Box, No. 6, St Andrew's Lane, Glasgow'.
37 See Cecil Sharp and Maud Karpeles (eds), *English Folk Songs from the Southern Appalachians* (London: Oxford University Press, 1932).
38 See Karina Williamson, *Contrary Voices: Representations of West Indian Slavery, 1657–1834* (Kingston, Jamaica: University of The West Indies Press, 2008); an appendix contains a collection of ballad-influenced songs, used for comment and satire.
39 Isabel Hofmeyr, *'We Spend Our Years as a Tale That Is Told': Oral Historical Narrative in a South African Chiefdom* (Portsmouth: Heinemann; Johannesburg: Witwatersrand University Press; London: Currey, 1993), pp. 160–61.

13: Nature, Landscape and Rural Life

1 John Burnside, 'A Science of Belonging: Poetry as Ecology', in Robert Crawford (ed.), *Contemporary Poetry and Contemporary Science* (Oxford: Oxford University Press, 2006), pp. 91–106 (p. 92).

2 See Antony J. Hasler, 'Robert Henryson', in Thomas Owen Clancy and Murray Pittock (eds), *The Edinburgh History of Scottish Literature* (Edinburgh: Edinburgh University Press, 2007), I: pp. 286–94 (p. 288).
3 See Douglas Gray, *Robert Henryson* (Leiden: E. J. Brill, 1971), p. 265.
4 Gavin Douglas, 'The Proloug of the Sevynt Buke of the Eneados', in Roderick Watson (ed.), *The Poetry of Scotland: Gaelic, Scots and English 1380–1980* (Edinburgh: Edinburgh University Press, 1995), pp. 109–12.
5 Allan Ramsay, 'Preface' to *The Ever Green* (Edinburgh: Thomas Ruddiman, 1724), pp. vii–viii.
6 Susan Manning, 'Robert Fergusson and Eighteenth-Century Poetry', in Robert Crawford (ed.), *'Heaven-taught Fergusson': Robert Burns's Favourite Scottish Poet* (East Linton: Tuckwell Press, 2003), pp. 87–112 (p. 98).
7 See Carol McGuirk, 'Augustan Influences on Allan Ramsay', *Studies in Scottish Literature*, 16.1 (1981), pp. 97–109.
8 John Sitter, 'Eighteenth-Century Ecological Poetry and Ecotheology', *Religion & Literature* 40.1 (2008), pp. 11–37; Gerard Carruthers, 'James Thomson and Eighteenth-Century Scottish Literary Identity', in Richard Terry (ed.), *James Thomson: Essays for the Tercentenary* (Liverpool: Liverpool University Press, 2000), pp. 165–90 (p. 174).
9 Lawrence Buell, *The Environmental Imagination: Thoreau, Nature Writing, and the Formation of American Culture* (Harvard: Belknap Press of Harvard University Press, 1995), p. 184.
10 Gerard Carruthers, *Scottish Literature* (Edinburgh: Edinburgh University Press, 2009), p. 83.
11 See Natasha Sumner, 'James Thomson's *The Seasons*, Gone Gaelic: The Emergence of a Poetic Trend', *Proceedings of the Harvard Celtic Colloquium* 30 (2010), pp. 236–58; Thomas O. Clancy, 'Gaelic Literature and Scottish Romanticism', in Murray Pittock (ed.), *The Edinburgh Companion to Scottish Romanticism* (Edinburgh: Edinburgh University Press, 2011), pp. 49–60.
12 See Thomas O. Clancy, 'Medieval Gaelic Nature Poetry Revisited', in Georgia Henley and Paul Russell (eds), *Rhetoric and Reality in Medieval Celtic Literature: Essays in Honor of Daniel F. Melia, CSANA Yearbook*, 11–12 (2014), pp. 8–19.
13 Derick S. Thomson, 'Mac Mhaighstir Alasdair's Nature Poetry and its Sources', in Derick S. Thomson (ed.), *Gaelic and Scots in Harmony: Proceedings of the Second International Conference on the Languages*

of Scotland (Glasgow: University of Glasgow, Celtic Department, 1990), pp. 95–115; Robert Crawford, *Scotland's Books* (Oxford: Oxford University Press, 2009), pp. 301–02.

14 Angus MacLeod (ed. and trans.), *Orain Dhonnchaidh Bhàin/The Songs of Duncan Ban Macintyre* (Edinburgh: Scottish Gaelic Texts Society, 1978), pp. 196–225. See Sorley MacLean, 'Realism in Gaelic Poetry', in *Ris a' Bhruthaich: Criticism and Prose Writings* (Stornoway: Acair, 1985), p. 19.

15 See Ronald Black, 'Alasdair mac Mhaighstir Alasdair and the New Gaelic Poetry', in Susan Manning (ed.), *The Edinburgh History of Scottish Literature* (Edinburgh: Edinburgh University Press, 2007), II: pp. 110–24 (p. 112).

16 Duncan Ban Macintyre, 'Oran nam Balgairean' ('*Song to the Foxes*'), trans. William Neil, in Watson, *The Poetry of Scotland*, pp. 330–33.

17 Crawford, *Scotland's Books*, p. 318.

18 See 'Social Stability in the Eastern Lowlands of Scotland during the Agricultural Revolution, 1780–1840', in T. M. Devine (ed.), *Lairds and Improvement in the Scotland of the Enlightenment* (Dundee: University of Dundee; Glasgow: Distributed by the University of Glasgow, 1979), pp. 59–70.

19 See Matthew Simpson, 'Robert Fergusson and St Andrews Student Culture', in Crawford, '*Heaven-taught Fergusson*', pp. 21–40 (pp. 34–36).

20 Robert Crawford, 'Robert Burns and the Mind of Europe', in Murray Pittock (ed.), *Robert Burns in Global Culture* (Lewisburg, PA: Bucknell University Press, 2011), pp. 47–60 (p. 51).

21 See Murray Pittock, '"The Real Language of Men" Fa's Speering? Burns and the Scottish Romantic Vernacular', in David Sergeant and Fiona J. Stafford (eds), *Burns and Other Poets* (Edinburgh: Edinburgh University Press, 2012), pp. 91–106 (pp. 94–95).

22 See Marilyn Butler, 'Burns and Politics', in Robert Crawford (ed.), *Robert Burns and Cultural Authority* (Edinburgh: Edinburgh University Press, 1997), pp. 86–112 (p. 92).

23 Alexander Pope, *The Major Works* (Oxford: Oxford University Press, 2006), pp. 293–94.

24 See Robert Crawford, *The Bard: Robert Burns, a Biography* (London: Pimlico, 2010), pp. 201–02.

25 Nigel Leask, *Robert Burns and Pastoral: Poetry and Improvement in Late-18th Century Scotland* (Oxford: Oxford University Press, 2010), p. 225.

26 See Susan Manning, 'Ossian, Scott, and Nineteenth-Century Literary Nationalism', *Studies in Scottish Literature*, 17.1 (1982), pp. 39–54.

27 See Fiona Stafford, *The Sublime Savage: A Study of James Macpherson and the Poems of Ossian* (Edinburgh: Edinburgh University Press, 1988).
28 Patrick Geddes, 'The Scots Renascence', *Evergreen*, 1 (1895), pp. 131–39 (p. 37).
29 See Louisa Gairn, *Ecology and Modern Scottish Literature* (Edinburgh: Edinburgh University Press, 2008), p. 30.
30 Alasdair MacIlleathain, 'Duanag don triuir Ghaidheal a th' ann am priosan Dhun Eideann' ('*A Poem to the Three Highlanders who are in the Edinburgh Prison*'), in Donald Meek (ed.), *Tuath is Tighearna – Tenants and Landlords: An Anthology of Gaelic Poetry of Social and Political Protest from the Clearances to the Land Agitation (1800-1890)* (Edinburgh: Scottish Academic Press for the Scottish Gaelic Texts Society, 1995), pp. 119–21.
31 See Donald Meek (ed.), *Caran An-t-saoghail/The Wiles of the World: Anthology of Nineteenth-Century Gaelic Verse* (Edinburgh: Birlinn, 2003), p. xxvii.
32 Mary MacPherson, 'Farewell to the New Christmas', in Watson, *The Poetry of Scotland*, pp. 488–93.
33 Hugh MacDiarmid, *Selected Essays*, ed. Duncan Glen (London: Jonathan Cape, 1969), p. 173.
34 Robert Crawford, 'Modernism as Provincialism', in *Devolving English Literature* (Edinburgh: Edinburgh University Press, 2000), pp. 216–70.
35 W. N. Herbert, *To Circumjack MacDiarmid: the Poetry and Prose of Hugh MacDiarmid* (Oxford: Clarendon Press, 1992), p. 34.
36 Hugh MacDiarmid, *Selected Prose*, ed. Alan Riach (Manchester: Carcanet, 1992), p. 10; 22.
37 Louisa Gairn, *Ecology and Modern Scottish Literature*, p. 93.
38 Edwin Morgan, 'Edwin Muir', in *Essays* (Cheshire: Carcanet New Press, 1974), pp. 186–93 (p. 193).
39 Edwin Muir, *The Estate of Poetry* (London: The Hogarth Press, 1962), pp. 8–9.
40 See Terry Gifford, *Green Voices: Understanding Contemporary Nature Poetry* (Manchester: Manchester University Press, 1995), pp. 73–74.
41 Sorley MacLean, 'Realism in Gaelic Poetry', p. 19.
42 Kenneth White, cited in Tony McManus, 'Kenneth White: a Transcendental Scot', in Gavin Bowd, Charles Forsdick and Norman Bissell (eds), *Grounding a World: Essays on the Work of Kenneth White* (Glasgow: Alba, 2005), pp. 9–23 (p. 17).

43 Kenneth White, *The Wanderer and His Charts* (Edinburgh: Polygon, 2005), p. 207; Kenneth White, 'Valley of Birches', in *The Bird Path: Collected Longer Poems, 1964–1988* (Edinburgh: Mainstream Publishing, 1989), p. 160.

44 Kathleen Jamie, interviewed by Lilias Fraser, *Scottish Studies Review*, 2.1 (2001), p. 20; Attila Dósa, 'Kathleen Jamie: More than Human', in *Beyond Identity: New Horizons in Modern Scottish Poetry* (Amsterdam: Rodopi, 2009), pp. 135–45 (p. 141).

45 John Burnside, 'Rewilding: Who Are We to Dictate What Species Live Where?', *The New Statesman* (28 August 2013).

46 Kathleen Jamie, quoted in Kirsty Scott, 'In the Nature of Things: An Interview with Kathleen Jamie', *The Guardian* (18 June 2005).

14: Nation and Home

1 In Benedict Anderson's established definition – see his *Imagined Communities: Reflections on the Origin and Spread of Nationalism* (London: Verso, 1983).

2 See Michael Billig, *Banal Nationalism* (London: Sage, 1995).

3 In reference to ethnosymbolism, see, among others, the theories developed by John A. Armstrong, Anthony D. Smith and John Hutchinson.

4 Alan Riach and Douglas Gifford (eds), *Scotlands: Poets and the Nation* (Manchester: Carcanet Press, 2004), p. xx.

5 See Andrew Galloway, 'The Borderlands of Satire: Linked, Opposed, and Exchanged Political Poetry During the Scottish and English Wars of the Early Fourteenth Century', in Mark P. Bruce and Katherine H. Terrell (eds), *The Anglo-Scottish Border and the Shaping of Identity, 1300–1600* (New York: Palgrave Macmillan, 2012), pp. 15–31.

6 Robert Baston, *Metrum de praelio apud Bannockburn/The Battle of Bannockburn*, trans. by Edwin Morgan (Edinburgh: Scottish Poetry Library with Akros Publications and the Mariscat Press, 2004).

7 One of the latest instalments in the scholarly controversy about the poem is Màrtainn MacGriogair's 'Ar sliochd Gaodhal ó Ghort Gréag: An dàn 'Flodden' ann an Leabhar Deadhan Lios-mòir', in Richard A. V. Cox and Gillian Munro (eds), *Cànan & Cultar/Language & Culture: Rannsachadh na Gàidhlig 4* (Edinburgh: Dunedin Academic Press, 2010), pp. 23–35.

8 In Ronald Black (ed.), 'A Manuscript of Cathal Mac Muireadhaigh', *Celtica*, 10 (1973), pp. 193–209 (194–200).

9 Ed. by J. Carmichael Watson in 'Cathal Mac Muireadhaigh Cecinit', in Eóin Ua Riain (John Ryan, ed.), *Féil-Sgríbhinn Eóin MhicNéill* (1940; repr. Blackrock: Four Courts, 1995), pp. 167–79. Corrections in Angus Matheson, 'Poems from a Manuscript of Cathal Mac Muireadhaigh', *Éigse*, 10 (1961–63), pp. 270-78, & 11 (1964–66), pp. 1–17 (part 1, p. 270).
10 Leith Davis, 'Gender and the Nation in the Work of Robert Burns and Janet Little', *SEL: Studies in English Literature 1500–1900*, 38:4 (1998), p. 640.
11 Many of his poems can be found in A[lexander] Maclean Sinclair (ed.), *Clàrsach na coille/The Harp of the Wood: A Collection of Gaelic Poetry* (1881), 2nd rev. ed. by Hector Macdougall (Glasgow: Alexander MacLaren, 1928).
12 In Michael Newton (ed. & trans.), *Seanchaidh na Coille/The Memory-keeper of the Forest: Anthology of Scottish Gaelic Canadian Literature* (Sydney, NS: Cape Breton University Press, 2015, pp. 390–95, also see 389.
13 See Scott Hames (ed.), *Unstated: Writers on Scottish Independence* (Edinburgh: WP Books, 2012).
14 www.theguardian.com/books/2014/sep/23/carol-ann-duffy-poem-scottish-independence-referendum-september-2014.

15: Protest and Politics

1 Edward Dorn, *Collected Poems* (Manchester: Carcanet, 2012), p. 543.
2 Christopher Hitchens, 'Introduction', in Christopher Hitchens, *Arguably* (London: Atlantic Books, 2011), pp. xv–xix.
3 Wilson McLeod, *Divided Gaels: Gaelic Cultural Identities in Scotland and Ireland, c. 1200–c. 1650* (Oxford: Oxford University Press, 2004), but see Pía Coira, *By Poetic Authority: The Rhetoric of Panegyric in Gaelic Poetry of Scotland to c. 1700* (Edinburgh: Dunedin Academic Press, 2012).
4 Wilson McLeod, 'Language Politics and Ethnolinguistic Consciousness in Scottish Gaelic Poetry', *Scottish Gaelic Studies*, 21 (2003), pp. 91–146.
5 Douglas Gifford and Alan Riach (eds), *Scotlands: Poets and the Nation* (Manchester: Carcanet and Edinburgh: The Scottish Poetry Library, 2004), pp. 20-28.
6 John Lorne Campbell (ed.), *Highland Songs of the Forty-five* (Edinburgh: Scottish Gaelic Texts Society, 1984 [1933]), pp. 100–01.
7 John MacInnes, 'The Panegyric Code in Gaelic Poetry and its Historical Background', in Michael Newton (ed.), *Dùthchas nan Gàidheal: Selected Essays of John MacInnes* (Edinburgh: Birlinn, 2006), pp. 265–319.

8   Annie M. MacKenzie (ed.), *Òrain Iain Luim: Songs of John MacDonald, Bard of Keppoch* (Edinburgh: Scottish Gaelic Texts Society, 1964), pp. 228–29.
9   Gifford and Riach, *Scotlands*, p. 81.
10 Gifford and Riach, *Scotlands*, pp. 86–87.
11 Gifford and Riach, *Scotlands*, p. 88.
12 Ronald Black (ed.), *An Lasair: Anthology of 18th Century Scottish Gaelic Verse* (Edinburgh: Birlinn, 2001), pp. 292–99.
13 Black, *An Lasair*, pp. 294–95, ll. 40–46.
14 Gifford and Riach, *Scotlands*, pp. 104–05.
15 Tom Leonard (ed.), *Radical Renfrew: Poetry from the French Revolution to the First World War by Poets Born, or Sometime Resident in, the County of Renfrewshire* (Edinburgh: Polygon, 1990).
16 Michel Byrne, '"Chan e chleachd bhith an cabhsair chlach": Am Bàrd Gàidhlig 's am Baile Mòr bhon 17mh Linn chun an 20mh', in Sheila M. Kidd (ed.), *Glasgow: Baile Mòr nan Gàidheal – City of the Gaels* (Glasgow: Department of Celtic, University of Glasgow, 2007), pp. 55–88.
17 Sorley MacLean, 'The Poetry of the Clearances', in Sorley MacLean, *Ris a' Bhruthaich: The Criticism and Prose Writings of Sorley MacLean*, ed. by William Gillies (Stornoway: Acair, 1985), pp. 48–74.
18 Wilson McLeod, 'Gaelic Poetry and the British Military Enterprise, 1756–1945', in Carla Sassi and Theo Van Heijnsbergen (eds), *Within and Without Empire: Scotland Across the (Post)colonial Borderline* (Newcastle: Cambridge Scholars Publishing, 2013), pp. 61–76.
19 John MacAskill, *We Have Won the Land: The Story of the Purchase by the Assynt Crofters Trust of the North Lochinver Estate*, Foreword by Jim Hunter (Stornoway: Acair, 1999).
20 McLeod, 'Language, Politics and Ethnolinguistic Consciousness in Scottish Gaelic Poetry'.
21 Ronald Black (ed.), *An Tuil: Anthology of 20th-Century Scottish Gaelic Verse* (Edinburgh: Polygon, 1999), pp. 520–25.
22 alanbissett.com/2012/01/13/my-contribution-to-the-debate-on-scottish-independence.

16: Love and Erotic Poetry

1   Antonia Fraser (ed.), *Scottish Love Poems* (Edinburgh: Canongate, 1975), pp. ix–xvii.
2   Thomas Crawford (ed.), *Love, Labour and Liberty: the Eighteenth-Century Scottish Lyric* (Cheadle: Carcanet, 1976), p. 5.

3 See Liam McIllvanney, *Burns the Radical: Poetry and Politics in Late Eighteenth-Century Scotland* (East Linton: Tuckwell, 2002), p. 169, and Peter Wagner, *Eros Revived: Erotica of the Enlightenment in England and America* (London: Secker & Warburg, 1988), p. 162.

4 See Priscilla Bawcutt and Janet Hadley Williams, 'Introduction: Poets "of this Natioun"', in Bawcutt and Hadley Williams (eds), *A Companion to Medieval Scottish Poetry* (Cambridge: D. S. Brewer, 2006), p. 17.

5 'Ane Schort Treatise conteining some Reulis and Cautelis', Ch. VII, in *The Essays of a Prentise, in the Divine Art of Poesie* (Edinburgh: Vautroullier, 1585).

6 Cf. Joanna Martin, *Kingship and Love in Scottish Poetry, 1424–1540* (Aldershot: Ashgate, 2008), p. 2.

7 See Julia Kristeva, *Tales of Love*, trans. Leon S. Roudiez (New York: Columbia University Press, 1987), p. 9.

8 Sally Mapstone, 'Older Scots Literature and the Court', in Thomas Owen Clancy and Murray Pittock (eds), *The Edinburgh History of Scottish Literature* (Edinburgh: Edinburgh University Press, 2007), I: pp. 273–85, 274. See also Sally Mapstone, 'Kingship and *The Kingis Quair*', in Helen Cooper and Sally Mapstone (eds), *The Long Fifteenth Century: Essays for Douglas Gray* (Oxford 1997), pp. 51–69 (pp. 62–63).

9 Martin, *Kingship and Love in Scottish Poetry*, p. 2.

10 Bawcutt and Hadley Williams, 'Introduction: Poets "of this Natioun"', pp. 1–18 (p. 10).

11 Anne M. McKim, '*Orpheus and Eurydice* and *The Testament of Cresseid*: Robert Henryson's "fine poeticall way"', in Bawcutt and Hadley Williams, *A Companion to Medieval Scottish Poetry*, pp. 105–17 (p. 115).

12 Jacqueline A. Tasioulas (ed.), *The Makars: The Poems of Henryson, Dunbar and Douglas* (Edinburgh: Canongate, 1999), pp. 213–14.

13 Sarah M. Dunnigan, *Eros and Poetry at the Courts of Mary Queen of Scots and James VI* (Basingstoke: Palgrave MacMillan, 2002), p. 55.

14 McKim, '*Orpheus and Eurydice* and *The Testament of Cresseid*', p. 116; see also Antony J. Hasler, 'Robert Henryson' in Clancy and Pittock, *The Edinburgh History of Scottish Literature*, I: pp. 286–94 (p. 293).

15 See William Gillies, 'Gaelic Literature in the Later Middle Ages: *The Book of the Dean* and beyond', in Clancy and Pittock, *The Edinburgh History of Scottish Literature*, I: pp. 219–25 (p. 224).

16 See Thomas O. Clancy (ed.), *The Triumph Tree: Scotland's Earliest Poetry AD 550–1350* (Edinburgh: Canongate, 1998), pp. 274–81; Osborn

Bergin, *Irish Bardic Poetry* (Dublin: Institute for Advanced Studies, 1970), §21; and Wilson McLeod and Meg Bateman (eds), *Duanaire na Sracaire/Songbook of the Pillagers: Anthology of Medieval Gaelic Poetry* (Edinburgh: Birlinn, 2007), pp. 18–31, 168–73.

17 See McLeod and Bateman, *Duanaire na Sracaire*, pp. 286–91.
18 Malcolm MacLean and Theo Dorgan (eds), *An Leabhar Mòr/The Great Book of Gaelic* (Edinburgh: Canongate, 2002), p. 271.
19 Dunnigan, *Eros and Poetry*, p. 6.
20 George Buchanan, *Ane Detectioun of the duinges of Marie Quene of Scottes*, trans. Thomas Wilson (1571), sigs. Q4.
21 Dunnigan, *Eros and Poetry*, pp. 6–7.
22 Ronald Black (ed.), *An Lasair: Anthology of 18th Century Scottish Gaelic Verse* (Edinburgh: Birlinn, 2001), pp. 278–71, 493–94.
23 For examples, see Derick S. Thomson (ed.), *The MacDiarmid MS Anthology* (Edinburgh: Scottish Academic Press, 1992), pp. 41, 47–53, 57–8, 101, 248–49 and Black, *An Lasair*, pp. 28–29.
24 Black, *An Lasair*, pp. 316–17.
25 R. D. S. Jack, 'Critical Introduction' to R. D. S. Jack and P. A. T. Rosendaal (eds), *The Mercat Anthology of Early Scottish Literature 1375–1707* (Edinburgh: Mercat, 1997), pp. xxx, xxxvii.
26 Marshall Walker, *Scottish Literature since 1707* (London and New York: Longman, 1996), p. 95.
27 See Thomas Crawford, 'Burns, Love and Liberty', in Carol McGuirk (ed.), *Critical Essays on Robert Burns* (New York: G. K. Hall, 1998), p. 99.
28 Andrew Noble and Patrick Stuart Hogg (eds), *The Canongate Burns* (Edinburgh: Canongate, 2001), pp. 956–57.
29 Edwin Morgan, 'Scottish Poetry in the Nineteenth Century', in Edwin Morgan, *Crossing the Border* (Manchester: Carcanet, 1990), pp. 96–97.
30 *Whistle-Binkie* (Glasgow: David Robertson, 1878), p. 301
31 Kirsteen McCue, 'Women and Song 1750–1850', in Douglas Gifford and Dorothy MacMillan (eds), *A History of Scottish Women's Writing* (Edinburgh: Edinburgh University Press, 1997), pp. 58–70, p. 61. See also Valentina Bold, 'Beyond "The Empire of the Gentle Heart"', in the same volume, pp. 246–61.
32 Eliza Cook, *Eliza Cook's Journal*, no. 174, VII (London: John Owen Clarke, 1852), p. 276, quoted in McCue, 'Women and Song 1750–1850', p. 67.
33 Amanda Gilroy and Keith Hanley (eds), *Joanna Baillie: A Selection of Plays and Poems* (London: Pickering & Chatto, 2002), p. 263.

34 Donald Meek (ed.), *Caran an t-Saoghail: The Wiles of the World* (Edinburgh: Birlinn, 2003), pp. 254–55.
35 Sorley MacLean, *Caoir Gheal Leumraich/A White Leaping Flame*, ed. Christopher Whyte and Emma Dymock (Edinburgh: Polygon, 2011), pp. 152–53.
36 MacLean, *Caoir Gheal Leumraich*, pp. 124–25, 132–33, 134–35.
37 Sydney Goodsir Smith, *Collected Poems* (London: John Calder, 1975), p. 185.
38 Christopher Whyte, '"Now you see it, now you don't": Revelation and Concealment in the Love Poetry of Edwin Morgan', *Glasgow Review* 2 (1993), pp. 82–93.
39 Edwin Morgan, *Nothing Not Giving Messages: Reflections on Work and Life* (Edinburgh: Polygon, 1990), pp. 178, 162.
40 Edwin Morgan, *Collected Poems* (Manchester: Carcanet, 1990), p. 169.
41 Cf. Christopher Whyte, 'Queer Readings, Gay Texts: From *Redgauntlet* to *The Prime of Miss Jean Brodie*', Eleanor Bell and Gavin Miller (eds), *Scotland in Theory: Reflections on Culture and Literature* (Amsterdam: Rodopi, 2004), p. 152.
42 Liz Lochhead, *Dreaming Frankenstein* (Edinburgh: Polygon, 1984), p. 16.
43 Carol Ann Duffy, *Selected Poems* (London: Penguin, 1994), p. 22, originally *Standing Female Nude* (London: Anvil, 1985). See Deryn Rees-Jones, *Carol Ann Duffy* (Devon: Northcote House, 2001), pp. 30–44.
44 Jackie Kay, *Other Lovers* (Newcastle-upon-Tyne: Bloodaxe, 1993), p. 40.

17: Faith and Religion

1 Colin N. Manlove, *Scottish Fantasy Literature: A Critical Survey* (Edinburgh: Canongate, 1994).
2 Thomas O. Clancy (ed.), *The Triumph Tree* (Edinburgh: Canongate Books, 1998), pp. 188–89. Most other Gaelic poems referred to can be found, with translation, in Meg Bateman, Robert Crawford and James McGonigal (eds), *Scottish Religious Poetry: An Anthology* (Edinburgh: St Andrew Press, 2000).
3 Key factors are mapped in Michael Lynch, *Scotland: A New History* (London: Pimlico, 1992), pp. 171–202.
4 R. L. Thomson (ed.), *Foirm na n-Urrnuidheadh: John Carswell's Gaelic Translation of the Book of Common Order* (Edinburgh: Oliver & Boyd for the Scottish Gaelic Texts Society, 1970), pp. 10–11.

5   Edwin Morgan, 'Ioannis Calvini Epicidium/Elegy for John Calvin', in Bateman, Crawford and McGonigal, *Scottish Religious Poetry*, p. 62.
6   See Marie-Louise Sjoestedt, *Gods and Heroes of the Celts*, trans. Myles Dillon (Mineola: Dover, 2000), especially chapter 3, 'The Mother-Goddesses of Ireland'.
7   See Attila Dósa, 'Poets and Other Animals: An Interview with John Burnside', *Scottish Studies Review* 4:1 (2003), pp. 9–23, reprinted in his *Beyond Identity: New Horizons in Scottish Poetry* (Amsterdam, New York: Rodopi, 2009).

18: Scottish Poetry as World Poetry

1   Translated extracts from *The Kingis Quair* appeared in the *Revue poétique* (Paris, 1835), and from Dunbar and Douglas in the Croatian-Slovenian poet Stanko Vraz's posthumously published *Děla* (1868). These appear to be the only translations from the makars before the twentieth century, which saw complete translations of *The Kingis Quair* (France, 1969; Japan, 1976), Dunbar's *Tretis of the Twa Mariit Wemen and the Wedo* (Japan, 1980–81; Italy, 1989), Henryson's *Morall Fabillis of Esope the Phrygian* (Japan, 1986), *The Testament of Cresseid* (Japan, 1988; Italy, 1998) and *Orpheus and Eurydice* (Japan, 1992), and Barbour's *The Bruce* (Spain, 1998). Selections also appeared in anthologies of world or anglophone writing in Belgium, Georgia, Germany, Hungary, Italy, Netherlands, Poland, Slovenia and Russia. For full bibliographical details of these and subsequently mentioned translations, see the Bibliography of Scottish Literature in Translation (BOSLIT) www.nls.uk/catalogues/boslit. I am also indebted to Dr Yuko Matsui (Aoyama Gakuin University) for information on Japanese translations.
2   Du Bartas was returning a favour after James partially translated his *L'Uranie* and *La seconde Sepmaine* in 1584. See Sarah M. Dunnigan, 'The Return of the Repressed', in Gerard Carruthers, David Goldie and Alastair Renfrew (eds), *Beyond Scotland: New Contexts for Twentieth-Century Scottish Literature* (Amsterdam: Rodopi, 2004), pp. 111–32 (p. 124).
3   Apart from James VI (translated primarily as a prose writer), no translation of the Castalian Band has been traced before the twentieth century, when Sir Robert Ayton appeared in the Polish anthology *Poeci języka angielskiego* (1969), and Alexander Montgomerie in the Georgian anthology *Šotlandiéri poezia* (1979).

4   George Buchanan, *Psalmorum Davidis paraphrasis poetica, nunc primùm edita* (Geneva: Apud Henricum Stephanum, & ejus fratrem Robertum Stephanum, 1566).
5   See I. D. McFarlane, *Buchanan* (London: Duckworth, 1981), p. 194, and Raymond Lebègue, *La Tragédie religieuse en France: les débuts (1514-1573)* (Paris: Champion, 1929), p. 252.
6   See McFarlane, *Buchanan*, pp. 198-202.
7   See Astrid Stilma, 'Tyrants and Translations: Dutch Interpretations of George Buchanan's Political Thought', in Caroline Erskine and Roger A. Mason (eds), *George Buchanan: Political Thought in Early Modern Britain and Europe* (Farnham: Ashgate, 2012), pp. 111-30.
8   See Robert von Friedeberg, 'Buchanan and the German Monarchomachs', and Alan I. MacInnes, 'The Reception of Buchanan in Northern Europe in the Seventeenth Century', in Erskine and Mason, *George Buchanan*, pp. 131-50, 151-70. *Baptistes* was translated twice into German (1583, 1585). There were also two French translations (1590, 1613).
9   As suggested in James Porter, '"Beatus ille qui misertus pauperis": The Historical Importance of Jean Servin's Settings of Buchanan's Psalm Paraphrases', in Philip Ford and Roger P. H. Green (eds), *George Buchanan: Poet and Dramatist* (Swansea: Classical Press of Wales, 2009), pp. 113-36 (p. 126).
10 See J. A. Van Doorsten, *Poets, Patrons, and Professors: Sir Philip Sidney, Daniel Rogers, and the Leiden Humanists* (Leiden: University of Leiden, 1962), pp. 38, 43.
11 Du Bellay also translated Buchanan's ode on the siege of Metz, 'Ad Henricum II. Franciæ de soluta urbis Medionatricum obsidione' (c. 1553). See McFarlane, *Buchanan*, pp. 165, 487.
12 See Gilbert Waterhouse, *The Literary Relations of England and Germany in the Seventeenth Century* (New York: Haskell House, 1966), p. 60.
13 McFarlane, *Buchanan*, pp. 116-17.
14 See Philip Ford, '"Poeta sui sæculi facile princeps": George Buchanan's Poetic Achievement', in Ford and Green, *George Buchanan*, pp. 3-18.
15 For a fuller treatment of the reception of Scottish neo-Latin poetry, see Paul Barnaby and Tom Hubbard, 'The International Reception and Literary Impact of Scottish Literature of the Period 1314 until 1707', in Thomas Owen Clancy and Murray Pittock (eds), *The Edinburgh History of Scottish Literature* (Edinburgh: Edinburgh University Press, 2007), I: pp. 164-67 (166-67).
16 The earliest known translations of Ramsay and Fergusson appear in the Georgian anthology *Šotlandiéri poezia* (1979).

17 See Margaret M. Cameron, *L'Influence des 'Saisons' de Thomson sur la poésie descriptive en France (1759–1810)* (Paris: H. Champion, 1927), and Lawrence Marsden Price, *English Literature in Germany* (Berkeley, CA: University of California Press, 1953), pp. 73–84.

18 See Yu. D. Levin, *The Perception of English Literature in Russia: Investigations and Materials* (Nottingham: Astra Press, 1994), pp. 155–95, and Ernest J. Simmons, *English Literature and Culture in Russia (1553–1840)* (Cambridge, MA: Harvard University Press, 1935), pp. 167–74.

19 See Zsuzsanna Varga, 'Sporadic Encounters: Scottish–Portuguese Literary Contacts since 1500', in Tom Hubbard and R. D. S. Jack (eds), *Scotland in Europe* (Amsterdam: Rodopi, 2006), pp. 203–20 (p. 205), Katia Kretkowska, 'Scotland in the Life of the Polish Country Estate, 1790–1830', in T. C. Smout (ed.), *Scotland and Europe, 1200–1850* (Edinburgh: J. Donald, 1986), pp. 166–86 (p. 169), and María Eugenia Perojo Arronte, 'Spanish Romanticism and the Struggle for Legitimation', in Denise Merkle, Carol O'Sullivan, Luc van Doorslaer and Michaela Wolf (eds), *The Power of the Pen: Translation and Censorship in 19th Century Europe* (Münster: LIT Verlag, 2010), pp. 191–212 (p. 197).

20 For further details, see Howard Gaskill (ed.), *The Reception of Ossian in Europe* (London: Continuum, 2004), and Paul Van Tieghem, 'Ossian et l'ossianisme', in his *Le Préromantisme: études d'histoire littéraire européenne*, 3 vols (Paris: Rieder, 1924–47), I: (1924), pp. 197–287. For the German reception, see also Wolf Gerhard Schmidt (ed.), *'Homer des Nordens' und 'Mutter der Romantik': James Macphersons Ossian und seine Rezeption in der deutschsprachigen Literatur*, 4 vols (Berlin: De Gruyter, 2003–04), and Price, *English Literature in Germany*, pp. 112–35.

21 Peter McCarey, 'Ossian, Scott and Byron in Russia', in his *Hugh MacDiarmid and the Russians* (Edinburgh: Scottish Academic Press, 1987), pp. 1–16 (pp. 1–5).

22 Two poems by Ruaraidh MacThómais were translated into Italian in the Florence journal *Il Bimestre*, 22–23 (1972), p. xxxii.

23 See Price, *English Literature in Germany*, pp. 140–41.

24 See Kirsteen McCue, 'Schottische Lieder ohne Wörter?: What Happened to the Words for the Scots Song Arrangements by Beethoven and Weber', in Hubbard and Jack, *Scotland in Europe*, pp. 119–36.

25 For the undated Italian translation, see Anna Benedetti, *Le traduzioni italiane da Walter Scott e i loro anglicismi* (Florence: Olschki, 1974), p. 26.

26 See Tom Hubbard, 'European Reception of Scott's Poetry: Translation as the Front Line', in Murray Pittock (ed.), *The Reception of Sir Walter Scott in Europe* (London: Continuum, 2006), pp. 268–84 (pp. 272, 284).

27 See Martin Procházka, 'From Romantic Folklorism to Children's Adventure Fiction: Walter Scott in Czech Culture', and Mirosława Modrzewska, 'The Polish Reception of Sir Walter Scott', in Pittock, *The Reception of Sir Walter Scott in Europe*, pp. 173–89, 190–203.

28 See Hubbard, 'European Reception of Scott's Poetry', p. 282, and Levin, *The Perception of English Literature in Russia*, p. 246.

29 See Varga, 'Sporadic Encounters', p. 210, and Lia Noêmia Rodrigues Correia Raitt, *Garrett and the English Muse* (London: Tamesis, 1983), p. 79.

30 See Levin, *The Perception of English Literature in Russia*, p. 245, and Procházka, 'From Romantic Folklorism to Children's Adventure Fiction', p. 186.

31 See Raitt, *Garrett and the English Muse*, p. 78.

32 See Modrzewska, 'The Polish Reception of Sir Walter Scott', pp. 194–97, José Enrique García-González and Fernando Toda, 'The Reception of Sir Walter Scott in Spain', in Pittock, *The Reception of Sir Walter Scott in Europe*, pp. 45–63 (p. 56), and Mary E. Ambrose, '*La donna del lago*: The First Italian Translations of Scott', *Modern Language Review*, 67 (1972), pp. 74–82 (p. 79).

33 A rare exception is Mikhail Lermontov, who took pride in his and Byron's joint Scottish ancestry (see McCarey, 'Ossian, Scott and Byron in Russia', p. 11 and Levin, *The Perception of English Literature in Russia*, p. 297).

34 See Levin, *The Perception of English Literature in Russia*, p. 272.

35 Richard A. Cardwell, 'Introduction', in *The Reception of Byron in Europe*, 2 vols (London: Thoemmes Continuum, 2004), II: pp. 1–10 (p. 9).

36 See Raitt, *Garrett and the English Muse*, p. 40; Levin, *The Perception of English Literature in Russia*, p. 289; and Joanne Wilkes, '"Infernal Magnetism": Byron and Nineteenth-Century French Readers', in Cardwell, *The Reception of Byron in Europe*, I: pp. 11–31 (p. 29). For other references in this section, see Cardwell, *The Reception of Byron in Europe*, passim.

37 Iain Galbraith, '"Your Scottish dialect drives us mad": A Note on the Reception of Poetry in Translation, with an Account of the Translation of Recent Scottish Poetry into German', in Hubbard and Jack, *Scotland in Europe*, pp. 137–52 (p. 139). 'Tam o' Shanter' has been suggested as a

source for the 'Walpurgisnacht' section of Faust, see William Macintosh, *Burns in Germany* (Aberdeen: Milne and Hutchison, 1928), p. 14.
38 French, German, Russian, Dutch and Norwegian; for details, see the Bibliography of Scottish Literature in Translation.
39 See Robert Crawford, 'Robert Burns and the Mind of Europe', in Murray Pittock (ed.), *Robert Burns in Global Culture* (Lewisburg: Bucknell University Press, 2011), pp. 47–62 (pp. 50, 55).
40 See Mario Verducci, *Giacomo Leopardi e Robert Burns, ovvero, il retroscena inglese del 'Sabato del villaggio'* (San Gabriele: ECO, 1993).
41 See, in particular, Silvia Mergenthal, 'Burns and European Identities', in Pittock, *Robert Burns in Global Culture*, pp. 63–72.
42 For a more chronologically detailed account, see Paul Barnaby and Tom Hubbard, 'The International Reception and Literary Impact of Scottish Literature of the Period 1707–1918', in Susan Manning (ed.), *The Edinburgh History of Scottish Literature*, II: pp. 33–44 (pp. 38–41).
43 The 1960s saw the publication of monographs by Kenneth White (France, 1964), Edwin Muir (France, 1968, and Japan, 1969) and Hugh MacDiarmid (East Germany, 1968 and 1969).
44 Rare exceptions include the Burns translator Heinrich Julius Heintze, who also published a joint anthology of verse by Robert Tannahill and William Motherwell (1841). Motherwell, Alan Cunningham and James Hogg also appeared in Eduard Fiedler's anthology *Geschichte der volksthümlichen schottischen Liederdichtung* (1846) and Ferdinand Freiligrath's *Rose, Distel und Kleeblatt* (1863).
45 Denis Saurat, 'Le Groupe de la "Renaissance ecossaise"', *Revue Anglo-américaine*, 1 (1924), pp. 295–307. This includes translations from MacDiarmid previously published in *Scottish Chapbook*, 2.1 (1923), pp. 13–14.
46 In his *Antologiia novoi angliiskoi poezii* (1937). See Alexander Mackay, 'MacDiarmid and Russia Revisited', in Carruthers, Goldie and Renfrew, *Beyond Scotland*, pp. 59–94 (p. 78).
47 Young's 'For the Old Highlands' was translated into Breton, with MacDiarmid's 'Little White Rose', in *Al Liamm*, 21 (1950), pp. 11–13. French selections from Forbes appeared in *Marsyas*, Sept.–Oct. 1950, pp. 1618–20.
48 See Carla Sassi, 'Prismatic Modernities: Towards a Re-Contextualisation of Scottish Modernism', in Emma Dymock and Margery Palmer McCulloch (eds), *Scottish and International Modernisms: Relationships and Reconfigurations* (Glasgow: Association for Scottish Literary Studies, 2011), pp. 184–97.

49 See, in particular, David Damrosch, 'Kafka Comes Home', in his *What is World Literature?* (Princeton, NJ: Princeton University Press, 2003), pp. 187–208.
50 See, in particular, Anne-Marie Le Bon-Dodat, 'Introduction', in Edwin Muir, *Poésie et prose*, trans. Anne-Marie Le Bon-Dodat (Paris: Seghers, 1968), pp. 7–11; and Carlo Izzo, 'Introduzione', in Edwin Muir, *Un piede nell'Eden e altre poesie*, trans. Marina Pellizzer (Turin: Einaudi, 1974), pp. v–xvii.
51 See Jan Östergren, 'Bångstyrigt snille – skrivende rebell ...', in Hugh MacDiarmid, *En drucken man beskådar tisteln och andra dikter*, trans. Jan Östergren (Stockholm: Folket i bilds lyrikklubb, 1984), pp. 5–9, Paul Borum, 'Efterskrift', in Hugh MacDiarmid, *Den slags poesi jeg vil have: digte*, trans. Paul Borum (Aarhus: Husets Forlag, 1992), pp. 83–86, and more recently, *La Rose au Risque du Chardon: anthologie de poèmes anglais et écossais inédits en français*, ed. and trans. Jacques Darras (Brussels: Éditions du Cri, 2003), pp. 9–18. This last anthology includes the first complete translation of *A Drunk Man Looks at the Thistle* into French (pp. 19–102).
52 For an overview of post-1970 translations of Scottish poetry, see Paul Barnaby and Tom Hubbard, 'The International Reception and Literary Impact of Scottish Literature of the Period since 1918', in Ian Brown (ed.), *The Edinburgh History of Scottish Literature*, III: pp. 31–41 (pp. 32–33). See also Paul Barnaby, 'Three into One: Twentieth-Century Scottish Verse in Translation Anthologies', *Translation and Literature*, 9 (2000), pp. 188–99, and 'Scotland Anthologised: Images of Contemporary Scottish Identity in Translation Anthologies of Scottish Poetry', *Scottish Studies Review*, 3.1 (2002), pp. 86–99.
53 See Sassi, 'Prismatic Modernities', pp. 191–92.

19: The Literary Environment

1 Robert Crawford, *Devolving English Literature* (Edinburgh: Edinburgh University Press, 1992).
2 See the announcement by the Scottish Studies Working Group, 'Scottish Studies across the Curriculum', *The Scottish Government* (1 March 2012), www.scotland.gov.uk/News/Releases/2012/03/scottishstudies01032012; and the response by the Educational Institute of Scotland in Andrew Holton, 'Union Warns over Plans for Scots Literature Question', *Herald* (5 November 2012), www.heraldscotland.com/news/13079667.Union_warns_over_plans_for_Scots_literature_question/.

3   See 'Is there a writer in the house?', the Scottish Arts Council Archive website, www.scottisharts.org.uk/1/artsinscotland/literature/features/writersinresidence.aspx.
4   In Daniel O'Rourke (ed.), *Dream State – The New Scottish Poets* (Edinburgh: Polygon, 1994), p. 206.
5   Giles Foden (ed.), *Body of Work: 40 years of Creative Writing at UEA* (Framlingham: Full Circle, 2011), quoted in Sarah Keating, 'Can Great Writing Be Taught?', BBC Radio 4 (1 December 2011), news.bbc.co.uk/today/hi/today/newsid_9652000/9652745.stm.
6   Roderick Watson, 'History of Creative Writing', Creative Writing, University of Stirling, creativewritingstirling.wordpress.com/about/.
7   Jennie Renton, 'Norman MacCaig: An Interview', *Textualities* (1987), textualities.net/jennie-renton/norman-maccaig-an-interview.
8   The first issue of the *Rialto* in autumn 1984 included four poems by Carol Ann Duffy, who published her first collection in 1985.
9   The *London Review of Books* has published poems by John Burnside, Robert Crawford and Robin Robertson, for example. It was founded in 1979 by the Scottish academic Karl Miller, who edited the fortnightly journal until 1992.
10 James Robertson, 'Becoming a Writer', in Paul Henderson Scott (ed.), *Spirits of the Age – Scottish Self-Portraits* (Edinburgh: The Saltire Society, 2005), p. 351.
11 Trevor Royle, *The Macmillan Companion to Scottish Literature* (London: Macmillan, 1983), p. 98.
12 David Miller and Richard Price (eds), *British Poetry Magazines 1914–2000: A History and Bibliography of 'Little Magazines'* (London and Newcastle: The British Library and Oak Knoll Press), p. 124.
13 Joy Hendry, 'About *Chapman*', *Chapman*, www.chapman-pub.co.uk/about.php.
14 Quoted in David Purves, 'Poems, Stories, Plays in the Scots Language', *Lallans Magazine*, www.electricscotland.com/poetry/purves/lallans.htm.
15 Robert Crawford, 'Introduction', in Robert Crawford, Henry Hart, David Kinloch and Richard Price (eds), *Talking Verse: Interviews with Poets* (St Andrews and Williamsburg: Verse, 1995), pp. 8–9.
16 Crawford et al., *Talking Verse*, p. 102.
17 'Gairfish Prepares to Dive into Cultural Pool', *Herald* (29 July 1989), www.heraldscotland.com/news/11927064.Gairfish_prepares_to_dive_into_cultural_pool/.
18 Miller and Price, *British Poetry Magazines 1914–2000*, p. 227.

19 'Liz Lochhead Interviewed by Emily B. Todd', in Crawford et al., *Talking Verse*, pp. 117–18.
20 After this failed financially, it was taken over by the city council and became the Centre for Contemporary Arts in 1992, and hosts work in all the art forms.
21 Shore Poets, shorepoets.org.uk/about-shore-poets.
22 'Kathleen Jamie Interviewed by Richard Price', in Crawford et al., *Talking Verse*, pp. 101–02. For a discussion of Scottish authors and publication within and outwith Scotland, see also Jane Potter, 'Literary Publishing: 1945–2000', in David Finkelstein and Alistair McCleery (eds), *The Edinburgh History of the Book in Scotland* (Edinburgh: Edinburgh University Press, 2007), IV: pp. 269–73.
23 See Ian Stevenson, 'The Role of the Scottish Arts Council', in Finkelstein and McCleery, *The Edinburgh History of the Book in Scotland*, IV: pp. 67–70; and Trevor Royle, 'Walter Cairns Respected and Leading Figure in Scottish Literature', *Herald* (14 January 2003), www.heraldscotland.com/news/11907320.Walter_Cairns_Respected_and_leading_figure_in_Scottish_literature/.
24 See Simon Ward, 'The Development of the Bookshop', in Finkelstein and McCleery, *The Edinburgh History of the Book in Scotland*, IV: pp. 83–91; and Tam Dalyell's obituary for James Thin, in the *Independent* (5 June 1997), www.independent.co.uk/news/people/obituary-james-thin-1254230.html.
25 Pamphlet publishing in Scotland has been encouraged by the annual Callum Macdonald Memorial Award for poetry pamphlet publication, established in 2001. www.nls.uk/about-us/awards/2012-callum-macdonald-memorial-award.
26 For the first twenty-five years of the Scottish Poetry Library, see *This House, This Poem … This Fresh Hypothesis: A Brief History of the Scottish Poetry Library* (Edinburgh: Scottish Poetry Library, 2005).
27 See Robyn Marsack, 'On the National Poet's First Year', in Anne Varty (ed.), *The Edinburgh Companion to Liz Lochhead* (Edinburgh: Edinburgh University Press: 2013), pp. 9–13.

Further Reading

Since the *Companion* covers a very long time scale, the following list is meant to act only as a starting point to further, more detailed research. It includes, with very few exceptions, monographs only. Investigations of individual aspects and authors of Scotland's poetry are available in the individual chapters of the list of volumes included in the 'General' section.

Bibliographical Sources

Glen, Duncan, *The Poetry of the Scots: An Introduction and Bibliographical Guide to Poetry in Gaelic, Scots, Latin, and English* (Edinburgh: Edinburgh University Press, 1991).

National Library of Scotland, Bibliography of Scottish Literature in Translation (BOSLIT), www.nls.uk/catalogues/boslit.

Scottish Poetry Index: An Index to Poetry and Poetry-Related Material in Scottish Literary Magazines, 1952–, 9 vols (Edinburgh: The Scottish Poetry Library, 1994–2000).

Scottish Poetry Library Online catalogue, www.scottishpoetrylibrary.org.uk/library/online-catalogue.

General

Bateman, Meg, and Catherine Kerrigan (eds), *An Anthology of Scottish Women Poets* (Edinburgh: Edinburgh University Press, 2007).

Brown, Ian, Thomas Owen Clancy, Susan Manning and Murray Pittock (eds), *The Edinburgh History of Scottish Literature*, 3 vols (Edinburgh: Edinburgh University Press, 2007).

Buchan, David, *The Ballad and the Folk* (London: Routledge & Kegan Paul, 1972).

Carruthers, Gerard, and Liam McIlvanney (eds), *The Cambridge Companion to Scottish Literature* (Cambridge: Cambridge University Press, 2012).

Corbett, John, *Language and Scottish Literature* (Edinburgh: Edinburgh University Press, 1997).

Craig, Cairns (gen. ed.), *The History of Scottish Literature*, 4 vols (Aberdeen: Aberdeen University Press, 1987).

Crawford, Robert, *Bannockburns: Scottish Independence and Literary Imagination, 1314–2014* (Edinburgh: Edinburgh University Press, 2014).

Crawford, Robert, *Scotland's Books: A History of Scottish Literature* (Oxford: Oxford University Press, 2009).

Dunnigan, Sarah, and Suzanne Gilbert (eds), *The Edinburgh Companion to Scottish Traditional Literatures* (Edinburgh: Edinburgh University Press, 2013).

Gifford, Douglas, and Dorothy McMillan (eds), *A History of Scottish Women's Writing* (Edinburgh: Edinburgh University Press, 1997).

Gifford, Douglas, Sarah Dunnigan and Alan MacGillivray (eds), *Scottish Literature in English and Scots* (Edinburgh: Edinburgh University Press, 2002).

Hall, Simon W., *The History of Orkney Literature* (Edinburgh: John Donald, 2010).

Kinsley, James (ed.), *Scottish Poetry: A Critical Survey* (London: Cassell, 1955).

Norquay, Glenda (ed.), *The Edinburgh Companion to Scottish Women's Writing* (Edinburgh: Edinburgh University Press, 2012).

Riach, Alan, and Douglas Gifford (eds), *Scotlands: Poets and the Nation* (Manchester: Carcanet Press, 2004).

Smith, Mark R., *The Literature of Shetland* (Lerwick: The Shetland Times, 2014).

Stroh, Silke, *Uneasy Subjects: Postcolonialism and Scottish Gaelic Poetry* (Amsterdam: Rodopi, 2011).

Thomson, Derick S., *The Companion to Gaelic Scotland* (Glasgow: Gairm, 1994).

Thomson, Derick S., *An Introduction to Gaelic Poetry* (Edinburgh: Edinburgh University Press, 1993).

Watson, Roderick, *The Literature of Scotland*, 2 vols (Basingstoke: Palgrave Macmillan, 2007).

Pre-1700

Aitken, Adam J., Matthew P. McDiarmid and Derick S. Thomson (eds), *Bards and Makars: Scottish Language and Literature: Medieval and Renaissance* (Glasgow: University of Glasgow Press, 1977).

Bateman, Meg, and Wilson McLeod (eds), *Duanaire na Sràcaire/Songbook of the Pillagers: Anthology of Medieval Gaelic Poetry* (Edinburgh: Birlinn, 2007).

Bawcutt, Priscilla, *Dunbar the Makar* (Oxford: Clarendon, 1992).

Bawcutt, Priscilla J., and Janet Hadley Williams (eds), *A Companion to Medieval Scottish Poetry* (Woodbridge: Boydell & Brewer, 2006).

Boardman, Stephen I., and Eila Williamson (eds), *The Cult of Saints and the Virgin Mary in Medieval Scotland* (Woodbridge: Boydell Press, 2010).

Bruce, Mark Paul, and Katherine H. Terrell (eds), *The Anglo-Scottish Border and the Shaping of Identity, 1300–1600* (Basingstoke: Palgrave Macmillan, 2012).

Calin, William, *The Lily and the Thistle: The French Tradition and the Older Literature of Scotland: Essays in Criticism* (Toronto: University of Toronto Press, 2014).

Carpenter, Sarah, and Sarah M. Dunnigan (eds), *'Joyous Sweit Imaginatioun': Essays on Scottish Literature in Honour of R. D. S. Jack* (Amsterdam: Rodopi, 2007).

Clancy, Thomas Owen (ed.), *The Triumph Tree: Scotland's Earliest Poetry AD 550–1350* (Edinburgh: Canongate, 1998).

Crawford, Barbara E., *St Magnus Cathedral and Orkney's Twelfth-Century Renaissance* (Aberdeen: Aberdeen University Press, 1988).

Dunnigan, Sarah, *Eros and Poetry at the Courts of Mary Queen of Scots and James VI* (Basingstoke: Palgrave, 2002).

Frank, Roberta, *Old Norse Court Poetry: The Dróttkvætt Stanza* (Ithaca, NY: Cornell University Press, 1978).

Goldstein, R. James, *The Matter of Scotland: Historical Narrative in Medieval Scotland* (Lincoln: University of Nebraska Press, 1993).

Gribben, Crawford, and David George Mullan (eds), *Literature and the Scottish Reformation* (Aldershot: Ashgate, 2009).

Hasler, Antony, *Court Poetry in Late Medieval England and Scotland: Allegories of Authority* (Cambridge: Cambridge University Press, 2011).

Houghton, Luke, and Gesine Manuwald (eds), *Neo-Latin Poetry in the British Isles* (London: Bloomsbury Academic, 2012).

Jack, R. D. S., 'The Language of Literary Materials', in Charles Jones (ed.), *The Edinburgh History of Scots* (Edinburgh: Edinburgh University Press, 1997), pp. 213–63.

Kindrick, Robert L., *Henryson and the Medieval Arts of Rhetoric* (New York: Garland, 1993).

Kratzmann, Gregory, *Anglo-Scottish Literary Relations, 1430–1550* (Cambridge: Cambridge University Press, 1980).

Mainer, Sergi, *The Scottish Romance Tradition c. 1375–c. 1550: Nation, Chivalry and Knighthood* (Amsterdam: Rodopi, 2010).

Mapstone, Sally, *Older Scots Literature* (Edinburgh: John Donald Publishers, 2005).

Martin, Joanna, *Kingship and Love in Scottish Poetry, 1424–1540* (Aldershot: Ashgate, 2008).

Ò hAnnracháin, Tadhg, and Robert Armstrong (eds), *Christianities in the Early Modern Celtic World* (Basingstoke: Palgrave Macmillan, 2014).

Petrina, Alessandra, *The Kingis Quair of James I of Scotland* (Padova: Unipress, 1997).

Poole, Russel Gilbert, *Viking Poems on War and Peace: A Study in Skaldic Narrative* (Toronto: University of Toronto Press, 1991).

Rickard, Jane, *Authorship and Authority: The Writings of James VI and I* (Manchester: Manchester University Press, 2007).

Robinson, Jon, *Court Politics, Culture and Literature in Scotland and England, 1500–1540* (Aldershot: Ashgate, 2008).

Ross, Sarah C. E., *Women, Poetry, and Politics in Seventeenth-Century Britain* (Oxford: Oxford University Press, 2015).

Royan, Nicola (ed.), *Langage Cleir Illumynate: Scottish Poetry from Barbour to Drummond, 1375–1630* (Amsterdam: Rodopi, 2007).

Shire, Helena Mennie, *Song, Dance and Poetry of the Court of Scotland under King James VI: Musical Illustrations of Court-Song* (Cambridge: Cambridge University Press, 1969).

Waugh, Doreen, and Alison Finlay, *The Faces of Orkney: Stones, Skalds, and Saints* (Edinburgh: Scottish Society for Northern Studies, 2003).

Williams, Janet Hadley, and J. Derrick McClure (eds), *Fresche Fontanis: Studies in the Culture of Medieval and Early Modern Scotland* (Newcastle upon Tyne: Cambridge Scholars, 2013).

Post-1700

Alker, Sharon-Ruth, Leith Davis and Holly Faith Nelson (eds), *Robert Burns and Transatlantic Culture* (Farnham: Ashgate, 2012).

Andrews, Corey E., *Literary Nationalism in Eighteenth-Century Scottish Club Poetry* (Lewiston, NY: Edwin Mellen Press, 2004).
Angeletti, Gioia, *Eccentric Scotland: Three Victorian Poets: James Thomson ('b.v.'), John Davidson, James Young Geddes* (Bologna: CLUEB, 2004).
Black, Ronald (ed.), *An Lasair: Anthology of 18th Century Scottish Gaelic Verse* (Edinburgh: Birlinn, 2001).
Black, Ronald (ed.), *An Tuil: Anthology of 20th Century Scottish Gaelic Verse* (Edinburgh: Polygon, 1999).
Blankenhorn, Virginia S., *Irish Song-Craft and Metrical Practice since 1600* (Lewiston, NY: Edwin Mellen Press, 2003).
Byrne, Michel (ed.), *Collected Poems and Songs of George Campbell Hay (Deòrsa Mac Iain Dheòrsa)* (Edinburgh: Lorimer Trust/Edinburgh University Press, 2000).
Campbell, John Lorne, and Francis M. Collinson (eds), *Hebridean Folksongs* (Oxford: Clarendon Press, 1969–81).
Carruthers, Gerard, 'Poetry Beyond the English Borders', in Christine Gerrard (ed.), *A Companion to Eighteenth-Century Poetry* (Oxford: Blackwell, 2006), pp. 577–89.
Carruthers, Gerard (ed.), *The Edinburgh Companion to Robert Burns* (Edinburgh: Edinburgh University Press, 2009).
Christianson, Aileen, and Alison Lumsden (eds), *Contemporary Scottish Woman Writers* (Edinburgh: EUP, 2000).
Crawford, Robert, *Devolving English Literature* (Edinburgh: Edinburgh University Press, 2000).
Crawford, Robert, *Robert Burns and Cultural Authority* (Edinburgh: Edinburgh University Press, 1997).
Davis, Leith, *Acts of Union: Scotland and the Literary Negotiation of the British Nation, 1707–1830* (Stanford: Stanford University Press, 1998).
Davis, Leith, Ian Duncan and Janet Sorensen (eds), *Scotland and the Borders of Romanticism* (Cambridge: Cambridge University Press, 2004).
Dósa, Attila, *Beyond Identity: New Horizons in Modern Scottish Poetry* (Amsterdam: Rodopi, 2009).
Dunbar, Rob, 'The Poetry of the Emigrant Generation', *Transactions of the Gaelic Society of Inverness* 64 (2008), pp. 22–125.
Dymock, Emma, and Margery Palmer McCulloch (eds), *Scottish and International Modernisms: Relationships and Reconfigurations* (Glasgow: Association for Scottish Literary Studies, 2011).

Dymock, Emma, and Wilson McLeod (eds), *Lainnir a' Bhùirn – The Gleaming Water: Essays on Modern Gaelic Literature* (Edinburgh: Dunedin Academic Press, 2011).

Fazzini, Marco, *Crossings: Essays in Contemporary Scottish Poetry and Hybridity* (Venice: Supernova, 2000).

Fielding, Penny, *Scotland and the Fictions of Geography* (Cambridge: Cambridge University Press, 2009).

Gairn, Louisa, *Ecology and Modern Scottish Literature* (Edinburgh: Edinburgh University Press, 2008).

Leask, Nigel, *Robert Burns and Pastoral: Poetry and Improvement in Late Eighteenth-Century Scotland* (Oxford: Oxford University Press, 2010).

Leonard, Tom, *Radical Renfrew: Poetry from the French Revolution to the First World War* (Edinburgh: Polygon, 1990).

Lyall, Scott, *Hugh MacDiarmid's Poetry and Politics of Place: Imagining a Scottish Republic* (Edinburgh: Edinburgh University Press, 2006).

Lyall, Scott, and Margery Palmer McCulloch (eds), *The Edinburgh Companion to Hugh MacDiarmid* (Edinburgh: Edinburgh University Press, 2011).

McCulloch, Margery Palmer, *Scottish Modernism and Its Contexts 1918–1959: Literature, National Identity and Cultural Exchange* (Edinburgh: Edinburgh University Press, 2009).

McGonigal, James, *Beyond the Last Dragon: A Life of Edwin Morgan* (Dingwall: Sandstone Press, 2010).

McGuire, Matt, and Colin Nicholson (eds), *The Edinburgh Companion to Contemporary Scottish Poetry* (Edinburgh: Edinburgh University Press, 2009).

Mackay, Peter, Edna Longley and Fran Brearton (eds), *Modern Irish and Scottish Poetry* (Cambridge: Cambridge University Press, 2011).

MacLachlan, Christopher (ed.), *Crossing the Highland Line: Cross-currents in Eighteenth-Century Scottish Writing* (Glasgow: Association for Scottish Literary Studies, 2009).

MacLachlan, Christopher, and Ronald W. Renton (eds), *Gael and Lowlander in Scottish Literature: Cross-currents in Scottish Writing in the Nineteenth Century* (Glasgow: Scottish Literature International, 2015).

Macleod, Michelle, 'Language and Identity in Modern Gaelic Verse', in Ian Brown and Alan Riach (eds), *The Edinburgh Companion to Twentieth-Century Scottish Literature* (Edinburgh: Edinburgh University Press, 2009), pp. 167–80.

McMillan, Dorothy, and Michel Byrne (eds), *Modern Scottish Women Poets* (Edinburgh: Canongate Classics, 2003).

Meek, Donald E., 'The Role of Song in the Highland Land Agitation', *Scottish Gaelic Studies*, 16 (1990), pp. 1–53.

Meek, Donald E. (ed.), *Caran An t-saoghail/The Wiles of the World: Anthology of Nineteenth-Century Scottish Gaelic verse* (Edinburgh: Birlinn, 2003).

Moore, Dafydd (ed.), *Ossian and Ossianism* (London: Routledge, 2004).

Newton, Michael (ed.), *Dùthchas nan Gàidheal: Selected Essays of John MacInnes* (Edinburgh: Birlinn, 2006).

Nicholson, Colin, *Edwin Morgan: Inventions of Modernity* (Manchester: Manchester University Press, 2002).

Nicholson, Colin, *Poem, Purpose and Place: Shaping Identity in Contemporary Scottish Verse* (Edinburgh: Polygon, 1992).

Pittock, Murray (ed.), *The Edinburgh Companion to Scottish Romanticism* (Edinburgh: Edinburgh University Press, 2011).

Pittock, Murray, *Poetry and Jacobite Politics in Eighteenth-Century Britain and Ireland* (Cambridge: University Press, 1994).

Pittock, Murray (ed.), *Robert Burns in Global Culture* (Lewisburg, PA: Bucknell University Press, 2011).

Pittock, Murray, *Scottish and Irish Romanticism* (Oxford: Oxford University Press, 2008).

Riach, Alan, *Hugh MacDiarmid's Epic Poetry* (Edinburgh: Edinburgh University Press, 1991).

Ross, James, 'The Sub-literary Tradition in Scottish Gaelic Song-poetry', *Éigse* 7 (1953–55), pp. 217–39, and 8 (1955–57), pp. 1–17.

Sergeant, David, and Fiona J Stafford (eds), *Burns and Other Poets* (Edinburgh: Edinburgh University Press, 2012).

Somerville-Arjat, Gillean, and Rebecca E. Wilson (eds), *Sleeping with Monsters: Conversations with Scottish and Irish Women Poets* (Edinburgh: Polygon, 1989).

Stafford, Fiona J., *Starting Lines in Scottish, Irish, and English Poetry: From Burns to Heaney* (Oxford: Oxford University Press, 2000).

Stafford, Fiona J., and Howard Gaskill (eds), *From Gaelic to Romantic: Ossianic Translations* (Amsterdam: Rodopi, 1998).

Thomson, Derick S., *The New Verse in Scottish Gaelic: A Structural Analysis* (Dublin: University College, 1974).

Whyte, Christopher, *Modern Scottish Poetry* (Edinburgh: Edinburgh University Press, 2004).

Notes on Contributors

Paul Barnaby is editor of the Walter Scott Digital Archive at Edinburgh University Library where he is responsible for modern Scottish literary manuscripts. Previously editor of the Bibliography of Scottish Literature in Translation (BOSLIT) and Postdoctoral Research Fellow for the Reception of British and Irish Authors in Europe project, he has published on the international reception and translation of Scottish literature.

Meg Bateman is a senior lecturer at Sabhal Mòr Ostaig in Skye, part of the University of the Highlands and Islands. She has co-edited and translated several anthologies of Gaelic material and has published four collections of her own poetry, the most recent being *Transparencies* (2013).

Ronald Black is Gaelic Editor of the *Scotsman* and a former lecturer in Celtic in Glasgow and Edinburgh universities. He has published two anthologies of Gaelic poetry and an edition of Johnson and Boswell's tour. He is currently working on a book about the relationship between Alastair mac Mhaighstir Alastair (Alexander MacDonald) and the Campbells.

Gerard Carruthers is Francis Hutcheson Professor of Scottish Literature at the University of Glasgow. General Editor of the new Oxford Edition of the Works of Robert Burns, his publications include (as co-editor with Liam McIlvanney) *The Cambridge Companion to Scottish Literature* (2012); *Scottish Literature: A Critical Guide* (2009); and *Robert Burns* (2006).

Thomas Owen Clancy is Professor of Celtic at the University of Glasgow. He has written widely on Celtic and, especially, medieval Gaelic literature, bringing Scotland's pre-1350 poetry to the attention of scholars and the general public, notably through the edited anthology *The Triumph Tree: Scotland's Earliest Poetry, AD 550–1350* (1998). He is series co-editor of *The International Companions to Scottish Literature*.

Attila Dósa is a Senior Lecturer at the University of Miskolc in North Hungary. After graduating from Debrecen University, he conducted postgraduate work at Oxford as a Soros Scholar. His *Beyond Identity: New Horizons in Modern Scottish Poetry* (2009) received a HUSSE Book Award in 2011.

Emma Dymock is affiliated to the University of Edinburgh where she currently teaches Gaelic poetry and culture. She co-edited *Caoir Gheal Leumraich/White Leaping Flame: Sorley MacLean Collected Poems* (2011) and is preparing the *Sorley MacLean–Douglas Young Correspondence* and *Naething Dauntit: The Collected Poems of Douglas Young* for publication in 2016.

Ian Duncan is Florence Green Bixby Professor of English at the University of California, Berkeley. Author of *Scott's Shadow: The Novel in Romantic Edinburgh* (2007) and *Modern Romance and Transformations of the Novel* (1992), he co-edited *Scotland and the Borders of Romanticism* (2004) and *The Edinburgh Companion to James Hogg* (2012), and is a general editor of the Collected Works of James Hogg.

Roberta Frank, Marie Borroff Professor of English at Yale University, is author of *Old Norse Court Poetry* (1978) and more than fifty articles on aspects of early English and Norse language, literature, and history. Her edition of the Orkney poem *Málsháttakvæði* will appear in volume III of *Skaldic Poetry of the Scandinavian Middle Ages* (2016).

Louisa Gairn is Lecturer at Aalto University, Finland. Author of *Ecology and Modern Scottish Literature* (2008), which was shortlisted for the Robin Jenkins Literary Award, she has contributed to *The Edinburgh Companion to Contemporary Scottish Literature* (2007), *The Edinburgh Companion to Hugh MacDiarmid* (2011) and *Kathleen Jamie: Essays and Poems on Her Work* (2015).

Suzanne Gilbert is a Senior Lecturer in English at Stirling University and publishes on eighteenth- and nineteenth-century Scottish literature, ballads and chapbooks. She and Ian Duncan are general editors of the

Stirling/South Carolina Research Edition of *The Collected Works of James Hogg* and she co-edited *The Edinburgh Companion to Scottish Traditional Literatures*.

William Gillies is a Visiting Professor at Harvard University. He was Professor of Celtic at Edinburgh University from 1979 to 2009. His main research interests are in the history of the Gaelic languages and literatures and he is currently working on the Books of Clanranald and the Book of the Dean of Lismore.

Roger Green was Professor of Humanity in the University of Glasgow between 1995 and 2008, and is now Honorary Research Professor in Classics. As well as various studies of classical Latin literature he has worked intensively on the poetry of George Buchanan and related Scottish neo-Latin topics.

Sìm Innes is Lecturer in Celtic and Gaelic at the University of Glasgow. He works on Scottish Gaelic literature and folklore. He has a particular research interest in the pan-Gaelic bardic poetry tradition of late medieval and early modern Scotland and Ireland.

Ronnie Jack is a Fellow of the Royal Society of Edinburgh. He held a Personal Chair of Medieval and Scottish Literature from 1987 until 2004 in the English Department of Edinburgh University. His books include *The Italian Influence on Scottish Literature* (1972) and *The Road to the Never Land* (1991).

Sheila Kidd is Senior Lecturer in Celtic and Gaelic at the University of Glasgow. Her research interests lie primarily in eighteenth- to early twentieth-century Gaelic literature, particularly nineteenth-century Gaelic periodical publishing and the literature of the Highland diaspora. She is also researching the social domains of Gaelic language usage in the eighteenth and nineteenth centuries.

Scott Lyall is Lecturer in Modern Literature and Programme Leader for English at Edinburgh Napier University. He is author of *Hugh MacDiarmid's Poetry and Politics of Place: Imagining a Scottish Republic* (2006), co-editor of *The Edinburgh Companion to Hugh MacDiarmid* (2011), and editor of *The International Companion to Lewis Grassic Gibbon* (2015) and the forthcoming *Community in Modern Scottish Literature*.

Derrick McClure has chaired the Scottish Government's Ministerial Advisory Group on the Scots Language, the ASLS Language Committee and the Forum for Research in the Languages of Scotland and Ulster. Author of four books and over a hundred articles on Scottish linguistic and literary topics, his translations includes *Sangs tae Eimhir* (Sorley MacLean's *Dàin do Eimhir*) and poetry from Gaelic, Italian, Sicilian, Provençal and other languages.

James McGonigal is Emeritus Professor of English in Education in the University of Glasgow. He co-edited *The Midnight Letterbox: Selected Correspondence of Edwin Morgan 1950–2010* (2015), and earlier wrote an award-winning biography, *Beyond the Last Dragon: A Life of Edwin Morgan* (2010, 2012). He is one of the poet's literary executors.

Peter Mackay is a Lecturer in Literature in the School of English at the University of St Andrews. Author of *Sorley MacLean* (2010), and of a collection of poems, *Gu Leòr* (2015), he has also co-edited an anthology of Scottish Gaelic bawdy, erotic and transgressive verse, *An Leabhar Liath* (Luath, due out 2016). He is a BBC/AHRC New Generation Thinker for 2015.

Michelle Macleod is a Senior Lecturer in Gaelic Studies at the University of Aberdeen. She has written extensively on modern Gaelic literature, across the genres. As the socio-linguistic context for Gaelic changes at pace, she has a particular interest in exploring manifestations of the modern Gael in the literary text. She is the co-editor of *The Companion to Gaelic Language* (EUP) and editor of *Dealbhan-chluiche Thormoid Chaluim Dhòmhnallaich* (AUP).

Wilson McLeod is Professor of Gaelic at the University of Edinburgh. He has published widely on medieval and modern Gaelic literature; Gaelic education, sociolinguistics and language policy; and on minority languages issues more generally.

Robyn Marsack was a freelance publishers' editor until taking up the post of Director of the Scottish Poetry Library in 2000. She is a member of various literary boards, including that of Carcanet Press (since 2004), and chaired the Literature Forum for Scotland from 2011 to 2013. She is an editor, critic and translator.

Alessandra Petrina is Associate Professor of English Literature at the Università degli Studi di Padova, Italy. Author of *The Kingis Quair* (1997) and *Cultural Politics in Fifteenth-century England: The Case of Humphrey, Duke of Gloucester* (2004), she has recently edited *The Medieval Translator: In principio fuit interpres* (2013); *Machiavellian Encounters in Tudor and Stuart England* (2013) and *Natio Scota* (2012).

Alan Riach is Professor of Scottish Literature at Glasgow University, general editor of the *Collected Works* of Hugh MacDiarmid, author of *Representing Scotland in Literature, Popular Culture and Iconography* (2005) and co-author with Alexander Moffat of *Arts of Resistance* (2008) and *Arts of Independence* (2014). His fifth book of poems is *Homecoming* (2009).

Carla Sassi is Associate Professor of English Literature at the University of Verona. She specialises in Scottish and Postcolonial studies. Her publications include *Why Scottish Literature Matters* (2005); as a co-author, *Caribbean–Scottish Relations*(2007); as a co-editor, *Within Without Empire: Scotland across the (Post)colonial Borderline* (2013).

Brian Smith is archivist at the Shetland Museum and Archives. He is the author and editor of many books and articles about Shetland and Orkney.

Silke Stroh is Assistant Professor of English, Postcolonial and Media Studies at Münster University. Author of *Uneasy Subjects: Postcolonialism and Scottish Gaelic Poetry* (2011) and *Gaelic Scotland in the Colonial Imagination: Anglophone Writing from 1600 to 1900* (2016), her other research areas include modern anglophone Scottish literature, diaspora studies, transnationalism, film, and anglophone African and black British writing.

Index

'A' Ghriadach Dhonn' ('*The Brownhaired Girl-child*') (anon), 147
abecederian format, 24
Aberdeen, University of, 26
Adam of Bremen, 34
Adams, J. W. L., 28
Adamson, Patrick, *De Papistarum superstitiosis ineptiis*, 29
Adomnán of Iona, 24
  Life of Columba, 27
Akros (magazine), 205
'Alba gan díon a ndiaidh Ailín' ('*Scotland is defenceless after Ailean*') (anon), 146
Aleander, Jerome, 26
Alexander, William, *Aurora*, 52
Alfred, A Masque (play), 58
allegory, 19–20, 21, 117, 118
alliteration, 39, 114, 116, 133
American speech rhythms, 87
Amhlaoibh of the Lennox, 8, 9, 12
amour courtois tradition, 52, 172, 176
'An spaidsearachd Bharrach' ('*The Barra Saunter*') (anon), 147

'An Tánaiste Tais' ('*The Gentle Tanist*'), 55
Andersen, Flemming, *Commonplace and Creativity*, 128
Anderson, Basil R., 41
Andrew of Wyntoun, 110
Anglo-Saxon poetry, 25
Angus, James Stout, 'Eels', 40
Angus, Marion, 77, 129, 140, 153, 180, 186
  'The Wild Geese', 63
animals, treatment of, 134, 135, 136
Annand, J. K., 206
anticlericalism, 187
Aonghus, Lord of the Isles, 9
'Ar sliocht Gaodhal ó ghort Gréag' ('*The Gaels from the land of Greece*') (anon), 147
Arany, János, 195
Arbuckle, James, 58
Argyll, 8, 12, 71
Argyll, Duke of, 157
Argyll, Earldom of, 48, 51, 147
Ariosto, Ludovico, *Orlando Furioso*, 50
Aristotelian concepts, 17, 18, 19
Aristotle, *Rhetoric*, 17

Arnold, Matthew, 67
Arnórr jarlaskáld Þórðarson, 32, 33–35
'art' poetry, 73
Arthur, King, 18
Asclepiad metre, 26
Asloan Manuscript, 45
Association for Scottish Literary Studies, 200, 208
assonance, 23
Augustan pastoralism, 134, 135
Augustanism, 55, 57
autobiographical poetry, 139
Ayton, Robert, 51
Aytoun, W. E., *Lays of the Scottish Cavaliers*, 70

Bacach, Eachann, 53
Baillie, Joanna, 'A Proud Lover's Farewell to his Mistress', 175
ballads, 121–31
    'ballad-epic', 67
    broadside ballads, 123, 130
    Caribbean adaptations, 131
    definition, 126
    female poets, 149
    formulaic recurrences, 128
    literary, 70
    metre, 126
    as 'narrative song', 123
    oral, 123, 126, 130–31
    stanzas, 126–27
    use of Scots language, 128
Bamforth, Iain, 91, 188
Bannatyne, George 170
Bannatyne Manuscript, 45, 47, 117, 170
Bannerman, Anne, *Poems*, 68
Bannockburn, Battle of, 25, 145
Barbour, John, *The Bruce*, 16, 17, 19, 109–10, 145, 156
Barclay, John, *Argenis*, 20
bard baile ('village poet') tradition, 151
Barr, John, 161
Barry, Thomas de, 26
Bartholin, Thomas, *Antiquitatum Danicarum*, 39, 40
Baston, Robert, 25
    'Metrum de Praelio apud Bannockburn' ('The Poem of the Battle of Bannockburn'), 145
Bateman, Meg, 85, 91, 167, 176
    Aotromachd agus dain eile/ Lightness and other poems, 92
    'Cànain' ('Language'), 86
bawdy poetry, 169, 171
beast fables, 21–22, 132, 133, 136
Beat Poets, 88
Beattie, James, 'The Minstrel', 60
Beccán mac Luigdech, 9
Beccán of Rum, 9
Bede, 24
Beerbohm, Max, 'Enoch Soames', 41
Belli, Giuseppe, 187
Bellum Bothuelianum, 30
Benson, Larry, 18
Bernard of Arbroath, 25
Bernstein, Marion, 73, 161
    'On the Franchise Demonstration of the 6th Inst', 72
    'A Woman's Plea', 72
Biblical themes, 24, 27, 185
'binding rhyme', 24

Bissett, Alan, 'Vote Britain!: My Contribution to the Debate on Scottish Independence', 167, 168
Bjarni Kolbeinsson, Bishop, 32, 33, 36–37
Black, Ronald, 79
Black Death, 26
Blackwood's Edinburgh Magazine, 67, 69, 72
Blair, Robert, 61
Blamire, Susanna, 149
Blind Harper, the *see* Clàrsair Dall, an
Blind Hary, *The Wallace*, 17, 18, 20–21, 111–12, 145, 156, 161
Bloodaxe publishers, 209
Bochanan, Dùghall (Dugald Buchanan), 107
  'Là a' Bhreitheanais' (*Day of Judgement*), 186
  Spiritual Songs, 61
Boethius, 19
Bold, Alan, 125
Bonar, Horatius, *Hymns of Faith and Hope*, 199
'Bonny Barbara Allan' (popular ballad), 130
book festivals, 209
Book of the Dean of Lismore, 11, 12, 45, 47, 48, 157, 171, 187
Bowd, Gavin, 209
Bower, Walter, 25
Brackenbury, Roz, 209
Braes, Battle of the, 71
British Empire, 64, 72, 164
British Romanticism, 67–69
Bronson, Bertrand H., 126
Brooks, Cleanth, 129, 130

Brooks, Cleanth, and Warren, Robert Penn, *Understanding Poetry*, eds, 129, 130
Brough of Birsay, 32
Brown, Anna Gordon, 122
Brown, George Mackay, 42, 186
Bruce, George, 74, 75
Bruce, Michael, 60
Bruno, Giordano, *Eroici Furori*, 50
Buchan, David, 121
Buchan, John
  The Northern Muse, 77
  Poems Scots and English, 77
Buchanan, Dugald *see* Bochanan, Dùghall
Buchanan, George, 26, 27–28, 30, 190–92
  Baptistes, 191
  De Jure Regni apud Scotos, 28, 157, 158, 191
  De Sphaera, 28
  dramas, 27
  'Elegy on John Calvin', 184
  Elegies, 28
  Franciscanus, 27, 28, 192
  Jephthes, 191
  Miscellanea, 28
  Portuguese Inquisition, 27
  Psalm poems, 27, 28, 45, 192
  and Ruddiman, 57
  satire, 192
  secular poems, 28
  Somnium, 27, 190
Buchanan, Robert, 162, 163
Buell, Lawrence, 134
Bulter, Rhoda, 42
Burns, Elizabeth, *Held*, 167
Burns, Robert
  'Address to Beelzebub', 137

278   INDEX

Burns, Robert (*cont.*)
   'Auld Lang Syne', 63
   ballads, 122
   Byron and, 66
   Chalmers and, 68
   'Epistle to Davie', 118
   'Hallowe'en', 117
   'The Holy Fair', 117, 187
   'Holy Willie's Prayer', 187
   impact of Bible, 185
   influence of, 60, 198–99
   'Is there for honest poverty', 63
   'Love and Liberty', 118
   love poetry, 174
   Macpherson and, 62
   The Merry Muses of Caledonia, 174
   as national icon, 144
   on nature, 132
   'The Ordination', 117
   poetic form, 111, 109, 120
   protest and politics, 160, 161
   'A Red Red Rose', 144
   on rural life, 136–37
   satire, 117, 187
   Scottish identity, 63, 150, 151
   Stanza form, 120
   'Tam o' Shanter', 63, 111, 180
   'To a mouse', 137
   translations of, 63, 198–99
   and *The Wallace*, 20
Burnside, John, 87, 92, 132
   Common Knowledge, 186
   The Light Trap, 142, 189
Butlin, Ron, 90
Byron, Lord
   Childe Harold's Pilgrimage, 66
   Don Juan, 66, 197
   'English Bards and Scotch Reviewers', 66
   translations of, 196–97
   'Vision of Judgement', 187

Caimbeul, Aonghas (Angus Campbell), 62, 63
Caimbeul, Aonghas (Angus Campbell, 'Am Puilean'), 'Am Fear Nach Ainmich Mi' ('*The One I shall not Name*'), 187
Caimbeul, Donnchadh (Duncan Campbell), 62
Caimbeul, Maoilios (Myles Campbell), 91
'Caismeachd Ailein nan Sop' ('*War-Song for Ailean nan Sop*'), 49
Caithness, earldom of, 32
Cambridge, Gerry, 208
Campbell, Angus *see* Caimbeul, Aonghas
Campbell, Anna/Agnes, 48
Campbell, Duncan *see* Caimbeul, Donnchadh
Campbell, Myles *see* Caimbeul, Maoilios
Campbell, Thomas, 66, 161
   Gertrude of Wyoming, 67
Campbell MacPhail, Calum *see* Caimbeul MacPhàil, Calum
Campbells of Argyll, 51
Campbells of Glenorchy, 48
Carcanet Press, 208
Cardwell, Richard A., 197
Carmichael, Alexander, *Carmina Gadelica*, 75, 182, 183
Carrick, John Donald and Rodger, Alexander, *Whistle Binkie, or the Piper of the Party*, 69, 175
Carruth, Jim, 209

Carruthers, Gerard, 135
Carswell, Bishop, 184
Cassells, John, 72
'Castalian band', 49, 50–53
Catraeth (Catterick, North Yorkshire), 7
Catrìona, daughter of Eachann Mòr MacLean of Duart, 48
causa finalis, 17, 20
Caxton, William, 16
'Celandine' (Sutherland), 41
'Celtic Christianity', 188
'Celtic Twilight' movement, 138, 139, 175
Cencrastus (magazine), 206
Chaimbeul, Anna of Scalpay, 'Ailein Duinn' ('O Brownhaired Allan'), 173
Chalmers, Margaret, *Poems*, 68
Chan Ky-Yut, 89
Chapman (magazine), 206
Chapman, Walter, 209
Chaucer, Geoffrey, 16, 20, 45
  Anelida and Arcite, 113
  Troilus and Criseyde, 112
Chepman and Myllar Press 44
Child, Francis J., *The English and Scottish Popular Ballad*, 122–27
chivalric Romances, 16, 17, 18, 151
Chréstien, Florent, 192
Christian Humanism, 15, 17, 21
Christian motifs, 18–19, 24–25, 34, 84, 158, 182, 186, 191
Chronicon Elegiacum, 25
Chronicon Rhythmicum, 25
Church of Scotland, 182
Chyträus, Nathan, 192
cianalas, 163, 175
Ciaran Mabach, an, 53

clan panegyric, 54, 149, 159
clan poetry tradition, 45, 46, 53
Clanchy, Kate, 93
  Newborn, 92
  Slattern, 92
Clàrsair Dall, an (Roderick Morison, 'the Blind Harper'), 53, 55
  'Cumha Choire an Easain' ('*Corrienessan's Lament*'), 56
Classical Common Gaelic, 55
Classical Gaelic poetry, 6, 8, 94, 98
Classical Irish verse, 7, 12
classical mythology, 78
The Clearances, 70, 71, 137, 138, 141, 152, 163
Cockburn, Ken, 189
Coiscéim publishers, 91
Coleridge, Samuel Taylor, 'Christabel', 67
Colla Uais, 48
Collection of Old Ballads (ed. anon), 122
Columba, St of Iona, 9, 11, 23, 180, 183
  Adiutor laborantium, 24
  'Altus Prosator' ('*Creator on High*'), 23–24, 183
Comh-Chruinneachidh Orannaigh Gaidhealach ('Eigg Collection'), 46
Congalach mac Maíle Mithig, 11
Conn, Stewart, 188
cosmopolitanism, 153, 154
Craig, Alexander of Rosecraig, *Amorous Songes*, 52
Craig, David, 54
Crawford, Robert
  on Burns, 198

Crawford, Robert (*cont.*)
   on *The City of Dreadful Night*, 74
   on language, 88, 89, 90
   Masculinity, 92
   on nature, 136
   on praise poetry, 8
   'Scotland', 92
   Talkies, 89
   Testament, 154
   The Tip of My Tongue, 89
   Verse magazine, 207
Crawford, Thomas, *Love, Labour and Liberty: the eighteenth-century Scottish lyric*, 169
Creative Scotland, 212
Crichton, James, 28
Crockatt, Ian, 219n4
Crofters' War, 139
cross-cultural fertilisation, 24, 31, 57, 60
Crowe, Anna, 209
Cruickshank, Helen, 77, 153
Cú Chuimne, *Cantemus in omni die*, 24
Culloden, Battle of, 54, 159
cultural hybridism, 34, 83, 85–86, 91, 201
Cunningham, Allan, 67

Daiches, David, 54
Dál Riata, 8
Dame Scotia, 147
Dante, 17
   La Divina Commedia, 19
The Dark Horse (magazine), 208
Darradarljod (anon), 39
David I, King, 9

Davidson, John
   Ane Breif Commendatioun of Uprichtness, 113
   'Ayrshire Jock', 138
   Ballads and Songs, 70
   Fleet Street Eclogues, 73
   MacDiarmid and, 75, 181
   Modernism, 87
   'The Rev Habakkuk McGruther of Cape Wrath, in 1879', 187
   Testaments, 162
   'Thirty Bob a Week', 73, 74
de la Motte, Antoine, 57
De Luca, Christine, 42
decasyllabic couplet, 111–12
Decker, Jeremias de, 191
Deleuze, G. and Guattari, F., 83, 88, 90
Delille, Jacques, 192
Delitiae Poetarum Scotorum huius aevi illustrium ('Delights of Famous Scottish Poets of This Age'), 29, 45, 192
descriptive realism, 135
devotional poetry, 10, 12
dialect verse, 40–43, 78
diasporic poets, 65, 66, 152, 161, 163, 181
Diderot, Denis, 193
Din Eidyn, 7
Dòmhnall Dubh rebellion, 48
Dòmhnall Ruadh Chorùna (Donald MacDonald)
   'Air an Somme' ('*On the Somme*'), 75
   'Òran a' Phuinnsein' ('*Song of the Poison*'), 76
   'Voice of the Trenches', 75
Domnall Brecc, 7, 8

Doric poetry, 69, 77, 80
Dorn, Edward, 156
Douglas, Gavin, 16, 57
    Eneados, 16, 44, 56, 111, 112, 115, 133
drama, 27, 47, 56, 57, 112, 129, 191
dream poems, 20
dream-vision, 47
'dróttkvætt', 33, 34, 35
Drummond, William of Hawthornden, 58, 83
    Biblical translation, 185
    Flowres of Sion, 52
    History of Scotland during the Reigns of the Five Jameses, 148
Dryden, John, 57
Du Bellay, Joachim, 192
    Deffence et Illustration de la Langue Francaise, 50
Duffy, Carol Ann, 155, 182, 209
    Feminine Gospels, 92
    Mean Time, 91
    'Oppenheim's Cup and Saucer', 177
    Other Country, 91
    Poet Laureate, 212
    'Prayer', 183
    Selling Manhattan, 186
    Standing Female Nude, 177
    The World's Wife, 92, 167
Dunbar, William, 16, 17, 27, 180
    bawdy poetry, 171
    'Complane I wald, wist I quham til', 110, 111
    'The Flyting of Dunbar and Kennedy', 146
    The Goldyn Targe, 16, 113
    poetic form, 110
    'rediscovery', 133
    and religion, 184
    satire, 147
    'The Thrissil and the Rois', 113, 132, 145, 146, 157
    The Tretis of the Tua Mariit Wemen and the Wedo, 114
Dundee, University of, 205
Dunn, Douglas, 83, 88, 89, 90, 91, 203
    Dante's Drum-kit, 92
    Elegies, 92
    The Happier Life, 87
    Love or Nothing, 87
    Northlight, 92
    St Kilda's Parliament, 87
    Terry Street, 87
    The Year's Afternoon, 92
Dunnigan, Sarah, 172, 173

Easy Club, 17
echoic (serpentine) elegiac couplets, 24
ecology, 78, 92, 132, 136, 140–43, 180, 188–89
ecopoetics, 140
Edinburgh
    Butlin and, 90
    Gaelic nobility in, 51
    literary magazines, 205
    plague, 26, 28
    printing, 44
    Romantic poetry, 68
    and Scottish Renaissance (c20) 80, 84
Edinburgh Book Festival, 208, 209
Edinburgh Castle, 7
Edinburgh Festival, 207
Edinburgh Miscellany, 58
Edinburgh Review, 205

Edinburgh, University of, 202, 203, 204
Edinburgh University Press, 210
Edward I, King, 17
'Eigg Collection' see *Comh-Chruinneachidh Orannaigh Gaidhealach*
Eimhir, wife of Cù Chulainn, 81
elegiac couplets, 24, 26
elegiac metre, 26, 29
elegies
    Chronicon Elegiacum, 25
    Mairghread nighean Lachlainn (Margaret MacLean) and, 55
    mock-elegies, 119
    Mugrón and, 11
    Murchadh MacCoinnich and, 46
    nature motif in, 172
    Thomas Campbell and, 67
Eliot, T. S., 5, 74, 162
    The Waste Land, 181
Elliot, Jean, 'The Flowers of the Forest', 149, 159
English poetry, 30, 45, 91, 107, 111
Enlightenment, 54, 59, 61, 62, 64
epic poetry, 50, 63, 67, 70, 71, 111, 194, 196 see also Barbour, *The Bruce*
epigrams, 30, 51, 192
Erasmus, 26, 27
'erfidrápa' (memorial ode), 33
Eriugena, John Scotus, 188
    Carmina Gadelica, 183
Ermengarde/Ermengarda see Ermingerðr, Viscountess
Ermingerðr, Viscountess, 35–36
Estienne, Henri, 191

'Ettrick Shepherd' see Hogg, James
eulogies, 36, 46, 51, 55
Evans, Sally, 208
The Evergreen (magazine), 138
    experimentation, 109

faith and religion, 179–89
    ancient Gaelic, 182
    'cosmic impiety', 187
    'cosmic piety', 183
    impact of migration, 181, 182
    male authority, 185
    mariology, 185
    and nature 183, 189
    pantheism, 185
    place of women, 185
    and social justice, 188
    'sons of the manse', 188
Falkirk, Battle of, 59
fascism, 79, 81
female poets
    contemporary, 91, 154, 167
    faith and religion, 186
    in Gaelic, 13, 167
    gender politics, 92
    on industrialisation, 161
    Land Agitation, 163
    love and erotic poetry, 172, 175
    and national identity, 68, 149–50, 153
    war poetry, 76
    see also individual poets
feminism, 72, 92, 161, 167, 177
Fergusson, Robert, 60
    'Auld Reekie', 111
    'A Drink Eclogue', 112
    'An Eclogue, To the Memory of Dr William Wilkie', 136
    'Braid Claith', 119–20

'Eclogues', 112
'Elegy, on the Death of Scots Music', 119–20
English poetry, 62
'The Farmer's Ingle', 62
'The Ghaists: a Kirk-yard Eclogue', 112
'Hallow Fair', 117
impact of Bible, 185
'Leith Races', 117
satire, 117, 160
Fernaig Manuscript, 45, 46
Ferreira, António, *Castro*, 191
Fielding, Penny, 68
Fifth Crusade, 6
Finlay, Alec, 189
Finlay, Ian Hamilton, 89, 205
Fionnlagh an Bard Ruadh, 47
'Fíor mo mholadh ar MhacDomhnaill' ('*True my Praising of MacDonald*') (anon), 146
First World War, impact of, 75–76, 164
Fletcher, Andrew, 126
Flodden Field, Battle of, 44, 149, 151, 157
Folk Revival, 123, 129, 130
folksong tradition, 46
Foulis, John (Follisius), 26
Fowler, William, 45, 49, 50
Fraser, Antonia, *Scottish Love Poems*, 169
Fraser, G. S., 80, 165
Fraser Darling, Frank, 140
Frater, Anna (Anne), 209
    Fon t-Slige/Under the Shell, 154
Frederick, Prince of Wales, 159
Free Church, 182

Freebairn, Richard, 30
Freiligrath, Ferdinand, 198
Friel, Raymond, 208
Fulton, Robin, 188

Gaeldom, 146, 147, 148
Gaelic poetry, 94–108
    alliteration, 98
    bardic, 51–53
    and the Clearances, 163
    decline of culture, 84–85
    diasporic, 65, 66
    early, 9, 12
    language, 16, 153, 166
    love poetry, 175
    metrical structure and types, 96, 98–108
    and national identity, 146
    panegyric code, 60
    public role, 64
    rhyme, 96–98
    rhythm, 94, 95–96
    spaidsearachd genre, 147
    unpopularity at court, 51
    urban descriptions, 163
Gagnier, Regenia, 74
Gairfish (magazine), 207, 208
Gairm (magazine), 206
Gallimaufray (magazine), 205
Garioch, Robert, 165
    'The Cannie Hen', 120
    'Embra to the Ploy', 120
    'To Robert Fergusson', 120
    Selected Poems, 187
    Seventeen Poems for Sixpence, 80
Garrett, Almeida, *Camoes*, 196
Gay, John 58
    The Shepherd's Week, 134

Geddes, Alexander, 62
- 'Epistle to the President, Vice-Presidents and Members of the Scottish Society of Antiquaries', 62
- *Three Scottish Poems with a Previous Dissertation on the Scoto-Saxon Dialect*, 62

Geddes, James Young, 161, 162
- *The New Jerusalem and Other Verses*, 162
- *The Spectre Clock of Alyth and Other Selections*, 162

Geddes, Patrick, 138
gender politics, 92, 149
'geopoetics', 142–43
George II, King 159
Gessner, Salomon, 193
Gille-Brighde Albanach, 6–7, 10, 12
Gillies, William, 12
Gillis, Alan, 205
Glasgow, 72–73, 82, 90, 161, 166, 181, 189, 207
Glasgow Group, 87, 203
Glasgow publishers 65, 72
Glasgow Renaissance, 87
Glasgow School of Art, 203
Glasgow, University of, 58, 90, 202, 208
Glasgow Weekly Herald, 72
Glasgow Weekly Mail, 72
Glen, Duncan, 205
'Glorious Revolution', 55
Gobha, Iain (John Morison), 186
Gododdin, kingdom of, 7
Goethe, Johann Wolfgang von, 197
- *The Sorrows of Young Werther*, 61, 62, 193

Golagros and Gawane (anon), 16, 17, 18, 114
Gordon, George *see* Byron, Lord
Gorman, Rody, 85, 91, 176, 188
Graham, James, 1st Marquis of Montrose, 148
- 'On the Death of Charles I', 148
- 'Lines Written on the Eve of his Execution', 148, 158

Graham, John J., 41
Graham, John of Claverhouse, 30
Graham, Laurence, 41
Graham, W. S., 205
- *Malcolm Mooney's Land*, 84
- *The Nightfishing*, 84

Grameid, 30
'Graveyard School', 61
Gray, Alasdair 203, 205
- *Lanark*, 73

Gray, Thomas, *The Fatal Sisters*, 39, 40
Greek, ancient, 23, 25, 29, 56, 78
Greig, David, *The Strange Undoing of Prudencia Hart*, 129
Grieve, C. M. *see* MacDiarmid, Hugh
Griffin, Roger, 77
Grimble, Ian, 60
The Gude and Godlie Ballatis, 47, 185
Gunderloch, Anja, 121
Gutter (magazine), 210

Habbie stanza, 119, 120
Hadfield, Jen, 42
Hagedorn, Friedrich von, 192

Haldane Burgess, J. J.
   'Da oobin (moaning) wind', 41
   Rasmie's Buddie, 41
   'Scranna', 41
Hallr Þórarinsson, 36
Hamilton, Elizabeth, 161
Hamilton, Janet, 69, 72, 161, 181
Hamilton, William of Bangour, 59
Hamilton, William of Gilbertfield, 20, 119, 161
Haraldr hárfagri, 38
Harris, Emmy Lou, 130
Hart, Henry, 207
Hasler, Antony, 133
Hay, George Campbell (Deòrsa mac Iain Dheòrsa), 79–82, 85, 108, 120, 165
   Kailyaird and Renaissance, 120
   'Mochtàr is Dùghall', 81, 82
   'Prìosan da Fhèin an Duine?' ('Locked in the Human Cage?'), 188
Hay, William, 26
Hebrew, 23
Hebrides, migration to, 51
'Helicon' stanza, 115
Henderson, Hamish, 129
   Elegies for the Dead in Cyrenaica, 80, 165
Hendry, J. F., *The New Apocalypse* anthology, ed., 80
Hendry, Joy, 206
Henryson, Robert, 57, 180
   'beast fable' genre, 132
   Morall Fabillis, 21–22, 133
   Orpheus and Eurydice, 113
   'The Preiching of the Swallow', 184
   'rediscovery', 133
   'Robene and Makyne', 133
   The Testament of Cresseid, 113, 171, 190
Herbert, W. N., 88, 89, 90, 92
Herd, David, *Ancient and Modern Scots Songs*, 122
Herd, Tracey, 205
Herder, Johann Gottfried, 66, 193, 194
   Volkslieder, 195
'heroic' poetry, 8, 39
Highland Clearances *see* Clearances
Hitchens, Christopher, 156
Hjörungavágr, Battle of, 36
Hobsbaum, Philip, 203
Hodgart, M. J. C., 124
Hofmeyr, Isabel, 131
Hogg, James
   The Mountain Bard, 67, 151
   The Private Memoirs and Confessions of a Justified Sinner, 180
   The Queen's Wake, 67, 151
   Holland, Richard, *The Buke of the Howlat*, 16, 20, 114, 132, 146
Homer, 107
homosexuality, 26, 93, 169, 188
Horace, 17, 58
Hudson, John, 208
Hudson, Robert, 49
Hudson, Thomas, 49, 50
Hugh of St Victor, 19
humanism, 26, 188 *see also* Christian Humanism; Scottish Humanism
Hume, Alexander, 49
Hume, Anna, 47, 50

Hume, David, 28, 61
Hutton, James, 136
hybridisation, cultural, 85–86, 91

Iain Lom (John MacDonald), 53
   'A Dhòmhnaill an Dùin' ('*O Donald of the Dun*'), 46
   'Crùnadh an dara Rìgh Teàrlach' ('*The Crowning of King Charles II*', 148
   'Cumha Mhontròis' ('*A Lament for Montrose*'), 148
   'Cumha Morair Hunndaidh' ('*Lament for the Marquis of Huntly*'), 148
   'Là Inbhir Lòchaidh' ('*The Battle of Inverlochy*'), 149
   'Òran an Aghaidh an Aonaidh' ('*A Song Against the Union*'), 159
Icelandic poetry, 31–37
identity
   Gaelic, 81, 82, 85–86, 185
   Highland, 66, 137
   and landscape, 132, 133, 138
   local, 148, 149
   national, 144–55, 200
industrialisation, 66, 72–73, 75, 141, 161–63, 199, 200
'Informationists', 90
Ingibjörg, widow of Þorfinnr, 32
Iona, 11, 23, 24
Ireland, 6, 7, 9, 23, 48, 61, 107

Jack, R. D. S., 174
Jacob, Violet, 129, 140, 153, 186
   Songs of Angus, 77
Jacobitism, 59, 63, 149 150, 159

James I, King
   Kingis Quair, 15, 19, 20, 112, 170, 171
James IV, King, 44
James V, King, 26, 27, 44, 46, 47–49
   'Christis Kirk on the Greene', 56, 115, 116
James VI, King
   Ane Metaphoricall Invention of a Tragedie called Phoenix, 173
   Ane Schort Treatise, Conteining some Reulis and Cautelis to be Observit and Eschewit in Scottis Poesie, 50, 109
   as anti-Gaelic, 44, 51
   dislike of stanzas, 115
   Lepanto, 190, 191
   political censorship, 170
   promotion of poetry, 49, 50–53
Jamie, Kathleen
   ballad form, 129
   and Creative Writing course, 203
   and ecology, 87, 142
   Jizzen, 92
   literary magazines, 205, 207
   Mr and Mrs Scotland Are Dead: Poems, 1980–1994, 143
   The Overhaul, 189
   publishers, 209, 210
   The Queen of Sheba, 92
   protest poetry, 167
   Sightlines, 189
   The Tree House, 143

Jamieson, Peter, 41
Jamieson, Robert, 122
Jamieson, Robert Alan, 42
Jeffrey, Francis, 205
Johnson, Dr Samuel, 160
Johnson, James, *Scots Musical Museum*, 122
Johnson, Laureen, 42
Johnson, Samuel, 61
Johnston, Arthur, 28, 29, 30
Johnston, Duncan *see* MacIain, Donnchadh
Johnstone, Brian, 209
Jómsvíkingadrápa (Kolbeinsson), 36–37, 39
Jonson, Ben, 58
József, Attila, 87
Juvenal, 23
Juvencus, 25

Kailyard school, 76, 77, 132, 133, 137–40
Karpeles, Maud, 130
Kay, Jackie, 91
    feminism, 167
    Other Lovers, 93, 178
    'Swim', 178
Kelman, James, 205
Kennedy, William, 'First Love', 175
Kennedy-Fraser, Marjory, *Songs of the Hebrides*, 75
Kentigern, St, 25
Kerr, Roderick Watson, 164
King, Adam, 28
Kinloch, David, 90, 93, 207
Kirkhall minster, 32
Klopstock, Friedrich Gottlieb, 192
Knox, John, *Book of Common Order*, 184

Krakumal ('Kraka's poem') (anon), 39
Kravitz, Peter, 205
Kuppner, Frank, 84, 89–90
    A Bad Day for the Sung Dynasty, 89
    The Intelligent Observation of Naked Women, 89
Kynaston, Sir Francis, 190

Lallans (Lowlands) poetry, 76, 201
Lallans (magazine), 206
Lamb, Helen, 188
Land Agitation, 163
landscape, 70, 71, 135, 137, 140
Langland, William, *Piers Plowman*, 114
Latin
    dramas, 57
    Holland on, 16
    heritage, 55
    metre, 34
    paraphrases of Psalms, 45
    poetry in, 23–30
    Scottish Humanism and, 56
    translation from, 16
Leask, Nigel, 137
Leavis, F. R., 5
Lee, Joseph, 'The Green Grass', 164
Leech, John, 29, 30
Legends of the Saints (anon), 110
Léonard, Nicolas-Germain, 192
Leonard, Tom, 73, 87, 88, 89
    Intimate Voices, 88
    Radical Renfrew, 88, 161
    Reports from the Present, 166
    Six Glasgow Poems, 80, 88
leonine rhyme, 25
letters in verse form, 119

Lindsay, Christian, 147
Lindsay, Maurice, *Modern Scottish Poetry* ed., 80
Lines Review, 207
'Linn nan Creach' ('The Age of Forays'), 48
Linnaeus, Carl, *Systema Naturae*, 134
literary environment, 202–12
literary magazines, 204–08, 210
Little, Janet, 68
    The Poetical Works of Janet Little, the Scotch Milkmaid, 149
Livingstone, Duncan *see* MacDhunlèibhe, Donnchadh
Livingstone, William *see* MacDhunlèibhe, Uilleam
Llyfr Aneirin (Book of Aneirin), 7
local newspapers, and dialect verse, 40
Lochhead, Liz
    ballad form, 129
    The Colour of Black and White: Poems 1984–2003, 154
    Dreaming Frankenstein, 92, 177
    education, 203
    feminism, 177
    The Grimm Sisters, 92
    Mary Queen of Scots Got her Head Chopped Off, 167
    Memo for Spring, 167
    public readings, 208
    Scots Makar, 1, 92, 154, 212
Lomax, Alan, 130
Loose, Gerry, 188
Lorris, Guillaume de, *Roman de la Rose*, 117

love and erotic poetry, 169–78
    Classical Gaelic tradition, 171
    and control, 170
    court poetry, 170, 171
    Gaelic, 173
    homoeroticism, 173, 176–77
    hybridism, 176
    oral tradition, 173, 174
    and nature, 172
Lowland poets, hostility to Gaels, 146, 147
Lumsden, Roddy, 91
Lyndsay, Sir David of the Mount, 20, 22, 45, 46–47
    Ane Dialog Betwix Experience and ane Courteour, 147, 190, 191
    Ane Satyre of the Thrie Estaitis, 157
    The Complaynt, 46
    'The Deploratioun of the Deith of Quene Magdalene', 113
    The Dreme, 46, 47, 113
    satire, 147
    Squyer Meldrum, 111
    The Testament and Complaynt of Our Soverane Lordis Papyngo, 46, 113

Mac a' Ghobhainn, Iain *see* Smith, Iain Crichton
Mac a' Ghobhainn, Iain (John Smith), 163
mac Ailein, Iain (John MacLean), 55
mac an Ollaimh, Giolla Coluim, 'Ní h-eibhneas gan Chlainn Domhnaill' ('There is no Joy without Clan Donald'), 147

Mac an t-Saoir, Domhnall
    (Donald MacIntyre)
    'Aeòlus agus am Balg' ('*Æolus and the Bellows*'), 79
    Bardic Crown National Mod, 79
    'Òran na Cloiche' ('*The Song of the Stone*'), 79
    poetic form, 107
Mac an t-Saoir, Donnchadh Bàn
    see Macintyre, Duncan Ban
Mac an t-Saoir, Seumas, 'Òran don Ollamh MacIain' ('*A Song to Dr Johnson*'), 160
mac Fhearchair, Iain (John MacCodrum), 60, 151
mac Iain Dheòrsa, Deòrsa see Hay, George Campbell
mac Iain mhic Ailein, Iain Dubh (John MacDonald), 55
mac Mhaighstir Alasdair, Alasdair (Alexander MacDonald), 46, 58, 59, 62, 150, 151, 158, 159
    'Birlinn Chlann Raghnaill' ('*Clanranald's Galley*'), 60, 63, 151
    'Moladh Mòraig' ('*The Praise of Morag*'), 59
    'Òran a' Gheamhraidh' ('*Song of Winter*'), 135
    'Òran a Rinneadh sa Bhliadhna 1746' ('*A Song Composed in the Year 1746*'), 158, 159
    'Òran an t-Samhraidh' ('*Song of Summer*'), 135
    self-published, 60
Mac na Ceàrdaich, Dòmhnall see Donald Sinclair

mac Theàrlaich Òig, Lachlann (Lachlan MacKinnon), 55
MacAmhlaigh, Dòmhnall (Donald MacAulay), 79, 91
    'Fèin- Fhìreantachd' ('*Selfrighteousness*'), 187
    'Soisgeul 1955' ('*Gospel 1955*'), 187
MacAonghais, Iain (John MacInnes), 71
    'Oran mu Dhaoine Posda a bhios a sgròbadh a chèile' ('*A Song about a Married Couple who attack one another*'), 72
MacAulay, Donald see MacAmhlaigh, Dòmhnall
Macaulay, Thomas Babington, *Lays of Ancient Rome*, 70
MacCaig, Norman, 80, 84, 91, 165, 166, 186, 204
    Riding Lights, 83
MacCodrum, John see mac Fhearchair, Iain
MacCoinnich, Coinneach (Kenneth Mackenzie), 62
MacCoinnich, Murchadh Mòr mac mhic Mhurchaidh (Murdo MacKenzie), 46
MacDhùghaill, Ailean Dall (Allan MacDougall), 61
    'Òran do na Cìobairibh Gallda' ('*Song to the Lowland Shepherds*'), 64, 65
MacDhùghaill, Raibeart (Robert MacDougall), 65
MacDhunlèibhe, Donnchadh (Duncan Livingstone), 75

MacDhunlèibhe, Uilleam
    (William Livingstone), 163
  'Fios chun a' Bhàird'
    ('A Message for the Poet'),
    71
MacDiarmid, Hugh (C. M.
    Grieve), 74, 75–81
  'An Apprentice Angel', 187
  ballad form, 129
  To Circumjack Cencrastus, 206
  'Direadh I', 140
  *A Drunk Man Looks at the
    Thistle*, 77, 153
  'The Eemis Stane', 184
  *Golden Treasury of Scottish
    Poetry*, 78
  In Memoriam James Joyce, 78
  influence of Davidson, 181
  influences on, 162
  language of, 88, 89
  Modernism, 77, 87, 139
  'Of John Davidson', 75, 181
  Penny Wheep, 140
  'Prayer for a Second Flood', 187
  religion, 185
  Sangschaw, 140
  'Scotland, Small?', 92
  Scottish Literary Renaissance
    (c20), 75–81, 164
  Scottish Scene, 140
  socialism, 153
  and Tait, 41
  Three Hymns to Lenin, 165
  translation, 199, 200
MacDonald, Alexander *see* mac
    Mhaighstir Alastair, Alastair,
    58
MacDonald, Callum, 207
MacDonald, Cicely/Sìleas *see*
    Sìleas na Ceapaich
MacDonald, Coll Ciotach, 51
MacDonald, Donald *see*
    Dòmhnall Ruadh Chorùna
MacDonald, John *see* Iain Lom
MacDonald, Iseabail Mhòr, 51
MacDonald, John *see* mac Iain
    mhic Ailein, Iain Dubh
MacDonald, Dòmhnall Gorm
    Òg, 46
MacDonell, Alasdair Ronaldson,
    64, 65
MacDonnell, Fionnghuala, 48
MacDonnell, James (Seumas nan
    Ruaig), 48
MacDougall, Allan *see*
    MacDhùghaill, Ailean Dall
MacDougall, Robert *see*
    MacDhùghaill, Raibeart
MacEoghain, Athairne, 184
MacFadyen, John *see*
    MacPhaidein, Iain
Macfarlan, James, 181
MacFarlane, Murdo *see*
    MacPhàrlain, Murchadh
MacFhionnlaigh, Fearghas, 85
  'Laoidh nach eil do Lenin' ('A
    Hymn which is not to
    Lenin', 183
MacGill-Eain, Somhairle *see*
    MacLean, Sorley
MacGillivray, Pittendrigh, *Bog
    Myrtle and Peat Reek*, 77
MacGregor, Eoin Dubh, 47
MacGregor, Martin, 12
MacIain, Donnchadh, (Duncan
    Johnston), 75
MacIlleathain, Iain (John
    MacLean), 64
  'Cumha for Donnchadh
    MacAonghais', 152

'Òran molaidh do Alasdair MacDhòmhnuill, Tighearna Ghlinne-Garadh' ('*Praise-song to Alexander MacDonnell of Glengarry*'), 151
MacIlleBhàin, Crìsdean *see* Whyte, Christopher
MacInnes, John *see* MacAonghais, Iain
MacInnes, Dr John, 55
Macinnes, Morag
   Alias Isobel, 42
   Street Shapes, 42
MacIntyre, Donald *see* Mac an t-Saoir, Domhnall
Macintyre, Duncan Ban (Donnchadh Bàn Mac an t-Saoir), 59, 140
   'Mòladh Beinn Dóbhrain' ('*The Praise of Ben Dorain*'), 60, 135
   'Rainn gearradh-arm' ('*Verses on Arms*'), 151
MacKay, John *see* Pìobaire Dall, am
MacKay, John of Mudale *see* Mhuthadail, Fear
MacKay, Peter, 91
MacKay, Rob Donn, 60, 62, 188
   'Marbhrann do Chloinn Fhir Taigh Ruspainn' ('*The Rispond Misers*'), 188
Mackay Brown, George
   Fishermen with Ploughs, 84
   Loaves and Fishes, 84
Mackenzie, Kenneth *see* MacCoinnich, Coinneach
MacKenzie, Murdo *see* MacCoinnich, Murchadh Mòr mac mhic Mhurchaidh
MacKenzie, Rob A., *Fleck and the Bank*, 188
MacKinnon, Lachlan *see* mac Theàrlaich Òig, Lachlann
MacKintosh, Ewart Alan 'Departure of the 4th Camerons', 164
MacLachlainn, Eoghann (Ewen MacLachlan), 60, 107
MacLachlainn, Iain (John MacLachlan), 'A Ghlinn ud shios' ('*Oh yon Glen below*'), 70, 71
MacLachlan, Dr John, 'Seo nam shìneadh air an t-sliabh' ('*Here on the Moor as I Recline*'), 175
MacLean, Alexander of Coll, 64, 65
MacLean, John *see* mac Ailein, Iain
MacLean, Margaret *see* nighean Lachlainn, Mairghread
MacLean, Roderick, 27
MacLean, Sorley (Somhairle MacGill-Eain), 79, 165
   'An Cuilithionn' ('*The Cuillin*'), 81, 153
   'Ban-Ghàidheal' ('*A Highland Woman*'), 187
   'Calbharaigh' or '*My Een are Nae on Calvary*', 163, 188
   'Coin is Madaidhean-allaidh' ('*Dogs and Wolves*'), 81
   Communism, 81
   'Dàin do Eimhir', 81, 175, 176
   'Hallaig', 141
   innovation, 80, 108
   and MacDiarmid, 78

MacLean, Sorley (*cont.*)
   on religion, 185
   socialism, 153
   'Tìodhlacadh sa Chlachan'
      ('*Funeral in the Clachan*'),
      187
   writer in residence, 203
MacLeod, Christina *see* NicLeòid,
   Ciorstai
Macleod, Fiona (William Sharp),
   138
MacLeod, Kenneth *see* MacLeòid,
   Coinneach
MacLeod, Mary *see* nighean
   Alasdair Ruaidh, Màiri
Macleod, Neil, 181
MacLeòid, Coinneach (Kenneth
   MacLeod), 75
MacLeòid, Ruairidh Mòr of
   Harris, 51
MacMhuirich, Cathal, 46, 51
   'Do ísligh onóir Gaoidheal'
      ('*The Honour of the Gael is
      Lowered*'), 148
   'Saoth liom do chor, a Cholla'
      ('*I Grieve for your
      Condition, Colla*'), 148
MacMhuirich, Niall Mòr,
   'Soraidh slán don oidhche
   a-réir' ('*Hail and farewell to
   last night*'), 52
MacMhuirich, Seumas Bàn *see*
   Macpherson, James
MacNeacail, Aonghas, 176
   *Laoidh an donais oig/Hymn to
   a young demon*, 91
MacNeil, Kevin, 176, 188
   These Islands, We Sing, 42
MacPhaidein, Iain (John
   MacFadyen), 163
MacPhàil, Calum Caimbeul
   (Calum Campbell MacPhail),
   'Oran do Luchd-fuatha na
   Gailig' ('*Song to the Haters of
   Gaelic*'), 70
MacPhàil, Dùghall, 'An t-Eilean
   Muileach' ('*The Isle of Mull*'), 163
MacPhàrlain, Murchadh (Murdo
   MacFarlane), 'Is Mise Guth
   nan Innse Gall' ('*I am the
   voice of the Hebrides*', 91
Macpherson, George, 127
Macpherson, James
   landscape, 194
   The Poems of Ossian, 61, 66,
      137, 150, 193–95
MacPherson, Mary *see* Nic a'
   Phearsain, Màiri
MacThòmais, Ruaraidh (Derick
   Thomson), 79
   Àirc a' Choimhcheangail'
      ('*The Ark of the
      Covenant*'), 187
   *An Dealbh Briste/The Broken
   Picture*, 82
   *Creachadh na clarsaich/
   Plundering the Harp*, 154
   'Dh'fhalbh siud is thàinig seo'
      ('*That went and this
      came*'), 86
   Gairm magazine, 206
   and identity, 86
   and landscape, 135
   'Leòdhas as t-Samhradh'
      ('*Lewis in Summer*'), 187
   *Meall Garbh/The Rugged
   Mountain*, 154
   poetic form, 55, 108
   *Saorsa agus an Iolaire/
   Freedom and the Eagle*, 154

'Srath Nabhair' ('*Strathnaver*'), 187
Maeshowe, Orkney, runic inscriptions, 36
Magnús the Good, King of Norway, 34
Magnus, St, 32
Mainland, Jim, 42
Màiri Mhòr nan Òran *see* Nic a' Phearsain, Màiri
Maitland, Robert, *Ane Ballat of the Creation of the World*, 117
Maitland, Sir Richard, 147
Maitland, Thomas, 28
Maitland Folio and Quarto, 45
Malcolm III, King, 32
Mallet, David, 58
Málsháttakvæði, 37–39
Manlove, Colin, 180
Manning, Susan, 133
Mannyng, Robert, *Chronicle of England*, 109
mansongr, 37
Mapstone, Sally, 170
Margaret, St, 26, 33, 145
Markings: New Writing and Art from Dumfries and Galloway (magazine), 208
marriage alliances, 48
Marwick, Ernest W., 42
Mary, Queen of Scots, 27, 44, 52
'Casket Sonnets', 47, 172
McCarey, Peter, 90, 91, 195
McCue, Kirsteen, 175
McCulloch, Margery Palmer, 78
McGonagall, William, 69
McGrath, Tom, 208
McGuire, Matt and Nicholson, Colin, 83
McLane, Maureen, 122

Meek, Donald, 75
Melville, Andrew, 28
Melville, Elizabeth, Lady Culross, *Ane Godlie Dreame*, 47, 149
'MhicPhàrlain an Arair' ('*MacFarlane of Arrochar*'), 49
Mhuthadail, Fear (John MacKay of Mudale), 59
Miller, David, 205, 206
Milton, Colin, 76
'minor literature', concept of, 83
Miracula Nynie episcopi, 24, 25
Modernism, 74–82, 87, 89, 129, 139–40, 200–01
Moireasdan, Aonghas (Angus Morrison), 'Dun Èideann' ('*Edinburgh*'), 163
'Moladh Beinn Dóbhrain' ('*The Praise of Ben Dorain*', 56
Moniack Mhor writing centre, 211
monologues, 68, 73, 84, 164
Montgomerie, Alexander, 49, 173
The Cherrie and the Slae, 50, 56, 117, 157, 185, 186
The Solsequium, 50
Montgommery, Mary *see* NicGumaraid, Màiri
Moore, Thomas, 66
Morgan, Edwin
on anthologies, 175
Cathures, 87
'The Fifth Gospel', 187
first Makar, 1, 154
'For the Opening of the Scottish Parliament', 88
From Glasgow to Saturn, 87, 154
Instamatic Poems, 87
and MacDiarmid, 87
'Message Clear', 187

Morgan, Edwin (*cont.*)
   on Muir, 141
   'On John MacLean', 166
   'Pelagius', 188
   and religion, 185
   science-fiction, 87, 90
   The Second Life, 177
   and Second World War, 165
   Sonnets from Scotland, 87, 154
   on Stevenson, 76
   Themes on a Variation, 87
Morison, John *see* Gobha, Iain
Morison, Roderick, 'the Blind Harper' *see* Clàrsair Dall, an
Morrison, Angus *see* Moireasdan, Aonghas
Morrison, David, 205
Motherwell, William, 128
   Minstrelsy, Ancient and Modern, 122
Mugint (probably of Whithorn), 24
Mugrón, abbot of Iona, 11
Muir, Edwin, 83
   'The Good Town', 165
   'The Horses', 141
   Journeys and Places, 78
   on modernity, 78
   The Narrow Place, 78
   pastoralism, 140
   religion, 185, 186
   'Scotland 1941', 180
   and Scottish identity, 153
   Scott and Scotland, 78
   translations, 200
Muir, Willa, 121, 126, 129
Mulrine, Stephen, 203
Murray, Charles, 164
   Hamewith ('homewards'), 77
Murray, David, *Celia*, 52

The Muses' Welcome, 29
music, importance of, 50

'The Nabob' (Blamire), 149
Nairne, Carolina, 175
Napoleon, 62
Napoleonic wars, 66
nature, 20, 24, 56, 132–37, 139–43, 172, 183
Neaves, Lord Charles, 'Let Us All Be Unhappy on Sunday', 187
neo-classicalism, 57
neo-Latinists, 27, 190, 192
Neo-Platonic theology, 183
New Apocalypse movement, 80
New Criticism, 130
New Edinburgh Review, 205
The New Penguin Book of Scottish Verse, 183
New Shetlander (magazine), 41, 42
New Writing Scotland, 208
Newman, Steve, 129, 130
Ní Mheic Cailéin, Iseabail, 172
Nic a' Phearsain, Màiri (Mary MacPherson), 141, 152, 163, 182, 246
   'Òran Beinn Lì' ('Song of Ben Lee'), 71
   'Soraidh leis an Nollaig ùir' ('Farewell to the New Christmas'), 139
NicDhòmhnaill, Catrìona, 'Mo Chalman ('My Dove'), 186
NicEalair, Anna, 'Luinneag' ('Song'), 186
NicGhille-Bhàin, Catriona *see* Whyte, Katherine
NicGumaraid, Catrìona, 167
NicGumaraid, Màiri, 91, 167

NicLeòid, Ciorstai (Christina MacLeod), 'Cuimhneachan 1914–1918' ('*In Memory of 1914–1918*'), 76
Nicolson, L. J., 41
nighean Alasdair Ruaidh, Màiri (Mary MacLeod), 53, 149
nighean Lachlainn, Mairghread (Margaret MacLean), 52, 55, 149, 150
nihilism, 75
Niles, John Jacob, 130
Norse verse, Orkney Earldom, 31–40
Northwords Now (magazine), 210
nostalgia, 66, 71, 76, 84, 137–39, 149, 161

Ó Dálaigh, Muireadhach Albanach
    Classical Gaelic poetry, 6, 8–10, 12, 171, 172
    'Éistidh riomsa, a Mhuire Mhór' ('*O Great Mary, Listen to Me*'), 185
    'Mairg thréigeas inn, a Amhlaoibh' ('*Woe to him who neglects me, Amhlaoibh*'), 146
Ó hEóghusa, Eochaidh, 48
Ó Maoil Chiaráin, 13
Ó Maoil Chiaráin, Fearchar, 'The Blackthorn Brooch', 14
O'Brien, Sean, 205
octosyllabic couplets, 109, 110, 111, 120
Óengus, 10, 11
O'Gallagher, Niall, 85
oil industry, 31

Old Norse, 31–40
Old Testament, 24
Oliphant, Carolina, Baroness Nairne, 69
Opitz, Martin, 192
oral tradition, 37, 39, 40, 46, 55, 123, 126
'Òran Arras' ('*The Song of Arras*'), 75
'Òran na Comhachaig' ('*The Song of the Owl*'), 49, 56
Orkney, 31–40
Orkneyinga Saga, 33
Orléans, 26
O'Rourke, Donny, *Dream State, the New Scottish Poets*, ed., 92, 154, 209
Ossian, 61, 62, 193–95
Otterburn, Adam, 26
Ovid, 29
Owain, king of Dumbarton, 8

panegyric code, 53, 54, 55, 59, 60
Panter, Patrick, 26
pantheism, 194
Parker, Henry, Lord Morley, 50
pastiche, 120
pastoral poetry, 29, 57, 58, 133–34
pastoral revivalism, 62
Paterson, Don, 87, 92, 188, 203
Paterson, Ninian, 30
patronage poetry, 44, 47, 48, 53
Peblis to the Play (anon), 115, 116
Pelagius, 188
Pepys, Samuel, 130
Perceval, 16, 18
Percy, Thomas, *Reliques of Ancient English Poetry*, 122, 195
Peterson, Jack, 42

Petrarch
  Canzoniere, 50
  Trionfi, 50
Petrarchan model, 52, 148
Pìobaire Dall, am (John MacKay, 'the Blind Piper'), 55, 60
Pitcairne, Archibald, 55, 58
  The Assembly, 56
  Babell, 56
  Selecta Poemata, 30
Pittock, Murray, 68
'Poem '72', 208
'poethical' approach, 154
poetry prizes, 212
Poetry Scotland (magazine), 208
Polygon publishers, 209
Poor.Old.Tired.Horse. (magazine), 89, 205
Pope, Alexander, 57, 60, 133, 134
  Essay on Man, 137
portraiture, 9, 10
Portuguese Inquisition, 27
praise poetry, 6, 8–12, 29, 33–36, 53, 105, 135, 146 *see also* panegyric code
Price, Richard, 89, 91, 205, 206, 207, 208
  Contraflow on the Super Highway, ed. with Herbert, 90
primitivism, 137
The Proclaimers, 167
protection, prayers for, 24
protest and politics, 156–68
  embedded messages, 157
  Gaelic poetry, 158
  industrialisation and urbanisation, 161–63
  land and Clearances, 163
  local and linguistic, 165, 166

Scottish Wars of Independence, 156
  Union of the Parliaments, 159
Protestant poetry, 47, 113, 157, 179, 182, 184–85, 187
Psalms, 24, 28, 45, 47, 107
public poetry, 72–73, 208–09

querelle des femmes, 171, 172

'Radical Renfrew' tradition, 73
Ragnarr loðbrók, 36
  'Deathsong', 39
Ramsay, Allan, 56, 58, 109, 116
  'Elegy for Archibald Pitcairn', 57
  'Elegy on Maggy Johnston', 119
  The Ever Green, 133
  The Gentle Shepherd, 57, 112, 133, 134
  'The Monk and the Miller's Wife', 111
  pastoral poetry, 133
  poetic form, 111
  Poems, 119
  Tea-Table Miscellany, 122, 130, 174
  The Vision, 118
Ransford, Tessa, 207
rationalism, 21, 57, 197
realism, 75, 133, 135, 177
referenda, 92, 93, 154
Reformation, 45, 47, 157, 180, 182, 184–85
Reid, Alastair, 188
Reid, Charlie, 167
Reid, Craig, 167
Renaissance, the (c15–c17), 16, 17, 26, 28, 44, 117, 121, 146, 160
Renaissance, Scottish (c20) *see* Scottish Renaissance

Rendall, Robert, 42
Restoration, 57, 148
Revelation, Book of, 24
rhyme, 10, 23, 24, 25, 34
Rhyme Royal, 113
Riach, Alan, 90
Riddell, Alan, 207
Ritch, Paul, 42
Robert I, King, 20
Robertson, Alexander of Struan (Tighearna an t-Sruthain), 59
Robertson, James, 204
Robertson, James Logie ('Hugh Haliburton'), 77
Robertson, Jeannie, 129
Robertson, Robin, 91, 201
Robertson, T. A. ('Vagaland'), 41
'Da Sneug wal', 41
Rögnvaldr Brúsason, Earl of Orkney, 33, 34
Háttalykill, 39
Rögnvaldr Kali Kolsson, Earl of Orkney, 32, 33, 35–36
Rollock, Hercules, 28
Romantic Nationalism, 194
Romanticism, 16–20, 66, 68, 134, 141, 151, 152
Ronaldson MacDonell, Alasdair of Glengarry, 64
Ros, Uilleam (William Ross), 60, 173
Ross, Alexander, 60
Helenore, or The Fortunate Shepherdess, 62, 112
Ross, Raymond, 206
Ross, William *see* Ros, Uilleam
Rothach, Iain, 164
Rousseau, Jean-Jacques, 193
Discourse on Inequality, 137
Ruddiman, Thomas, 56, 57

'Rule Britannia', 58
rural themes, 132–43
Russell, Jessie, 161

satire, 9, 62, 65, 147, 181, 186, 187, 192
Saurat, Denis, 199
Saxby, Jessie M.E., 41
Scot, Sir John of Scotstarvit, 29
Scotia Review (magazine), 205
Scotichronicon (Bower), 25
Scots Language Society, 206
Scott, Alexander, 22, 47
On Patience in Love, 118
Scott, Sir Walter
The Antiquary, 69
on ballads, 122, 128
European Romanticism 196
The Lady of the Lake, 67, 151
Lay of the Last Minstrel, 66, 67, 138, 151
Marmion, 151
The Minstrelsy of the Scottish Border, 67, 122, 138, 151, 195–96
'Sir Patrick Spens', 195
The Pirate, 40
Scott, Tom, *A Wee Cock o the Midden*, 120
Scott, Willie, 129
Scott Forbes, Lillias, 199
'Scottis' language, 16
Scottish Arts Council, 200, 203, 210, 212
Scottish Humanism, 56, 57
Scottish International (magazine), 205
Scottish Poetry Library, 200, 206, 211
Scottish Referendum (2014), 1, 2

Scottish Religious Poetry: An Anthology, 183
Scottish Renaissance (c20), 75–80, 108, 120, 123, 139, 153, 164, 182, 199–201
    second wave, 80, 83, 120, 139, 153, 164
Scottish Review of Books, 210
Scottish Rights of Way movement, 138, 139
Scottish Studies, 200
Scottish vocabulary, increase in, 15
Scottish Wars of Independence, 145, 156
Second World War, impact of, 80, 82, 165
Sempill, Robert of Beltrees, *Life and Death of the Piper of Kilbarchan*, 56, 118, 119
sentimentalism, 69, 91
Servin, Jean, 192
Seumas nan Ruaig *see* MacDonnell, James
Sharp, Cecil, 130
Sharp, William *see* Macleod, Fiona
Shepherd, Nan, 153
Sheriffmuir, Battle of, 54, 59
Shetland, 31, 40–43, 68
Shetland Arts Trust, 43
Shetland movement 41
Shetland News, 40
The Shetland Times, 40
Shirrefs, Andrew, *Jamie and Bess*, 112
Shore Poets, 209
Sìleas na Ceapaich (Cicely/Sìleas MacDonald), 55, 149
    'Do Rìgh Seumas' ('*To King James*'), 150

Sinclair, Donald (Dòmhnall Mac na Ceàrdaich), 78
    'Là nan Seachd Sìon' ('*The Day of the Seven Elements*'), 79
    'Slighe nan Seann Seun' ('*The way of the Old Spells*'), 79
Sinclair, James, 42
Sinclair, Lise, 42
skaldic form, 31–38
Skinner, Reverend John, *The Christmas Bawing of Monymusk*, 116, 117
Smith, Adam, *Theory of Moral Sentiments*, 136
Smith, Alexander, 181
    'Glasgow', 73
Smith, Charlotte, *Elegaic Sonnets*, 68
Smith, Iain Crichton (Mac a' Ghobhainn, Iain), 79, 84, 85, 108
    'A' Chailleach' ('*Old Woman*'), 187
    'Deer on the High Hills', 142
    'Mas e Gàidhlig an cànan' ('*If Gaelic is the language*'), 166, 167
Smith, John *see* Mac a' Ghobhainn, Iain
Smith, Mark Ryan, 42
Smith, Sydney Goodsir, *Under the Eildon Tree*, 80, 176
Smollett, Tobias, 'The Tears of Scotland', 159
Snjófríðr, 38
Snorri Sturluson, 33, 36
socialism, 41, 60, 87, 153, 154, 165, 188
Somerled, 25
song-collections, 109

Songcatcher (film) (dir. Maggie Greenwald), 130
sonnets, 47, 50, 52, 68, 80, 87, 162, 172
Sorley, Charles Hamilton, 164
Soutar, William, *Seeds in the Wind*, 80
Southfields (magazine), 208
Soviet ideology, 87
Spanish Civil War, 81
Spark, Muriel, 128, 186
Speirs, John, 80
Spence, Alan, 188
Spence, Lewis, 'Great Tay of the Waves', 77
Spenserian forms, 50, 57, 62
St Andrews, University of, 92, 203
St Mungo's Mirrorball, 209
St Nynia (Ninian), hymn for, 24
StAnza Festival, 209
stanza form, 112–18
Statius, *Silvae*, 28
Stevenson, Robert Louis
    A Child's Garden of Verses, 69
    'To S. R. Crockett', 76
    'The Scotsman's Return from Abroad', 76
    'Song of Rahero: A Legend of Tahiti', 70
    Songs of Travel, 69
    Underwoods, 69, 76, 120
Stewart, George, 40
Stewart, John of Baldynneis, 49, 50, 173
    Ane Schersing Out of Trew Felicitie, 50
Stewart, John Roy, 59
Stirling, University of, 203, 204
Stone of Destiny, 79
Strathcarron, Battle of, 7
Stroh, Silke, 86
Suard, Jean-Baptiste-Antoine, 193
supernatural, 125, 180, 186
surrealism, 80, 181, 197
Sutherland, earldom of, 32
Sutherland, Stella, 41
symbolism, 80, 140, 180
Symon, Mary, 77
Symson, Andrew, *Octupla*, 30
synecdoche, 10

The Taill of Rauf Coilyear (anon), 16, 17, 18, 114
Tait, Bob, 205
Tait, John M., 42
Tait, William J., *A Day between Weathers*, 41
'Tàladh Dhòmhnaill Ghuirm' ('*Lullaby for Donald Gorm*'), 46
Taliesin, 8
Tannahill, Andrew, 166
Tannahill, Robert, *The Soldier's Return*, 67
temperance movement, 181
Third Eye Centre, Glasgow, 208
Thom, William, 161
Thomas of Ercildoune (Earlston) 'True Thomas', 125
Thomson, Derick *see* MacThòmais, Ruaraidh
Thomson, James, 57, 62, 192–93
    pastoral poetry, 134
    'Rule Britannia', 159
    The Seasons, 58, 134–35, 192–93
Thomson, James ('B. V.'), 75, 87
    The City of Dreadful Night, 73, 74, 162, 181
Þorfinnr Sigurðarson the Mighty, Earl of Orkney, 32, 33–35

300 INDEX

Tighearna an t-Sruthain *see* Robertson, Alexander of Struan
Torfæus, Thormod, 39
Tiughraind Bhecain 'Beccán's Final Verses', 9, 10
Todd, Ruthven, 80
Torfæus, *Orcades*, 39
Traill Dennison, Walter, 41
transnationalism, 55, 58, 77, 83
Turgot, Anne-Robert-Jacques, 193
Tymoczko, Maria, 214 n.14
Tytler, Alexander Fraser, 122

Ulster, 48, 58
Union of Parliaments, 149, 150, 159
Union of the Crowns, 44
United States of America 130
urban themes, 72–73, 75, 82, 87–88, 139–40, 161, 163
Urien, King of Rheged, 8

Vagn Akason, 36
van Hout, Jan, 192
Varty, Anne, 1
Vernacular Revival, 111, 112, 118
Verse (magazine), 207
Viking Age, 32, 33, 36–39
Virgil
    Aeneid, 16, 111, 133, 192
    Georgics, 134

Wace, *Roman de Brut*, 109
Wales, 6, 7
warfare as theme, 30, 76, 200

Warren, Robert Penn, 129
Watson, James, 119
    A Choice Collection of Comic and Serious Poems, ed., 56
Watson, Roderick, *The Poetry of Scotland: Gaelic, Scots & English 1380–1980*, 3
Wedderburn, Robert, *Complaynt of Scotland*, 147
Weöres, Sándor, 87
Whiggism, 55, 58
White, Kenneth, 90, 91, 142, 189
Whyte, Betsy, 129
Whyte, Christopher (Crìsdean MacIlleBhàin), 5, 80, 85, 93, 153, 154, 176, 177, 188, 201
Whyte, Hamish, *Mungo's Tongues*, 181
Whyte, Katherine (Catrìona NicGhille-Bhàin), 75
Wilkie, William, 136
Williams, William Carlos, 88
Wilson, Florens, 27
    De Tranquillitate Vitae, 29
Wittig, Kurt, 16, 54
Wordsworth, William, 60
The Working Man's Friend (magazine), 72

Y Gododdin, 7, 8
Yates, Mike, 127
Yeats, W. B., 138
Young, Douglas, 91, 199
    Fife Equinox, 120
Young, Edward, 61
    Night Thoughts, 193
Yule, Alexander, 28

www.ingramcontent.com/pod-product-compliance
Lightning Source LLC
Chambersburg PA
CBHW052053230426
43671CB00011B/1893